Whataya Gonna Do?

A Memoir of Laughter, Love
and Life After Brooklyn

Gary Floyd

BLUE FORGE PRESS
Port Orchard, Washington

Whataya Gonna Do?
Copyright 2022
by Gary Floyd

First eBook Edition July 2022
First Print Edition July 2022

ISBN 978-1-59092-939-1

All rights reserved, including the right to reproduce this book or portions thereof in any form whatsoever, except in the case of short excerpts for use in reviews of the book.

For information about film, reprint or other subsidiary rights, contact: blueforgegroup@gmail.com

This is a work of fiction. Names, characters, locations, and all other story elements are the product of the authors' imaginations and are used fictitiously. Any resemblance to actual persons, living or dead, or other elements in real life, is purely coincidental.

Blue Forge Press is the print division of the volunteer-run, federal 501(c)3 nonprofit company, Blue Forge Group, founded in 1989 and dedicated to bringing light to the shadows and voice to the silence. We strive to empower storytellers across all walks of life with our four divisions: Blue Forge Press, Blue Forge Films, Blue Forge Gaming, and Blue Forge Records. Find out more at www.BlueForgeGroup.org

Blue Forge Press
7419 Ebbert Drive Southeast
Port Orchard, Washington 98367
blueforgepress@gmail.com
360-550-2071 ph.txt

This book is dedicated to Candy. With regard to my artistic passions, you have always been my greatest fan. Thank you for your steadfast love and support.

Acknowledgements

There are many folks who have influenced me greatly over the years. I wish to formally acknowledge some of the ones who lit a particular fire in me.

First and foremost is a very special shout-out to Glen Campbell. We all need our heroes because they give us something grand to aspire to. Glen did that in spades. He was my very first hero, and always remained the most powerful. Glen implanted in me an enormous desire to sing and play the guitar. As anyone who ever picked up a musical instrument will tell you, it isn't nearly as easy as it looks. During those first few years when the going got tough (and my fingers were aching), Glen's amazing presence gave me the strength and determination to keep going. Music and playing the guitar changed my life in ways that I couldn't even begin to imagine. I owe a great deal to my hero, Glen Campbell. Rest in peace Glen. You are one of a kind and you are greatly missed.

Another very special shout-out goes to S. Hamill Horne (aka "Ham"). Though he was not the original founder of my old Pennsylvania summer camp (Camp Choconut), he served as its director for over twenty-five years. During his long tenure, he made an indellable impact on the lives of thousands of young boys aged nine through fourteen. As I was fortunate enough to be a part of this man's orbit for twelve consecutive summers, the effect he and Camp Choconut had upon me is immeasurable. Ham taught us to love and respect the land, to get along with our many diverse neighbors, and to recognize the rewards of hard work. Mostly, he taught us how to stand on our own two feet, and to value ourselves as good and decent human beings. I can't even imagine what my life would have been like without those blissful summers in the hills of northeastern Pennsylvania. Thank you so much Ham Horne. For me (and so many others,) you were a game changer.

I also wish to acknowledge my first professional mentor and close

6 *Whataya Gonna Do?*

personal friend, George Behrend. To this day, I have no idea why you hired a guy who had absolutely no previous chemistry work experience (and no propensity for the field, whatsover). Somehow, our personalities just clicked, and it was to be the start of a life-long friendship. To George I owe my ability to be frank and forthright, as well as my desire to create relationships that go well beyond the surface. I also owe my bold and wry sense of humor to George, as we were absolutely cut from the same cloth in this regard. It was George's influence that taught me to approach new situations (and people) with enthusiasm and curiosity. In short, he made me a far more approachable and welcoming individual. Your long and enduring friendship has meant the world to me. I miss you like crazy.

    I'd be remiss if I didn't mention my brother Mitch. Though we have both had our ups and downs throughout the years (or because we have), you will always remain one of my closest friends and confidants. As we both know, our father wasn't always the easiest guy to get along with. I can't imagine what some of those times would have been like, however, if you and I hadn't experienced them together. Our years of playing music together at all those seedy New York nightclubs were a source of great joy (mostly) as well. Thanks for always being such a special part of my life.

    With regard to acknowledgements, I could never forget my partner in crime, Mr. Pete Evans. With a soul for music that outstripped even my own, I will never forget our trials and tribulations (as well as our successes and victories) while trying to be a Country Music band in the Big Apple. Whether we made ten dollars or two hundred dollars (or nothing at all), I wouldn't trade those nights for all the money in the world. A "get rich quick" scheme it was not, but the pride I felt when our group performed at O'Lunney's and The Lone Star Cafe was absolutely priceless. Thanks for all the music and our wonderful friendship.

    Speaking of music, I also want to acknowledge all those great pickers we met during our band days back in New York. You guys were some of the best musicians I've ever met. Listening to you folks (and playing with some of you) has been both an inspiration as well as an absolute joy. To Ray Gentek, Larry Campbell, Buddy Lane, Gary Hayes, Dave Keyes, Skeeter Starke, Jeremy Harris, Justin Mobrey, I salute you all.

    To my good buddies of the last seven years, Keith and Nathan. You guys came along when I most needed you. You made me realize that friendship endures, even though marriages often don't. I can't imagine my life without the wonderful friendship that we've built. I am blessed to have you guys in my life.

A big thank you to my book club pals at Lake Washington Readers. Not only did you bestow upon me the joy of reading, you also inspired me to write a book of my own. Thanks guys (and gals).

Last but certainly not least, to Jennifer and Brianne at Blue Forge Press. Thanks so much for making this dream a reality.

Whataya Gonna Do?

A Memoir of Laughter, Love
and Life After Brooklyn

Gary Floyd

1
Through the Façade

When I was a kid, I had no idea that people could actually see past the façade my father constantly tried to put forth. I was sure that he kept the moody and often volatile sides well hidden, saving the bulk of his real self for his family during private moments. Out of politeness people certainly never made comments to the contrary, but that didn't mean they weren't thinking them. While in my forties this became shockingly apparent to me during a trip back to New York with my brother. We thought it would be fun to look up our old judo instructor Cliff Yost. We took judo lessons under Cliff's tutelage for a goodly number of years starting about age nine or so. My parents were thinking that some martial arts training might serve us well on the mean streets and schoolyards of Brooklyn. I'm not sure if it ever really served its intended purpose, but judo was certainly an interesting sport that definitely toughened you up.

Approaching Cliff's house that afternoon we were in luck, as he was just heading out the door when we arrived. When last we had seen Cliff, my brother and I were in our mid-teens. Nevertheless, he instantly recognized the two grown-up forty-somethings that had unexpectedly dropped by. "Gary, Mack!" he shouted. After all those years we didn't even have to introduce ourselves.

Cliff absolutely loved people. He loved meeting them, talking to them, and above all, regaling them with his wonderful and extremely colorful stories. Cliff had about the warmest, friendliest, and most engaging personality of just about anyone I've ever met. When he asked how you were doing, you got the feeling that he truly wanted to know. It was wonderful to see him after all those years, and we spent quite a few minutes getting caught up. No longer in the judo business, his current line of work was that of an agent who represented entertainers working New York City's nightclub scene. Given his winning personality, I have no doubt he was quite good at it.

12 *Whataya Gonna Do?*

Mack and I brought him up to speed as to our various careers and families, and the conversation progressed in a very lively manner. We also talked about the many colorful folks that crossed our path during the old judo school days. So many fascinating characters who went on to lead very interesting lives. Cliff did have an appointment to get to that day, so we had only a finite amount of time to reminisce.

Before getting on his way, however, his face suddenly turned very serious. In a strikingly solemn tone, he then asked, "How's your dad?"

Seeing the way his demeanor had obviously taken a turn, we asked why such a somber inquiry. Maintaining his serious outlook, he revealed that our father just never seemed very happy. That's when it hit me. Wow, other people could actually see what was going on with our dad. They could actually see through the façade. It was quite the "aha" moment for me, and something I'll never forget.

When we're kids, we want more than anything for our lives to be what we consider normal. Normal is everything at that age. We want two parents, a roof over our heads, food on the table, and a loving environment. Ideally, it would be like the old TV shows we were so fond of back in the sixties. Parents that loved each other (even though they were never overly demonstrative) and showed kindness, patience, and understanding toward their kids. A truly loving and supportive upbringing, with parents that were infinitely wise and obviously well-grounded.

Needless to say, I was quite taken aback by Cliff's most unexpected question. Upon reflection, I simply replied that Dad was about the same. I told Cliff that the reason Dad never seemed very happy was a very simple one. He never really was. As can be surmised, Cliff Yost was a very perceptive and intuitive fellow. It did cause me to wonder, however, how many other people noticed the same thing over the years. It's hard to get people to tell you these kinds of things, so most of the time you'll probably never know. I guess that's why it's so illuminating to talk to a guy like Cliff Yost every once in a while.

In the forward, I mentioned the long-lost cousins with regard to Mom's passing. It is fascinating to finally talk to our relatives as one adult to another, as opposed to when you were a kid. Although fourteen years my senior, Neil was the youngest of the three cousins. During our conversation, he also added some interesting insight as to my father. As I mentioned, these are my dad's eldest sister's sons. Their mom was Maizy, who unfortunately met her demise at a very early age. Maizy had been out to a Broadway show with her gal pals one cold and icy NYC winter night. Owing to financial realities, the gals only did this once a year. As such, this was their big night to howl. As Maizy was descending the steeply elevated subway train platform that night, she slipped and came crashing down to the sidewalk below. In the fall she hit her head and never regained consciousness. As amazing as it sounds, she died very quickly and quite unexpectedly beneath that train platform in NYC that night. In the blink of an eye, the cousins had lost their mother. Neil was five at the time, and his older brother Steve was eleven.

In the wake of such a terrible tragedy, my dad's younger sister Doris pitched in immediately. She was there every night with groceries, cooking dinner for the kids in lieu of their mom. She did whatever she could, as I suppose she figured this is what family is all about. Even as a kid I recall that Doris truly had a heart of gold.

To hear Neil tell it, however, my father most decidedly did not. "What your father did for us during those horrible initial days and months was exactly nothing," to quote him as accurately as I can recall. I grew up with my father, so I guess this didn't surprise me terribly. Still, to hear such a story about your father's selfish and uncaring nature is unsettling. What's even more astounding is that Dad always liked and very much respected this side (his side) of the family.

These cousins went on to lead very productive and successful lives, despite the untimely and tragic loss of their mom. And to their credit, they still maintained a relationship with my father despite the hard feelings they no doubt had to suppress.

II
Memories

It never ceases to amaze me how some people remember just about everything, while others remember almost nothing. I recall a fellow from Lowe's a few years ago who advised me for almost an hour on which parts I needed to replace an aging bathroom shower stall. When I returned only one day later to purchase these parts, he had no recollection of our conversation whatsoever. Didn't ever remember having met me.

On the other hand, when I found myself suddenly divorced after twenty-five years, I started frequenting a particular watering hole at the end of my workday. When I say frequenting, I mean I wound up in this place a few times during a two- or three-week span. This was in an effort to drown my sorrows with a couple of pre-dinner gin and tonics. I gave up that habit quickly, however, and my next visit to this watering hole probably took place about six months later.

Immediately upon being seated in the bar area, a very friendly and attractive young waitress inquired as to whether I wanted a gin and tonic.

Absolutely astounded, I asked how in the world she knew that.

She replied that she remembered me from the last time I was in.

"For gosh sakes that was about six months ago," I told her.

She said, "Yeah, I remember."

So one guy doesn't remember an hour-long discussion only one day earlier, and another person remembers my drink order from six months ago. Remarkable.

As for me, my earliest memories go back to about age four. The eerie part is that I not only remember these things, but they seem like only yesterday. These interactions come back to me clear as a bell, and I even remember how the conversations made me feel.

For a couple of years prior to my entering kindergarten in the public school system, my mom enrolled me in a private nursery school. Not a fancy place by any means, and probably pretty cost-effective considering

16 *Whataya Gonna Do?*

our socio-economic status, but I remember it being a pretty decently run program. As we were nearing the end of my first term, I told the teacher that I was planning to bring my camera the next day so I could take some pictures. For some reason, this amused her greatly to the point where she laughed aloud. To this day I'm still not quite sure what she found so amusing. Perhaps it was the thought of such a young child claiming to own a camera and knowing how to use it. Perhaps it was just too grownup a thought for a four-year-old to conjure up. Hard to say. In any case, I can also vividly recall how truly astounded she was the next day when I brought my little Brownie camera (loaded with real film) to school with me. Black & White mind you, but an honest to goodness camera, nonetheless. Believe it or not, I still have a few of the pictures I took that day. To be completely fair, I don't remember the names of the other kids anymore. But I do have the pictures.

Another of my first memories is still quite vivid, although not nearly so flattering. It had to be among my most formative years because it concerns my potty training (or the lack thereof). My family was packed in the family car one afternoon and we were heading back home after a day of adventure. Apparently, I should have seen to my potty responsibilities before getting into the car, but a little kid is never perfect where this is concerned. While still en route for home, nature unfortunately began to take its course. Even now I still recall feeling embarrassed at my impropriety, not to mention being pretty uncomfortable. What to do, what to do. My parents had been thrown into a sudden quandary. It was Dad that actually arrived at the solution. He realized that we weren't actually too far from his mom and dad's place at the time, so best to head over there and take care of my immediate needs.

Perhaps the reason this seemingly insignificant incident has remained with me for so long, is that it happens to be my last recollection of my grandpa Jack. Don't ask me why, but there was an old raggedy pair of my underwear in the glove compartment of the car. (Perhaps this situation had arisen on previous occasions.) The plan was to use this tattered pair of briefs when we got to grandma and grandpa's place. There were no cell phones in those days, of course, so the folks were naturally surprised at our "drop-in." Mom and Dad quickly communicated the problem, I was then cleaned up, and the new (old) underwear was brought to bear.

As for me, I was good as new. Grampa Jack, however, was not pleased. I can even recount the concerned expression on his face when he admonished my mom and dad for putting me in the old raggedy underwear. He then emerged from the bedroom carrying packages of fresh underwear that he had recently purchased for my brother and me. Why my granddad was buying underwear for us I cannot imagine, but such was the case. "Why did you use that old pair of underwear when I just bought the kids brand new ones," he scolded. Believe it or not, I remember thinking, how were my mom and dad to know that Grampa was going to buy us new underwear? Was this issue of underwear a recurring theme? Perhaps having new underwear constantly on hand is a safety measure that everyone with young kids needed to observe. Perhaps it was one of those issues that young parents argue over with their older more experienced parents. Who knows? As for me, an embarrassing situation had been averted, and I no longer felt like one of the great unwashed. A little ashamed that I had caused such alarm, but I suppose these things are not at all uncommon in the life of a child.

Having an incredible memory is both a blessing and a curse. It's nice to remember the camera story, but I could certainly do without the potty recollections.

I don't actually remember that much about Grandpa Jack (other than my hygienic faux pa above). I must have been about three or four when he passed. What I do remember is the starched white button-down shirts he always wore. I'm not sure why men of that era couldn't bring themselves to dress in comfortable clothes when they weren't working. In those days it was important not to look like a bum. Nowadays it seems people go to great lengths (and expense) to look like one.

Aside from the starched white shirt, I remember his old wooden desk with the candy drawer. Apparently, the man had quite the sweet tooth, and he always kept an ample supply of hard candies in that locked desk drawer. During our visits, the highlight for my brother and me was when he invited us to select a piece of candy from that well-protected drawer. "Take one," he would say, despite the fact that the drawer was filled with goodies.

My parents would then emphasize, "Take *one*." The question of quantity was obviously not debatable. This didn't seem at all fair at the time, but I'm guessing it was born of a post-depression mindset. Kind of a "waste not, want not" philosophy. (I recall my mom's parents had a very similar mindset.)

The only other thing I remember about Grampa Jack was that he always seemed very old to me. Certainly not unusual for a small child to think this way about the grandparents, but I got the same impression many years later while looking at photos of him. Perhaps this was a consequence of toiling for many years in a dangerous and very unhealthy work environment. Grampa Jack worked in a hat factory with probably little to no safety equipment. He breathed the dust-infested air every day of his working life, and eventually succumbed to lint poisoning. Kind of the city equivalent of working in a coal mine. Much like coal dust, the lint clogged

18 *Whataya Gonna Do?*

the lungs of its victims, eventually shutting them down completely. Can't imagine it was a pleasant way to go, and impossible to imagine that such conditions existed back in those days. As for Grandma Rose (Jack's wife), I have absolutely no recollection of her at all.

III
Ah, the Old Days

Nowadays I like to tell people that Brooklyn is a great place to be from. We all have to start off somewhere, and as far as I'm concerned, it's a good thing we don't have to wind up there. But it did make me humble and painfully aware that life can be harsh, unforgiving, and a constant struggle. I mean no disrespect to the fine folks who presently inhabit the land I once called home. But to be perfectly fair, today's Brooklyn (with its overflow of upwardly mobile Manhattan wannabees) is nothing like the Brooklyn I experienced for twenty-plus years starting in the late 1950s.

To quote my favorite comedian of all time, Mr. Rodney Dangerfield, "My neighborhood was tough."

"How tough?"

"My neighborhood was so tough that the guys bowled overhand."

In the 60s, 70s, and 80s (and probably beyond), Brooklyn was comprised mainly of blue-collar, working-class families from a variety of cultural backgrounds. It was often called a melting pot, but I've always felt this to be quite the misnomer. Personally, I've always viewed it more as a separatory funnel. For those without a chemistry background, a separatory funnel is a rounded pear-shaped glass apparatus with a stopper at the bottom. The fatter more rounded end is at the top, and the part that tapers is down below. A solution containing two immiscible liquids (liquids that will not blend into each other) is poured into the top of the separatory funnel and left to form their own separate layers. The heavier/denser liquid will form the bottom layer, while the lighter and less dense liquid will sit up at the top. Once these disparate liquids come completely to rest within the funnel, you can actually see a line clearly separating the one layer from the other. Extrapolate this metaphor to Brooklyn's many different ethnic and racial cultures, and you begin to get the picture.

My family was a part of the Jewish contingent. We occupied specific neighborhoods which usually involved large multiple-dwelling apartment houses. Very few of us owned homes, with just about everyone opting to rent. Our members typically toiled behind desks in an effort to perform all manner of office administration functions. Utilizing pens, paper, typewriters, or other office machines, they dutifully put in their eight hours each and every day from Monday to Friday. The streets immediately adjoining us were occupied by the Italians. As opposed to massive apartment dwellings, our Italian neighbors preferred the reclusion of small individual "private" houses. It wasn't uncommon for grandma and grandpa to live with the family as well, and very often Italian was spoken every bit as much (or more) than English. A great many of these folks originated in the southern part of Italy, Sicily in particular. No office or desk work for them, thank you very much. These robust men sprung from a long line of laborers and were quite adept at working with their hands. Those that were not employed in some form of construction were the ones who became cops and firemen.

Did the Jews and the Italians get along, one might ask? Absolutely. The Italian kids enjoyed beating us to a pulp in the schoolyard at three o'clock, and we got even by marrying their sisters when we grew up. So yes, we got along just fine. So, there you have it. A bunch of nerdy Jewish bookworms surrounded by a large contingent of wild and fiery Sicilians. Along various borders were the Irish. Their temperament was rather akin to the Italians, so no real conflict issues to speak of between these two segments.

Now add to the funnel the Blacks and the Puerto Ricans. While their neighborhoods were equally as well defined, they were quite separate and apart from the Jews, Italians, and Irish. These neighborhoods struck us as downright scary, and we didn't venture into them without a very compelling reason. Although racial tensions have eased somewhat in more recent years, getting the races to exact harmony with each other was a losing battle back in those days. Unemployment, despair, and frustration ran high in these neighborhoods, and ill feelings often spilled over when the funnel was too vigorously shaken.

It is a very sad phenomenon indeed when prejudice is transferred from generation to generation. No one is born with racial prejudice, but I've seen just how easily the ideas of the old guard become the thoughts of the new. And no one is immune. As a kid growing up in a Jewish family, we were taught that black people were violent, unpredictable, and not to be trusted. It was said that our Italian neighbors were largely illiterate, not all that bright, and easily taken to brawling. The Irish were all out getting drunk, and as far as the Puerto Ricans were concerned, well you just stayed as far away from them as possible (for no particular reason).

Perhaps if we all could have stayed in our separate and distinct alcoves, we'd have gotten along just fine. Herein lies the problem, however. Since our neighborhoods were adjoining, our school classes contained Jews, Italians, and Irish alike. To populate the funnel even more, the Black and Puerto Rican kids were bussed into the white neighborhoods, as these schools were much more highly regarded. I never got the impression that they wanted to be in our schools, and I certainly never felt that they were at all welcome there.

Without a doubt, the most volatile combination was the Blacks and the Italians. Since both deeply resented one another (and that's probably understating it significantly), it was well understood that each was expected to rejoin their separate and distinct geographic stations once the school day was over. And since the school was usually in the Italian neighborhood (or near enough to it), that meant that the Black students had better be gone by about 3:30 or so. And woe to any who were not. In a nutshell, this is how I remember my formative school years. Of course, there were exceptions to the various generalities I've put forth, but tension was certainly a constant, with so many vastly different racial and ethnic components in the mix.

We didn't often talk about issues of racial and cultural harmony in school, but I do recall a very eye-opening discussion one day during a high school English class. This particular instructor was a very open and outspoken fellow, and by no means afraid to broach the delicate subjects of race and culture. He asked various students in the class if they would consider dating someone from outside their particular race or culture. My ears really perked up when he asked one of the Puerto Rican girls whether she'd consider dating a white (non-Puerto Rican) boy. Her response was that she might, but he'd really have to be something special. The reason that the white non-Hispanic boy needed to be so special was because of the strong response she knew she'd get from her father. As a Puerto Rican dad, he had the same prejudices against white people that we might have had about Puerto Ricans. And because I was taught that whites were higher on the totem pole than Puerto Ricans, I automatically assumed that a Puerto Rican father would be proud to have his daughter date a white boy. A status symbol, in fact, as it was universally accepted (or so I believed) that white people were the pinnacle of society.

I don't know about the other white students in class that day, but that discussion certainly took me down a notch or two. People are people, I realized. Our basic thoughts and feelings don't really vary all that much. Despite any obvious outward appearances, we're not so very different in the end.

IV
Early Lessons

I'd have to say that the most lasting lessons I learned in school had very little to do with the subject material presented. While elementary school surely did teach us to read and write, as well as a fair bit of basic math and history, the main lessons were about hierarchy and social structure. Even as a young first grader I had heard the word "democracy" used quite a bit. I didn't really know what it meant, but supposedly we were living in one. Nevertheless, our first-grade teacher (and all the others to follow) made certain we understood that democracy had no place in the classroom. Clearly, the teacher was the undisputed King, while the rest of us were mere subjects. If the King said jump, the only point of clarification was to determine how high.

    For reasons that I can't fathom, my first day of the first grade was not the actual first day of the term. Perhaps I had been ill and destined to start a day or two late. Though I can't recall the reason, I can surely remember standing in front of the room while the teacher announced to the rest of the class that we have a new student. "This is Gary and he'll be joining our class today," Ms. Notrika enthusiastically announced from behind her desk. I felt pretty self-conscious just standing there during my introduction until I heard a friendly voice call out from the first row of desks. "Hi Gary," came the voice of my old nursery school buddy Randy. I was so happy to see someone I knew among this sea of unfamiliar faces; I immediately returned his greeting. "Hi Randy," I echoed! But just as I did so, about twenty-five kids immediately put their index finger to their lips, and there came a resounding *ssssshhhhh*. That self-conscious feeling instantly returned as I had already acted inappropriately. I hadn't been in the room for more than five minutes and I had already done something wrong.

    Little did I know at the time that acting inappropriately in school was to be a constant challenge for me. What in the world did I do, I pondered? Perhaps the teacher had been on the phone (a real hard-wired phone) when I returned Randy's greeting. That could certainly explain the immediate need for total quiet. Whatever the reason, I thought it best not to ask, while simply remaining quiet. I'd get the actual explanation later on when things settled down.

To this day I wish I'd never gotten the actual story at any time. The actual story was that you had to be quiet all the time while in class, regardless of whether you had anything on your mind or not. The only time you were permitted to speak was when you first raised your hand and were recognized by the teacher. Then and only then could you vocalize what might be going through your head. As I say, there was no getting this environment confused with a democracy. In my six-year-old mind, I was already wondering how in the world was I ever going to make this work. Talking was my specialty. I was very good at it, and up until that point, not at all shy in so doing. Now it was suddenly unacceptable. Man, was I in trouble. This was the start of many unhappy parent/teacher conference nights, as well as the end of my freedom as I knew it.

Another wonderful and critical lesson we learned in school was the art of basic survival. That is to say, the art of actually surviving throughout the entirety of our school years. Case in point, Mr. Frankie Farella. It wasn't long before Frankie and I were introduced. Frankie was a scraping fellow first-grader, but unlike my old pal Randy, Frankie's intentions were anything but friendly. He sized me up immediately, thus determining that I was an easy-going and good-natured kid. More importantly, one that would easily succumb to his particular form of terrorism. Unlike Frankie, my physical frame was rather slight, and I probably gave up a few inches to him in height as well. And unlike Frankie, I was not a bully who was determined to inflict hardship on those I judged to be weaker.

Suffice to say that it didn't take long before Frankie informed me that he was going to teach me a few lessons of his own out in the schoolyard at 3:00. For those who recall the movie The Shawshank Redemption, think of Andy Duphrane's encounters with the "Sisters" during his formative years at Shawshank. Every day there would be fresh bruises, though I never told anybody who was responsible. And every day there was the repeated announcement from Frankie that we were again going to meet at 3:00 out in the schoolyard. This probably went on for about a week until I just couldn't take it any longer.

Normally I never would have prevailed upon my father for help in matters such as these, but desperate times required desperate measures. This was one of the few times, however, when my father really surprised me with a sincere and well thought out solution to my dilemma. Instead of pointing out my inadequacies (as was his usual response), he reached into his closet and extracted a long thin black belt. While convinced that he was going to use it on me as a form of reprimand, he instead began rolling it into a tight coil starting at the end closest to the holes. From our nearby toolbox, he extracted a roll of black electrical tape and then proceeded to wrap the coiled end of the strap tightly with the tape. Once the "handle" had now been established, there remained a length of belt (toward the buckle) of about eighteen inches or so.

Satisfied that the newly formed weapon would do the trick, he rolled it up the rest of the way and told me to put it in the pocket of my jacket. He then gave me the best advice he has ever given me. In a low but deadly serious tone, he stated the following. "The next time that son of a bitch tries to bother you, you take that belt out of your pocket and wallop him one right over his stupid head." While my father's advice may not have always been entirely sound, I had to admit that he was making sense this time.

Though I didn't exactly feel like Sylvester Stalone when I headed off to school the next day, I would have to say that I did have a certain feeling of renewed confidence. I was rather hoping that just the sight of this awesome weapon would send Frankie packing, but if it was absolutely necessary to use it, then so be it. Like clockwork, Frankie announced his usual intention at the end of the school day. Oh well, so much for that thought. Showtime once again. When 3:00 rolled around, Frankie took up his usual position just outside the school grounds. As usual, he placed his books on the ground, ready for another afternoon's fun and festivities. And as usual, a big circle formed as all the curious and happy onlookers waited with great anticipation for their usual afternoon's entertainment.

I can still hear the murmurs that echoed through the ranks, as I extracted the great equalizer from my jacket pocket. "Whoa, he's got a strap," the word quickly circulated. I have to admit, it wasn't just any strap. With the shiny belt buckle flapping prominently, and the sleek black electrical tape around the handle, it must have been an awesome sight. I held it to my side but certainly in full view of Frankie. I wanted him to be in no doubt that this time I meant business. Immediately, the expression on his face changed from exuberance to extreme concern. Naturally, I was hoping that this extreme concern would translate into his calling the whole thing off. What I didn't count on was the fact that he couldn't call it off at this late juncture, for fear of losing face. Any effort on his part to turn tail and head home would result in being seen as a coward.

Despite his obvious misgivings, he surged forward anyway. It's now or never I thought. At that point, I closed my eyes, wheeled around, and delivered a perfect strike. It was probably more the sound of the steel buckle striking the top of Frankie's head, as opposed to the actual pain, but with one blow the great Goliath fell to his knees. The roar from the crowd echoes in my head still. And much like David, one blow was clearly all that was needed. Almost immediately Frankie burst into tears. He quickly grabbed up his books and ran home, all the while howling like a wounded dog.

Once you injure a bully's pride it's like breaking a stallion. They are thoroughly beaten, and they simply have no fight left. Just to be on the safe side, I carried that mighty strap around for the next month or so. As it turned out, I needn't have done so. Admittedly, I was more than a bit concerned about what Frankie would say when he saw me in school the next day (the day after his profound whooping). His only words to me that next morning were "Hi Gary" (which he delivered with a broad smile on his face). We were friends from that point on.

Every once in a while, some kid in school would come up to me and ask if I still carried that strap with me. I'd say, "Maybe." Naturally, there were other confrontations as my school career advanced. I'd like to say that I was every bit as triumphant as I was with Frankie, but the mean streets of Brooklyn are no fairy tale (as Morgan Freeman would say).

V
Humor and Dancing

Ever ask yourself why so many comedians are Jewish. Think about it. Rodney Dangerfield, Henny Youngman, Jerry Seinfeld, Joan Rivers, Woody Allen, Jackie Mason, Mel Brooks, Milton Berle, Jack Benny, Groucho Marx, the list goes on and on. Now also consider how many of these folks hail from the east coast (New York in particular). Just about all of them. A coincidence? I doubt it. Humor has a number of purposes. For one, it can deescalate a bully. After all, do you really feel like pulverizing someone when they're making you laugh? And the reverse is that perhaps you can maneuver out of potentially dangerous situations by filling your opponent with laughter. After all, if they find you hysterical, are they really going to want to clean your clock.

We're all given certain tools and skills that enable us to survive and even prosper in this life. Some people are physically imposing and possessing of great strength. Some are very fleet of foot (a handy thing when trying to stay one step ahead of possible danger). Some people are very clever and know just what to say and when to say it. The ability to make people laugh, however, is a very powerful tool indeed. When used skillfully it is quite endearing, and a very good way to break down barriers.

Just about everyone likes to laugh. I've heard it said many times that people who laugh actually live longer. Let's face it. Life is often stressful, and laughter can go a long way to relieving that stress. Using it skillfully, however, is an art. And like any art form, it must be honed over time. If taken to excess, or not used strategically, it can surely backfire. From the perspective of someone who has always chosen the comedic route in life, to this I can surely attest.

Fast-forwarding to the third or fourth grade (I can't remember exactly which), I can recall a time when my attempt to be quick with a quip certainly could have met with disaster. In this case, I was fortunate to have survived it unscathed.

28 *Whataya Gonna Do?*

The way I was raised, there was an unwritten law when it came to girls. Say it with me, "No matter what the situation, *You Never Hit A Girl.*" Although this was not biblical, it may as well have been. If it were one of God's commandments, it would have come right after, "Thou Shalt Not Kill," or perhaps before. As a kid, I'd be the first to admit that this was not always an easy rule to live by. It was, however, absolute and non-negotiable. To violate this sacred law was to invite scorn, disgust, and snickering for many school years to come. Your buddies who used to greet you warmly and with respect, now avoided you like the plague. You were an embarrassment and thus an outcast. Your social standing could now be measured in negative numbers. Such was the fate of any school-aged boy who dared to violate this sacred law of non-contact when it came to the fairer sex.

Now it came to pass during that third or fourth-grade year, that one of the boys in our class became quite enraged with a petite little gal named Debbie. I never cared much for Michael as a rule. He was always trying to be Mr. Tough Guy, frequently starting fights to assert his physical superiority over the rest of us.

Michael was indeed a tough guy until he made the mistake of tangling with Debbie. While I wouldn't go so far as to say that Debbie was totally innocent with regard to Michael's consternation, I would say that she did have several important things going for her. For one thing, she was as cute as a button. I doubt there was one guy in the class that didn't have a major crush on her, myself definitely included. Next, she had a brain, and in the teacher's eyes, she could do no wrong. She was also the type who made friends very easily, and all the other girls in the class loved her. Personality-wise she was always a ray of sunshine. In terms of looks, she was pretty, slim, and damned appealing. In short, any boy that figured on harming her in any way needed to have his head checked. Even if Debbie decided to haul off and clobber you for no reason (not that she ever would have), you'd be best advised to laugh it off and go on about your business. Surely, no jury would ever convict her.

I don't recall exactly what Debbie found so intolerable regarding Michael's behavior on this particular day, but I can assure you that most of the guilt was probably on Michael's side. Be that as it may, Debbie decided to bring Michael's wrongdoing to the attention of the teacher. While I have no doubt that Michael deserved to be reprimanded, I am by no means a fan of tattling. While it can certainly be argued that Debbie's actions were brave and commendable, tattling crosses a certain line for me.

While we can debate issues of morality for quite some time, suffice to say that Michael was less than pleased with Debbie's decision to blow the whistle. What is that expression about pride coming before the fall?

Had Michael exercised better judgment, he would have swallowed his pride and taken his lumps. Being the tough, ornery and intractable fellow that he was, he instead decided to teach Debbie a lesson she'd never forget. Had the tattler been any of us dudes, no one would have even batted an eyelash when Michael announced his desire to take revenge. When he announced his intention to clean Debbie's clock, however, many an eyebrow was raised.

Murmurings filled the classroom throughout the entire afternoon. Is Michael actually serious about beating up Debbie, we all wondered. This baffled inquiry came from all directions. Surely Michael can't be serious about hitting a girl, for no boy in his right mind would do such a thing. While we were all convinced that Michael was just trying to throw a scare into Debbie, she was sure as heck not pandering to his faux bravado. And perhaps that's truly what made Michael go off the deep end when push came to shove. He would have been well-advised to suck it up, go home, and hope for a better day tomorrow.

As you may have surmised, however, that's not the way it went down. True to his word, Michael immediately grabbed a hold of Debbie when school let out that afternoon. Bluffing he was not, as he proceeded to show her what made him such a tough guy. Michael couldn't possibly have realized just how serious a miscalculation he had made, but Debbie wasn't about to go down easily. This cute and petite little gal was a lot tougher than she looked, and she had every intention of giving the best possible account of herself. I felt sorry for her at first, as they grappled and hit the pavement hard. We all watched in horror as poor Debbie's skirt rose up around her waist during the struggle. Back then girls wore dresses and weren't particularly excited at the prospect of having their underwear visible to all.

Oddly enough, Debbie didn't seem the least bit embarrassed or humiliated. In fact, her face showed no fear whatsoever. Without losing a beat, she grabbed a handful of Michael's hair and held on like a bulldog. Clearly, Michael was not prepared for this particular tactic, as he was not accustomed to fighting with girls. As Debbie held on with a vengeance, Michael was clearly in considerable discomfort. At this point, I'm sure he began hearing the laughter and jeers from the large crowd encircling the conflict. Combined with the pain resulting from the hair being ripped from his head, the confrontation was pretty much decided right then and there. A lesson was learned that afternoon alright, but it was Michael who was on the receiving end. While Debbie emerged from this infamous battle looking like Joan Of Arc, Michael's image was that of a whipped puppy.

Perhaps the most memorable part of this tale for me came the next morning. We all gathered for class at 8:00 as usual, but we had a surprise adult guest that morning. It wasn't difficult to surmise the identity of this unexpected middle-aged lady, as she graced our presence on this most auspicious day. Certainly, she carried the expression of someone who was rather put out. Naturally, the assumption was that this in fact was Debbie's mom, and there would be hell to pay as soon as our teacher entered the room that morning.

As my desk just happened to be near where the probable Mrs. Debbie was now standing, she looked at me and asked which one was Michael's desk. Surely, she intended to give him a good going over as well. For some reason, Michael hadn't even shown up for school yet. (Probably needed to grab a few extra aspirin before class that morning.) While we were waiting for the teacher to arrive, curiosity eventually got the better of me. I politely asked if by any chance she was Debbie's mom. With stern and miffed expression intact, she quickly confirmed my suspicion.

In terms of appropriateness, I know my next comment to Mom was questionable at best. Regardless, it came sliding off my tongue with considerable ease and expediency. I looked over at her and said, "I half expected to see Michael's mom here this morning." The extremely puzzled and perplexed look that came over her face at that point is forever cemented in my brain. I'm sure to this day she never understood my Johnny Carson-like quip. Fortunately, just then our teacher arrived, and Debbie's mom quickly proceeded to the business at hand. It was just as well that I never had to explain that wisecrack. One of those times where discretion would have been a much wiser choice, as opposed to continuing to hone my comedic skills. Nevertheless, it still gives me cause to chuckle.

Despite the challenges of growing up in a tough inner-city environment, I'd have to say that I made the most of it during those elementary school years. I never did become one with the required hush-hush atmosphere, but I would say that I was likable enough, and got along well with my peers. I always had a best buddy during grades one through six, not to mention a girlfriend or two along the way. Our fifth-grade teacher (Mrs. Goldstein) threw us a party at school one day in advance of the upcoming holidays. There was cake, ice cream, and soda pop that afternoon, and we were even treated to music via someone's handy record player. As the pop tunes of the day reverberated across our classroom, the desks were slid toward the walls, thus providing ample floor space for the gals to dance.

Naturally, we boys stuck to more "manly" recreational forms, including cards and talk of sporting events. Though Mrs. Goldstein encouraged us to get up and join the girls, this seemed totally out of the question. It was inappropriate, not the least bit cool, and not to mention downright silly. Dancing was one of those ridiculous activities that somebody invented so that giggly girls could be giggly girls. Let them have their fun we thought. After all, they're not interrupting our card games and sports talk. And had it not been for one of the first epiphanies of my young life, the party probably would have continued along these lines.

Despite the obvious need to maintain my macho image, those giggly girls did look like they were having a pretty good time. And who's kidding who, I've always been very interested in girls. I started noticing them when I was about four, and by the fifth grade, they were certainly becoming more and more noticeable. Let's face it, they were actually pretty cute. Their hair was long and flowing, and their skirts were short and sexy. Slim attractive legs emerged from the bottom of those skirts, and sometimes those legs were decked out in colorful tights or sleek nylons. Quite the mysterious and attractive package they were, and now they were dancing a few feet in front of us. And once again, here was Mrs. Goldstein beckoning us to get up and take the plunge.

Though her plea once again fell on deaf ears among my male brethren, I suddenly experienced the aforementioned epiphany. All at once I said to myself, "Oh what the hell." I then proceeded to rise up out of my chair and make my way to the dance floor. With every male face staring at me in horror, I approached the nearest gal and began gyrating to the music as best as I could imitate. With the boys still in shock, the gals were suddenly catapulted into a state of ecstasy. And the particular gal that I had chosen as my partner had a look like she'd died and gone to heaven. The other gals were green with envy as they danced as close to me as possible.

It would be a very long time before I'd get so many elated smiles from so many adoring women as I did that afternoon. (Or perhaps I'm still waiting for that time.) It wasn't long, however, before I found myself going through the entire female rotation out on that makeshift classroom dance floor. By now the envious looks were forming on the faces of the rest of the boys. Holy cow they must have thought. Gary's out there having the time of his life, and all the girls think he's the greatest thing since sliced bread.

Ah, such a confident and pioneering fellow I was back in those days. It didn't take long before every other boy took up his place on the dance floor that afternoon. And what do you know? They were all having a good time as well. I guess my big payoff came a little later while dancing with a gal named Betty. (Funny I can still remember her name). "Once you started dancing, all the other boys also got up and danced," she remarked. Couldn't argue with her about that. That's exactly the way it happened. I know Mrs. Goldstein was pretty proud of me as well, but mostly I was proud of myself for being so brave and adventurous. I found out later in life that brave and adventurous were qualities I was certainly going to need.

VI
Who is That Man Singing?

Roundabout this time, a new and mysterious attraction was beginning to take shape in my still-forming brain. I had seen a man play the guitar once while I was still in nursery school. I recall that it made a very big impression on me even as a four-year-old, but I guess it was television that really sealed the deal some years later. My older brother, my dad, and I were returning from some activity one evening. As I walked through the door of our small Brooklyn apartment, my attention turned to my mom who was on the sofa watching TV. She had on one of the many musical variety shows that were popular at the time, and there was a man singing. By then of course I had heard many people sing, but there was something very unique about the way this man was crooning.

As I quietly entered the living room, I found myself absolutely captivated. The tune was clearly a sad one, and the emotion that came pouring out of this man was absolutely mesmerizing. In all my nine years I had never heard anyone sing like that. I didn't even know that it was possible to sing like that. I listened to the lamenting lyrics, "She just didn't know, that I would really go." I listened to the beautiful phrasing as he sang these haunting words. I had no idea why the fellow in the song was leaving the woman that he obviously loved. Listening to this man sing about it, however, was life-changing.

Toward the end of the tune, I turned to my mom and said, "Who is that man singing?"

While the subdued tone of Mom's response assured me that she was singularly unimpressed, she replied "Some new singer named Glen Campbell."

In terms of significance, this was right up there with Jonas Salk's development of the polio vaccine as far as I was concerned. Life was never going to be the same again. "Glen Campbell," I repeated. "I'm going to remember that name." And to this day (and for the rest of Glen Campbell's life), I most assuredly did. Not only was he someone who could sing any kind of tune beautifully, but he was also one of the best guitar players that ever lived. As the late country singer Merle Haggard once put it, how so much talent could be placed into one man was absolutely astounding. As I say, life took a very definite turn, and I now knew what I needed to do. I was going to make it my mission in life to play the guitar and sing like my new hero, Mr. Campbell.

Recognizing my budding interest in music, my parents agreed to sign me up for guitar lessons, while also investing in a twelve-dollar guitar. My dad worked as an accounts payable clerk at the post office and my mom was a secretary at a hospital. As such, a guitar in this price range just about fit the budget. I'm sure they also figured why spend good money on an instrument I might get tired of in a year or two anyway. Not that they had any extra money at the time, but I guess I couldn't really fault their logic. Nor did they have any way of knowing just how determined I was at that point.

Ronnie Paris was about thirty-five or so. He was good-looking and rather charming as I recall, and he taught guitar to a dozen or so kids in our apartment complex. Five bucks for an hour lesson, and best of all, he came to us. Well, at least he did so in the beginning. While an accomplished guitar player, Mr. Paris was every bit the stereotypical musician. By this, I mean that he was often flighty and rather unreliable. Unlike the other students Ronnie taught in our apartment complex, I was absolutely committed and deeply dedicated. I looked forward to my lesson every week and certainly put in my fair share of practice in between.

If I had to guess, I'd also say that Mr. Paris was a bit of a drinker. In any case, it wasn't long before his track record for showing up on lesson day was about fifty/fifty. While his other apartment students were probably thrilled when he didn't show, it made me extremely angry. From fifty/fifty, he then degraded to about ten/ninety in favor of not showing up. I remember playing ball with my brother in the back of our apartment house one afternoon on lesson day (my brother took lessons from Ronnie as well.) We knew it was time to come back inside for our guitar lesson, but we looked at each other and decided, he's probably not coming anyway.

My mom was mad when she got home later that afternoon. Not because we had missed our lesson, but because Ronnie Paris had called to say that he wouldn't be coming, and we weren't there to receive his call. (No cell phones, e-mail, or answering machines in those days.) Gee what a surprise, Ronnie couldn't make it. Sure glad we didn't give up our ball game that afternoon. My brother and I kinda chuckled, however, when my mom told us Ronnie had called to cancel. Big surprise.

A week or two later, Ronnie's wife called one afternoon to deliver the cancellation message. The poor woman had no idea what she was in for. It was I who took her call on this occasion and suffice to say that I had just about had it. I questioned her as to why Ronnie couldn't make it, and I emphasized my frustration with her nonchalant and dismissive answers. Toward the end of the exchange, I indicated to her that Ronnie wasn't going to enjoy our business much longer if he continued in this manner.

As far as Mrs. Paris was concerned, however, this nine-year-old kid had no business talking to her in such a disrespectful manner. In my defense, however, I would emphasize that I employed no foul language or name-calling, or any such childishness throughout the conversation. At most, it could be said that my words were probably pretty threatening in terms of Ronnie remaining our guitar teacher. But after all, what good is having a guitar teacher who doesn't show up most of the time.

Would you believe Ronnie actually called back later that night to tell my parents how rude I was on the phone with his wife? Not that he was sorry for missing all those lessons, or that he was conducting himself in such an unprofessional manner, but that I was rude to his wife. In fact, I was having the kind of conversation with her that I know my parents would have (had they taken her call). I don't recall any particular fallout from my parents following Ronnie's angry call, but a new teacher was finally then sought. As it turned out, there were to be many along my path to becoming a guitar player. A path that was destined to be a long and steady one.

More about the guitar playing later, but I'd have to say that the sixth grade (my final year of elementary school) found me riding quite the crest. My teacher that year was much more tolerant and accepting of my quirky sense of humor, as well as my need to be highly social. I had friends and was well-liked. I even had a girlfriend in the class who was probably the most popular gal in the school. To top it off, I was probably one of the few sixth graders in my school to have experienced his first passionate kiss (courtesy of said girlfriend).

My life was filled with joy and confidence, and the world certainly seemed my oyster. All things were possible and my outlook on life was strong. I guess if things had simply continued along these same lines, I probably wouldn't have felt the desire to write this book. Much like songwriters, however, I suspect sad or negative circumstances are more inspiring than happy ones. Unfortunately, there were great changes on the horizon. And sadly, these changes would alter the course of my outlook in some very profound ways.

VII
They Sure Talk Funny at Camp

One of the best things my parents ever did for me was to send me to summer camp starting at age nine. The entirety of those eight-week summers were spent in the beautiful, lush rolling hills and forests of northeastern Pennsylvania (about 20 miles south of the New York State border). I say it was one of the best things they ever did for me, but looking back, it was probably just as beneficial for them. For two entire months every year, they got a reprieve from the rigors of taking care of their frequently rambunctious kids. And for two glorious months every year, we didn't have to be under their constant watchful eye. It was truly a win/win.

Camp Choconut taught us to appreciate the land, how to sail a boat, swim in a lake, pitch a tent, and even swing an ax. Mostly it taught us how to get along with our fellow man, and how to stand on our own two feet. For those two pioneering summer months, we lived in primitive wooden cabins with six or seven of our same-aged bunkmates. Getting along meant that if a conflict arose with one of our roomies, it was up to us to work out the problem. After all, we'd have to see each other for a good part of every day, and it was often necessary to work together for the common goal. Sure, we had our occasional disagreements and conflicts, but those cabin bunk mates became some of the strongest friendships I've ever formed.

Although the camp director (Mr. S. Hamill Horne) advertised in the New York Times the year my parents happened to be camp shopping, it was the first time he had ever explored that particular marketing choice. And after my brother and I were signed on, it was the last time he ever advertised in any New York newspaper. I'm not sure what that says about my brother and me, but the fact remains.

The bulk of Camp Choconut's clientele consisted of well-to-do Philadelphia society types. My world would suddenly gain tremendous variety and complexity, as I'd soon be introduced to boys with first names

38 Whataya Gonna Do?

such as Blakesley, Urquart, Blair, Milby, Woodley, Reed, Chauncey, and Tumpy. Up till now I was convinced that people all lived in similar circumstances to my own. What else would a nine-year-old surmise? I was soon to be the recipient of the biggest culture shock I'd ever have. Lo and behold, there were kids that weren't like me at all. Kids that didn't grow up in the inner city, in crowded apartments with one bathroom. These kids mainly grew up in sprawling suburbs. In big spacious and luxurious houses with lots of grass and trees all around. Some that even grew up in great mansions with very prestigious and well-to-do neighbors. One summer we even had one of the Dupont kids. Would you believe his parents named him Lamont? There's no way you can make up stuff like that. Lamont Dupont, no kidding.

The camp was originally founded in 1898 and was very proud of its long and illustrious roots. In those days summer camps were reserved for the richest of the rich, the most affluent of society. It's funny how things have revolved back in that direction in the last thirty years or so. Check out the prices of eight-week sleepaway summer camp programs these days, and you'll see what I mean. One has to wonder how many parents can afford a $10K (per kid) bill these days to send their child (or children) to camp for the summer.

Despite its obvious affluent clientele, Camp Choconut was actually reasonably priced back in the late sixties and all throughout the seventies. Had it not been, my brother and I would never have been able to go there. There's a line from a Steve Wariner tune called "So Much Heart in The Heartland." He sings about the other kids making fun of him because he sounds like he's from Kentucky. "We took a lot of kidding—But looking back I'd take it all again. Because the ones that laughed the loudest turned out to be my very closest friends." Right on the button Steve.

My brother and I sounded like we'd just stepped off the boat at New York Harbor and taken up residence in the concrete jungle that is Brooklyn. "Trow me da bawl, trow me da bawl," we'd often say. And many other colorful phrases of similar style. As this was the way everyone we knew spoke, it was impossible for us to understand why our new society counterparts thought we were so hysterical. At best they would just bust a gut laughing. The meaner ones, of course, taunted us unmercifully. Clearly, we were not a part of their culture. And if we ever hoped to be, it was quite apparent that our rough edges would have to be smoothed out.

By contrast, their speech patterns seemed just as curious to me. They actually pronounced words that ended in "er" with an "er" sound at the end. "Never" for instance, was pronounced "nev-er" ("nev-ur.") This was in stark contrast to our version, which was of course pronounced "nev-a." Then there was the actual inflection. The best example I can give is "water." Their version: "wah-t-err." Our version: "waut-a." As in, "*I need a drink-a-waut-a.*" Despite these blatant initial disparities, in the end, we did manage to find common ground. After all, kids are kids, with many more similarities than differences. As I read about the current Donald Trump impeachment hearings (with the way our nation is so staunchly divided these days), it occurs to me that republicans and democrats could both take a page from my early summer camp experiences.

S. Hamill Horne (later to be known simply as "Ham") actually drove all the way from the suburbs of Philly, to meet us at our Brooklyn apartment prior to that first summer at camp. Being city kids my brother and I were both very sports-minded. Baseball, football, and basketball were our favorites, and we eagerly asked whether these sports would be provided at Camp Choconut. Clearly, these queries made Ham very uncomfortable. Almost in Ralph Cramden ("homina-homina") fashion, he tried his best to skirt around the issue. "Well, yes we have those things," he replied in an unsteady voice. But our real specialty is hiking, canoeing, and waterfront activities." This part he stated proudly.

My brother and I both looked at each other in bewilderment. Hiking and canoeing? What is this guy talking about? And camping, what does that even mean? It was English that we were all speaking, but you never would have known it at that point. And though we were certainly in for a new and very unique experience, somehow this "Ham" guy seemed an honest and genuinely sincere fellow. By the time the meeting was over, and despite our obvious skepticism, my folks had signed on the dotted line. It was to be the start of a twelve-year adventure that changed the course of my life in ways that I couldn't possibly imagine or measure.

It was around this time that my relationship with my father started to become quite strained. On the one hand, Camp Choconut was building very positive feelings of self-esteem and confidence. I was also given a great deal of freedom at camp, even though there was a very definite structure to the daily routine. Camp brought great pride in one's accomplishments both individually and as a group. Strapping on a forty-pound pack, and hiking through the woods for a few miles was hard work to be sure. But it just as certainly brought a feeling of tremendous pride. Starting out as a complete non-swimmer at the beginning of my first summer, then eventually being able to cover nearly a quarter of a mile across the lake at summer's end, was also a huge milestone. The successes and victories came quickly and resoundingly while at camp.

Back on the home front, however, there was quite a different story developing. There was a growing tension between my father and me, as I struggled to maintain the newfound individualism and sense of self that I unearthed at camp. To help secure the framework of a new cabin, I could climb a ladder and drive nails into wooden beams while at camp. To provide a hole for the leg of a wooden walking bridge, I could drive a pickaxe into the ground while at camp. I could sit in the stern of an aluminum canoe while guiding it safely through the rapids of the Delaware River while at camp. Despite these milestones, I'll never forget the tension I felt after returning home after one particular summer.

Not long after I got back, my father asked me to help him with a household project. Why my dad attempted household projects in the first place, I'll never know. He failed miserably at just about all of them. There was the one where we attempted to tile the bathroom floor. By the time that one was done, there were large and irremovable smudges of ugly construction adhesive all over the newly tiled surface. There was the one where my father and grandfather attempted to install a large mirror in my parent's bedroom. That one resulted in a good part of the wall in my bedroom collapsing in an avalanche of plaster. There was the one where my dad wanted to paint the walls of the corridor that led to the bathroom from the entrance of the apartment. I thought it would be a good idea to mask off the ceiling before painting the two walls. Dad didn't agree, thus we managed to smear paint all over the ceiling in an effort to get the job done as quickly as possible. Needless to say, that one was not a work of art either.

My favorite (though not a household project) was the time he tried to spruce up the paint job on our old DeSoto automobile. He did this via cans of spray paint purchased from the auto parts store. As I recall, that job didn't take too long either. A few streaks here, and a few swishes there. It then only remained for him to stand back and admire his artistry. With great pride in his lovely paint job, he then invited our mom to come take a look. At the sight of it, she let out a blood-curdling scream. Need I say more. Suffice to say, Norm Abrams of This Old House, my father was not.

So naturally, I was uneasy when he requested my help in mending the closet door in the corridor (the same corridor we had previously attempted to paint). There was a thin "U-shaped" metal strip that ran up and down the front edge of the closet door. I guess it was there so that you wouldn't see the unfinished raw edge of the wooden door. Over time the glue that held it on had given up the ghost, and the metal strip had become detached from the wood. Our mission was to secure it back onto the front edge of the door, such that it would once again rest firmly in place.

Looking back at it, had we a few appropriate size clamps and the proper adhesive, we probably could have secured it back in place quite nicely. Our simple tool kit was wholly inadequate, however, so our plan was to simply nail it back in place. To accomplish this, we'd have to drive a series of nails through the metal strip and into the narrow edge of the wood.

Worth a shot perhaps, if the wood hadn't become too badly rotted over time (and could actually hold the nail firmly). In the end, I'm not sure we ever got to that point.

    My dad asked me to select a nail from the thousands we had stored in a large metal can. I carefully selected a roofing nail because of its large diameter head. Although not the thinnest nail in the can, my thought was that the large diameter head might help press the metal strip down into the wood. That was my theory, anyway. Upon scrutinizing my nail choice, however, Dad proceeded to go into a rage. "What are you, some kind of an idiot?!" he bellowed. At times like this, I knew it was always best to stay silent and accept his admonishment. To try and justify my nail choice would have been foolhardy.

    He then went on to inform me in no uncertain detail, that I had returned from camp very stupid this year. "I don't know what went on in the camp of yours this summer," he repeated. "But you came back really stupid this time." Naturally, those words affected me very deeply, but Dad was often prone to these kinds of outbursts. As I wasn't of an age where I could adequately protect myself at this point, I simply retreated to my room while Dad continued to struggle with that closet door. "Son of a *this*" and "son of a *that*" came pouring from the corridor in a loud and endless stream. In the end, I think he gave up in disgust. I recall the state of the door being pretty much unchanged after the whole incident had finally concluded. I guess he wasn't able to find the right nail either.

VIII
Help; I Can't Swim!

As I mentioned, I was one of the only non-swimmers at our fancy "hoity-toity" summer camp when I first arrived in 1968 at the age of nine. Sure, we had been to the ocean at Coney Island in Brooklyn many times, but nobody actually teaches you how to swim in the ocean. The ocean is all about splashing around in the waves and trying not to get pulled in by the famous "undertow." Mostly it was about cooling off on a hot New York summer day, setting up the big beach umbrella on the sand, and getting an ice cream or two before the day was out. Unfortunately, this did not qualify me (or in any way prepare me) to venture out into the deep waters of Lake Choconut.

On the first day of camp, it was necessary to separate the men from the boys with regard to swimming ability. One of our first tasks was to pass the "Area Test." This involved wading into the lake from the shallow end, then approaching the main dock as the water quickly got deeper. The water was a good fifteen or twenty feet deep by the time you got to the main dock. From there you had to swim about twenty yards to the floating dock. Once at the floating dock, all that remained was to swim the twenty yards back to the main dock, and the Area Test was complete. Piece of cake. At least that's how it looked when I watched the kid just ahead of me do it. With seemingly little effort this young man easily drifted out to the main dock. He then did a nice little crawl stroke to the floating dock, while completing the course in much the same manner. The whole ordeal took him less than five minutes.

Although I had never before swam in water over my head, this fellow made it look like a walk in the park. This provided me with quite a false sense of security, as I now envisioned accomplishing the task in similar style. Suddenly it was my turn, and I began to wade out into the water. As long as I could feel my feet still touching the bottom I was just fine. In an instant however the ground was gone, and I wasn't even to the main dock yet. As treading water was a skill that I did not yet possess, panic set in almost instantly. I began flapping around wildly in an effort to keep myself from going under, all the while convinced that I would certainly drown.

At the age of nine, I was going to die in the pristine waters of Lake Choconut on my first day of camp. And try as I might, there wasn't a damned thing I could do to prevent it. It was one of the most terrifying moments of my young life. Fortunately, the waterfront counselor (Willard Foote) instantly recognized that I was in trouble. In front of the entire camp, he dove into the lake and pulled me to safety. Fifty kids and several counselors all looking on, while the nine-year-old dork from Brooklyn had to be fished out of the lake so as not to drown. To this day it was one of the most humbling experiences I've ever had.

Why was I the only one in the entire place who couldn't pass a simple swimming test? Why was everyone else proficient in this area except me? It wasn't fair. I felt totally alone and totally inadequate. All I wanted to do at that moment was to go back to my cabin and forget that the place even had a lake.

I decided that swimming was just not going to be my thing. And for the rest of that first summer, it wasn't. I avoided the lake whenever possible, only quickly dunking in and out when it was absolutely required. Unfortunately, there was the matter of "waterfront detail." These were required morning sessions down at the lake a couple of times a week for an hour and a half at a crack. These "details" were designed mainly for instruction, so Mr. Foote made it his mission to teach me some basics on how to swim (and how not to drown).

Though I was a less than willing participant, Willard decided to start with the Elementary Backstroke. Looking back, I guess that was an excellent choice as it killed two birds with one stone. As the name implies, elementary backstroke is done by floating on one's back. The simultaneous leg and arm motions are then added to propel the swimmer forward through the water. But floating on your back is a pretty good way not to drown in it of itself, thus a very handy skill indeed for a non-swimmer. You might say the leg and arm movements are icing on the cake, as they will eventually get you from point A to point B.

The best thing about being able to float on your back is that the feeling of panic and sudden terror when your feet no longer touch the bottom is now gone. In essence, I guess I could now swim, and I didn't need to be afraid of the lake and its deep water any longer. I certainly wouldn't say that I was as comfortable in the water as everyone else, but at least I was no longer going to plunge to a watery death.

By the last couple of weeks of that first summer at camp, Willard was convinced that my elementary backstroke was worthy of conquering the Area Test. Though it still took a bit of convincing, I agreed to give it another shot. This time the feeling of being in water over my head didn't throw me into a panic, and I quickly shifted into elementary backstroke mode. From the main dock, I was actually quite surprised by how quickly I glided across to the floating dock. With newborn confidence (and knowing that there was no turning back at this point), I slowly glided back to the main dock, finally clutching onto the steel ladder for dear life. And with that, the entire ordeal was over. I could now legitimately claim that I was no longer a non-swimmer.

I think Willard Foote was actually prouder than I was. In any case, it was a good feeling to know that nobody was ever going to have to dive into a lake to save me again. And for the final two weeks of that first summer, that was vindication enough. There was a much larger aquatic challenge that lie ahead, but for now, the Area Test of 1968 would surely suffice.

The lake at Camp Choconut was particularly pristine. Though not the largest lake on the planet, it was surrounded by lush, wooded rolling green hills. During the summer, the water was both inviting, as well as a great comfort on very warm days. As it was located entirely on privately held land, there were also no houses along its banks, save for the one owned by the landowners themselves. Yet somehow everyone in the entire county seemed to know that it sported some of the best fishing of any lake in the entire area. We pulled quite a few large-mouth bass out of that lake during our summers at Choconut. To accomplish this, however, we needed to operate a canoe. And to prove ourselves worthy of operating such a vessel, we now needed to pass the dreaded "Lake Test."

When someone first pointed out what was involved in accomplishing this challenging feat, I thought they were out of their mind. As I stood on the main swimming dock, my buddy pointed to a tiny wooden shelter that seemed clear across the lake. In a very casual tone, he informed me that this was where you needed to swim in order to pass the Lake Test. That's crazy I thought, as I gazed across the lake at that little wooden shelter barely visible from where I was standing. Turns out it was actually about a quarter of a mile, but to me, it might as well have been the English Channel (not that I'd ever seen the English Channel). Sure, I could now elementary backstroke myself about twenty or thirty yards, but this distance was insane. Insane or not, it was another one of those things at camp that everyone could easily do.

This was now becoming a familiar theme. Things that everyone else could somehow do, and that I couldn't. Even though the counselor stayed right beside you the whole time in a rowboat (in case you got into trouble along the way), I was not assuaged. I was absolutely convinced I'd plummet swiftly to the bottom in a state of total exhaustion, should I attempt this extremely foolish and dangerous feat. For this reason, I decided to forego the attempt during most of my second summer at camp. Though the counselors assured me I could do it, and some of the other kids teased me about not being able to do it, the thought was just too frightening.

There was only one other kid in camp that second summer who hadn't yet accomplished the Lake Test, and that was Henry Wood. Henry was quite the laughing stock among our group, and throughout the entire camp as well. Despite this, I figured as long as there was at least one other "non-Lake Test" kid in camp, I'd be okay. Then one day it happened. From out of the blue, even dorky Henry Wood somehow summoned up the courage to give it a shot. Perhaps Henry was just not bright enough to realize how dangerous it would be, but he was actually going to give it a try.

So one sunny afternoon Henry jumped in and began the arduous trek across the lake toward that tiny wooden shelter. In my heart of hearts, I hoped Henry would panic or just get too tired. I longed to see him pulled from the water at some point and hoisted into that little aluminum rowboat. But as I watched from the dock, I could see Henry slowly and persistently paddling his way across. My heart sank when he finally reached the little wooden shelter that still seemed so far away. Henry Wood had made it. Dorky Henry Wood had actually made it. At this point, I knew there would be no sympathy left for me at all at Camp Choconut. All I heard for the next several days was, "If Henry Wood can do it, anyone can do it." And if I chose not to do it now, I might easily replace Henry as that dorky laughing stock.

With this great bit of inspiration ringing in my head, I knew I had to take the plunge. That next afternoon I suddenly found myself in the water starting out beside that little aluminum rowboat. The words still echoing in my head, "If Henry Wood can do it, anyone can do it." It became my mantra as I paddled and elementary back stroked through the water. Every time things got tense, I looked around for the little rowboat and was comforted when I saw it right there beside me. Even if my strength gives out I'm not going to drown, I reasoned. Surely, I could make it back over to the boat if need be. Amazingly, however, I never needed to reach for the boat. The counselor kept shouting that I was doing just fine, so I kept paddling and backstroking. I don't remember how long it actually took me to get to the little wooden shelter that afternoon. All I can say is that it seemed like an eternity. But that was okay, as the Lake Test had no specific time limit. It was just a question of getting there.

I'm not sure if I can describe the overwhelming feeling of relief when my feet finally touched the muddy bottom near that little wooden shelter (which suddenly wasn't that small anymore). Holy cow, I can actually stand up now. I can finally stop paddling and backstroking. I had actually made it to the other side and lived to tell the tale. It was a bit surreal as I recall. Now the dock where I had started looked very small, and very far off in the distance. Had I actually traversed the entire distance from start to finish? And if so, how in the world did I do that? What had initially seemed like an impossible task had now been conquered. And no one even seemed all that surprised (except for me of course). Get in the boat, the counselor invited. And with that, he happily rowed us back to the dock in triumph.

It took Henry Wood to finally get me off the dime, but this was undoubtedly a major achievement. From a little boy who couldn't swim at all when he first arrived at age nine, I was now a ten-year-old kid who was just as capable of passing the Lake Test as any of my senior peers. I was right up there with all of them. Would you believe that during my last summer at Camp Choconut at the age of 21, I actually became the waterfront director. I now held the same job as Willard Foote had manned twelve summers previously (the year I first arrived as a nine-year-old non-swimmer).

So many lessons learned at Camp Choconut that would follow me in all the years to come. The Lake Test taught me that anything was possible, no matter how impossible it might seem at first. It also taught me not to let fear get in the way of trying new things and approaching formidable challenges. The Lake Test was truly out of my comfort zone when I was ten years old back in 1969. Somehow I found a way to break out of that comfort zone and expand my horizons. These days when people talk about getting out of their comfort zone, I tell them that I have no idea where my comfort zone is anymore. In many ways, I think I've lived most of my life outside my comfort zone. And that's just fine with me.

IX
The Saga of the Stick

Back at home in Brooklyn, I was starting to make some significant strides in music. My guitar playing was coming along nicely, and at age eleven my parents even convinced me to take up the violin as well. I didn't care much for this idea at first because I didn't think the violin was manly. As such, I was quite surprised to discover how much I enjoyed it. I even joined my high school orchestra some years later, and that turned out to be a lot of fun as well.

Not everything was hunky-dory at home, however. I'm not sure if it was the stress of his job or some form of depression, but Dad was starting to have some pretty volatile mood swings. Not that much was known about these things back in the early seventies, nor did people even wish to discuss it. As for my brother and me, we preferred to think that it was just a normal phase that fathers went through. Of course, we knew other fathers who weren't prone to these kinds of violent and abusive patterns, but when you're a kid, the last thing you want to believe is that your situation may be unusual. We'd often hear our parents arguing at night, but some of the things that Dad would say to Mom seemed above and beyond the call (even from a child's point of view). The scary part was that we never really knew what was going to trigger him, but when he went off, it was best to give him a very wide berth.

There had been some burglaries in our building, so Dad decided to step up security measures as best he could. One such measure was to cut down a length of wood in an effort to shore up the kitchen window that led out to our terrace. Once the "stick" (as it was now called) was fit into place, it would be very difficult to open the window, even if the intruder could somehow gain access to the terrace. Of course, a determined burglar could break the window and gain entry (regardless of the stick), but Dad was convinced that his ingenuity and handiwork would get the job done.

I'm not sure from where this thin piece of wood originated. Perhaps it was a leg from an old piece of furniture, but I do recall that it was made from a very hard wood. So hard in fact, that my father had a heck of a time sawing through it (in his efforts to obtain just the right length). After a great deal of toil and many phrases beginning with "son of a—" the stick was finally ready to be fitted into place.

At that point, my father walked into the living room and announced that the stick was now in the window, and woe to anyone caught removing it for any reason. His exact words were, *"If anyone takes that stick out of the window, you might even say, I'm gonna get wild."*

"Okay Dad," we half-heartedly grunted, as his point had been made.

A few days later my brother's wise-guy friend Howie came for a visit during the afternoon while Dad was still at work. As my father had permanently banned Howie from our home, his visits could only take place when Dad was not present. The reason for Dad's extreme dislike for Howie is a whole other story, but suffice to say that these feelings ran quite deep. Upon entering our apartment, Howie immediately noticed the new development with regard to the stick in the window. A curious guy by nature, he was naturally very interested to know what it was doing there.

In addition to being a wise-guy, Howie also specialized in being a troublemaker. Quickly sizing up the import my father placed in this new security measure, he seized the opportunity to have a little fun with the old man. Unbeknownst to my brother and me, Howie secretly removed the stick and tossed it behind the piano in the living room. Yet another characteristic example of a guy who loved to stir up trouble, while bucking the system in any way he could. And as he was already on my father's top ten hated list, why miss out on a golden opportunity such as this.

As was key to Howie's plan, Mack and I failed to realize that the all-important stick was now missing. My dad on the other hand noticed it immediately. That evening while Mack and I were in our bedroom watching TV, Dad suddenly approached. *"Awright, somebody took the stick out of the window,"* he announced. *"Which one of you doity bums took the stick out of the window?"* he angrily accused. I think he went back to reinvestigate the scene of the crime at that point; thus he didn't return until a few minutes later.

During his brief absence, Mack and I noticed that our new cassette tape recorder was all plugged in, and just happened to have a fresh cassette tape already loaded. The little plastic microphone was even poised and ready to go. All that remained was to simultaneously push the play and record buttons, and we'd be ready to rock and roll. At that instant, we looked at each other with the same thought in mind. Hey, this might be good. Should we turn the tape recorder on? Oh yeah! What the hell, he'll never even know it's rolling. In an instant, the necessary buttons were activated, and we went live.

It wasn't long before Dad reentered the room with a full head of steam. And for the next twenty minutes or so he unleashed a tirade the likes of which we had never heard before. Of course, there was always the danger of his becoming violent at times like this. Yet somehow the thought of having that tape recorder rolling added an element of excitement that superseded all thoughts of physical peril. The decibel level of his voice rose to an incredible level as he shouted insults and threats one after the other.

I suppose he needed to make good on his promise of getting "wild," but this was probably the wildest we had ever seen him. His tone reached unprecedented proportions as he proceeded to assault our character in every possible manner. It was as if we were murder suspects in an interrogation room. I can't recall all the specifics these many years later, but a particular favorite was the part where he shouted, "*If anybody ever takes that stick out of the window again, I'm not gonna say a woid.*" Then, "*I'm just gonna take that stick, and I'm gonna Swat it over one of yis backs.*" And, "*Then I'm gonna say ha, ha, ha, you didn't put the stick back where it belonged.*"

Like a prizefighter that had just gone eighteen rounds, I guess he eventually hit a point where he had punched himself out. He then retired back to the living room in a state of total exhaustion. I should mention that during his twenty-minute tirade, he was actually in and out of our room several times. Though we left the tape recorder rolling the entire time, there were gaps between his explosive narrative (due to these periodic departures and reappearances).

Naturally, when we played the tape for wise-guy Howie the next day, he thought it was absolutely hysterical. And due to my father's altered state that night, I was inclined to agree. We decided that it would be fun to compile a complete comedy routine based on my father's caustic ramblings. A dramatic opening was inserted at the beginning, announcing "The Saga of The Stick" (complete with piano background). To fill the various gaps, we created dialogue between Mack, Howie, and me. Fitting our dialog perfectly within the gaps involved careful timing, as we did not want to accidentally erase any of the vital moments. By the time we were done, our project had a wonderful introduction, an incredible body, and a goodly amount of humorous and entertaining quips. There was a section in which Dad shouted "*I'm gonna break heads.*" A short pause enabled us to insert, "What's he gonna break?" Just then his angry narrative continued, "*Heads, I'm gonna break heads.*"

By anyone's definition, the thing was absolutely hysterical. Between people trying to keep their composure (because they were laughing so hard), they would often ask if he was really that mad about a stick. Some said our dad was carrying on like we'd committed murder. No one could believe that somebody could get that angry over something so seemingly trivial. As many times as I listened to it, it was also hard for me to believe that all this was over a stick in the window. Mack had an on-again-off-again girlfriend at the time named Tina who had no sense of humor whatsoever. It was the first time I had ever seen Tina laugh. And not just "tee hee." This absolutely dry and lifeless gal nearly busted a gut.

For us, it was our way of removing ourselves from the craziness of the situation. I guess it probably wasn't nice or in any way respectful to display our father's lunatic ramblings to all our buddies, but damn it was funny. And instead of looking back on the whole thing from a sad and tragic perspective, it just became a funny story that will always give us a good laugh. In the end, perhaps no real harm done. I'm pretty sure that Dad never heard "The Saga of The Stick."

X
Judo School Time

Around the same time that I was being introduced to Camp Choconut, my parents thought it would be a good idea to give us a leg up on some of the local Brooklyn street toughs. As mild-mannered and peace-loving kids, Mack and I never looked for fights and tried to avoid them whenever possible. As such, we were often viewed as an easy target by our more aggressive and more streetwise schoolmates. As in the previous case of Frankie Farella, we'd eventually rise to the occasion when our backs were up against the wall. But in general, we tolerated a lot of abuse from the neighborhood ruffians. So one afternoon, my dad hauled us off to Cliff Yost's "Fighting Arts" Judo School. I'm thinking he probably found this place via the Yellow Pages and must have liked the look of the ad. Whatever means he used to find it, neither Mack nor I had any idea what Judo was, and we were skeptical, to say the least.

The only thing we knew about Martial Arts was what we saw on TV and in the movies. But these representations were made to look spectacular and were also largely based on the skills of Karate and Kung Fu. Both of which had nothing whatsoever to do with Judo. So what was Judo? A Japanese word that roughly translated into "The gentle art of the gentle way." But as we observed what was going on in that "dojo" (judo school) on that first day, we saw nothing that looked in any way gentle. Guys were vigorously wrestling with one another in an attempt to throw their opponent to the ground, thus achieving "a theoretical kill."

From a standing position, the body can be leveraged to lift one's opponent from his feet and somersault him through the air, thus landing him squarely on his back. We were soon to discover that there were a great variety of ways in which to accomplish this. There were arm throws, leg throws, hip throws and shoulder throws, all designed to land the opponent helpless on the mat. And if one's opponent didn't land squarely enough to achieve the theoretical kill, then there were various methods of holding the man down on the mat while securing his body such that he couldn't escape. And if this wasn't sufficient, the match could also be won by choking one's opponent into submission (or unconsciousness), or by leveraging the opponent's arm such that they'd either have to concede or risk having it broken. Throws, hold downs, chokes, and arm locks. Any of these (or a combination) of these techniques could achieve the theoretical kill and win you the match. Sound gentle?

Yet somehow to watch the really good players compete, there was almost a grace and elegance to it. And even more amazingly, most of the time nobody actually got hurt. The key to this hidden element of safety was that great care was taken to first teach all beginning judo students how to fall correctly and safely. Falling is an unnatural feeling for most people, and most react with panic. Feeling the ground coming up fast, the natural tendency is to reach down with arms extended outward. While this seems like a better alternative than slamming one's head and body into the ground, the typical result is broken arms or wrists.

When being hurled through the air in judo, the correct technique is to try and land on your side (as opposed to flat on your back). Since most judo players are right-handed, you will mainly be falling on your left side. The legs will come down first, so the left leg should remain extended while the right leg should be cocked at the knee. The arms should remain at your side. At the point of impact, the left arm should rotate downward with force (with palm open and loose at the elbow), slapping the mat vigorously with the inside of the hand. The result is that it winds up sounding much worse than it actually is. The open hand slapping down on the mat makes quite a racket. In reality, if the fall is handled in just this way, there is no pain or injury whatsoever. The fallen player simply gets right up and the two continue to grapple.

To the untutored, it looks horrible, although it's actually quite a bit safer than it seems. In all the years that Mack and I practiced judo, I don't actually recall people getting hurt very often. I'm not saying it couldn't happen, but it usually didn't. Of course, there were accidents from time to time, but these usually didn't result in serious injury. If, however, somebody got it in his head to be really nasty, they could indeed hurt you quite badly.

There was always the infamous "Makikomi" (pronounced Mock ee comb mee). I should add that while throwing your opponent to the ground, it is important that you pull back a bit with your arms thus supporting your opponent's body at the point of impact. This reduces the downward force and is considered good judo etiquette. When one seeks to Makikomi however, additional force and follow-through are applied at the point of impact. This increases the severity of the fall and is designed to let your opponent know that their safety and well-being are not your prime concern. In the most extreme case, the "thrower" will actually use his body to come down hard on his opponent at the completion of the throw. This not only maximizes impact, but most of the time it serves to completely take the wind out of your opponent. I've been on the receiving end a time or two, so I know it's not much fun. But as I say, this is the vast exception and most judo players I've met were actually pretty good guys.

How accomplished a judo player you are can be easily surmised by the color of the belt you've earned. During the early years, your instructor will promote you as he sees fit. He will rank you in accordance with the other players in your dojo. Naturally, he will not want to promote you too quickly, as your rank will reflect upon the caliber of his dojo. As the various dojos will often compete with one another during large organized intercity contests, it is important that you represent your school and instructor well.

These contests were my idea of purgatory. I sincerely hope that there isn't actually a hell because if there is, I would be playing in these contests for all eternity. Hundreds of participants all gathered in a huge gymnasium with their supporters sitting in the stands. Picture a well-publicized heavy-weight boxing match, and you begin to get the idea. Two guys going at it while people are screaming at the top of their lungs. "Get him, kill him, rip his head off!" At least that's how I remember it. I remember one particular match when one of the moms was not happy with the referee's decision. Often during these contests no one actually gets thrown cleanly (or held down or choked into submission), so it is the referee's job to appoint the winner. And this particular ref did not call the match in favor of her son. So, Mom walked out onto the mat in a huff and slapped the referee squarely in the face. Her son was a much better sportsman than she was. In fact, he congratulated his opponent when the match was over. Mom took it a bit more personal. In retrospect, many of the parents took these matches way more personally than they should have.

When I first started competing in these contests, I was very quickly introduced to a guy who would become my nemesis. His name was Frankie Palosi (why did I have so much trouble with kids named Frankie?) Anyway, Frankie Palosi was the twelve-year-old New York State champion at the time. During my first match with him, it was not hard to see why. Frankie had a deadly shoulder throw at his disposal known as "marote seianagi" (pronounced ma row tay – say a nog gee). In fact, his nickname was "Marote Frankie." Before it was my turn to play him, I watched the three or four others that came before me. They were flying over Frankie's shoulder like sides of beef being slammed down onto a butcher block.

As I watched with great interest, I was determined not to become yet another carcass of beef. But as the match began, I quickly saw just how skilled Frankie was with his deadly shoulder throw. He had a way of lulling you in while moving you forward, then suddenly dropping down while turning his body 180 degrees. Using your momentum, he'd easily topple you over his shoulder. In an instant, you were laid out and ready to be trimmed. Before I even knew it, he had performed this trick on me three times, and the match was over almost as quickly as it began. Not knowing what had hit me, I slowly walked back to the edge of the mat. The top player from my school immediately walked up to me and told me not to take heart. I had just played the state champ, and it wouldn't get any more difficult than that. This gave me a little bit of comfort, but such an ungraceful defeat was still a bitter pill to swallow.

    I was to grapple with Frankie Palosi many more times in my brief judo career. Although the results were usually pretty similar, there came a fateful day. While Frankie was famous for Marote, I had developed a little weapon of my own. Mine was simply called a "Foot Sweep." As I mentioned, there were such things as leg throws. More specifically in my case, the Foot Sweep was a foot throw. By using either one of your feet to literally sweep your opponent's feet out from under him, it is possible to send him flying through the air in spectacular fashion.

    Though it's hard to describe on paper, I have at times launched my opponents three or four feet into the air, eventually crash landing them hard on the mat below. This technique seems to come from nowhere, taking the opponent completely by surprise, while absolutely laying them out at the end. To throw someone squarely and convincingly on their back will earn you a full point, and thus win you the match. The dreaded foot sweep could often accomplish this. At the very least it would earn you a half-point. And though the match would continue, you were now firmly in the lead.

    On this particular day (about a minute or so into the match), from out of nowhere I let loose with one of my famous haymaker Foot Sweeps. To Frankie's astonishment, his body was now hurling through the air with great velocity, eventually landing most ungracefully and unceremoniously with a tremendous thud. And oh, the roar that went up through the crowd when they saw the champ crashing down on the mat like a ton of bricks. What was even better was the look of horror on Frankie's father's face at that point. As far as his dad was concerned, it might have been he who was now lying crumpled on that mat.

    As Jackie Gleason used to say, "How sweet it is." For the senior Mr. Palosi was one smug S.O.B. "My son Frankie this, my son Frankie that." Now his son Frankie was actually losing the match. Mr. Palosi's face now showed a look of total desperation, as he shouted to his son that there was very little time left in the match. It was a sweet moment indeed.

Unfortunately, I didn't get to enjoy it for very long. I would love to say that I finally emerged victoriously and was carried off the field in triumph on the shoulders of my supporters. I'd love to say it, but it just didn't happen that way. Not long after my glorious Foot Sweep, Frankie managed to hold me down on the mat, thus snatching victory out of the jaws of defeat.

No, I didn't win the match that day. But I did teach both senior and junior Palosi some respect. And for a short time, I made them extremely nervous indeed. I'd even like to think that Frankie received a thorough admonishment from his father as to how he could let someone come so close to beating him. One thing was for certain. I came about as close as anyone did that day. And what did I have to lose. He was the national champ.

XI
The Crosses We Bear

When we're young none of us like to think that we may be different in some way. For a great many of us, that rule carries over well into our adult years. But as young people, we especially strive to believe that we are part of the much-desired group known as normal. While "normal" has certainly shifted greatly over the years, it probably still includes things like having a reasonably well-adjusted family, a roof over our heads, food on the table, and being of sound mind and body. If any of these conditions are somewhat out of alignment, however, it can certainly be cause for concern.

I mentioned Mack's wise-guy friend Howie concerning "The Stick." Long story short, Howie's dad was a gangster, and his mother was a hooker. The two were already divorced when Howie was still in elementary school, so he lived in our apartment building with his "working" mom. As far as Howie was concerned, however, his life was as normal as any other kid in our building. And if you ever tried to convince him otherwise, you'd do so at your own peril. Never mind that his dad was always at home any hour of the day including Monday thru Friday. (In those days it was very rare for anyone to work at home). And despite his seemingly unemployed and carefree lifestyle, he lived in a very fashionable part of the city known as Forest Hills. And never mind that at any hour of the day Howie's mom might insist that Howie immediately vacate the apartment for an hour or two. He even told me on one occasion that she was going to the racetrack one afternoon, as rent funds were coming up short that month. And wouldn't you know it, her horse came in.

Speaking of "out of alignment," I ran into a very friendly fellow in my elementary school one day who had a very odd-looking front tooth. Save for the funky tooth, he was a good-looking kid of about age eleven or twelve. As I recall, he was also very well-liked by his teachers and peers. Still, I couldn't help but notice that strange-looking tooth. Upon closer inspection, I also noticed that it had turned green. Up till that point, I had never seen a green tooth before, thus I had no idea what it meant. I quickly learned that this was the telltale indication of a tooth that was dying, and poor Tommy would probably lose it in fairly short order. Most unfortunate, as it was one of his prominent top front teeth. Quite taken aback, I whispered to my buddy next to me if he had noticed Tommy's green tooth. I guess I wasn't as discreet as I thought, as Tommy clearly overheard my comment. "If you've got something to say to me, why don't you come here and say it to my face," Tommy immediately demanded. Looking back, I'm sure I could have displayed a great deal more consideration and discretion regarding Tommy's tooth. But kids aren't always well endowed with these particular attributes.

Tommy must have endured many derisive comments regarding that tooth and was probably always on high alert when he sensed one was coming. Naturally, I was a bit embarrassed when he called me to the carpet on it. He even insisted that I meet him after school that day to settle the matter out in the schoolyard. An unsightly discolored and dying tooth would probably make most of us self-conscious. Something I probably should have figured out at the time, but as far as Tommy was concerned, his appearance was perfectly normal. And if for any reason you didn't agree, then he'd settle it with you in the best way he knew.

We all know that expression about people who live in glass houses. With regard to having a weird physical malady, it turns out Tommy and I actually shared that burden. The big difference was that his was readily visible to the naked eye, while mine was not. Fortunately for Tommy, his issue could have been resolved via some dental surgery. Perhaps a false tooth, or an implant of some sort. In my case, however, I have sadly come to accept that there really is no viable solution to my condition.

Even at a very early age, I had frequent stomach aches and pain in my gut that was often quite debilitating. The pain would often result in desperate races to the bathroom, with bowel movements that were anything but comfortable (or brief). One of my earliest memories of this condition was about age four or so. My parents wanted to reward Mack and me with a trip to the ice cream shop one evening on our way to grandma's house. Mack had done something that angered my parents just prior to ice cream time, and as his punishment, he'd have to forego the treat that night. He was most distressed at the time, but my parents were insistent. Though I felt a bit guilty, I accepted the ice cream and we proceeded to grandma and grandpa's. Ice cream rental would have been a better name for that shop in this case because my stomach proceeded to explode upon arriving at the grandparent's place.

After dominating their only restroom for the better part of an hour, I finally emerged looking like I had just gone ten rounds with George

Foreman. A lactose intolerance perhaps? Maybe, but over the years I've had countless similar attacks following meals consisting of all kinds of foods. I've had countless stomach attacks over the years even when no food was involved at all. Much like Howie and Tommy, however, if anyone ever suggested to me that there might actually be something wrong, I'd deny it vehemently. Not being normal in a physical sense was bad enough, but being abnormal because of bathroom habits was absolutely intolerable. There was no way I was ever going to own up to that.

As a peace-loving guy, however, I didn't respond by calling people out on the schoolyard. I'd simply react as though they had no idea what they were talking about. I'd defend my delicate stomach constitution with a vengeance, explaining to the inquisitive that this was perfectly normal for me. After all, it's the way I've always been, so it must be normal for people like me.

What I didn't realize at the time was that people notice everything that seems a bit out of the ordinary. Even though my stomach wasn't as immediately visible as Tommy's tooth, it certainly didn't take too long for people to sleuth it out. What I also didn't realize at the time, was that parents could be just as self-conscious about their child's maladies. After all, our kids are a reflection of us. If our child has a nasty and embarrassing stomach condition, might people think that we are somehow the cause? And as it happens, my affliction probably did come from Dad's gene pool. And that particular pool got a bit shallow when it came to disorders of the gastrointestinal system. My brother and I chuckled about Dad's frequent bathroom "needs" on many occasions. If I knew what was to come, there's no way in the world I would have found it in any way amusing.

When I was an adult and had a family of my own, Mom and Dad came to Seattle one week for a visit. Though Dad and I never related well to each other about anything, I took the opportunity to ask him about his ongoing stomach battles. I knew the subject had to be approached delicately, as Dad was not the most forthcoming of individuals, especially when it came to information of a deeply personal nature. In a casual and understanding tone, I asked if his stomach issues had gotten any better over the years. I told him that mine were being pretty stubborn at this point in my life, and I was wondering if perhaps things would ease up as I got older. I don't know why, but I was really hoping for an insightful and helpful response.

Even if the answer was no (things haven't really gotten better with age), at least I'd have a clue as to what might lie ahead. I guess I should have predicted his response which was basically, "What stomach issues?" Again, trying to be delicate, I mentioned that he and his stomach often seemed at odds. Despite this preliminary prompting, I was again met with denial (as if this was a peculiar inquiry to a condition for which he was completely unfamiliar). In short, he played dumb. Am I just imagining that he and his tummy were often at odds? Believe me, I am not. But like Tommy's tooth or Howie's parents, it was probably something he simply never came to terms with. He did offer one short tidbit on this subject, however. He casually noted that very few physical things actually get better with age. I suppose I couldn't argue with that.

Throughout my teens and into my young adult life, I recall people making frequent polite inquiries as to my poor stomach. Mostly, it seemed to come from feelings of genuine concern. Where did Gary go? Is he okay? Has he been in the bathroom all this time? Is he ill? The voices were always hushed and put forth with polite discretion. Nevertheless, I heard them either directly or through those close to me. And, of course, I would assuage any and all concerned that they needn't worry about me. I was just fine. Why wouldn't I be? What reason was there to indicate otherwise? Couldn't they see that this was simply "my normal," and they should all just go on happily about their business?

I know now that what they were observing probably seemed like a giant elephant roaming about the room. But elephants can get pretty ornery when you approach them too directly. And the funniest part of all is that I actually believed in my heart of hearts, that there was truly nothing wrong with me. I really never stopped to analyze why I was the only one that had to deal with these frequent and disruptive stomach issues. I simply preferred to believe that it was something that everyone battled from time to time.

One summer at camp when I was about eleven or twelve, we set out for a five or ten-mile hike up and down the dusty dirt roads of northeastern PA. It was a hot sunny August afternoon with temperatures probably hovering in the nineties. By the time we reached our campsite in the late afternoon, suffice to say we were pretty spent. Delighted to finally shed our forty-pound backpacks, we easily shifted into relax mode. The hard part was over and now we could have fun for the next couple of days. But for some reason, I wasn't feeling all that great. I didn't even understand why I wasn't feeling all that great. I just knew I wasn't.

At that moment one of the older boys approached me with sheer joy in his heart. After Bint Toland had put down his pack, he immediately changed out of his jeans and into a lightweight pair of shorts. He then informed me that he now felt absolutely wonderful. "I feel just great," he joyfully announced. He turned to me and said, "Don't you feel just great?"

I answered him honestly. "No, I don't."

He then turned to me like I was from Mars. With a look of utter confusion appearing on his face, he said "Why don't you feel great? I do."

And the odd part was that I really had no idea why I didn't feel great. But in fact, I didn't even feel good. At that moment, my gastrointestinal system suddenly put forth a gaseous burst that was distinctly audible. At least that answered the question as to why I didn't feel great.

Not realizing that this was an unfortunate condition over which I had little to no control, Bint Toland was immediately repulsed. His expression then changed to one of total disgust, as he stormed away muttering loudly as he went. He even informed several of my cabin mates about the vile and disgusting act I had just committed. The physical pain I was already experiencing was now compounded by the emotional pain that Bint added to the mix. If I really thought about it, I could probably recall many such incidents throughout my childhood.

It certainly can be a truly embarrassing issue, while at the same time, often resulting in great pain. At a minimum, it leaves one feeling worn out and generally unwell. It zaps your energy while often disrupting your best-laid plans. I got sick a lot when I was a kid, and although I didn't think about it at the time, I'm now convinced that my stomach was adversely affecting the natural absorption of nutrients throughout my body. It's as good a theory as any. Of course, these were just the physical ramifications. The emotional ones were every bit as debilitating.

This pattern of issue and denial continued to play out into my early twenties, upon which time I received my first full-time job. Not only was Norm Bestrum my first real boss, but he also became my mentor and lifelong friend. In addition to jump-starting my career, Norm also took a deep personal interest in my professional journey, as well as my general wellbeing. And much to Norm's credit, he was not someone to shy away from discussing potentially sensitive issues. If there was something he needed to bring up with you, he'd just put it out there. He wasn't cruel or insensitive about it. He was simply direct and extremely matter-of-fact.

So when he approached me one day to engage in a very serious discussion, I was caught quite off guard. Without a great deal of fanfare, he simply stated that he'd been observing my frequent use of the company restroom. "I see the way you're constantly in and out of the bathroom," he stated. "What's going on with you is just not right." As usual, I feigned ignorance while attempting to understand what would prompt such an off-the-wall statement. So he took a breath and simply repeated, "I see what's been going on with you and the bathroom, and what's going on just isn't right." As I say, Norm was more than just a boss to me, so his opinions had to be respected (or at least acknowledged). My assertion that this was normal for me, and how it's always been this way, made no headway with Norm whatsoever. Sticking to his guns he asserted, "You may have always been this way, but it's just not right."

How could I possibly respond to that? Norm was one of the sharpest and most intelligent men I'd ever met in my life. As such, his assertions were not quickly dismissed. And I knew that to do so at this point would be foolhardy. The message had officially been delivered, and this time it was undeniable. For the first time in my life, I finally gave up the pretense of feigning ignorance. I finally had to admit to myself that my body may indeed be suspect in this regard. That didn't make it any less humiliating, but it did make it real. Alright, I resolved. If this is some form of physical malady and a potential threat to my health, then I need to do something about it.

There are specialists for this, Norm informed me. "You need to get an appointment with one of these guys and have it thoroughly checked out." While I knew he was absolutely right, getting it "checked out" didn't sound like it was going to be much fun.

Several weeks later, I could see the look of relief on Norm's face when I told him of my impending appointment with a gastroenterologist. I must admit it also brought me a certain sense of calm, though I had no idea of the arduous journey that was now beginning.

Upon arriving on appointment day with much fear and dread, I was quickly ushered into the examining room. After being told to remove my clothes and don the special gown, I sat on the examining table awaiting the presence of His Royal Highness, the gastroenterologist. Admittedly, I had no idea what these guys did, what kinds of examinations they performed, or what equipment they used to perform them. All I could see was that the room looked like any other medical treatment facility I'd ever experienced.

The doc and his nurse entered simultaneously. I was immediately concerned upon noticing that they were both giggling like schoolchildren. I was even more concerned to discover that the source of their amusement was the previous patient (apparently an older lady treated in the room next to mine). I couldn't imagine what would cause such jocularity while treating this poor woman, but it was certainly unsettling that both doc and nurse found it so amusing. I immediately wondered if they'd be chuckling about me after my exam.

After their little joke was over, the doc introduced himself and asked about my condition. He nodded affirmingly at my responses and told me that he would be performing a procedure known as a partial (or limited) colonoscopy. Basically, he'd introduce a long and seemingly bulky scope into the anus. This would enable him to probe deeply inside a goodly length of the bowel. Fitted to the end of the scope was a tiny camera which enabled the doc to visualize the bowel as it moved along. Yikes, no wonder the old woman next door panicked.

This procedure is done without anesthetic and although uncomfortable, I was told it would be tolerable. Whether or not it was actually tolerable is a matter of opinion, but there was certainly no turning back at this point. My opinion was that it hurt like hell when that scope was introduced, and pretty much during the entire procedure. The only time it ever stopped hurting was when it was withdrawn. I can't say exactly how long the actual procedure took. Probably about ten or fifteen minutes, but it seemed like an eternity. One of those surreal moments when you can't believe what's happening to you is really happening. Anyway, I bore it like a trooper and noticed no discernable reaction on the doc's face at any time along the way.

When the procedure was finally complete, the doc gave a slight "Hmm." He then instructed me to put my clothes back on and meet him in the consulting room. Delighted to be done being probed in this manner, I did as I was told. When we started to talk, his questions mainly concerned my eating habits and what kinds of foods I gravitated toward. After advising that I should add more green vegetables and roughage to my diet, he began to describe a condition known as Irritable Bowel Syndrome.

The fact of the matter was that he found nothing unusual during my examination, and Irritable Bowel Syndrome was his only explanation. At that point, I demanded to know exactly what was meant by this heinous condition (often abbreviated I.B.S).. After the pain of his exam, I figured I was entitled to a goodly explanation. I wanted to know what it is, what causes it, and most importantly, how it is cured.

Unfortunately, this is when it started becoming painfully obvious that the medical community has a wonderful way of naming things of which it has very little knowledge. To us cynics in the non-medical community, we can only assume that this is done in an attempt to make the medical practitioners appear more knowledgeable. Leprosy, for instance, was a name invented in the old days to indicate that someone had a skin condition. What actually caused it, or how to treat it was not known. But it had a name by God, and therefore we could identify it, thus letting patients know when we spotted it.

So, as I demanded more specific information about Irritable Bowel Syndrome, the spottier the answers became. We don't really know what causes it, the wise practitioner advised, although there are any number of working theories. Perhaps it's genetic, but perhaps not. Sometimes a change in diet or lifestyle will ease the symptoms, but sometimes not. Perhaps stress is the culprit, but not always. The one thing the doc was good and sure of, however, is that there is certainly no cure. "But don't worry, I didn't see anything in there that's going to kill you," he proudly

66 *Whataya Gonna Do?*

concluded. "And by the way, please pay the receptionist on your way out."

Since this first experience back in my twenties, I've been seeing various gastroenterologists and other noted specialists for the last forty years. All told, I've probably racked up at least a dozen of these guys and gals over the years. There have been a great variety of tests, some more painful than others, and I can't tell you how many digital rectal probes I've endured. In the end, all with no tangible results to speak of. A friend of mine who sells surgical instruments refers to these folks as scope jockeys. From my perspective, it's not hard to see why. I can't tell you how many times I've been told everything looks just fine when the scope failed to reveal anything even remotely out of whack. And when you insist that you're anything but fine, you're pretty much dismissed out of hand. As we all know, however, medicine is not an exact science. Quite often there are no answers to the issues that plague us. In the end, we are often left up to our own devices, thus we plod on as best we can.

XII
With Friends Like That...

It is said that one of the easiest times in our lives to make friends is during those formative years in school. And why not. You're with the same group of kids each and every day, all day long. Since you're in the same class, it also stands to reason that you don't live far from one another. So it's no wonder that some pretty lasting bonds are formed during these years. And since these relationships started out at such a young age, it allows us to boast that these folks are our oldest and dearest friends.

I attended a wedding recently where the bride had several childhood friends in attendance. During the speech portion, one of these old friends proudly informed the crowd that she and the bride had first met in kindergarten. Granted, it's easier for this kind of thing to take place when people don't stray far from where they were born. Even so, a friend since kindergarten is something worth boasting about. During my elementary school years, I too was blessed with a couple of these very special friendships. Though for reasons that I will now explain, they both had a relatively short expiration date. Despite their limited longevity, however, these relationships formed a very significant part of my young life.

Steven lived in the same apartment building as I did, and we were in the same class from the third to the sixth grades. Though long on intelligence, Steven lacked a bit of basic common sense. He and I shared a similar sense of humor, and he was very well-liked among his classmates. Quick with a quip, always ready with a smile, and equipped with a moppy pile of blond hair, Steven was a likable sort indeed. I recall some of the gals in class taking quite a shine to him as well.

Steven and I would meet down in the lobby of our apartment building every morning, and we'd start our day by walking to school together. He'd most often head down to my apartment when the school day was over, either to hang out or get together for a game or two of basketball. Though our friendship was very important to me, it was thoroughly tested on a couple of occasions. One such time was when he and I were accosted after school by a group of local toughs. Rather than hang tough and put up a united front, however, Steven decided his safest option was to join forces with the bullies, while leaving me to fend for myself.

Naturally, this made for a very rough afternoon for me, but it allowed Steven to survive the confrontation completely unscathed. Or so he thought. After the thugs were finally finished pummeling me, I extended the same courtesy to Steven even before we returned home. He probably wound up taking a worse pounding from me than he would have gotten from the bullies, had he done the honorable thing in the first place. When his mom got wind of the story, she asked me to explain why Steven came home crying (if I was the one who got beaten up). With absolutely no reservation, I explained to her that I cleaned his clock as a result of his "Benedict Arnold-like" behavior. She never questioned me for a second. That was one of my first experiences with the concept of betrayal. Getting beaten up wasn't fun, but it often came with the territory of growing up in the big city. Having your best friend turn on you like that, well that was something else entirely. That was much harder to reconcile. As I say, a smart kid, but common sense and loyalty were not Steven's strong suit.

Not long after that very unpleasant incident, we went on a long class trip. I think it was the one where they drove us all the way to our state capitol in Albany. The goal was for us to learn a little bit about our government while journeying to the place where governing is exercised. This involved about a five-hour stretch (both coming and going) on the big yellow school bus. Naturally, we all chose seat partners and paired off in accordance with our usual well-established friendships.

I don't recall who I sat next to on the ride up to Albany, but I distinctly recall sitting by myself on the way back. Steven and I weren't even talking anymore by now. Though I hadn't noticed (or cared to notice), Steven was also sitting alone during the trip back. About three-quarters of the way home, our teacher (Mr. Brewster) came by and casually sat down next to me. I knew he was going to ask me about Steven, though I had no desire to discuss it. "I couldn't help notice that you and Steven are both sitting by yourselves," he commented in a curious and caring manner. He was concerned as to why we were no longer friends, further adding that good friends are hard to find. I still didn't want to recount the story for him, but I certainly agreed that good friends are indeed hard to find. As Mr. Brewster continued to press me for details, I volunteered only this. I told him that I didn't want to say what happened, for fear that he would lose respect for Steven. Though my respect for Steven had greatly diminished, I was determined to take the high road. I would not besmirch his character before our teacher.

Despite our differences, we eventually resumed our friendship shortly thereafter, and the incident was never mentioned again. We were put in different classes for our seventh grade (Junior High School) term, but still continued to see each other around the apartment building. Eventually, he found other friends, while becoming even more popular with the ladies. My last impressions of Steven were of someone who was starting to get a pretty big head, while rapidly losing his former good-natured and pleasant self.

While working at a summer camp somewhere in upstate New York (at the age of seventeen), his life was abruptly cut short by a drunk driver. A victim of his own chronic lack of common sense, Steven was apparently walking along a quiet country road all alone on a dark night. The car came out of nowhere and the badly inebriated driver probably never even saw him. The only saving grace was that he was probably killed instantly. For years following his death, I would frequently ride up and down the elevator of our apartment building alongside his mom or dad. The looks on their faces always suggested business as usual, but I couldn't even imagine being in their shoes. One day I finally got up the nerve to ask his mom how she was doing. "How should I be doing," she replied in a half-hearted manner. That was the extent of our conversation.

My other great pal in elementary school was Peter Issacov. I met him right around the same time I met Steven. Our apartment complex consisted of two large nineteen-story buildings that each contained about two hundred apartment units. Whereas Steven and I lived in the one, Peter resided in the other. As the two buildings sat directly across from one another, with only a grassy lawn to separate them, it was a pretty simple matter to traverse from one to the other. They were affectionately known as "Building 1" and "Building 2." I recall spending many an afternoon over at Peter's apartment under the kind and warm supervision of his mom. Unlike my mom, Peter's mother was a stay-at-home "homemaker/housewife." Our little apartment community had many of these stay-at-home moms. As I think about it, being a full-time working woman, my mom was definitely in the minority.

I don't know if I ever asked Peter what kind of work his father did, but whatever it was, it provided a sufficient lifestyle such that his wife didn't need to work. As I mentioned, Peter's mom was a very nice lady indeed, and she always went out of her way to make me feel warm and welcome. She also seemed highly intelligent and struck me as quite educated. Had she ventured out into the working world, I have no doubt she would have met with success. Though I probably met Peter's dad only once or twice during all those years (and briefly at that), I know that he was also a smart guy and equally well-schooled.

To be honest, the Issacovs always seemed a bit out of place to me in this highly blue-collar and mainly working-class environment. I never got the feeling that such obviously astute and well-bred people belonged in this community of secretaries and clerks. Another thing that made them interesting was the combination of their ethnicities. Peter's dad (Abraham) was Jewish, while Maria (his mom) was Italian and Catholic. My earlier joke about growing up and marrying the bully's sister really did pan out from time to time. Though technically half Jewish, Peter always identified as Catholic. He often talked of his upcoming catechism and observed all the regular Catholic holidays. Perhaps Abraham wasn't a practicing Jew, as Peter's Catholic upbringing never seemed to be an issue.

Regardless of creed, Peter was a product of his well-mannered and highly refined parents. More than a bit on the nerdy side, he was regarded as being the class genius. No subject was out of Peter's reach, and he was an absolute champ come exam time. Academically, you could count on Peter to come out on top every time. But for all his sheer intelligence, he was actually a very humble, well-adjusted, and extremely approachable kid. In fact, Peter was probably one of the nicest kids I've ever met. He had a kind word for everyone and a natural ability to put people at ease. Though his intelligence was obvious, you somehow never felt threatened by it. You were more likely to hope that it would rub off on you if you hung around with him.

Though he was one hell of a nice kid and always a genuine pleasure to be around, it would be a stretch indeed to suggest that the girls ever got that excited about him. Sure, they liked him well enough, but never in a way that made their hearts go pitter-patter. Suffice to say that rugged (or boyish) good looks were not Peter's strong suit. Perhaps it was his nerdy appearance and studious manner that made him so non-threatening.

Though he always seemed more than willing to participate in our usual schoolyard sports activities, he was usually about the last one chosen whenever it came to picking teams. While he could certainly help you with your math or history homework, his blinding speed or basketball jump shot accuracy was never destined for the record books. I guess we all have our gifts and hitting a baseball out of the park will probably have to remain on Peter's bucket list. While it certainly wasn't for lack of trying, one does require a basic physical coordination for these kinds of activities. It's too bad you can't learn to be a great athlete by acing it on a test. But if you could, Peter would have been an all-star.

If you are destined only to be a so-so baseball player, however, it's probably a good idea to at least incorporate some basic principles of safety into your game. I say this as I recall one afternoon when Peter and I were in the fifth grade. Being a rather sports-minded group, the guys in our class decided to get up a baseball game after school that day. Turnout was good, sides were chosen up, (with Peter probably coming in dead last), and we quickly got down to business.

Things were rolling along quite well, and everyone was getting into the spirit. When it became my turn at bat, I eagerly took up my position alongside the plate. I should mention that Peter and I wound up on the same side. This added to the fun for me and made the game that much more exciting. With my favorite bat cocked and ready to go, I was a force to be reckoned with. And if I do say so myself, I was an unusually decent baseball player for a kid my age. Though I was thin, I was quite athletic and could easily send a baseball hurling well into the outfield.

I remember taking a few practice swings before settling into my stance. I don't recall whether I swung at the first pitch, or whether I waited for the second or third. When it suddenly looked right, my bat automatically began to rotate with great force. This one was right where I wanted it, thus I prepared to launch it into outer space. My bat came around with great extension, as I followed through for maximum rotation. My first reaction was that of extreme exhilaration. There was no doubt whatsoever that I had pulverized the incoming projectile. About a half-second later, however, I got one of the weirdest feelings I've ever had. All of a sudden, my brain conjured up serious concerns about whether that impact was actually the result of bat to ball. Somehow things just didn't feel quite right. While there was no doubt that my bat had definitely connected with something solid, there was not the familiar spring of a baseball being launched skyward.

A very uneasy question then began to conjure up in my mind. If my bat didn't actually make contact with the ball, then what did I hit? It didn't take too much longer to uncover the sickening answer to that question. (No doubt I had my eyes closed at the actual point of impact). But now that they were open, the first thing I saw was my good buddy Peter clutching his head, while his body was very quickly heading toward the ground. No wonder it didn't feel like a baseball. The impact of bat to human skull is a very different sensation indeed (or so I discovered). Suddenly I got a very nauseating feeling in my gut. Everyone was now gathered around Peter, who at this point seemed to be unconscious and laying on the ground. There was great turmoil and a sudden concern for locating an adult or a policeman. He was clearly alive, albeit probably in quite a state of shock.

As for me, I was frantically searching to make some kind of sense out of this extremely sudden and bewildering turn of events. Slowly I became aware that Peter had decided to neatly arrange the unused baseball bats during the time I was at-bat. Naturally, I had no knowledge of this during the heat of the moment. As I say, I WAS AT BAT! Of all the times to choose to tidy up, man did he ever pick the wrong one. By now some of the kids were attempting to help him up, so that he could be taken home to his mom. As for me, I was now entering a state of panic. The realization that I had just clobbered my best friend with a baseball bat had filled my conscience. How bad was he hurt? Did I cave in his skull? Would there be brain damage? Could he actually die from such an injury? It was like a terrible dream unfolding right in front of me, only it was real.

Eventually, I saw Peter being led off back to his apartment building where his mother was sure to have a coronary. Two guys were necessary to keep him steady, as he was not walking completely under his own power. I would have liked to help him, but I was terrified that some of the kids would start to blame me. He would be home shortly and there was nothing I could do at this point anyway. I slowly walked back to my apartment building feeling like someone who had just committed a violent and heinous crime.

When I got back home, I tried to act like nothing was wrong. I waited for dinner as usual, although I had no appetite. I debated several times whether to call Peter's house but was terrified at what I might find out. Finally, I could stand it no longer. With my heart in my throat, I dialed Peter's number. If I live to be a hundred, I'll never forget the sound of his mom's voice that evening when she answered the phone. I was a fifth-grade kid and she was an adult, but it was she who was absolutely frantic. It scared the hell out of me. Adults were supposed to keep calm in the face of calamity, and Peter's mother sounded like someone had died. More specifically, like Peter had died.

Though I don't remember her exact words, it was something to the effect of *"I don't know where Peter is,"* and *"There was an accident,"* then, *"They took him to the hospital!"* She was sobbing by the time she got to the last part. Her next words to me were, *"Do you know what happened?!"*

My reply could probably be listed among the greatest cowardly responses of all time. I said, "I don't know... I think someone might have hit him with a baseball bat." Needless to say, she found no comfort in my gutless explanation. The rest of that evening passed excruciatingly slowly. I don't know if my parents ever got wind of what was going on. At last, it was time for bed, and I tried to put it out of my mind during the night. I don't remember being too successful on that score.

The next day also unfolded very slowly, but at last, I found myself seated in my classroom. To my extreme delight and with great relief, I also discovered Peter sitting in his usual spot. By now, of course, word had spread like wildfire. It wasn't long before the teacher asked Peter what had happened the previous afternoon and if he was okay. With my heart rate still very much elevated, Peter announced that it actually wasn't as bad as it initially seemed. As it initially seemed pretty darned bad, I was finally able to let out a great sigh of relief.

As it turned out, the only real damage was that one of Peter's baby teeth had been knocked out. Since we eventually lose these anyway, we somehow managed to dodge a very big bullet that day. In my heart of hearts, I knew that the accident really wasn't my fault. That wouldn't have been of great comfort, however, had Peter's injuries been more serious. What he was thinking (when he decided to arrange those bats while the game was in progress) I'll never know, but I'd like to think that he learned a very valuable lesson that day. Never a good idea to take your eye off the ball (so to speak) during the heat of a baseball game. You might think that tidying up the unused bats at a time when it was safe to do so, might simply be common sense. For Peter, however, yet another of life's many formative bumps in the road. Although he never blamed me, I felt bad just the same.

Over the years I've had ample time to consider the similarities between my two elementary school friends (Peter and Steven). Steven was bright but didn't have a great deal of common sense in most matters. Peter was brilliant but lacked a certain acumen when it came to physical pursuits. In Steven's case, it proved fatal at the age of seventeen. I'm pleased to say that Peter is very much alive and well. He currently lives in Dallas, TX, and I was able to connect with him (no pun intended) via telephone a number of years ago. Naturally, he went on to become a very successful lawyer, and he now sits on several boards of directors as well.

Not long after I tracked him down, I needed to fly somewhere for business. And as it turned out, my flight involved a rather lengthy stopover in Dallas. What luck, I thought. Now I'd have an opportunity to see Peter again after all these years. I e-mailed him many times before my trip, asking if he'd like to meet at the Dallas/Fort Worth Airport. I never got a reply. I went on my trip having never heard back from him. I hoped he might be there anyway when my flight got in, but there was no sign of him. When I returned home to Seattle, I finally saw an e-mail from him. Sorry I couldn't meet you he replied, but I had a dentist appointment that day.

During the years we were friends, Peter and I were inseparable. As such, I must say I took his rejection somewhat to heart. Had his plans included being at Seatac Airport for four hours, I surely would have rescheduled my dentist appointment. I don't think I'd have let anything get in the way of a reunion with such a valued friend that I hadn't seen in thirty years. I could only conclude that not everyone shares my sense of nostalgia, or the importance I place on personal relationships (whether current or past). Perhaps he does blame me for the baseball bat incident! Just kidding of course. I doubt he even remembers it. I do wish him well.

As a footnote to the Peter story, I can only remember one time during our entire association that I ever ruffled his feathers. I remember it because it was so out of character for Peter. Being such an easy-going and mild-mannered dude, it was awfully hard to get him into a lather about anything. But without intending to, I managed to do it one afternoon.

Peter and I were both taking guitar lessons from the same guy at that time. While I was always extremely enthusiastic about my musical pursuits, it became all too clear to me that Peter was not. We were hanging out at his apartment (in his room) one afternoon and trying to figure out what fun thing we wanted to do. While rummaging through his closet for some game we might like to play, I spotted his guitar. It was almost identical to the one I had at home, as it was also purchased by the guy who provided us both with lessons. This was great, I thought. Let's pull out the ole guitar so that Peter and I could take turns playing it. This was my idea of fun. It was Peter's idea of purgatory.

All of a sudden, his face took on a look that I had never seen before or would ever see again. In a deadly serious and frighteningly solemn tone, he then demanded that I, "Put the guitar away." He never actually raised his voice, but the venom prompting his words was both obvious and chilling. I had never seen my friend react to anything in such a negative way, so my first thought was that he must not have heard me quite right. If I just casually repeated that we have some fun with his guitar, he'd then react in a way that was much more characteristic of the Peter we all knew and loved. Not a good plan. His reaction to my second request was even more striking than his first one. It was as if Peter's closet had been declared a crime zone, and none of the evidence was to be disturbed. "*Put the guitar away*," he slowly repeated with even greater angst. No doubt about it, the guy meant business. As such, I certainly wasn't going to try it a third time. Had I foolishly done so, I have no doubt that he would have asked me to leave. And as he'd never done that before, it would probably have weighed very heavily on our friendship.

My best guess was that his mom and dad were putting great pressure on him to learn the guitar, and this was not sitting well with him. I believe his reaction to me that afternoon was actually born of a panic attack. In any case, I "Put the guitar away."

XIII
Parental Expectations

I truly believe that we can learn as much from bad parenting as we can from good. We're much more blessed if the lessons can be gleaned from good parenting, but unfortunately, not everyone is so blessed. I've had people tell me that their parents loved them absolutely unconditionally. That whatever they chose to do in life, their parent's love and support were a given. Granted, I haven't actually met that many of these people along my journey, but those I did encounter were very well adjusted, and typically went on to lead very productive lives.

I've always tried to emulate these kinds of positive parenting examples in bringing up my own daughter. As such, I am very proud that she graduated with a bachelor's degree from the University of Washington. I must admit that I've always been a bit dubious as to her selected degree program (Woman's Studies). Still, this is where her scholastic path eventually led her, and a B.S. degree in any discipline is a significant accomplishment indeed.

Having spent quite a few years in school myself, I've learned a couple of things. The first is that people very often do not settle into a career that involves those subjects they studied in school. The second is that many folks return to school to pursue interests that surface later on in life. In light of these circumstances, I never sweated the "Women's Studies" curriculum. And I certainly never let her choice of academic disciplines get to a point where it could come between us. I surely made the odd career suggestion every once in a while, as most parents do. But like most suggestions to our kids, they usually fell on deaf ears. In the end, it's their life and they must navigate it in the way they deem fit.

As an extremely musical person, I've also known families whose kids developed a huge interest in music. I was hoping that this would be the case with my daughter, but by the time she turned fourteen or fifteen, it became abundantly clear that it wasn't in the cards. I do get wistful when I hear stories about families that play and sing together, and I've certainly met a bunch of these over the years. What a wonderful bond this would provide, regardless of whether it led to musical careers or not. Am I disappointed that my daughter didn't go in this direction? Sure. But do I love her any less, or do I ever communicate my disappointment to her in this regard? Of course not. We all have a right to be who we are, and who we are should never be a disappointment to our parents (as long as we're good and decent people).

And I must say, I wasn't totally surprised when my daughter informed me (while still in high school) that she was gay. I guess I had seen that one shaping up for a while. But honestly speaking, it's a conversation I would rather not have had to deal with. Though I do give myself high marks for taking the news in stride, I can only imagine how this scenario would have played out had I ever needed to hold such a conversation with my father. Suffice to say, I'm very glad it wasn't necessary. But as I was well aware, I was most definitely not my father. Instead of reacting in a decidedly negative manner, here was an excellent opportunity to exercise the aforementioned concept of unconditional love. While I did advise her that a gay lifestyle was probably more complicated than a straight one, I also let her know that it would never affect the relationship that she and I had. And I'm very proud to say that it most certainly hasn't. Nor is it ever likely to.

Here is one thing I most definitely learned from questionable parenting. It is a very dangerous dynamic when a parent tries to live vicariously through their kids. Often in these cases, the love is no longer unconditional. It is now contingent on some area that the parent deems of paramount importance. Perhaps it comes from a deficiency the parent feels in their own life. Or perhaps a parent that excels in some area of their life, wants to see their child excel in much the same way. In either case, the parent's sense of self-esteem and accomplishment is now reflected in their child's success.

Parents who've become highly successful professionals, academics, or businesspeople can certainly present a very high bar for their kids. In more extreme cases, some parents become highly paid entertainers or sports stars. Requiring their children to follow in those kinds of footsteps can be a daunting challenge indeed. Likewise, a parent who fails to achieve a high level of success can also harbor great expectations with regard to their kids. A good example is a parent who never went to college and thus places tremendous expectations that their kids will be the first in their family to achieve this particular milestone. Or a parent that never particularly excelled in athletics, who now has an overwhelming need to see their child do so. I certainly don't think that having high hopes for our kids makes us bad people. After all, we all want to see our kids succeed in everything they do. There is, however, a fine line between a desire to witness our child's success, versus transferring our own hopes and dreams onto our children.

Thirteen was a particularly bad year for me. It's a tough age for a lot of kids anyway, but my relationship with my father took a disastrous turn at this point. It was a turn that took us completely off track, and unfortunately never really righted itself. By now Dad had gotten way too consumed with the judo school. Though my brother and I could easily have taken the train to the dojo on judo nights, it was something that my father attended religiously. For him, it represented two nights out per week, as well as every Saturday afternoon. What's more, the judo school was a place that he enjoyed more than anywhere else. And though you wouldn't always know it from his reactions, watching his kids play judo was his greatest joy. If he had looked at it simply from that perspective, however, we would all have been a lot better off. Instead, it became an obsession. He watched with intense scrutiny, noting each and every event in his mind. I recall that he was often the only parent sitting there observing, but that certainly never deterred him.

Immediately following every class was his analysis of what we did right, as well as a litany of what we did wrong. If there were more "rights" than "wrongs" on a particular night, then the car trip back home wasn't too unpleasant. If there were things he didn't like, however, suffice to say that it would be a very long ride back home indeed. Though he himself had never stepped out onto a judo mat in his entire life, he was nonetheless a self-proclaimed expert. And as such, his critique was absolute and non-disputable. Any attempt to argue would serve only to exacerbate his angst. Thus, the best strategy was to sit there and let him rant. And boy, could he rant. The only thing that interrupted his pontifications was our arrival back home (and the presence of our mom). He surely knew better than to display such critical behavior in front of her.

As I mentioned previously, there were frequent "contests" that came along in judo. Most of the time we grappled with players from different "dojos," but one particular contest involved only those from our own school. Still, it was a big deal with trophies awarded to the winners, and many guests in attendance to cheer on their friends and family participants. Among my particular age category, I was very heavily favored to win that day. In fact, I expected to do just that. Not that this gave me any particular feeling of pride or joy, it was just something I was expected to do. And if I put in a decent performance, then it would keep Dad happy and off my back.

As I was battling my last opponent that afternoon, however, the earth suddenly tilted ever so slightly off its axis. Truth be known, it shouldn't even have been a battle at all. The person I was squaring off against was a guy I could probably beat 999 out of 1,000 times. He wasn't even a particularly good player. But as I say, the earth picked this moment to tilt rather unexpectedly. Not only did he level me from out of nowhere, but he did it with the technique that was my trademark. If you recall the famous "Footsweep" from earlier, that's exactly what he clobbered me with.

To this day, I'm sure this guy (I don't even remember his name) still brags to his friends about the time he hit me with that amazing Footsweep. And I wouldn't even blame him if he did. Normally he wouldn't have been able to execute a Footsweep like that even in his wildest dreams. But on this fateful day, he couldn't possibly have pulled it off with any greater expertise. My legs went flying out from under me, and my entire body took flight. Though in an absolute state of shock, I was still able to land in a way that prevented him from scoring a full point. Thus, the match continued. Though I was highly stressed at the notion of suddenly finding myself behind, there was ample time to put things back to rights. It was simply a question of remaining calm and regathering my composure.

About a half-minute or so following my opponent's "Hail Mary" Footsweep, I connected with a convincing shoulder throw that sent him sprawling to the mat. And with that, the match was now all tied up and we were right back to square one. Though this calmed me down quite a bit, I was getting pretty tired. At this point, the thing to do was to attack more than my opponent, as this would land me the victory via the referee's decision. Certainly not the way I was hoping to win, but any way it got into the "W" column at this point was fine with me.

For the rest of the match I attacked, and I attacked. And if I wasn't quite so tired, my aggressions would have appeared far more convincing. But I was clearly running out of steam, and with every attack came my opponent's attempted counterattack. At last the bell sounded, and the match was finally concluded. As we faced each other on the mat, the referee's decision came swiftly. He pointed clearly in the direction of my opponent, who was suddenly overcome with joy at having pulled off the upset of the century. As for me, I felt like crawling under the nearest rock. How could I possibly have just lost to this joker, who normally couldn't beat me even on his best day? Apparently, his best day had now arrived, as he somehow emerged victorious. It was one of the lowest times in my life, and I was absolutely devastated. I remember thinking that life couldn't possibly get any worse than this. I've since learned never to tell myself things like that.

I have always been my least forgiving and harshest critic, and I probably still am. The simple fact is that nobody can beat me up better than I can do it myself. I knew Dad wasn't going to take the loss well, but I honestly wasn't even thinking about that at the time. I felt so bad that I probably wouldn't even hear Dad's obligatory tirade, which was sure to dominate the drive back home.

I remember getting changed back into my street clothes and preparing for the miserable ride home. As I leaned over the trunk to deposit my gear, however, I suddenly felt a crashing blow on my back and shoulders. "That's for losing," he then snarled. What went through my head at that point seemed absolutely inconceivable. My father's anger had actually bubbled over to the point of lambasting me while my back was turned. Naturally, there was a fair bit of pain involved, but the thought of what my father had just done was entirely overwhelming. Sure, I figured the usual caustic lecture was coming, but this had taken things to a whole new level. This was absolutely unprecedented, as we were now in totally unchartered waters. Not only did it cross a very dangerous line, but it totally shattered it. I knew right then and there that things between my father and me would never again be the same.

I remember telling this story to a bible study group a number of years ago. It's not an easy story to tell, but I was trying to make a point about parenting. I was actually quite taken aback at the response I got. The shock and horror in the room were palpable. To me, it was just a very sad moment in my past. To my bible study audience, it was horrific. The bottom line was that I never felt close to my father ever again, as the relationship had been permanently damaged from that point on. I'm sure the caustic lecture part did indeed follow after we got into the car, but I have no memory of it whatsoever.

If there is any positive to this sad tale, it's that the event served to shape my own parenting in years to come. Knowing how devastating an experience like this could be for a young person's sense of self, I vowed never to react in such a manner toward my own child. A tough way to acquire such parental expertise. Nevertheless, it got the message across.

XIV
My Name's-a-Not-a Pizza, It's-a Piazza

That expression about "When It Rains It Pours" has often been the case in my experience. Just before the ill-fated judo contest, I'd had a violin/piano lesson that pretty much blew up in my face. No issues with the violin part, as I was getting pretty comfortable on the fiddle. The problem came during the piano portion of the lesson. I'll talk more about Professor Piazza a bit later, but for now, suffice to say that he was a most intense individual who was prone to occasional fits of temper.

While I was always pretty comfortable with instruments that revolved around strings, the hard and unyielding keys of a piano never really gave me a warm and fuzzy. If I set my mind to it, I could learn to play the notes in the right succession, but I would never say that I was actually making music on the piano. And I would never say that I ever felt "one" with this very imposing and rather alien instrument. My job was to learn the tunes that Professor Piazza assigned to me, so for the most part that is what I did.

For some reason, however, on this particular day, Piazza decided to throw me a curveball. Toward the end of the lesson, he suddenly stuck a piece of music in front of me for the first time and asked me to play it as best I could. I knew this wasn't going to be a winner, so I protested immediately. "I've never seen this before," I explained. "I need time to take it home and practice it." But despite my objections, he insisted I give it a try right then and there. It now felt like I was being asked to walk across a bed of hot coals. It was certainly going to be painful, but just how painful was yet to be determined. As it turned out, very damned painful.

As I began plunking uncomfortably through the tune, I quickly hit a wrong note. Immediately Professor Piazza pointed out my error in no uncertain terms, and the fun continued. It wasn't long before I hit the very same wrong note, only this time Piazza was less forgiving. Clearly, he was becoming upset as I was now testing his patience. By the third or fourth time I "clunkered" the same wrong note, he began shouting loudly and angrily. In addition, the color of his face went from its normal pale white to crimson. Suffice to say that with each additional blunder, a complete avalanche of rage and total frustration was brought forth.

By now Piazza was screaming at me at the top of his lungs, to the point where I thought he was going to throw a coronary. Very much in line with my father, patience was not Piazza's strong suit. I'd been taking music lessons from him for several years by that point, but I had never seen him blow a gasket quite to this extent. Nor had I ever experienced him being so utterly unfair with regard to his scrutiny and criticism. As I said, it was a piece of music that I had never seen before.

To this day I wish I'd had the strength to tell Piazza exactly where he could stick that particular piece of sheet music. Or in a more adult manner, simply to let him know that he was being totally unreasonable and that he needed to back off. Looking back, there were a lot of ways I could have effectively handled it. But during my thirteenth year, I was simply not equipped to deal with it. Thus, there was no way I was going to work up the gumption to tell the old man that he was totally out of line. So, I just sat there and took it.

In the end, I think Piazza eventually stormed off in disgust. Obviously, he now thought of me as something you find wiggling around in the dirt when you turned over a rock. In my heart of hearts, I knew that he was being totally unfair and that I had nothing to feel bad about. After all, I was asked to play that piece of music for the first time that afternoon, and despite my misgivings, I still gave it the old college try. "E" for effort you might think. His response, however, was more like I was a miserable failure who should quickly get out of his sight.

As music had become my passion, this naturally took quite a toll. From that day on I never had any further desire to play the piano again. My father had been out doing a little shopping during the music lesson that Saturday afternoon, so he never got the full effect of Piazza's tirade. I'm not sure how he got wind of it, but somehow, he did learn that the music lesson did not go well. And Dad being Dad, I didn't feel as though I could adequately explain it to him. And even if I could have put it into words, my experience with Piazza had already taken the wind out of me.

It was at this point that we went on to the next giant failure, the above-mentioned disastrous judo contest. I think I'd have to say that this probably turned out to be one of the worst days of my childhood. By the time this day was over, two things had occurred. The first was that I felt totally worthless. The second was that I no longer trusted my father. It's a terrible thing to think that a parent may not have your best interests at heart. It's also a terrible thing for a kid to realize that you no longer trust one of the two most important people in your life. After all, your mom or dad should be someone with whom your trust should never waiver. What's more, I felt powerless to change any of it.

Not long after the events of this horrendous day, I was accosted by a local bully from the neighborhood. Much like the animal kingdom, perhaps he singled me out after spotting possible weakness. Regardless of his reasoning, the guy proceeded to pummel me unmercifully. The irony was that he wasn't actually all that imposing. No doubt he simply sensed that I had no fight left in me whatsoever. It was as if I were standing on the tracks with the train bearing down on me, yet I was powerless to move.

The strategy for both my brother and me during these years was to simply tell Dad as little as possible. If there was anything he wanted to know, the answer was that things went "just fine" (whether they actually did or not). What the heck, that was the answer he wanted anyway. So why not give him what he wanted and provide anything additional strictly on a need-to-know basis. This became a basic survival skill, and we became quite adept at it. This was true even of our mom, as it often got her through some potentially sticky situations as well. Darwin called it "Survival of The Fittest." No doubt Darwin spoke from experience.

Getting back to our illustrious childhood music teacher (Professor Michael Piazza), the man was a colorful character indeed. If you haven't already surmised it by now, he was an extremely stubborn and thoroughly irascible fellow. In fact, he was one of the most intractable individuals I've ever met. It wasn't too long after the great piano meltdown that he got into a giant argument with my father over money. Perhaps it was for the best, but that was the last we ever saw of him. My brother had missed a lesson due to illness, and Piazza wouldn't let him make it up. Piazza had a strict rule that all lessons missed must be made up prior to the end of the month for which they were scheduled. Since there wasn't time to make up this particular lesson by the end of the month, Piazza wouldn't let him make it up at all.

I'll never forget the ferociousness of the battle that ensued, and my feelings of utter amazement at witnessing such an unprecedented level of unyielding stubbornness. It is said that pride goes before the fall. That was certainly true for Professor Michael Piazza that day. Dad was just about to sign us both up for another year of lessons when this vicious argument ensued. In his ridiculous zeal to uphold a seemingly arbitrary monetary policy, Piazza lost two paying customers for good. I guess that's the price you pay for having an uncontrollable temper.

The sad part is that he was a phenomenal music teacher when he wasn't "going Postal." He was my first and only classical violin teacher, and always took great care to make sure I played accurately and with good technique. With some teachers or mentors, your desire to perform well is brought on by a deep sense of respect, and not wanting to disappoint them. Their approval is very important in your life, and your goal is to always make them happy. Such was not the case with Piazza. Our desire to keep him happy was a result of not wanting to hear his frequent and annoying musical metaphors.

There was always the one about misspelling his name. "If you leave out-a the "a" in a-Piazza, it would-a be a-Mr. Pizza," he'd pontificate. "My name's-a-not-a pizza, it's-a Piazza. If I try to cash-a the check at-a the bank and it-a says a-Mr. Pizza, they'd a-never cash-a the check." In other words, any note played incorrectly (or inadvertently omitted) would just make the whole thing wrong. Then there was our personal favorite, the one about the opera singer. "There's an opera singer. She's a-singing a beautiful-a song, then all of a sudden she a-chokes." (And to emphasize the choking part, he'd then go into a mock coughing spasm). The punchline to this one was: "The singer, she's a-singing a-beautiful-a song. But-a she a-chokes. The whole-a thing is a-ruined. She's a-gotta start-a the whole-a thing over." Bottom line, if you didn't want to hear these tired and pedantic parables ad-nauseam, best to play the tunes perfectly.

Piazza tried to teach us a little on the guitar as well. Although he was one heck of a violinist and pianist, by his own admission, the only reason he taught guitar was because of Elvis-a Presley. Suffice to say that strumming the ole six-string was not Piazza's strong suit. As he was well into his seventies at the time, I'd venture to say that he's probably long gone by now. Rest in peace Professor Piazza. And try to have a little patience with the folks you meet in the next life. After all, you may need to hang with them for a long time. And nobody's "a-perfect."

XV
Ah, Junior High

I was thinking about that expression "God Never Gives You More Than You Can Handle." I don't wish to be disrespectful in any way, but I think that expression is a bunch of baloney. For one thing, I don't think it's God who's actually dishing out the stuff that we need to "handle." I think stuff just happens. As a friend of mine recently put it, life sometimes hands us an absolute gut punch. Perhaps it's God who gives us the strength to regather ourselves when we're doubled over and gasping for breath. It's a similar thing with stress. Everyone's got it. It's just a question of how we deal with it. Clearly, some people are a lot better at it than others. The good news is that we can all train ourselves to deal with it more effectively if we so choose. And let's face it. The next test of our newly improved stress management skills is probably right around the corner. It's like an appetite. We can ruin one, but there will always be another coming right up behind it.

Just prior to those challenging and thoroughly stressful junior high school years, the students in my elementary school were given a particular aptitude test. This test was to determine whether we had to spend two years or three years in junior high school. It was known as the Special Progress program (or S.P. for short). Hmmm, two years versus three years in a school where the inmates often ran the asylum. It didn't take me long to arrive at that decision. So you can imagine the sigh of relief I breathed upon learning that I passed this all-important exam. Quickly checking the box indicating my choice of the two-year program, I submitted my paperwork accordingly.

If there was any grade you really wanted to skip, it was certainly grade eight. Like money falling from the sky, this was a rare opportunity indeed. A letter from my new junior high school arrived shortly, indicating that I would soon be a member of class 7SPE1. The "7SP" (7th Grade Special Progress) part sounded just fine, but I had no way to know at the time that the "E1" part actually referred to the three-year version. For some reason, the powers that be had screwed up and put me in the wrong class. Fortunately, I found this out before the start of the new term, and a resolution strategy was devised.

Turns out that there were three "two-year" SP classes that term (7SP2A, 7SP2B, and 7SP2C). The three or four of us (who were victims of this misclassification error) were thus divided up among the three "two-year" classes. By the luck of the draw, I was the only one slated to join class 7SP2C. In effect, I was on my own with regard to making certain that the transition proceeded smoothly. This made for quite a first week of junior high.

My homeroom teacher did her utmost to make the process as cumbersome and painful as possible. When she took the roll for the first time, naturally I wasn't on the official class list. Yippie, I now had to explain to her (in front of the other thirty or forty kids) about the mistake that was made, and how I was now assigned to her class. But a kind and understanding woman she was not. She then informed me that I was not a part of her class, and I should proceed to the "three-year" SP class to which I had been originally assigned. On my first day of junior high school, I was basically told that I was not welcome. In front of a big bunch of kids I'd never met before, I was then instructed to leave the room and head for the office of the assistant principal. Clearly, my perspective new homeroom teacher wasn't going to allow me into her class without express authorization from "On High." My first day of junior high was already off to a lovely start.

Although Mr. Assistant Principal attempted to be understanding, he clearly explained that there were procedures that had to be followed in the event of a mishap such as this. He also offered nothing in the way of an apology for the inconvenience I was now experiencing (especially considering that none of this was a result of my doing). I was eventually allowed to rejoin class 7SP2C that day, but with the understanding that I wasn't yet an official member of the student roster. Ms. Home-Room Pain in The Ass continued to make that quite clear.

In fact, the entire day proceeded in much the same manner. Science, English, Social Studies, Foreign Language, Art Appreciation. They all treated me like an intruder, as I wasn't on any of their student lists. In all fairness, some were much friendlier and far more accommodating than Homeroom Czar. These forward-thinking and understanding instructors simply penciled me into the roster. Still, there were a couple that also sent me back to Mr. Assistant Principal for further clarification.

God Never Gives You More Than You Can Handle? By the end of that first day of junior high school, I was having a breakdown. As I noted previously, I wasn't teeming with strength and confidence at this point in my life. By the last visit to Mr. A. P. that day, I was a basket case. I didn't understand why things had to be so difficult. It's curious indeed, but it often seems that we're most tested when we're already in a weakened state. In the end, it took more than a week for that little clerical error to be fully rectified. All the while, Homeroom Czar remained steadfast that I was not a part of her class. When word from "On High" finally did come down, then and only then was she assuaged.

XVI
What a Wisenheimer

If the reader will permit me to jump ahead just for a moment, I often recall the words of a wonderful therapist I ran into in my late twenties. Upon noting my constant propensity to effect humor, her view was that my attempts to be funny were actually a façade that I put forth. To this day, I'm not sure if she had a point or not. I can say, however, that there is a grand distinction between being funny and being a "wise guy." While the former can quite often be harmless (or even quite useful), the latter is often less so.

As a positive and most beneficial example of humor put to good use, consider the following example of a large corporate dinner gathering that would occur in my distant future. As a young and newly appointed employee of a large sales organization, I was seated directly across from the president (as well as several other corporate dignitaries). Having had little experience with this firm, my contribution to the evening's conversation was scant at best. Despite this, I was determined to make an impression upon the company's top brass. When the president pointed out the muscular physique of our waiter (and his ability to handle an enormous tray stacked to the brim with plates of food), an opportunity then presented. "You should have seen him before he took this job," I quickly chimed in. At that, our esteemed president turned to me and smiled. "He was a ninety-pound weakling before he took the job," Mr. President then kidded. With the blessing of our esteemed leader, it was now safe to continue this amusing characterization. I noted that bullies probably kicked sand in the poor young man's face while at the beach. And with that, our exalted company leader then took a few minutes to converse directly with me. Obviously, he was impressed by my off-the-cuff witticisms regarding our buff waiter. So much so, that he took a few moments to get to know me a little better. In this case, a little levity went a long way.

As a kid, however, I often learned that it didn't pay to establish oneself as being a "wise guy." We had just finished lunch one hot afternoon at my old summer camp and were lazily heading back to our cabins for rest hour. It was one of those really hot and humid northeastern Pennsylvania afternoons, and we were all moving with a great deal of effort. Lunch had been heavy, which didn't do much for our get up and go either. One of those afternoons where I was really looking forward to a blissful summer snooze. Very much like the way a pride of lions must feel after gorging on a gazelle in the blistering African sun.

It was a relatively short walk from the dining room back to our cabins, and I was only about twenty or thirty feet from the door when it happened. Before I describe the actual situation, however, I must bring to your attention a certain conveyance that existed at our camp during that particular summer. I have no idea where this rolling contraption came from, as this was the first summer I had ever seen it. But make no mistake, it was substantial. It resembled something a horse might pull back in the old days. Some sort of bulky wooden cart with big wooden spoked wheels, and two long steel pipes extending out from the front. Very much in the style of an old milk cart. Something that Tevye might have hauled around in his role as a dairy provider in Fiddler on The Roof.

Suffice to say the thing was particularly clumsy and weighed a ton. Though it did have the two big wheels in the back, getting this thing rolling on a grassy surface was no easy feat. Uphill was even less exciting. I remember the feel of those long pipes on my hands when I tried pulling this monstrosity around one day just for kicks. A guaranteed prescription for sore muscles and blisters. Definitely something you would not want to make a habit of doing. About the only fun you could have with this monster was to point it downhill, get up a little momentum, and watch as it hurled and clanged its way down to the bottom. I'm thinking that was exactly what must have happened one day, as the thing was oddly situated precisely at the bottom of such a hill.

As I said, I was headed back to my cabin after lunch, and there was that ancient milk cart smack dab between me and my destination. My obvious plan was to jog right (or left) so as to avoid the thing, while making my way inside for a little afternoon shut-eye. Indeed, that was the plan. But like that old saying about "the best-laid plans," it didn't pan out that way. Right about the "jog" point, I heard a loud voice sing out from behind me, "Hey Gary." Instantly I recognized that loud voice. It was the voice of one of my favorite counselors, Ned Livingston.

Normally Ned and I got along just famously. I was one of the more athletic kids at camp (with a particular affinity for basketball), and Ned largely shared my interest in sports. We often hung out on the basketball court together, happily passing the time shooting hoops. Unfortunately, I was also a pretty intuitive kid, thus I instantly surmised the reason for Ned's calls. Ned was behind me, and the horse and buggy thing-a-majigger was just ahead of me. I knew in a flash that Ned was about to tell me to grab a hold of the behemoth and haul it back up the hill to where it might have belonged. And naturally, I wanted no part of that plan. As a result, my devious mind instantly kicked into gear. My approach was to pretend that I didn't hear Ned calling. After all, if I didn't hear Ned, how could I possibly be expected to carry out his laborious assignment.

Another anxious shout followed, *"Hey Gary!"*

At that point, I started chanting to myself, "I don't hear Ned calling. There's no Ned. Certainly, there's no Ned calling my name."

A third frantic shout soon echoed, *"Hey Gary!"*

This time I think my head went into a little singsong. "I don't hear Ned, no siree. I don't hear Ned, calling me." Honestly, I don't remember if there was a fourth "Hey Gary" or not. My only recollection at that point was the feeling of being slammed from behind, much like a quarterback getting lambasted by the defense behind the line of scrimmage. Down I went on the grassy ground with Ned on me like wolves to a kill. The expression on his face at that moment was no more encouraging, as his lips were curled into a menacing snarl.

Prior to this point, I had never even seen Ned lose his temper, much less being at a point where he looked like he was going to commit murder. I had no idea the guy was even capable of achieving such a level of anger. I guess it just took the right amount of prodding, which I had obviously now provided. Though the look on his face suggested that my fate was sealed, I must say he somehow miraculously managed to summon restraint. After all, Ned was probably about eighteen or nineteen, and a pretty scrapping fellow. As for me, I was a scrawny pre-adolescent kid. Clearly, my plan of simply ignoring him was not a wise choice. After what seemed a considerable amount of time with my face buried in the dirt, he finally let me up. As I brushed the debris out of my hair and eyes, he then uttered the following. "If you ever pull something like that again, you will regret it." And I had absolutely no doubt as to the sincerity of his comment.

The last thing I remember about this brief but unpleasant encounter was the disgusted look on Ned's face, as he pulled that behemoth oxcart back up the hill all by himself. I felt pretty bad about the whole incident, as well as the prospect of losing Ned's respect and friendship. As I say, we had gotten along quite well up till that point. I don't remember if ole Ned ever forgave me for that impropriety or not, but I vowed never to let such a thing happen again. From now on, if I have to lug some unwieldy contraption up a hill (when I really want to take a nap), I'll bite the bullet and rest easy when the job is done. Well, maybe…

XVII
What Makes You Think Dairy is Any Easier?

I feel like I should talk a little about Mom at this point, as I've been relating much of my upbringing from the point of view of Dad's influence. Simply stated, my mom was about the best mom one could possibly hope for. She was kind, understanding, and had the patience of a saint. When she passed away recently, there was a general theme among the few relatives who remained. They all agreed that my mom was someone who would actually listen to you, and really try to understand where you were coming from. She truly cared about what you were saying and was genuinely interested in you as a person. I think the relatives absolutely nailed it. That was always the feeling I got with regard to Mom.

As a kind, understanding, and very patient person, my mom truly possessed all the major qualities that my father most decidedly lacked. One thing I told my mom before she died was that she was always someone we could talk to. Whatever the problem, we knew Mom was a safe harbor and a source of wisdom and practical advice. Most importantly, she was never one to judge. I guess that's what made her a safe harbor. We knew we could confide in her without hesitation. I'm not saying that she was perfect. On occasion, her temper would get the best of her as well. After all, my brother and I did accidentally smash our share of statues and lamps. But her episodes of temper were rare indeed. On the whole, she generally kept a calm head and a loving demeanor. Whereas my father typically flew into a fit of rage, Mom was always a voice of reason.

It is interesting how our perspective tends to change as the years advance. Having now reached my sixth decade, I often wonder just what it was that my mother saw in Dad. Clearly, there remain some unresolved issues between Dad and me, but I don't make this comment out of spite. I just can't imagine for the life of me, the forces that brought them together.

Mom was friendly and outgoing, while Dad kept to himself and typically regarded others as unworthy. As far as I've ever heard, my mom always treated my dad's side of the family with warmth and affection.

In fact, in talking to the long-lost cousins (Steve and Neil), they actually grew quite a bit closer to my mom than they ever were to Dad. Apparently, it was a big family back in the day, consisting of hundreds of aunts, uncles, and cousins. According to Steve and Neil, it wasn't unusual for well over a hundred family members to gather when there was some sort of get-together. On these occasions, Mom was typically friendly and ingratiating, while Dad was usually closed off in his own little cocoon. Neil still has strong feelings about my dad even to this day. He remembers being a little boy when he first met my dad, and how my dad generally ignored him. As a little kid, Neil would have loved for my dad to take some kind of an interest in him. If for no other reason than just to say hi, and to ask how he was doing every now and then. But apparently, my dad never made any such effort. I guess he just didn't consider it worthy of his time. At least that's how Neil interpreted it.

My dad's failure to show any interest following his older sister Maizey's (Steve and Neil's mom) untimely death, did nothing to undermine Neil's assertion. Under the circumstances, I suppose I can't blame him for feeling the way he does. Then there was Dad's older sister, Doris. By contrast, she showed up every night at the grieving family's home, bringing them groceries and cooking them dinner. What my father was doing at that time is anybody's guess.

Of my mother, I would say this without hesitation. Had she been part of the family during those tragic days, she would have joined Doris in a heartbeat to lend a helping hand. And though it pains me to say, in so doing, she probably would have had to endure considerable grief from my father. That was the basic difference between them. Mom had a kind heart, Dad did not. Mom saw the value of family. To Dad, family did not extend beyond his wife and kids. In his view, all others were extremely superfluous.

It is by no means an exaggeration to say that he had little to no regard for any member of my mom's family. In fact, it would probably be more accurate to say that he couldn't stand them. To be perfectly fair, my mom's younger brother Bernard was indeed no great prize. Nor was his Jewish American Princess wife Marsha, or their thoroughly spoiled son Ryan. Bernard was a pretty self-centered character himself, which is perhaps why he and my mom were not close. On the other hand, my mom's parents were wonderful people. My grandma Gussie could find the good in the most rotten of individuals. She loved having us over (despite my father's frequent rudeness), and cooked many wonderful dinners for us.

My favorite memory of my grandmother was during my nursery school years. For some reason, my mom couldn't pick me up on Tuesday afternoons, so grandma would come instead. Tuesdays were always a thrill for me because grandma would take me for pizza when she collected me from school. My grandpa Sam delighted in all his grandkids, and the pair always treated us with great kindness and generosity. In fact, my grandpa Sam was one of the nicest and most easygoing individuals you would ever have met. I remember at his funeral when relatives commented that they had never witnessed my grandfather ever losing his temper. Nor had I. I'm told that there were certainly times when he did, but I never saw it. I'm also told that if he ever did lose his temper, watch out. But again, not something I ever witnessed.

I suppose my grandmother's major Achilles heel was her outspokenness. She was never one to disguise her feelings or remain silent as to her opinions. Being a solid member of the Jewish community, I'll never forget her very audible shriek during the marriage ceremony with my second wife (a Christian). While repeating after the pastor with regard to "The Father, The Son, and The Holy Spirit," an alarmed voice seemed to cry out from the crowd. I paid it no mind at the time. Many years later, however, I learned that the voice was my devoutly Jewish grandmother blurting out, *"He said it!"* As I say, she was not one to keep her opinions to herself.

Perhaps it was this aspect of his mother-in-law that ruffled my father's feathers so profoundly. His feelings probably reached a climax when she eventually wore my mom down with regard to my brother being Bar Mitzvah'd. As my brother's thirteenth birthday was rapidly approaching, grandma had every intention of making sure that the all-important ceremony of Jewish manhood would be observed. Of course, this put Mom between a major rock and a hard spot with regard to her mom and her husband.

Bar Mitzvahs ain't cheap by any stretch, and considering that my brother and I had never even seen the inside of a Jewish temple, wholly unnecessary in Dad's view. In order to keep the peace, however, Dad finally relented in the end. Thus, a very costly Bar Mitzvah was convened, while at the same time widening the gap even further between my father and his in-laws. By the time I reached the age of Jewish manhood, even the premise of observing strict law had been totally abandoned. Nevertheless, the damage to family relations had already been done. All told, Dad was out about three-grand, just so my brother could have a meaningless party (for the benefit of the in-laws). That round was definitely awarded to grandma, with Dad left licking his wounds.

Truth be told, however, Dad had little use for his wife's parents even way before then. During one of our calmer moments when it was just him and me, I actually asked him about it. I tried to sound as non-threatening as possible as I probed for his reasons for disliking his in-laws so. I asked if there was anything specific that caused him to feel as he did, or was it simply a natural rivalry between a man and his in-laws. Although Dad seldom volunteered any information about himself, I would have to say that he usually did answer if asked. Concerning this particular question, there wasn't actually anything specific about his in-laws that summoned such rancor. It was more that he found them a general annoyance. "They knew I had a car, so your grandmother would sometimes ask me to drive her somewhere." This was one example he cited, although there were one or two others that I can no longer recall. Whatever the remainder of his reasons, suffice to say that they were just as innocuous as the "driving" example.

While we're on the subject of grandma, it occurs to me that she had a unique wisdom all her own. Though her formal education certainly culminated with high school, there was no doubt that the woman was clever. One evening when she was entertaining both my family and my uncle Bernard's family, she invited me to join the conversation in the living room. This was where my spoiled Cousin Ryan was now thoroughly occupying center stage. Much to grandma's chagrin, however, I remained at the dining room table so as to maintain a comfortable distance. When she further beckoned me to join them in the living room, I replied, "No thanks, I can hear Ryan perfectly well from here." As much as I hate to admit it, this is exactly the sort of response my father would have rendered. Unfortunately, there were far too many times when the apple didn't fall that far from the tree.

Did grandma respond with a quick and angry admonishment? As I say, the woman was quite clever. She simply turned to me with a deliberate and calculated look on her face. She then replied, "You know, you're just like your father." Suggesting such a direct comparison to my father was a death blow, and she knew it. Score another one for grandma. Game, set, and match.

I believe I was actually trying to say a few words about Mom, yet somehow, I managed to cycle back to Dad again. I suppose that figures, as he was so predominant in our family dynamic. But back to Mom. Although she worked a full-time job just as Dad did, she was still expected to cook all the meals and keep the house in order. Not the most equitable division of labor, but not atypical given the times. I remember one particular night when Mom was thoroughly exhausted and didn't feel like cooking. In an attempt to ease her burden, Dad suggested that she just make "dairy." To this day I have no idea what kind of meal "dairy" is, but the suggestion pretty much brought Mom to the end of her rope that night. She replied in an exhausted and exasperated voice, "What makes you think dairy is any easier than anything else?"

Mom was a secretary for the social services division of Maimonides Hospital in Brooklyn. During her long tenure at this post, she served several bosses with last names such as Yalowitz and Pagel. I never met Yalowitz, but I did meet Pagel a time or two. As a kid, most of us are pretty unaware of exactly what our parents do in their jobs. All I knew was that my mom's job involved a lot of typing. And when I say "typing" I mean on an IBM electric typewriter. I suppose she was mainly typing up Yalowitz's and Pagel's meeting notes and reports. In other words, translating their thoughts and ideas while rendering them into printed form.

As I got older, I began to realize that there was a definite distinction between a "job" and a "career." While Mom and Dad definitely had jobs, I would never say either of them really had a career. They did what they were told, and in return, they received a weekly paycheck. They didn't necessarily enjoy doing the things they were told to do, but this seemed to be the very definition of a "job."

By rendering her boss's thoughts and ideas onto paper, I can't imagine that my mom derived a great deal of satisfaction or fulfillment from her work. As I say, it was just a job. And for her efforts, she received an annual salary of about eight thousand dollars a year. Even back in the 1970s (and certainly into the eighties) this was not exactly a get rich quick scheme. The real shame of it was that my mother was a highly intelligent and extremely capable individual. Though her educational journey also ended with high school, she possessed a natural curiosity, as well as a general thirst for knowledge. In short, I believe she always knew that she could be more than she was. I think we all knew it. I think Dad certainly realized it too, and I believe the thought made him quite uneasy.

One evening while my brother and I were still teenagers, Mom made a grand announcement. She told us that she had been languishing and now felt the need to better herself. Her startling plan was to enroll in some courses at Brooklyn College. She was now ready to get this most ambitious ball rolling and see where it would eventually take her. Wow! This was big stuff indeed. My mom was actually going to college. She didn't exactly know what she was going to do there, but she was going to take the plunge, nonetheless. I think I was the proudest person in the room when she made this bold and thoroughly unexpected announcement. My mom was about to embark upon a new journey. No doubt she'd been thinking about it for some time, but thinking and doing are two very different things. And in my mind, if anyone could do it, Mom could.

It began with some general fun classes in art and music. I remember her bringing home a set of recordings one night and studying the way an operatic soprano sang about her need for coffee. She listened intently to those recordings night after night, while carefully considering the various musical aspects of the lady singer's need for caffeine. "Coffee, I've got to have coffee." And so, the woman crooned. I guess Mom scored pretty well in that class, as well as some of the others she initially chose. More importantly, it was giving her something to strive for, as well as a genuine sense of accomplishment. She was now rendering her own opinions, and not simply transcribing the thoughts of others. For the first time perhaps ever, she was now being encouraged to think independently. What a wonderful and empowering feeling that must have been. But as inspiring as it must have been for Mom, it was having quite the opposite effect on Dad.

As Mom started to weave her new tapestry, the fabric of Dad's world was beginning to unravel. First of all, she wasn't going to be home anymore to cook dinner on the nights she was at school. In her absence on those evenings, the rest of us would just have to fend for ourselves. For a husband that could barely boil water, this was not a happy thought. Secondly, and probably far more importantly, Mom was going to continue to feel more and more empowered (and in charge of her own destiny). And if she could actually see her way to completing a degree program, then she could very possibly carve out a whole new life for herself. Dad was very well aware of these facts, and the situation terrified him. With her newfound sense of self, his submissive and dutiful wife was bound to change. And would these profound changes extend to her feelings about him? Would she then seek greener pastures with regard to a more appropriate life partner, thus leaving him in the dust?

Dad was employed with the United States Post Office for pretty much his entire working life. Also a high school graduate, he took a job as an accounts payable clerk. From the way he described it (when he ever did talk about work), it sounded even more dull and mundane than Mom's job. What made it worse for Dad was that the Post Office was run in much the same manner as a branch of the military. Supervisors barked out orders and the workers snapped to. As in a military chain of command, you were expected to promptly carry out your superior's orders without question. In this kind of work, thinking was highly discouraged. Moreover, I got the definite impression that post office supervisors did not give a lot of thought to respecting the workers in their charge. Their method was simple. Crack the whip and get the worker bees moving.

For years we'd hear Dad lament over the dinner table about his miserable boss Thorpy. Thorpy must have been one miserable SOB, because every night Dad came home looking like that guy in Ben Hur that had been run over by the chariot. How he endured it for thirty years I'll never know, but it certainly never did anything for his rosy glow (or winning demeanor). At any rate, the thought of his wife changing her lot in life did nothing to inspire him. He made no bones about letting her know that her absence on college nights was a major league thorn in his side. He also took to chiding her (during their frequent heated discussions) with sarcastic barbs about being a "college woman." Clearly, if Mom was to accomplish her educational goals, she would certainly have to do it without his support. Somehow, I think she knew that right from the start.

Unfortunately for Mom, the train would eventually start to derail. She was rapidly reaching the point where fun courses alone do not a degree program make. A proper curriculum was going to involve some of the good ole core stuff, like math and science. As was required by the program, she signed up for an algebra class during one semester. Instead of listening to somebody crooning on about coffee, she now had to plug away at advanced algebraic equations on her non-school nights. Not wanting to sound chauvinistic, but math was never Mom's strong suit to begin with. The combination of trying to make sense of those tricky mathematical equations, coupled with my father's continued criticisms, proved too much for her in the end.

I do recall her taking a final exam for that math class, and I also remember that it caused her tremendous stress. I don't recall whether or not she received a passing grade, although I'm inclined to think that she did. In the end, it really didn't matter, as that math class was as far as her college journey would take her. As proud as I was when she announced her desire to enter college, I was absolutely devastated when she told us she was now quitting. Had she actually gotten support from my dad, she may have had the wherewithal to keep going. I guess we'll never know. One thing I was certain of, however, was that she had something to contribute to the working world (far beyond typing up Yalowitz's and Pagel's memos).

XVIII
All's Fair in Love And War

As a young child, it's a tough thing to hear your parents arguing, especially if the arguments are frequent and often intense. When my brother and I were about twelve and nine respectively, it seemed that our parents argued vehemently just about every night. When these battles would rage on (seemingly for hours), it was very hard not to wonder just what they were arguing about. In fact, they screamed at each other so loudly at times, I'm sure all our neighbors were well aware of their marital discourse.

As we had little alternative to overhearing their rantings, it did seem as though most of the trouble centered around the general theme of money. More specifically, the very concerning realization as to their lack of it. Though both my parents held full-time jobs, even their combined income was modest at best. As I mentioned, Mom brought home about eight thousand a year, while Dad scored about twelve thousand per annum at the post office. For a family of four back in the late 1960s and all throughout the 1970s, theirs was a combined income of roughly twenty thousand per year.

Gasoline was only about thirty-five cents a gallon back in 1970, which by today's standards seems like nothing. As such, it's very tempting to say that things were a lot cheaper back then. But thirty-five cents in 1970 would be about $2.40 in today's dollars. At this point in 2020, as I observe the pumps, gasoline is about $2.70 a gallon. So perhaps we were slightly better off in 1970, but I'm thinking that gas probably still seemed pricy even back then. And to make matters worse, our big clunky 1970s American cars typically did not fare well with regard to fuel economy. So even though gasoline may have been a bit cheaper fifty years ago (in real terms), driving around in a big honkin' V-8 powered behemoth only netted you about twelve to fifteen miles per gallon. With most of today's models delivering at least twice that level of fuel economy, it's easy to see that the good ole days might not have been all that great after all (at least in terms of driving). Bottom line, it probably seemed like a great expense to keep those old "70s-mobiles" gassed up and ready to roll.

Without going through the entire monthly budget, between the rent, car, doctor and dental bills, music and judo lessons for the kids, occasional dinners at the Chinese restaurant, and whatever other incidentals came along, suffice to say that money usually got tight by month's end. A particular source of consternation with regard to finances was the nagging issue of my father's teeth. Though he never took his dental hygiene for granted, there came a point when he started to have trouble with his gums. This required many painful visits to someone named Dr. Franzetti. Prior to these discussions of this particular dental specialist, I had never before heard of a periodontist. From the way Dad described it, however, not somebody you want to frequent. I have no idea why Dad was so afflicted with gum issues, but I can certainly attest that his visits to Dr. Franzetti were not cheap. So much so, that his bills tended to skew our family's finances in no small way.

Anyway, most of my parent's evening arguments seemed to revolve around these continuing financial concerns. There was always the question as to how they were going to meet these monthly fiscal obligations, and clearly, there was never enough money to adequately get the job done. It was like living under a giant black cloud all the time. A source of untold stress that never went away. Listening to it from the next room night after night, it was as if my parents had lost all affection for each other. Unkind words were often spoken as voices were raised in anger, and the tension in the apartment was palpable.

During these times the living room became a war zone, and you hunkered down as far from the action as possible while the battle raged. As bad as it was, I hoped in my heart of hearts that somehow these two grownups (whom I called Mom and Dad) actually still loved each other. This question truly came to the forefront for me one night. Oddly enough, on this particular evening, the argument didn't stem from money. This particular conflict concerned my father's feelings toward his in-laws.

While my brother and I tried our best to fathom why such bitter feelings were coming from such a seemingly innocuous source, my father continued to rage about the evils of Gussie and Sam. Truly this subject cut very deep, as it produced the most bitter and brutal argument of my recollection. The gloves had completely come off on this one, as the two seemed locked in mortal combat. In retrospect, it was probably more a case of Mom trying to fend off my father's brutal and relentless psychological onslaught. And it was all she could do just to keep her head above water.

At one point my dad hollered, "Your parents never gave me anything."

To this accusation, Mom replied, "They gave you Me." I truly thought that such a heartfelt and loving statement would put an end to this needless and crazy argument.

It was at this point that Dad once again rocked my world in a most unsettling way. Without missing a beat he then leveled, "I'm beginning to think that wasn't such a hot deal." Certainly, we were all quite familiar with Dad's propensity for cruel words during fits of anger, but this one took the cake. One of those surreal moments where you know you heard what you heard, but you just couldn't believe it really happened. In any case, this reduced Mom to tears (as one could well imagine). About the only positive thing I can say is that it finally ended that night's argument.

In a state of total exhaustion and bitter frustration, Mom headed off to bed. Her goal seemed to be to put as much distance between her and my father as possible. Not a bad idea considering the circumstances.

I'd like to think that Dad felt bad about spewing such cruel words that night. I'd also like to think that he apologized to my mom at some point shortly thereafter. The fact of the matter is, however, that I really don't know. If he did feel bad, and if he did apologize, I wasn't privy to it. Even though I was pretty young at the time, I learned a lot that night about the power of angry and cruel words. No doubt about it, words can indeed hurt.

XIX
Camp Choconut

During my early childhood years, I had two sources of blissful escape. One was my growing enthusiasm and rapidly expanding abilities with regard to playing music. The other was our annual summer sojourn to Camp Choconut. Nestled in the lovely green rolling hills of northeastern Pennsylvania, the concrete jungle of Brooklyn quickly melted away. As I mentioned previously, summer camp was a win-win for my parents as well as my brother and me. For two months out of every year, Mom and Dad rejoiced in relinquishing their parental responsibilities, while my brother and I reveled in not being under their thumb.

Camp Choconut presented great opportunities for success through personal fulfillment. Though it took a little while to get there, the transition from a "non-swimmer" to someone who could swim from one side of the lake to the other was colossal. For someone who had never before experienced hiking, to walk ten miles carrying forty or fifty pounds on your back was colossal. Learning how to gather wood from the forest to craft a campfire was colossal. And learning how to pitch a tent in order to survive for days on end in the wilderness was colossal. Admittedly, using the woods for a bathroom was not always colossal, but an interesting and necessary part of the training, nonetheless.

At Camp Choconut I learned how to use an ax as well as a knife. I learned how to use a sledgehammer and a steel wedge to split a good size log. And I learned what a pain in the ass it was to dig holes in the hard, rocky Pennsylvania soil. I learned how to use rope to join together long timbers to build a standing tower. Most importantly, I learned to love and respect the land. I learned that it was important to leave a campsite in better shape than when you arrived. I learned that it was okay to be alone with our own thoughts at times (a skill that serves me well to this day). And

I learned how to respect and get along well with others.

I discovered what a joy it was to pull a seventeen-inch bass out of the lake, using only a cheap fishing rod and a rubber worm. And somewhere along the line, someone taught me how to clean and prepare that fish such that it would make a wonderful dinner entree. I learned how to maneuver a canoe down a river filled with rapids, while somehow remaining upright (most of the time). Perhaps one of my greatest lessons was discovering that people who might have seemed very different from me at first, were actually not that different after all. We might have come from very different places in life, but in the end, we were all seeking the same things. The things that really mattered. Friendships that lasted for many years, growth and success that would guide us throughout our entire lives, and experiences that would stay with us forever.

I could fill this entire book with some of the unique characters I met at Camp Choconut during my twelve-year tenure. Characters who secretly went off into the woods during their free time to chop wood (just because swinging an ax into a tree trunk cleared their mind). Characters who possessed the physical strength of Samson (who could carry off half a tree trunk on their shoulders). Characters who could build or construct just about anything from scratch (just by using whatever materials happened to be handy). Characters who could quote literature verbatim. Characters who could pass the Bar Exam after a summer of studying in the middle of the woods for an hour a day. Characters who could make up spellbinding stories on the spot (that kids would remember for the rest of their lives). Characters who could make a kid feel an overwhelming sense of remorse (for some indiscretion or other), simply by the tone of their voice. Characters who could teach you how to cook a gourmet meal in the middle of the woods with nothing but a Dutch Oven and an open fire. Characters who could figure out how to build an entire wooden cabin (complete with shingled roof), even though they'd never done it before. Then there were the ones who could do all of these things.

I must admit that I was never a huge fan of the various British counselors that passed through Choconut during my time. The camp's director Hamill Horne (a.k.a. "Ham") was a firm believer in the "counselor exchange program." This was an organization that gave capable young men from all over the world the opportunity to travel to America to be a summer camp counselor for a couple of months. As a result, we had counselors from all over Europe, a few from Asia, and even one or two from Africa. Owing to the difference in culture, I'd have to say that these were some of the most memorable young men to grace our humble camp environment.

The Europeans came from places like Scotland, Norway, Sweden,

Denmark, Finland, Germany, and yes, quite a few from England. Those who were privileged to meet him will never forget our beloved German friend Dieter (pronounced Deeter). Dieter graced us with his unique and wonderful presence for a few summers. He was probably best remembered for both his absolute hatred of peanut butter, as well as his wild affinity for Fruit Loops. Mostly, he was a genuinely warm and gracious guy, with a damn good sense of humor. I'll never forget a very serious counselor meeting we had one night after the kids had gone to bed. Ham warned us about the perils of "roughhousing" with the kids. By engaging with them in this manner, you lose your dignity, Ham explained. And once you lose your dignity, the kids will no longer take you seriously. At that point, Dieter leaned over and whispered to me, "Hey – I lose my dignity in the first ten minutes of camp." It was all I could do not to chortle at that point. Dignity or not, the kids adored ole Dieter. And so did the rest of us.

I recall a very slight fellow from one of the Nordic countries named Yan Rougthhhhhh. The strange spelling of his last name is because I have no recollection of how it was really spelled. What I do remember is that it had to be pronounced as if you were hocking back a lugey. No matter how you pronounced it, however, Yan would always correct you (even though his corrected version always sounded just like the way you said it in the first place). I felt kind of bad for Yan because his English was extremely rudimentary compared with most of his European counterparts. This didn't seem to faze him too much as it turned out. Like Dieter, I recall he was rather well-liked, and always seemed to be in very high spirits.

Yan's big project that summer was to build a little wooden shed out back behind the dining hall. Yan had considerable experience working with his hands, as he had once toiled for a time at a kibbutz in Israel. Toward the end of lunch every day, the counselors would have to get up for a minute and describe the activity they were going to lead that afternoon. Afternoons were free time for the kids, and they could choose whatever activity sounded good. So each and every day after lunch Yan would proudly stand up and announce, "I'll be working on the shed." The accent with which he spoke would be very hard to emulate in written form. Suffice to say, it took us several lunches before we knew what he was actually talking about. And even when the kids did understand, it never really sounded all that exciting. So most afternoons would find Yan toiling away on that shed, mostly by himself. And again, I wouldn't say it ever fazed him. He always seemed as happy as... Well, as a guy happily toiling away while working on a shed. And if I recall, it turned out to be a perfectly nice shed!

One of the few British counselors that I did get along quite well with was a strappy and rugged young fellow named Clive Reginald. As had been my complaint with some of the other Brits I had met at Choconut, there was nothing pretentious or snobbish whatsoever about Clive. He was about as real as it gets, and we very quickly became good buddies during his one summer at camp.

There are a couple of things that stick in my memory about my buddy Clive. The first is that he and another counselor that summer both set their sights on the same gal who worked as the camp secretary. Being that Choconut was a boys only camp, there were few female members (or employees) with whom we could fraternize. The camp secretary, the occasional unmarried nurse, and maybe the odd kitchen worker being possible exceptions. But in general, it was pretty slim pickings during those Choconut summers.

It was, therefore, inevitable that the young and good-looking camp secretary was highly sought after by two eligible young men during that particular summer. And truth be told, the young and good-looking secretary was indeed enticing. Sensing that it could get in the way of their friendship, both Clive and his rival made a pact with each other at the very start of camp. Each agreed to observe a strict hands-off policy concerning the fair maiden. And if both had lived up to their promise, they probably would have remained good friends that summer. Factoring in that summer is eight weeks long, and there was only one available hottie at the camp, perhaps such a pact wasn't entirely realistic. As it turned out, not realistic at all. It didn't take long before Clive's rival swooped in on Ms. Hottie, pact be damned. The result was twofold. Rival young man and Ms. Hottie had quite the fling that summer, and the two young men never spoke again. Childish and ridiculous indeed, but that is how it panned out.

I previously mentioned a fellow who could build a large wooden cabin, never having done so before. Clive was indeed that remarkable fellow. What's even better is that Clive had never actually built any kind of structure before. To put things into perspective, Clive was studying to be an architect. When he was asked to build that large cabin that summer, he went into quite a panic. Ham chose him for the assignment, as he was well aware of Clive's future vocational aspirations. Who better to trust with such a high-profile and potentially costly project?

What Ham didn't know was that Clive's only architectural experience up to that point had been strictly on paper. But what beautiful drawings Clive drafted. He had every detail of that cabin outlined and spec'd in just so. Clearly, he knew his stuff. Now it was just a question of actually building it. Easier said than done, as Clive was soon to discover. He agonized over every step of the construction process, but slowly and steadily the edifice began to take shape. Though he probably lost many a night's sleep that summer due to worry, in the end, his cabin was truly a work of art. It went together beautifully (albeit the occasional glitch), but it stood proudly and served admirably for many years to come. If indeed my theory about success begetting future success is true, then I'm sure Clive has had a great number of architectural winners throughout his career. Way to go Clive! And best not to make any future pacts with regard to desirable maidens.

XX
Johnny Carson and My Dad

Though my guitar and fiddle playing were both coming along nicely, I was soon to discover that replicating other people's tunes was a far cry from creating my own. It is quite ironic that the skills needed to conquer the intricacies of a particular instrument do not necessarily lend themselves to forming one's own musical creations. In other words, just plunking out the black notes that are written down on white paper does not a creative musician make. It is quite possible to reproduce the written notes with extreme accuracy, without having a creative bone in your body. On the other hand, it is quite common that some of the world's greatest songwriters and musicians never even learn to read music. Not to say that it wouldn't have benefited them, it's just that they didn't need this particular skill in order to be creative. It's this creative facet that cannot be taught or learned. It's either a part of your DNA chain or it isn't.

In my case, I'm not sure whether it's actually there or not. In fifty years or so, I've perhaps written five or six tunes that I thought were any good. Talk to any noted songwriter, and they'll probably tell you that they can sit down and write a tune whenever they will themselves to do so. My friend Pete from our old band days was such a person. All he needed was a little quiet time and a notebook. Then stand back and witness the magic. And did he ever write some amazing tunes! I wish he'd really pushed them to the music industry folks, as I'm convinced that many of them would have been big hits. Throughout his life, he's written hundreds of tunes. As for me, I'm convinced it happens by Divine Intervention. The words and thoughts appear out of nowhere, and it is always a scramble to get them down before the inspiration goes away. There have been occasions where it left long before I ever had a chance to start writing. That's why it's vital that I capture such rare moments while they're actually unfolding.

Perhaps the first time I experienced such an inspiration was around age seventeen or so. I was still living with the folks back in the Brooklyn apartment when all of a sudden it hit. Dad had just gone off to bed and I was alone in my bedroom watching Johnny Carson on a Saturday night. This was making me quite depressed, as this was the best activity I could come up with. When this thought began to coalesce in my head, I quickly turned off the TV. I grabbed my guitar (which was never very far), as well as a pen and paper.

Little by little the lyrics began to filter down. And when they did, I quickly jotted them down. Mind you, Dad was trying to sleep in the next room, so I mouthed the words and brushed the strings of the guitar as softly as I could. As words continued to flow, my humdrum Saturday night was suddenly becoming strangely stimulating. Somehow or other I just knew that this was going to result in a real honest-to-goodness tune, and the thought was exciting and all-consuming.

I'd say I probably had about three-quarters of it written when all of a sudden I was jarred back into reality. I suddenly noticed my father standing in the doorway of my bedroom with a giant scowl on his face. As I had been in another dimension while in the process of writing the tune, it suddenly occurred to me that perhaps I wasn't being as quiet as I thought. At that point I went into a bit of a panic, as the last portion of the tune still needed to be written. And as I mentioned, this rare bit of divine inspiration wasn't going to hang around forever, thus time was of the essence. I decided that the best plan of action was to apologize as sincerely (and quickly) as possible for disturbing Dad's sleep, in the hope that he would release whatever spit and venom were forming. I could only hope that his impending lecture would be brief. Fortunately for me, it was.

Though his words were quite memorable, I was most grateful that he opted for brevity on this particular occasion. All he said was, "Gary, music is just a sideline." I knew there was more coming, but the clock was ticking. Once again I apologized profusely for disturbing his slumber while acknowledging his words of wisdom. Though he wasn't at all pleased, he made his reluctant retreat while still muttering to himself. I am very proud to say that I was able to complete the tune that evening. And if I may say so myself, a pretty decent song it turned out to be. To this day, I can still reel off a version of "I'll Just Turn On Johnny Carson" any time the mood strikes. And people still get a kick out of it. One of these days I'll throw it up on YouTube.

Here are those lyrics that formed in my seventeen-year-old brain back in 1977 or so.

I'll Just Turn On Johnny Carson

Well I had a date last Friday night.
It didn't work out like I planned.
Thought I had her just where I wanted,
right in the palm of my hand.

She turned to me and said, Hey Gary.
You didn't sweep me off my feet.
But give it some time and maybe you will,
but that remains to be seen.

So here I am alone tonight,
No better no worse than before
I'll just turn on Johnny Carson.
I think I need to laugh some more.

When this old world gets me down,
I get into my truck and go.
And fifty-five miles an hour
just seems a little too slow.
I didn't see the highway policeman,
the bum caught me by surprise.
He said I was doing sixty-five.
He took my license to drive.

So here I am alone tonight,
No better but worse than before
I'll just turn on Johnny Carson.
I think I need to laugh some more.

Now Johnny's pulled me through some rough spots.
Ed McMann and all the guys.
He made the long nights a little shorter.
Lord you know at least he tries.
So this Bud's for you John, Ed and Doc.
For all that you've done for me.
I hope I don't need you too much longer.
I'd like to bury that old TV set!

So here I am alone tonight,
No better no worse than before
I'll just turn on Johnny Carson.
I think I need to laugh some more.
Yeah I think I need to laugh some more.
I know I need to laugh some more.

Incidentally, the awkward date part, as well as the speeding ticket were real. As was the feeling of having nothing better to do than watching

114 Whataya Gonna Do?

Johnny Carson all alone on a Saturday night.

I was telling this story to my girlfriend recently, and at the ripe old age of sixty, it now presents a certain perspective. There is a poignant episode of M.A.S.H (the old TV show) where Hawkeye's father is undergoing a dicey operation back home in Maine. Major Winchester (played so masterfully by David Ogden Stiers) happens to overhear Hawkeye's conversation with the hospital. The two men then engage in a rare moment of sharing on a very personal level. Major Winchester confesses that he envies Hawkeye's relationship with his father. He says, "Whereas I have a father, you have a Dad." Hawkeye then feels compassion for Winchester, perhaps for the first time in their association. When Hawkeye says that he hates being ten thousand miles apart from his father, Winchester laments that "He and his father can be ten thousand miles apart in the same room."

I remember that dialog to this day because it resonated so strongly in my case. When I saw my father scowling through the doorway the night I wrote "Johnny Carson," I knew that we were ten thousand miles apart in that small Brooklyn apartment. I sometimes have a fantasy where I envision my father coming down to breakfast the following Sunday morning. He has a smile on his face and he's in good cheer. Dad then apologizes for being in such a grumpy mood the night before, and with great interest, he inquires as to the song I'd been writing. He says something like, "Hey—What was that song you were writing last night?" "It sounded interesting." He would then want to hear it and would fill with pride when I sang it for him.

In reality, the preceding evening was never spoken of again, and Dad has never once heard the tune. I doubt he would even have remembered my writing it. If I could talk to him now, I'd surely tell him how lucky he was to have had such a creative and musical son. I would tell him how thrilled I'd be to hear my own child sing a song of his or her own creation. I'd tell him what a tremendous source of pride that would give me. How it would be a wonderful opportunity for us to bond in such a personal and meaningful way. In my fantasy, that's what I would tell him. Instances like this one are an excellent argument for having meaningful and pertinent discussions while people are still around.

A few years before the Johnny Carson tune, I had a similar "Hawkeye/Winchester" experience. For several years immediately following summer camp, my family would spend the Labor Day week at a resort in the Catskill Mountains. When I say "resort," I mean that it was a rather modest hotel on some very pretty acreage in upstate New York. Though somewhat rustic, it offered a hundred or so guests a pleasant retreat from the hot and oppressive New York City summer. Best of all it was reasonably priced and featured a refreshing outdoor swimming pool.

Our friend Mike and his sister Tina (whom we had met at the judo school) even joined us for a few summers after my father mentioned the place to their dad.

Mike and Tina's father Nat was one of the kindest and most easy-going men I've ever met. During one of these summers, Mike and I were lamenting that his minibike would sure come in handy on the relatively isolated dirt road that led up to the hotel. Mostly free of everyday traffic, this winding up and down dirt road would be the perfect place to put the minibike through its paces. The only problem was that the minibike was currently about five hours away, all the way back in their Brooklyn apartment. To me, this seemed like a rather overwhelming obstacle, but to Mike, not so much. He casually mentioned that he and his father could easily drive back to the city that night, retrieve the bike and return to the resort the next day.

Of course, my first thought was that nobody in their right mind would drive ten consecutive hours just to retrieve a minibike for a few days of enjoyment. I looked at my friend like he was crazy and insisted that there was no way his father would ever agree to such a ridiculous inconvenience. Mike then looked at me like I was from another planet and assured me that his father would do it in a heartbeat. While inconceivable to me, not only did Mike's father agree to do it, but he also offered to do it by himself. Nat told his son that there was no need for him to come along if he didn't want to make the arduous trek back and forth to the city. I then explained to my father that Nat was going to drive all the way back to Brooklyn that night and return with Mike's minibike on the following morning. My father then looked at me like I was from another planet, assuring me that there was no way in the world Nat would do such a crazy thing.

Apparently, my father didn't know Nat as well as he might have thought. That night Mike informed me that he was indeed going to join his dad on the drive back to Brooklyn. After all, if his father was going to go to all that trouble for him, the least he could do was go along. And though Nat insisted it wasn't necessary, Mike joined him anyway. I could just see the two of them tooling down the road that night while having a great time laughing and talking. The fact of the matter was that they thoroughly enjoyed each other's company and got along just famously. For Nat, it wasn't about picking up a minibike so his son would have something fun to do. It was about doing something that would enhance his relationship with his son. Something that would deepen their already strong bonds. And for Mike, it wasn't just about ridding himself of any guilt that might have formed at his father's gesture to make such a trip. It was about an opportunity to spend ten uninterrupted and treasured hours with his father. As Winchester said, I had a father while Mike had a dad.

XXI
Barry's Stash

I started going to Camp Choconut when I was nine because that was the youngest age they accepted. Choconut, however, was not my first all-summer camp experience. My first sleep-away camp adventure (that would take me away from home for all eight weeks) came the previous summer when I was eight. Looking back upon that experience, it is indeed a wonder as to why I ever wanted to attend a summer camp again. Telling this story all these years later, it is almost surreal when I recount the events that took place during the summer of 1967.

Camp Reckro was part of the Jewish Federation of Camps. Given our ethnic persuasion, I suppose that is how my parents learned of it. I hardly know where to even begin. Being only eight, I had significant trepidation about spending an entire summer away from home. I was assured, however, that it would be a wonderful experience and I'd have a great deal of fun. I can still clearly remember the first day I arrived (after Mom and Dad high-tailed it back to the city). My first duty was to unload and organize my gear. I was told to carefully stow the items I'd need most in a wooden cubby that was to be mine for the summer. Never having been assigned this particular task before, how does an eight-year-old know what items he's going to need most? As a result, I took out way too many clothes (and other items) and proceeded to stuff them into my little vertical wooden cubby. When the grossly over-stuffed cubby would hold no more, I figured I had completed the task. It didn't look pretty, but at least the job was done. A quick inspection was performed by our two counselors when everyone had completed the job.

Those who had been to camp before had cubbies that looked neat and orderly, with all necessary items easily accessible and clearly viewable. The counselors looked at several of these cubbies, then commented to the group that "This was how a cubby should look." When he made his way to my cubby, he very quickly announced that "This is how a cubby should not look." Perhaps that should have been an omen, because that's pretty much how my entire summer went. A more experienced camper was then assigned to help me fix my cubby, as I was clearly out of my depth.

Never having spent the summer in a rustic cabin in the middle of the woods before, I arrived quite ill-prepared. The clothes my mom packed for me were far more geared to city life than to rugged outdoor adventure. I was totally disorganized and struggled just to keep up with the daily pace of camp life. Clearly, I was the embarrassment of the entire cabin. Eventually, I did get to a point where I knew where my essential clothing items were, even if I wore the same combination all summer long.

Several things remain in my mind from that fateful summer of 1967. The first is that I spent a good bit of it in the camp infirmary. For some inexplicable reason, I got sick a lot that summer. Perhaps the strain of adapting to such a radical new way of life (at such a young age) was a bit overwhelming. And perhaps this stress was doing bad things to my body. Whatever the explanation, I logged an inordinate amount of time that summer in the camp sickbay.

Perhaps my weak stomach was also a contributing factor, as I'm sure it didn't react well to these extraordinary circumstances. I recall one of the nurses taking my temperature with a rectal thermometer one day (as was the common method back in those days). Shortly after removing the long slim glass probe, and with a furrowed brow, she inquired as to whether I was going to the bathroom on a regular basis. Even at the tender age of eight, I still had the wherewithal to ask why she had posed such a curious question. Without going into tremendous detail, the thermometer didn't exit my body in a manner that could be described as "clean as a whistle." To the untrained eye, it might certainly have appeared that I was not observing regular bathroom habits. Most assuredly, this was not at all the case. Alternatively, perhaps this particular health care practitioner was dealing with her first case of the so-called "Irritable Bowel Syndrome."

Of course, I had never heard of I.B.S. at that point in my life, but these kinds of experiences were already becoming frustrating, humiliating, and somewhat frequent. And after all, what eight-year-old wants to be accused of being "unclean" with regard to observing normal and healthy bathroom hygiene. These painful memories come back to me whenever stomach docs ask me how long I've had this condition. I'm catapulted back to the summer of 1967, and an insensitive nurse's comment about the thermometer being "very dirty" after yanking it from my body. So I tell the docs that I can certainly trace it back to age eight.

The fact of the matter is that I can actually trace it back further than that. Suffice to say, I've probably been dealing with it all my life. Anyway, I was frequently sick that summer. On one particular stretch, I was so sick that they had to drive me into town to see a real doctor. There was a little girl at the camp who was also pretty sick at the same time, so two lady counselors drove the two of us sickies into town that day to visit the doc. I was the first to be examined, so I climbed up on the table and took off my shirt as per the doc's request. Deep breaths in and out while he manipulated the stethoscope. Say "Ah," as he worked the tongue depressor as per the usual examination routine. In the end, I probably had some sort of virus that just needed to run its course. More rest and lots of fluids were the probable verdicts, so I hopped off the table and took a seat.

It was now the little girl's turn to be examined, so I resigned myself to wait patiently while the doc now turned his attention to her. While contemplating the meaning of life (or whatever I was actually doing), I heard a faint voice out of the corner of my ear. "Tell the boy to leave the room" is what it sounded like. I didn't pay much attention, as I had no idea that I was the "boy" to whom the little girl was referring (or what she was even talking about for that matter). So I continued waiting contentedly in my chair when I heard the voice a second time. This time it was less faint, but the message was the same. "Tell the boy to leave the room," it repeated. I was probably about as befuddled as the doc until I suddenly realized what the issue was. The little girl had also been asked to remove her shirt, and in the presence of a little boy, this made her extremely uncomfortable.

I doubt she was much more than eight herself, and I guarantee that her chest looked pretty much like mine at this stage. Be that as it may, she was obviously very distressed at the prospect of bearing herself in my presence. The only thing my eight-year-old brain could conjure at that point was why she was getting so put out about having to take her shirt off for the doctor. After all, you didn't hear me complaining that I had to take my shirt off in front of her. It's funny to think about it now, but at the time I actually found it quite embarrassing. Eight years old and I already stood accused of being a Peeping Tom. The two lady counselors smiled and told me to look away. God's honest truth, I wasn't even looking at her to begin with. As I say, I was contemplating the meaning of life.

The other thing that stands out in my mind about Camp Rekro is quite a bit more disturbing. And this is indeed the memory that makes me wonder how I ever summoned up the courage to give summer camp another shot. Had Mom and Dad actually taken the time to seek out a reference or two on this place, there would have been no way in the world they ever would have shipped me off that summer.

There were two counselors assigned to our group. One was a fairly affable fellow named Barry Weingas (pronounced Wine Gas). I guess I'll always remember that name for obvious reasons. Mr. Weingas was kind of a tubby-looking guy, short and a bit round in the midsection. For a man perhaps in his low to mid-twenties, he was also sporting quite a bit of hair loss. The overweight balding thing probably made him look a bit older than he actually was. The name of the other counselor escapes me completely (probably because it wasn't something like Weingas).

One of the things that kept Barry affable, was a large supply of snacks and candy that he always kept on hand toward the top of his big steamer trunk. Barry had quite the sweet tooth and quite the proclivity for salty snacks. In short, Barry loved his junk food and made sure he was always well-stocked. Affable to be sure, but generous, not so much. Many's the time we'd be sitting around the cabin with Barry feeding his face with candy bars, crackers, nuts, you name it. Clearly, it was of no consequence that he had all this junk food at the ready, while the rest of us had no such access to such exotic snacks. To make matters worse, he'd often enjoy his snacks right in front of us, while completely neglecting to share any of them. I suppose this gave Barry quite the feeling of power and superiority within his narrow domain.

This routine probably went on for about three weeks or so. On one fateful day, however, Barry ventured out for a while and neglected to lock his steamer trunk. A careless mistake indeed, as he was quite meticulous about protecting his stash at all times. Not this time, however. Like crows to an unprotected loaf of bread, Barry's error was spotted almost immediately. In an instant, a chant went up that Barry had left his prized stash unprotected. And just like that determined flock of crows, we all descended upon Barry's trunk the moment the coast was clear.

Though I was certainly no saint, my parents had raised me to understand that stealing was wrong (even if it was just fat Barry's candy stash). Still, I thought there'd be no harm in taking a look. When I got up in front of that trunk, I was absolutely amazed. Jars of Planters Peanuts, all variety of candy bars, Good & Plenty, packs of gum and licorice, you name it. The guy pretty much had an entire candy store in that trunk. What a treasure trove of junk food, and all of the highest caliber. I recall my cabin mates diving in and helping themselves, reveling in the good eats and their great fortune in capturing it. This was truly a page out of Lord of The Flies.

While I was happy that we had found retribution for Barry's stinginess, I was still a bit reticent at the concept of laying claim to someone else's property. Sure, Barry was kind of a jerk for never having offered us any of his treats. But stealing is stealing and even given the circumstances, it just seemed wrong. At one point someone passed me Barry's jar of Planters Dry Roasted Peanuts. I loved peanuts then and I still do. Would you believe that my conscience allowed me to remove only a single solitary peanut from that jar? It's not actually stealing if it's only one peanut, I rationalized. I kid you not. My total take from this entire caper was one solitary Planters dry roasted peanut. Perhaps in addition to my good upbringing, there was the very definite fear that retribution would be forthcoming. Though certainly cause for concern, it didn't seem to be putting a damper on anybody else's good time.

Boy, do I hate being right sometimes, but retribution did indeed come. Did it ever. Naturally, Barry discovered the terrible truth about the status of his candy stash the moment he arrived back at the cabin. Picture that scene in the movie "One Flew Over the Cuckoo's Nest" where the guards arrive in the morning after R.P. MacMurphy and the boys (and girls) had ravaged the place with an all-out orgy the night before. Very much like that. Candy bar wrappers strewn everywhere, empty jars all over the floor, discarded Good & Plenty and Milk Dud boxes as far as the eye could see. Quite the pillage indeed. Suffice to say that Mr. Weingas was no longer affable. The next few minutes were somber. Barry stared in horror, tiny tears streaming from the corner of his pudgy eyes, as he surveyed his massive losses. But those tears were quickly replaced with fire, as he and counselor number two plotted their revenge.

What followed is a bit hard to describe, but truly one of the most terrifying moments of my eight-year life. In short, the cabin door was locked, and the two young men set about to teach us a lesson we wouldn't soon forget. They swiftly set upon us with fists and feet and began pummeling each of us in turn. As I looked around it seemed like bodies were flying in all directions. Some were slamming to the ground, others were careening into walls, while still others were clanging into the furniture. It was like something out of an old Clint Eastwood movie. The room quickly filled with the terrified sounds of little kids screaming, either in fear or out of sheer pain. Punches were landed, fists were delivered, feet were kicking, and all the while the body count laid out on the cabin floor was ever-increasing.

Crying and moaning were now emanating from all around me. Kids were now strewn about the cabin floor like casualties on a battleground. For some inexplicable reason, at that moment I found myself somewhere in the eye of the storm. Though it was raging in every direction I looked, somehow the walls were yet to collapse upon me. As there was no question that they soon would, I was now filled with a horrible dread.

In a moment of such absolute and unprecedented chaos, it is amazing what will sometimes occur to you. I have no idea from where it came, but I suddenly received a vision. It all happened so quickly that I scarcely had time to even think about it. What I remember most at that point was one of the counselors snatching the kid just in front of me, and violently hauling him forward by his shirt. As the poor fellow flew forward from the counselor's tremendous grasp, the boy's head smacked soundly into one of the steel posts that held the army-style bunk beds together. The blow struck the boy just above his eye with a terrible clang, and the poor lad cried out in pain. If I was going to enact my plan, this was certainly the moment.

Though in my heart of hearts I really didn't think it would work, it was nevertheless my only shot. With no further provocation or delay, I immediately fell to the floor and began moaning in pain just as all the other kids were now doing. It was the best painful moan I could muster, and I enhanced my pantomime by doubling over and rolling about a bit while on the cabin floor. Thank God there were two counselors dishing out the punishment that afternoon, as they were both somehow convinced that the other had gotten to me.

With my heart still pounding wildly in my chest, the massacre finally concluded. Though no one ever actually laid a finger on me that afternoon (much to my astonishment) the trauma was as real as that of the actual wounded. I could swear that the two twenty-something goons actually looked over their handiwork for a couple of minutes when the attack was over. I was certain that they would suddenly realize their omission with regard to me. Thank God that realization never came. The two finally turned and left, and only then did we start to feel remotely safe again.

Naturally, I waited until some of the other kids got up from the floor before doing so myself. I had no desire for any of them to realize that I survived the entire ordeal unscathed. Had the other kids found out, they might well have finished the job. Needless to say, after that we never raided anyone's foot lock again. And for the remainder of that summer, we also never got along with our two counselors again.

Camp Rekro was a bizarre place indeed, where corporal punishment was practiced on a routine basis. Funny how the camp brochure never mentioned that. I was also later to learn that they routinely censored our mail so that news of such events never reached our parents. When that summer was finally over, I told my mom and dad about some of the things that went on at this place. Honestly, I don't think they ever believed me. It's still a bit hard even for me to believe, but I'm sure the details of my account are more than adequate testimony to the authenticity of this horrible event. I can only hope that the authorities shut this joint down many years ago.

XXII
The Long-Lost Cousins

Both Stevie and Neil rose from humble beginnings, but went on to lead very productive and successful lives. My father's eldest sister Maizy actually had three sons. Neil was the youngest, Stevie was in the middle, and the eldest was named Harris. I think I only met Harris once since he was much older than my brother and me, and his family migrated to Boston while still a relatively young man. All I know about him was that he was some kind of a sales rep and traveled a lot. There were also rumors of his frequent womanizing (though he was a married man), and how he loved to regale the family with tales of his numerous sexual conquests. With regard to his relationship with the little woman back home, perhaps what happened on the road stayed on the road.

    As a result of the service we held for my mom, I was informed that Harris was no longer with us. Stevie explained that he is now the oldest brother in the family, as Harris had chosen to abruptly end his life via a self-inflicted gunshot wound several years back. Harris had apparently struggled with alcohol and marital issues, and at some point "the little woman" simply decided to dump his ass. For a man in his eighties, it was just too much for him to handle. Much to the dismay of those who loved and cared about him, he decided it would be best to depart this earth. And so he did.

    Neil opted for a rather traditional occupation and thus became a teacher. While in that capacity he met Bonnie (another teacher). Two highly prudent and extremely intelligent individuals, they fell in love and were soon married. Before long they saved up a bunch of money and bought a house out on Long Island. Of my cousin Neil, I would say two things. The first is that he is an extremely nice guy. Warm and personable as the day is long, he is a genuine and sincere human being. He had some very nice things to say about my mom during the service we held in New York. Not long before she died, my mom had said some really nice things about

Neil as well. His second distinction is that he is one of the most OCD individuals I have ever met.

When Mack and I were flying into New York for the service, we were both scheduled to arrive at Kennedy Airport somewhat late in the evening. In fact, it would have been around midnight by the time we got off the plane and collected our bags. As such, we agreed that it would be easiest to simply head for a nearby Kennedy Airport hotel on the night of our arrival. After all, why inconvenience anyone by making them do an airport run at that late hour, or by arriving at their house via taxi around one in the morning. So I explained to Neil that Mack and I would simply grab a convenient airport hotel room on our first night. And while midtown Manhattan hotels are a small fortune, a decent Kennedy Airport hotel could be had for about a hundred and a quarter a night. Split between Mack and me, not really so much for a decent night's sleep in New York (and without having to put anyone out).

When I explained this straightforward plan to Neil, however, he would have none of it. Turns out his home on Long Island is a hop, skip, and a jump from Kennedy Airport. As such, it didn't matter to him what time we were getting in. Since it would only take him twenty minutes to drive to Kennedy, he was absolutely adamant about picking us up and whisking us back to his place (the late hour be damned). Naturally, Mack and I thanked him profusely for his warm hospitality, while respectfully declining his most gracious offer. Undoubtedly, we'd be absolutely shot after traveling all day to the east coast and would much prefer a nearby hotel bed. The only problem was that Neil had already cemented "Plan A" into his head. And once there, it was damned near impossible to remove it.

After several lengthier phone conversations, Neil finally seemed to relent concerning the midnight airport pickup. I suppose he realized that Mack and I weren't easily going to change our minds. Despite this, there was no doubt that the deviation was weighing heavily upon him. A couple more tedious telephone conversations (as well as several lengthy voice mails) found him summing up the travel plans (with particular mention that he would not be picking us up at the airport). Why such a simple alteration plagued him so, was indeed a head-scratcher. Clearly, however, he was not used to having his plans altered. Ah well. Once we were finally reunited, we all got along just famously.

I saved Stevie for last because he was far and away the most interesting of the three brothers. Unlike his younger sibling, Stevie chose not to go on to higher education. As a young man who had lost his mom at a very early age, he probably figured his role was to get out there as soon as possible in order to make a living and provide for the family.

Stevie had an extremely warm and ingratiating side. When you were in his home, both he and his wife (Marty) welcomed you with open arms. He was truly a man who held family in very high regard, and he reveled in the time we spent together. Perhaps this was also because our trips to his home in the suburbs of New York City were relatively infrequent.

When it came to work, Stevie was an absolute dynamo. I believe he was driven by a tremendous impetus to rise above his humble beginnings. Having had to fight his way through the rough and mean streets of New York City as a child and a teenager, Stevie was determined to carve out a better life. He achieved his goal by working three different jobs at the same time. He ran the movie projector (that was a job back then) at various New York theatres. He was also one of those guys you see operating the TV cameras at sporting events around the city. And in the time that remained, he utilized his basement to repair televisions, radios, and other electronic equipment.

As he explained to me about fifteen years ago, he'd leave for work on Monday and wouldn't come back home until Thursday. Between gigs, he'd sleep in his car, while paying off the NYC meter maids so they wouldn't hassle him. He kept clothing everyplace he worked so that he'd always have a change of wardrobe handy. As for meals, I'm sure he frequented New York's abundant quick and relatively inexpensive food establishments. In essence, he lived like a vagabond, and his wife and kids only saw him on weekends.

This lifestyle probably didn't seem too unusual to Stevie, as I'm told that his dad led a very similar one. Perhaps not exactly the ideal routine for a family man, but it did land him in fairly good economic steed. And I suppose the nice house in the burbs must have seemed a worthwhile tradeoff for the brief time he was able to spend with his family. And after all, maybe it was the only life he knew.

As for me, I loved those once in a while visits to Stevie's house. I was a big fan of all things electronic back then (probably still am), so the opportunity to peruse that amazing basement of his was a rare treat. The expression "Like a kid in a candy store" certainly applied in this case. And though nothing was actually edible, the items on display in Stevie's basement were absolute ambrosia. Electronic gadgets and components as far as the eye could see. Stereos in every manner of completeness, recording equipment, radios, televisions, you name it. A regular Disneyland of electronic gadgets.

On one particular tour of this wondrous basement, I spotted something that positively stopped me in my tracks. Lo and behold, I was staring directly into the face of a huge and extremely professional-looking reel-to-reel tape recorder. Complete with lighted V.U. meters (see just below), a huge bank of switches for all manner of functions, and two large reels filled with layer upon layer of brown magnetic recording tape, I stood there absolutely mesmerized. My voice a combination of enchantment and sheer astonishment, I exclaimed to Stevie, "Holy cow! Where did you ever get that?"

It was, in fact, a professional piece of recording equipment that had fallen into a state of disrepair. The owner had brought it to Stevie in the hope of having it brought back to its full function and capability. In the process, however, it became apparent that some of the parts would be hard to find and thus costly. As this was the case, a deal was made whereby Stevie got to keep the tape machine in exchange for some other work he'd do for this particular fellow. Perhaps Stevie would repair it of his own volition, but more likely it would simply sit in the basement looking impressive but gathering dust.

Impressive was an understatement in my mind, as I was imagining all the fun and enjoyment I'd get from such an amazing piece of sound equipment. It didn't take Carl Jung or Sigmund Freud to surmise that by now I had fallen in love. No, it wasn't human, but I was in love, nonetheless. So imagine my astonishment when Stevie suggested right then and there that I should just take it home with me. His offer left me absolutely speechless. And though he said I should just take it; I didn't interpret that to mean he intended to give it to me for nothing.

God only knows what that thing must have cost when it was new. Sensing that this could possibly create an embarrassing situation for me, he suggested that we could work out a price later. Hard to imagine what kind of a price he could have had in mind, as I was a broke fourteen-year-old kid at the time. But like that famous line in *The Godfather*, it was an offer I couldn't refuse.

No doubt about it, this had turned into a truly wonderful day. Only one small problem, however. After our time together in the basement, Stevie eventually exited to return to his other guests. That simply left me and that tape recorder in Stevie's basement, with the remainder of the family (who were not privy to any of this discussion) happily conversing in the living room. As I mentioned, that old machine was huge and must have weighed about seventy pounds. It wasn't that I minded slogging it up the steps and carrying it out the door. The problem was that I was going to have to explain my actions in front of the entire family. No small matter for a painfully shy adolescent, who was now going to have to explain to about twenty-five people (including my mom and dad), why I was transporting this massive piece of equipment out of Stevie's basement. And owing to its formidable size, there was no way on earth I was going to make it look in any way subtle.

At this point, I need to mention that the Jewish culture is indeed a most distinct one. Within its vast subtext, there are a variety of ideas concerning what may or may not be appropriate societal behavior. In fact, among our people there is a particular word for someone who exhibits characteristics that might be considered selfish, rude, or self-serving. It is called being a "Schnorrer." A good example of a schnorrer is someone who doesn't bring anything to a potluck, but takes a goodly portion of the grub home in a large Tupperware (or doggie bag). It is interesting to note that while the schnorrer didn't think to bring any food to the gathering, they somehow remembered to pack a doggie bag.

This somewhat odd concept may not resonate loudly for those not of the faith, but I will assure you that it was very real in my world. For God's chosen people to accuse one another of such a heinous offense, this would surely be suitable grounds for a "Hamiltonian" style duel. As such, I was now faced with an enormous conundrum.

To be sure, there was no way on God's green earth I was leaving that highly prized tape recorder behind. But how to get it past that gauntlet of loud and inquisitive relatives, without being labeled a "giant schnorrer," was going to be one hell of a challenge. Alas, I had a brainstorm. The machine was very heavy and extremely unwieldy after all, so why not ask my older and more muscular brother to carry it out to the car for me. This not only made perfect sense, but it would also save me the humiliation and embarrassment of having to explain my curious undertaking.

It was at this point that my brother Mack delivered the most hilarious response I've ever heard him put forth. Without hesitation, he replied, "Oh no. I'm not gonna be a schnorrer." Mind you, up until that point, I had not even said the word "schnorrer" out loud. Interestingly enough, however, it was the first thing that occurred to Mack. Though his unwillingness to help me was indeed inconvenient, I must say that his response was absolutely hysterical (even during the heat of the moment). I guess we are all a product of our upbringing.

In the end, I simply bit the bullet. With great trepidation, I carried that monster up the stairs, through the crowded living room, and finally out to the car. Was it every bit the miserable task I expected it to be? You better believe it. Most memorable was my uncle Benny, who carried on like I was committing grand larceny. While Benny was far and away the most vocal, others good-naturedly probed as to what I was carrying, or just sat in silent wonder. To be certain, it was a long walk indeed through Steve and Marty's living room that afternoon. Ultimately, however, it proved to be well worth the humiliation. Though not a hundred percent mechanically sound, that machine did prove most useful. When we first started recording some of our tunes in the months and years to come, that tape recorder came through like a champ.

At the behest of my parents, I called Stevie one night to see if we could settle up concerning the matter of compensation. "How does nothing sound," he asked. He then explained that it was only going to sit in his basement anyway, as it probably wasn't cost-effective to repair it. In my most humble and grateful voice, I replied that "nothing sounded just fine."

Here's what that old Robert's reel-to-reel tape recorder looked like:

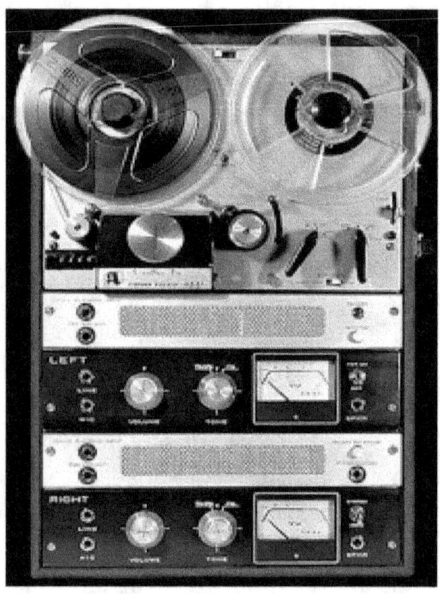

(Believe me, it was even more impressive in real life!)

As warm, friendly, and personable an individual as Stevie was, he also had his dark side. Lurking just below the exuberant and warm-hearted outer layer, was a fierce temper connected to a very short fuse. As a kid, I first became privy to this less than endearing characteristic one Sunday afternoon while viewing a slideshow from Stevie and Marty's recent family vacation.

Those of us of a certain age will remember slides and slide projectors. The opposite of a film negative, slides were those small square-shaped film images encased in a little cardboard border. These slides were then loaded into a circular plastic carousel which then connected to the top of the projector. With the click of a button, the carousel would rotate slightly so that each slide would be positioned in front of the lens. The machine would thus project a sharp and clear image onto a large white screen positioned several feet away.

All was going quite well at the start of the presentation, as we admired the beautiful images that streamed before us one at a time. No sooner had Stevie finished describing the details of the current image, when his expression quickly turned to one of extreme frustration. For when the very next slide appeared, it presented itself in an upside-down orientation. This vexed Stevie considerably, as his thought was that his wife had no doubt loaded some of the slides improperly. Indeed, if one were not concentrating fully when loading a slide projector, such a mistake would be easy to make. To hear Stevie tell it, however, he'd never loaded a slide upside down in his life. His wife on the other hand, well that was a very different story.

    With a noticeable grimace, he backed up the carousel and removed the improperly loaded slide. He then carefully reinserted it before resuming his presentation. Click, click, click, and a few more properly loaded slides were happily viewed. But then it happened again. More frustration on the part of Stevie, this time with the addition of sharp words directed at his wife. A few more good slides, then yet another upside-down one. At this point, Stevie could hold it together no longer. "She shows them to her friends, then doesn't put them back right!" he angrily bellowed.

    By now the rest of us could certainly feel Stevie's angst, which was amplifying steadily. It made for a very uncomfortable scene, leaving us hoping against all hope that we had seen the last of the upside-down slides. Unfortunately, this was not to be, as the problem continued to persist. The presentation then came to a sudden halt, with Stevie muttering loudly as he stormed out of the room. I remember his final angry and derisive words before exiting, "Let my wife clean up her own mess." Like most quick-tempered individuals, Stevie did calm down a short time later. But for those of us who hadn't seen this particular side of him, it was quite an eye-opener.

    The issue of Stevie's temper was apparently one that followed him throughout his entire life. He took great pride in describing himself as "Someone you don't fuck with." And from the look on his face when he said it, I can thoroughly believe it. As a youngster, he was one tough hombre when it came to navigating those lean and mean New York City streets. During our recent get-together for my mom's celebration of life, my ultra-tough cousin treated us to one of his more colorful and graphic tales.

    Seems one afternoon a gang of neighborhood street toughs decided to beat up his younger brother Neil. When Neil returned home quite a bit worse for the wear that afternoon, Stevie demanded to know what was up. When Neil explained the situation, Stevie was irate. He looked at his poor beat-up younger brother and said, "Show me the guys that did this." Together they retraced Neil's steps and came upon the brave souls who had earlier ganged up to pummel him. Stevie walked up to one of the young thugs and said, "Who's the leader of this gang?" One particular thug proudly announced that he was the leader. "You beat up my brother?" Stevie probed. Not bothering to wait for an actual reply, Stevie then hauled off and slugged the swaggering street urchin directly in the mouth.

By Stevie's account, the bully then staggered backward while tripping over a fruit stand. The remaining momentum from the thunderous blow culminated with the young thug flying directly through a plate glass window. With the haughty gang leader completely stunned and suddenly buried in an avalanche of glass, Stevie then shouted, "Who's next?" "There are plenty more windows." From what I understand, those hooligans never bothered Neil again. A pretty good story, one would have to admit.

So as I say, the three cousins all carved out a pretty successful life for themselves (Harris' eventual fate not-withstanding). And as a result, they all graduated from the rough and rugged city streets of Brooklyn, to the manicured lawns and two-story houses of the posh and peaceful suburbs. And that is precisely why we didn't get to see them very much. In essence, we now lived in very different worlds. The more time that went by, the more we lost track of each other. I was about fifteen when our families last got together. When we finally hooked up again to say goodbye to Mom, I was sixty. Hard to imagine, but it had been forty-five years.

XXIII
The Lionel Trains and Other Disappointments

"Don't get them toys, get them clothes." This was the mantra that my parents extolled upon the relatives whenever Christmas/Chanukah and birthdays rolled around. Though Mom and Dad weren't always in lockstep, unfortunately, they were absolutely united on this particular front. As a result, our toy selection always seemed rather sparse in comparison to our friends. On the other hand, my brother and I probably had a much greater selection of tasteless shirts (mainly owing to my Aunt Marsha). Not that I had any useful opinions about what constituted tasteful clothing as a kid, but the wacky shirts that arrived year after year from Marsha brought laughter even from my parents. I suppose Mom and Dad's concern for practical gifts, as opposed to childish and whimsical ones, is only natural. But given Marsha's questionable sartorial taste, I think I would have gotten much greater use out of the toys.

So imagine our astonishment when Dad arrived home one evening from work, carrying a big yellow cardboard box with colorful pictures of toy trains printed front and back. What prompted him to procure this totally unexpected prize, I'll never know. I don't recall it being anybody's birthday or even a holiday for that matter. Nevertheless, I'll never forget how proud he was when he arrived home with it. Perhaps he'd been very fond of toy trains as a kid and relished any opportunity to relive his youth. Or maybe someone at his work latched on to a "hot" batch of train sets. Or perhaps he just wanted to bring a smile to his family. Maybe it was all of the above.

In any case, it was a most unexpected and joyful surprise, to say the least. I was still pretty young at the time, so removing each unique train car from its particular cutout inside the box (not to mention a big pile of metal tracks) was truly a labor of love. Train sets were a hot item in the early seventies, so a big yellow box with the words "Lionel Trains" was sure to bring joy to any youngster's heart.

There was an amazingly lifelike black locomotive with fully functional wheels and smokestack, followed by a shorter black coal car. The additional cars were multi-colored and highlighted in a variety of industrial or agricultural themes. One of my favorites was the horse car with simulated wooden slats and windows on both sides. As the train rode along, the horse's heads would alternate popping out of the front and back windows on each side.

Another car was set up to hold wooden barrels (presumably of beer or whiskey), while others were configured to hold grains and other raw foodstuffs. There were flatbed rail cars, as well as units with big hoppers for hauling rocks and other building materials. And at the very end of the line was the obligatory little red caboose.

In addition to the standard complement of train cars and tracks, Lionel also offered an infinite selection of add-on accessories. These could be purchased separately to augment and spruce up the overall look of the set. There were bridges and tunnels, switches to divert the train to alternate tracks, and way cool towers with all manner of lights. I remember one particular light tower we added, where a rotating green and red tinted filter provided an alternating glow. Naturally, additional tracks could also be purchased (both straight and curving) to give the setup more breadth and diversity. I'd have to say that the Lionel train set was the coolest toy Dad ever got us. What possessed him I'll never truly know, but I do believe he had every bit as much fun playing with it as we did.

Like any beloved toy, however, there comes a time when you simply outgrow it. Even so, it stacked conveniently on the top shelf of our bedroom closet, where it remained for a goodly number of years. It was my hope that it would remain there somewhat permanently, but sadly that was not to be. When I was about sixteen or so, my mom proudly announced one night during dinner that she had cleaned house. In so doing, our prized train set had been unceremoniously relegated to the trash heap. Before we even had a chance to react, the garbage trucks had come, and that wonderful train set was reduced to a memory. The loss was devastating and quite ruined my dinner. Mom felt bad, but by now there was nothing she could do. "You never used it anymore" she implored. True enough, but that didn't mean I was ready to part with it. Ah well. The house was now a bit less cluttered.

Speaking of childhood disappointments, I recall two during my youth that were particularly resounding. Today they're actually pretty funny. The first has to do with that most beloved children's movie of all time, *The Wizard of Oz*. Way back before there were a zillion cable TV and movie channels (in fact before cable and the internet even existed), and before there were VCRs or Beta machines, our television viewing choices pretty much came down to about half a dozen broadcast channels. Naturally, there were the big three (CBS, NBC, and ABC). Then there were a couple of local networks (channels 5 and 11 in the greater New York area). And finally, we had the PBS channel which was WNET (channel 9 in our area).

So in this ancient time, when we couldn't summon up any show or movie whenever we wanted it, we made do with the limited choices that were put before us (commercials and all). As such, whenever The Wizard of Oz made its once only annual appearance on prime time, it was cause for great excitement. Whatever your daytime plans, you made darn sure you'd be back in the evening with plenty of time to tune in.

Such was the case on this particular Sunday evening when Mack and I huddled in our bedroom by the big black & white TV with great anticipation. The Wizard of Oz was about to come on. As it was such a grand event, the movie required a fitting introduction. Toward this end, a stately-looking gentleman wearing a suit was first presented. Apparently, it was this gentleman's job to introduce tonight's very special feature. As the man did indeed present as a very respectable and trustworthy figure, you knew his message would be one of great importance.

The stately gentleman briefly described the movie that would soon be presented, paying particular attention to one very noteworthy issue. Mr. "Stately" carefully explained that we would not see color during the beginning scenes of the movie. He then assured us that this would be through no fault of our television sets. The beginning scenes were in fact shot in black & white, thus there would be no cause for alarm.

I know now that the beginning scenes were actually filmed in a sepia tone (and not technically black & white), but I digress. In any case, we were not to worry. As soon as Dorothy opened the door looking out over the land of Oz, we would most certainly see color. I cannot even describe the feeling of excitement that these words conjured within me. I had never before witnessed color on our TV. For that matter, I had never seen color on any TV. This was really going to be something. Not only did we get to watch our very favorite movie, but we were also now going to watch it in "living color" (or so I was firmly led to believe).

With heart-pounding anticipation, I watched as the little wooden house was sent hurtling through the air. Twisting and turning within the great tornado, I was absolutely spellbound when it finally plopped safely down upon the land of the Munchkins. This was it. The moment was at hand! When Dorothy opened the door of that shanty wooden shack, lo and behold. Suddenly... Everything remained in black & white, and continued just that way. Bitter frustration reigned down upon me as there was no color in sight. Tears began streaming down my face, as I contemplated how the stately gentleman in the suit could possibly have lied to me.

In desperation, I went running into the living room to seek the counsel of my parents. I explained how the man assured us that there would be color, while in truth there was no color to be had. In a very calm and matter-of-fact voice, my father quickly replied that in order to see the color it was necessary to have a color TV. Obvious perhaps to an adult, but to a kid who's been assured that there would be color, not obvious in the least. In my most incredulous voice, I shouted, "The man didn't say it was necessary to have a color TV. All he said was that we'd see color." In today's world, one could probably sue that network for such an unsubstantiated claim. Back then, however, file it under the heading of "Life is Not Always Fair." Or perhaps, "Beware of Stately Looking Men in Suits."

My second amusing childhood disappointment has to do with the curious phrase "Limousine Service." My family was embarking upon our first and only flying vacation. Our coveted destination was Walt Disney World in Orlando, Florida. This would be the first time we'd ever been to Disney World, so that was exciting in it of itself. It was also going to be my first experience with airplane travel, so that was a pretty cool bonus.

In addition to these two monumental milestones, the itinerary also included "Limousine Service" from the airport in Orlando directly to our hotel. As a child raised in a very modest income environment, I certainly never had any occasion to ride in a limo. I'd seen limousines on television and in movies, and on occasion while picking up relatives at the various New York airports. I was aware that very special people rode in limousines, and that these folks seemed to lead very glamorous lifestyles. I certainly wasn't aware that everyday people like us could be treated to such luxury, but there was no mistaking that our travel papers definitely stated, "Limousine Service." Not only that, but my father recited the term multiple times when reviewing the trip itinerary.

At long last, we landed at the Orlando Airport. We then collected our luggage and made our way to the airport drive. As per the Wizard Of Oz incident, I waited with great anticipation. I observed with fascination as a great variety of elegant black and white limousines wove their way about, each collecting their very exclusive and privileged clients. These grand conveyances consisted of Lincoln Town Cars and long elegant Cadillacs, each with heavily tinted windows and leather upholstery. I was imagining that many probably had televisions in the back, and possibly even wet bars. (Not that a wet bar would do me any good, but it was an exciting prospect).

And as the menagerie of black and white stretch limos came and went, I waited with grand anticipation. At long last, a rickety tour bus pulled up where we were standing. Dad then announced, "This is us guys. Let's go." This is us guys, let's go??? What the hell was he talking about? This was no limo. It was a lousy, ordinary, noisy, cramped tour bus. Worse than that, it was now filling to capacity with other folks all crammed in on their way to different hotels. No leather upholstery, no exclusivity, no TV, no wet bar, no nothing. Just a typical crowded, run-of-the-mill, smelly tour bus.

    I didn't want to get Dad's nose out of joint, seeing as how he was usually pretty uptight on vacations anyway. But the disappointment on my face probably shone through like a beacon. With a tone of utter defeat, I said, "This isn't a limo, it's a bus." And just like in the "Wizard" incident, Dad calmly replied in a most knowing manner, "Yeah, when they say Limousine Service, they mean it's a bus." Then why don't they say "bus," I thought? Why do they have to call it "Limousine Service?" Another life lesson unfortunately learned the hard way. At least it wasn't told to me by a stately-looking man in a suit.

XXIV
Uncle Benny Was a Character

In terms of geographic proximity, my uncle Benny and my aunt Doris were far more accessible. You already heard about Doris with regard to the long-lst cousins. Her husband Benny was what you might call a professional "Chain-Yanker." By that, I mean that he absolutely lived to argue. Nothing brought Benny greater joy than a good, loud, no holds barred, winner-take-all argument.

I've read a bit about Ernest Hemmingway in my travels. I mention this because Earnest apparently had a nasty habit of clocking folks right in the mouth without the slightest provocation, but only if he liked them. In fact, it was his way of showing people that he held them in high esteem. Although he wasn't prone to violent displays, I think my uncle Benny was very much like that. If he liked you, he'd poke and prod until a source of significant disagreement could be reached. And once he set the hook, he'd settle back and carefully reel you in much like a prized marlin. As Benny was an absolute master concerning this particular pastime, his victims were hooked before they even knew they were being baited. Whether it was politics, world or local affairs, or the latest movie, Benny's need for conflagration was almost always satisfied.

The easiest target for achieving such a purpose was someone with a very limited sense of humor, as well as a complete inability to laugh at themselves. In other words, my dad. As a kid, I marveled at my uncle Benny's ability to play my father like a fine violin. Even when Dad was determined to resist Benny's unyielding taunts, the correct button would eventually be pushed, and they were off to the races. And once Benny had you, it was all over but the shouting (you should pardon the pun). Most of the time these extremely vocal arguments had no real resolve, as both parties were bound to remain vehement with regard to their respective positions. All the better for Benny, as he could be assured of a long and satisfying dispute. And like Hannibal Lector, Benny's heart rate remained slow and steady all throughout the turbulent clash, while Dad's usually went through the roof. Is it any wonder my dad was a particularly satisfying victim where Benny was concerned?

Of all the major-league fracases I witnessed between the two, my favorite had to be the one about Benny's job. As a kind of sales rep, it was Benny's responsibility to call upon the stores that supported his company's line of products. His job was to make sure that these items were displayed prominently and with panache. As such, Benny logged quite a few miles driving from store to store all over the New York metropolitan area. The big kicker here was that Benny was obliged to use his own car to get the job done.

So the argument basically boiled down to this issue of transportation. My father's staunch position was that Benny was being taken advantage of by his boss. The boss was getting all the benefits of Benny's hard work and extensive travel, while Benny was quickly burning out his nice car in the process. Not necessarily a problem if the boss was reimbursing him adequately for all the car expenses, but this was apparently not the case. The sly boss was more than happy to have Benny sacrifice his car while compensating him with only a modest salary.

To be sure, my father indeed had a point. Benny's position, however, was that he enjoyed his job thoroughly, and was truly grateful to the boss for affording him such a wonderful opportunity. As such, why quibble over a rapidly depreciating automobile or two. "He's exploiting you," my father admonished. "Who cares about the car, I love my work," Benny countered. And so it went, back and forth for what seemed like an entire afternoon.

At last the shouting was finally halted and it was time for Benny and Doris to head back home. Benny made his exit in wonderful spirits. By contrast, my father seethed for hours. Score another one for Uncle Benny. And since my father had no sense of humor when it came to Benny, there was absolutely no kidding him about it. Just prior to a future Benny and Doris visit, I joked to my dad that I'd retire to my room once the argument got going. With a rather perturbed expression, he turned to me and unequivocally stated, "There isn't going to be any argument." I prodded him no further.

In addition to provoking arguments, Benny had two favorite activities. One was ordering a corn beef sandwich at his favorite neighborhood deli. The other was spending time (and money) at a nearby OTB (Off Track Betting) establishment. At my mom's celebration of life, I learned that Benny's history of gambling went quite a bit further than two-dollar horse bets at the OTB. In his younger days he was a compulsive gambler, often going through his entire paycheck in pursuit of a fast buck.

Apparently, if it hadn't been for my aunt Doris, the couple would have been in rather desperate financial straits at several points during their long marriage.

While I have never understood the pull that gambling exerts on some people, I know it's probably just as strong as drugs, alcohol, or tobacco. And in much the same manner as these mind-altering substances, gambling probably has a very similar effect on one's psyche. Luckily for Benny, Doris did indeed possess a heart of gold. As practical and generous as she was, my guess is that she was just as forgiving. It stands to reason, as the two were married for more than forty years.

During my adolescence, it was Doris that afforded me one of the most powerful examples I'd ever receive on the issue of time and mortality. It was around this time that she became quite ill. The immediate family was then summoned to the hospital where she was spending her remaining days. Benny and Doris never had children of their own (I knew not why), so they doted on my brother and me all throughout our childhood. This was the woman that always showed up at our house with a strawberry shortcake because she knew we loved it. Now she was on her deathbed, and the family all visited with her in turn.

My parents told us that they preferred to talk with Doris alone, but that Mack and I could visit with her briefly when they were done. When Mom and Dad reappeared, my brother and I were then invited to say our parting words to our beloved aunt. The only problem was that Mack was sixteen and I was fourteen. What the heck do a couple of teenagers know about making peace with a treasured relative who was destined to depart this earth in fairly short order. In short, we had absolutely no idea what to say to her.

Upon entering her room, we barely even recognized the elderly and very sick woman lying in that hospital bed. She was thin and pale, and for the first time, not sporting the fashionable wig that she always wore. We were pretty much tongue-tied once we got past the initial greeting, thus we desperately searched for some form of meaningful conversation. The look of utter despondency on Doris' face didn't make it any easier.

It was a presidential election year, so my brother asked her who she'd like to see as the next president. Not the most pertinent topic at the time, but it was the best either of us could come up with given the circumstances. Doris simply shrugged and replied, "What difference does it make." That's when it hit me. As a fourteen-year-old, I had all the time in the world. My aunt Doris wasn't going to survive the week. The determination of our next president was only important if you were thinking in terms of the future. Clearly, Doris was not.

Up till that point, my brother and I never had to stare death directly in the face before. We were simply out of our element. I now realized that time was indeed relative, and subject to vast interpretation depending on what stage of life you were at. I'd love to say that we thanked her for all the strawberry shortcakes over the years, and for all their wonderful visits. In the end, I think we just sat there in quiet contemplation, before politely saying goodbye and making our exit. I'm sure she appreciated the effort, however, and I know she understood how awkward we must have felt. A few days later she was gone, but I'm very grateful for the opportunity for that final visit.

As should come as no surprise, Benny was your typical "life of the party" type. When he wasn't instigating arguments, he thoroughly enjoyed being the center of attention. He particularly loved regaling the relatives with his colorful and humorous tales. Like his wife, he also had a very generous nature, as well as a compassionate soul. Mack and I were visiting one afternoon (without my parents), when Benny received a phone call. We watched his face adopt a somber expression while being informed that a friend had just passed on. Though we continued our visit, Benny was clearly troubled and having a difficult time processing this sad and unexpected information. Truly his heart went out to his old friend, and the family he was leaving behind.

Even as a kid I could see that Benny was a man who felt things very deeply. Though he'd kid around till the cows came home, he was someone who truly cared about those close to him. And no one could possibly have been closer to him than his beloved wife of more than forty years. He was a broken man when Doris passed on. We didn't see much of Benny during the period immediately following Doris' funeral. But this grief-stricken stretch didn't last nearly as long as any of us would have figured.

When he re-emerged some months later, it was to deliver the startling announcement that he had found a new romance. Needless to say, this shocked the relatives good and proper. In my dad's view, his poor sister wasn't even cold in her grave yet, and here was Benny sporting his new and wonderful lady friend. While I had some inkling as to how Dad might have felt, I also knew that Benny was not the kind of man who could live alone. As a teller of tales and an instigator of great shenanigans, it was crucial for him to have a life partner. He needed someone with whom his boundless energy and enthusiasm could be reflected. And this role now fell to his new love, Ms. Lillian (or "Lil" as she preferred to be called).

Lil could not have been any more opposite from Doris even if she tried. Doris was a homebody whose focus was on her family and maintaining a tidy household. A high school graduate who probably never strayed more than fifty miles out of New York City in her entire life, it was fair to say that Doris was probably not the most worldly of individuals. Lil on the other hand had been all over the world. She was not only educated and savvy, but she was apparently also quite well to do. In fact, the rumor was that her net worth exceeded one million dollars (a very significant sum indeed back in those days). She was quick-witted and kept up quite nicely with Benny's extremely jocular and exuberant nature. I do not doubt that she yanked a few chains in her day as well. And much to my dad's chagrin, Benny seemed a happy man again. Not that he didn't want Benny to be happy, just not so quickly (and at Doris' expense).

When at last we were invited to meet Ms. Lil, my mom and dad were rather lukewarm, to say the least. Nevertheless, the invitation was accepted and we drove to Benny's old apartment (the same one he and Doris had lived in for so long). Apparently, Lil had now taken up residence there in Doris' stead.

As I recall, she was a most vivacious woman of about sixty-five or so. This suited Benny just fine, as he was rapidly approaching his seventieth year. Certainly, she was much more glamorous than Doris. This was quite apparent by the way she dressed, applied her makeup, and styled her hair. These things were obviously very important to her, as there was no doubt that she took great pride in her appearance.

Determined to put her best foot forward, she was not lacking in charm, elegance, or social grace. And as far as my brother and I were concerned, her best foot seemed pretty darned impressive. We noted that she had the look of a true socialite, and we were quite taken with her stories of trips to far-away places. As my family had never really gone anywhere that could be thought of as glamorous, we were riveted by her descriptions of such exotic destinations as Paris, Rome, and Greece. You name it, she had been there. Whereas Doris was plain-spoken and down to earth, Lil was sophisticated and cultured. And from the constant smile on his face whenever she spoke, it seemed that Benny delighted in these distinctions.

Perhaps it was all a bit too much for my father to take in, but I will admit that he remained sociable and polite throughout the visit. Not to say that he didn't put forth the occasional query, however. "Where are you two planning to live now that you're married," as an example. Unfortunately, the answer to that question was that Lil was planning to stay right there in Benny's old apartment. My parents pondered this with disturbing resolve. In other words, she was going to occupy this deeply personal space that once belonged to Doris. She'd avail herself of the comfortable furniture Doris had carefully picked out and arranged. And worst of all, she'd sleep in the same bed that was once the matrimonial domain of the former longtime couple. If Benny or Lil had an issue with any of this, they certainly didn't let on. But even if they didn't, they were probably the only ones who didn't. As for the rest of the immediate family, they most certainly did.

When Lil and Benny's afternoon dog-and-pony show was over, we said our polite goodbyes. The ride home in the car was mostly quiet, but clearly, Mom and Dad were less than content. Aside from the aforementioned ethical and moral concerns, there were also issues of a more fiscal nature.

As it turned out, Ms. Lillian had formally occupied a unit in the same large apartment building where Benny dwelled. In fact, that is indeed how they met. As Lil was planning to move into Benny's place on a permanent basis, she was only too happy to give up her own apartment. And why wouldn't she be? Little did we know that her plan also included having Benny continue to pay his normal rent, while she would now reside rent-free. And for that matter, she'd also have Benny pay for everything else (which he seemed more than willing to do).

What do you know, Ms. Lillian was a "Scheme-er." Benny was alone and miserable, which made him ripe for the pickings. Lillian sensed vulnerability and pounced. I guess this is why it's not a good idea to jump into new relationships while still on the rebound. But just in the way that Benny's boss had taken advantage of him (in terms of burning out his cars), Benny was just as happy to sacrifice his nest egg in return for the female companionship he so desperately required. In the end, this was indeed his downfall. While Lil's assets were indeed vast, Benny's nest egg was by no means inexhaustible. With no assistance whatsoever from his mercenary new wife, his resources began to run dry.

I left New York in my early twenties and unfortunately fell out of communication with Benny for quite some time. Of course, I had no knowledge of Benny's true plight until my brother and I decided to take a trip back to Brooklyn many years later. Naturally, we earmarked some time to reunite with Benny during this trip. Sadly, upon talking to a few of his neighbors, we learned that he had passed about two years prior. Ironically enough, Lil was still living in that same old apartment. Perhaps it was just as well, but she wasn't home at the time. Mack and I left a note on the door saying we had been there. Though the note included our phone numbers, no reply was ever forthcoming.

According to the long-lost cousins (mostly Stevie), poor Benny had become very ill and eventually needed to go into a care facility. Though his lovely wife certainly had the means (and then some) to put him in the very best facility that money could buy, she instead cast him to the wolves. Tragically, he was relegated to a very sub-standard facility, where he lived out his remaining days in misery.

More recently, the cousins informed me that Ms. Lillian was even more evil than we originally thought. Turns out Benny didn't actually blow his entire wad. The truth of the matter was that Lillian hid some portion of it so that the state wouldn't get it. While Benny suffered in a broken-down old age home for the rest of his life, Lillian added to her already sizable net worth. Perhaps there's a special place in the end for people like this. I have no idea what eventually became of Lillian, but I know she's long gone by now. Smart men, foolish choices?

XXV
My Dad's Happy Dance

I recall a time way back in my early years when Dad didn't seem so angry all the time. I was about seven or eight when he came home from work one day in a particularly good mood. My mom then gave him some additional good news about something I can no longer remember. His face lit up at that point as his joy overflowed. I never knew my father had a happy dance, but he began twirling around in the living room while snapping his fingers over his head. The most amusing part of this rare display was that it also included shouting the phrase "*Dippty, Dippty, Dippty Doo.*" I had never heard anyone utter that particular mantra before, which made the entire scene extremely entertaining. It was wonderful to see Dad in such high spirits, and the Dippty, Dippty, Dippty Doo Dance absolutely made the performance for me. I thought it was so cool that I immediately imitated the dance, making sure to include the finger-snapping and all the vocals. And as he was in such a good mood, he got quite a kick out of my impersonation.

Unfortunately, that was the first and only rendition of Dad's happy dance that I ever witnessed. Even so, it made a lasting impression. So much so that Dippty, Dippty, Dippty Doo became a standard part of our vernacular (at least among Mack and me). Our friends also thought it was pretty catchy, thus they began using it quite frequently as well. It didn't always require the twirling around part, as the phrase itself was colorful enough. Don't know where Dad came up with that one, but he had a way of introducing some rather unique lingo at times (to say the least).

While I will certainly admit that New Yorkers often have a unique inflection when it comes to the spoken word, to this day I've never heard anyone speak quite the way my father did. Describing it in written form would be futile. If you infused a sharp and piercing element into the voice of Donald Duck, you'd be somewhere in the ballpark. A jagged and harsh dissonance that often denoted a combination of anger and disgust. When so desired, the tone could also suggest self-righteous indignation, as well as an intractable finality. It was as though his message was unquestionable and absolutely indisputable.

As a teenager, I recall a day when Dad and I were riding down in the elevator of our Brooklyn apartment. He was loudly pontificating about something having to do with colleges, when the elevator stopped to pick up another passenger. As a middle-aged gentleman joined us, my father continued on without skipping a beat. It wasn't long before our passenger became annoyed at some of Dad's comments. So much so, that the man quickly involved himself in the discussion. He turned around to face my dad and told him that what he was saying wasn't true. He then backed up his assertion with an example from his own experience, leaving an opportunity for Dad to rebut.

As opposed to responding with civility, however, Dad simply gave the fellow one of his best disgusted looks. Seeing that no response would be forthcoming, the debate quickly ran out of fuel. As far as our elevator guest was concerned, Dad's message was abundantly clear. Any opinions outside of his own were totally unnecessary. I was probably about fifteen at the time, but the encounter left me feeling awkward and embarrassed. Though the gentleman was equally adamant, his comment was certainly respectful. Not sufficient reason to ignore him as if he didn't exist.

As for my father, I can only theorize as to why he seemed in such constant ill-temper. His job was undoubtedly weighing on him. As an accounts payable clerk at the main branch of the United States Post Office, he was clearly given little to no respect. The work was dull and mundane at best, and the bosses were constantly cracking the whip. This made his day an almost intolerable grind.

I've heard it said that being respected and appreciated are the essential elements for happy and fulfilled employees. A good salary and nice benefits don't hurt either, but the former is far more important. In stark contrast, to receive none of these things is to feel thoroughly undervalued and wholly disrespected. I can only imagine that this was how Dad felt throughout his entire working career. Perhaps it was this constant level of disrespect that was responsible for the way he approached others. Perhaps the man in the elevator was a good example of this. Perhaps the way he approached his own family was another example. Perhaps there were a lot of good examples.

One thing that always puzzled me about Dad was his constant identification with being a victim. Quite often he referred to himself as a "poor slob." A down-trodden individual doomed to remain a victim of his own circumstances. Perhaps this was just an excuse to remain dormant, to be spared the effort of rising above those humble circumstances. As a poor slob, the ability to effect change was simply not in his power. After all, folks like him were destined to remain downtrodden forever, and victims to all of life's oppressors. And to hear my father tell it, there was no shortage of oppressors. It's the government's fault, it's the president's fault, it's my boss's fault. The list went on and on. He also wasn't shy about blaming his wife and kids for his economic woes. Life would be so much easier if not for all these financially burdensome responsibilities, he often reflected.

Overwhelmingly, however, it was this precept of being a helpless victim that most shaped his persona. It gave him a negative view of people and the world around him. It justified his lack of effort to change that which held him back, in favor of the convenience of complaining constantly.

Another reason Dad saw himself as the perennial victim had to do with his ethnic background. Having been raised a member of the Hebrew faith, the concept of ethnic persecution was all too real. The slaughter of six million Jews during Hitler's regime (and all the atrocities that went along), were lessons not quickly forgotten. And I suppose it's not a stretch to think that people are out to get you if, in fact, there are dangerous and deadly people who are out to get you. Given such a perspective, I guess it's only natural to identify as a victim. And while I don't wish to minimize this concept, it is neither healthy nor productive to maintain this role ad infinitum. I'm not saying that there weren't plenty of folks still out there with little love or affection for Jews, but to be immobilized by this thought is no way to live.

As a somewhat slight and unimposing child growing up in a working-class Jewish environment, ethnic persecution was not a foreign concept for me either. I bore the brunt of many schoolyard altercations based on this premise, and I'm sure some of the emotional scars are still there. But unlike my dad, I somehow believed that my future was in my own hands. And when I'd hear Dad constantly complaining about the rotten blows that life was dealing him, it eventually made me angry. I started to wonder why he didn't rise up out of his chair, shut off the TV (or put down the newspaper), stop complaining, and do something productive to improve his lot in life. Whether it was going back to school at night, learning a new trade, or acquiring some new skills. Whatever it took to get out of that godforsaken post office job that was making him so miserable. But a victim does not have the resources to mobilize and regroup. Having perceived that their only option is to vent, they will do so as long as there is someone available to listen.

Having been born in 1959, I am considered a member of the late "Baby Boomer" generation. And like many working-class families of that era, a parent's most fervent wish was for their kids to achieve that which they had not. They simply wanted their kids to have a better life. A much easier and far more enriching existence than the one they experienced. And in those days, the way to achieve such a path was a college education. As such, a great many of us were destined to become our family's "first-time" college graduates.

Not only did a college degree guarantee a successful career path, but it could also catapult you to the very pinnacle of affluent society. Medicine, law, politics, business & finance, all these high prestige careers would now be within reach. There was no stopping someone with a college degree in those days. It was a sure road to a wonderful and prosperous life. Whether this was actually true or not, it mattered little. Our parents believed it with all their heart and soul, thus it became our reality. "You need to get good grades in school," they'd constantly stress. Good grades meant you'd get into a good college. And of course, a good college meant a good job and a good life. "We don't want you to have to struggle like we did," was another saying we'd often hear.

There were so many elements at play here. Most parents did want their children to have a better life. And for whatever reason, they saw college as an opportunity that was not available to them. Back then, there was also a certain mystique that went along with being a college graduate. Not only was it a great accomplishment, but it put you in a separate and elite class. With a university credential, you were now head and shoulders above the great masses of non-college-educated folks. It set you apart in a way that was not only prestigious, but also worthy of great admiration.

The other thing I remember about being a college man back in those days was that it didn't even matter what specific curriculum you chose. You could major in Art, Music, or Underwater Basket-Weaving for all anyone cared (not that it's my intention to minimize any of these fields). All that mattered was that you successfully completed the program and emerged with sheepskin in hand. And after all, there was no rule that stated you had to pursue a career in your chosen field of study. I can't even recall how many music majors I met in college who went on to become computer programmers.

My pain in the ass cousin Ryan graduated at the top of his class from The University of Arizona Law School. For some reason he took (and passed) the Bar Exam twice, yet never worked a day in his life in the field of law. When I last spoke with him, he was doing some form of computer network maintenance. In a similar vein, there was my old summer camp buddy Andy Warnack, who graduated with a degree in communications from Johns Hopkins University. Last I heard, he was selling airline tickets behind the counter at American Airlines. I guess that job would certainly involve a great deal of communication.

Then there was my extremely brainy friend Henry Aurbeck, who graduated with a Ph.D. in Marine Microbiology from Rutgers University. He used to tell me that careers involving the study of krill (and other such tiny marine creatures) were rather scarce in general. He wound up testing soil for the U.S. Department of Mines in Pittsburgh, PA. Not much marine microbiology to be examined there.

This microcosm not-withstanding, I suppose the expectation of venturing on to college gave me a certain hope for the future. I never felt like I was doomed to a life of hardship and drudgery. As far as I was concerned, playing the victim just wasn't for me.

As I mentioned previously, my mom worked as a secretary for the social services department of a large Brooklyn hospital. She'd worked there for quite some time when it suddenly became apparent that a much better position was about to open up in her department. Mom was quite familiar with the duties of this far superior post, and could probably have done the job admirably with one hand tied behind her back. She got along quite well with her boss (or so she thought), and thoroughly believed he would be most supportive in her efforts to move up the corporate ladder. The job would have meant a sizable pay increase, as well as a substantial boost to her status within the organization.

Although possessing only a high school diploma, Mom was convinced that her many years of "on-the-job" training would more than make up for any educational deficit. Unfortunately for Mom, her boss did not concur. When push came to shove, an outsider was brought in to fill the position. I don't recall what this individual's particular qualifications might have been, but his or her resume did indeed include a college degree. Not only did Mom lose out on the job, but she also had to suffer the indignity of training the newbie.

After that humbling experience, she never again allowed herself to get too hopeful about anything at work. It was quite clear that these kinds of opportunities were never going to come her way, so why become emotionally invested. A bitter disappointment indeed, and a very hard lesson learned. A college education might just have won the day for Mom. I guess we'll never know. Her boss was mentioned during our evening meals for years to come. From that point on, however, he was simply known as "That son of a bitch."

XXVI
Confidence and Unconditional Love

By the time I had gotten to my senior year of junior high school, things were clearly on the decline. The struggles with Dad were becoming almost intolerable, as he was also reaching the epitome of his angst. The judo school was becoming a bigger and bigger source of stress, as Dad became more and more verbally abusive with each successive defeat. Fortunately, he never again hit me for losing a match (at least not that I recall), but his disgust regarding my failure to excel was more than apparent.

After a while, it no longer became a question of trying to win a judo contest. The best I could hope for was to go down with a certain degree of dignity, simply from the standpoint of appeasing Dad. But just as victory and confidence beget greater victory and increased confidence, the opposite is equally as true. The losses (and the belittling that always followed) brought about despair and feelings of worthlessness. I remember confiding in a friend from my own judo school one afternoon when yet another contest was slipping from my grasp. I told him that I was worried about how my father was going to react. He looked at me like he couldn't believe what I had just said. With an incredulous tone, he simply replied, "Hey, you did your best." And, of course, he was right. Certainly, I wasn't going out there with the intention of losing. When it came right down to it, I always did my best. The simple fact was that I wasn't the world's best judo player. So why did that seem so obvious to my buddy, yet so foreign to my father?

My lack of confidence and withdrawn demeanor became easily recognizable among my classmates and teachers. For the first time in my life, I was now the kid in class who got picked on. I was also the kid on the street who got picked on. And unfortunately, this was also right about the time I took that nasty beating from the neighborhood bully. As I clearly lacked the ability to fight back, my life at school (and on the streets) was becoming hellish. Schoolmates that I had gotten along with just famously only the previous term, were now regarding me with disdain. No longer a part of their inner circle, they clearly wanted nothing more to do with me. I had lost their respect and now had to put up with their insults and abuse.

By the time the ninth-grade term was drawing to a close (and graduation was looming), there was talk of a party being organized by one of the gals in the class. Though it didn't surprise me, I was not invited. Not that I would have actually gone had I been asked, but nobody even mentioned it to me. Though I pretended it didn't matter, I'm pretty sure that I was one of the few students in the class who wasn't there.

During that last term, I also started experimenting with cutting classes. I figured if I kept a low enough profile, people wouldn't even notice that I was gone. I'd suddenly duck out when the coast was clear and catch the bus back home. As both my parents were away at work during the day, I'd just hang home and watch TV. I must say I got pretty good at ditching school, and for the most part, nobody was ever the wiser. If the other kids did notice I was gone, they probably didn't care enough to mention it. I don't recall ever getting into trouble on account of it. In essence, I became nearly invisible, maintaining just enough of a presence so as not to arouse suspicion. Somehow or other I still got my assignments done and managed to maintain passing grades. I was pretty intelligent after all, even if my stature had deflated.

Life became very isolating during this time, but that was better than being afraid of everyone and everything. It was extremely fortunate that I was in an accelerated two-year junior high school program. In fact, I think that's what probably saved me during this very dark time. If I had to put in the customary three years of junior high school, I truly believe that things would have spiraled out of control for me. As it was, I was barely keeping it together, but at least the end was in sight. High school would be a complete "do-over" if I could just make it to that point.

What is truly ironic about these two years in junior high, was that I had never met most of those kids before. And when it was over, I never saw them ever again. We were like two ships that passed in the night. They had come from a different elementary school, and they went on to a different high school. I have no idea what became of any of them, though I'm sure most went on to very successful careers. Perhaps what's even more interesting, is that I still look upon those guys with fondness. I remember that first term when many of them became good friends. We took some pretty cool class trips together in the seventh grade, and we had a lot of laughs. I thought they were some pretty nice guys, and I still believe that. Though it's not likely (as I haven't lived in New York for a very long time), I'd be absolutely tickled to run into them now. I'd love to know what ole Pauli, Angelo, Joey, Sal, and Pasquale are up to these days.

Those junior high school years took a heavy toll, but they instilled some very valuable insights as to the effects of successful parenting (or the lack thereof). For a great many kids, these early adolescent years can be some of the hardest and most challenging ones. Even so, most of my junior high school classmates seemed to navigate this tricky terrain with little to no difficulty. I marveled at the confidence many of them seemed to exude, and the ease at which they conducted themselves.

None of these kids had ever walked out onto a judo mat, much less sent larger kids sprawling "ass over teakettle" to the ground. But despite this, they still projected an air of confidence, as well as a great deal of self-assurance. These qualities alone were enough to dissuade the school troublemakers from giving them any grief. But even if a situation did arise, my ultra-confident school chums would have stood up to it admirably. The troublemakers would have undoubtedly moved on to less formidable targets. For that is what bullies do. They seek out weakness wherever they can find it, in much the same manner that predators seek out prey. As opposed to the animal kingdom, however, human beings have a choice as to which category they'll occupy. As one of my buddies often recites, "Be the predator, don't be the prey." While I don't particularly desire either of these two categories, the choice is certainly there.

These early lessons proved positively invaluable when I became a parent many years later. The obvious conclusion is that we must raise our children to be confident and self-assured people. I thoroughly believe that this is the greatest gift we can offer our kids. By instilling these positive qualities of inner strength and self-esteem, we give our children all the necessary tools to succeed throughout their life journey.

Skipping ahead briefly to my late twenties, I had the great fortune of hooking up with a wonderful therapist named Joanne when I first moved to Los Angeles. She told a small group of us one evening that it had been her great fortune to grow up with parents that loved and supported her unconditionally. As a therapist, she was all too aware that this was not the case for most of the folks she encountered in her travels. As such, she truly understood and appreciated how absolutely blessed she had been.

Even as an adult I had a very difficult time comprehending the concept of unconditional love. Is this to say that your parents will still love and support you if they don't agree with your career choice? They'll still love and support you if you don't excel in athletics? They'll still love and support you if you don't get straight "A"s in school? They'll still love and support you even if you choose not to go on to college? They'll still love and support you if you appear a little shy in public? They'll still love and support you if you tell them you're not heterosexual? Given my perspective, this was a very difficult concept to wrap my head around.

Joanne was an extremely enlightened therapist, as well as a highly intelligent and very capable individual. I have no doubt that she could have achieved anything she set her sights on. I'm equally as certain that she could have done quite well financially, had she chosen a higher paying profession. As a therapist who did not cater to the rich and famous, however, I very much doubt that her work was making her rich. There was no doubt in my mind, however, that it was providing a great deal of fulfillment and satisfaction. Perhaps that's one reason she was so good at it. I also do not doubt that her parents were indeed very proud of her. Of course, I'm not saying that we should be complacent or content if our kids are clearly heading down a negative or destructive path. But even if their life choices seem questionable at times, we should love and support them always. As a parent, that's our job.

Though I can count such examples of unconditional love on one hand (and have a couple of fingers left over), a definite instance was that of the husband of my ex-wife's closest friend. Though I had known Tyrell for many years, I only met his parents on a couple of occasions. From the brief encounters I had with his mom, she struck me as a bit high-strung and somewhat opinionated. Certainly, she was your typical "Type A" personality. Someone who found it hard to sit still for any length of time and was always actively involved in one activity or another. His dad, on the other hand, seemed pretty laid back and easygoing. I'd have to say that Tyrell certainly took after his dad, as he was one of the nicest and most easygoing dudes I've ever met.

Other than these cursory parental observations, I had little insight into their actual family dynamics. The couple (Louisa and Tyrell) visited us a number of times after we eventually relocated to Seattle. It was always great to see them, and we typically had a wonderful time together. I remember on one such visit, however, when we somehow got onto the topic of homosexuality (especially where it related to high school students). There was a recent news story that prompted this discussion, and this sparked some interesting feelings.

In essence, a high school student had confided in a counselor as to his sexual orientation. The school maintained a policy that such communications would be held in the strictest confidence, even if that meant keeping the information from the parents. This would give the student the freedom to be who he or she was, without fear of reprisal from parents who may disapprove. Prior to our discussion of this issue, I'd never seen Tyrell lose his cool over anything. I'd never even seen him get hot under the collar. I guess still waters run deep sometimes, as things got pretty tense rather quickly in this case.

Tyrell was incensed at the thought of his kid's school keeping such vital information from him. And to be candid, I'm not exactly sure why the thought upset him so. As a parent I guess he figured it was his right to be informed, should the school come to possess such personal information about his child. Whether he was right or wrong is a subject for another day. The reason it stood out in my mind, however, was because I knew full well that his child's sexual orientation would be of no consequence to him whatsoever. In my heart and soul, I knew darned well that Tyrell would love and respect his child regardless of orientation. And perhaps this is why Tyrell was so adamant about this issue of full disclosure. It probably never even entered his mind that a parent might reject their child over an issue such as this.

On the other hand, I understood the school's position perfectly. Considering how abusive my dad became when I didn't win a judo match, it is not a pleasant thought to consider how he would have reacted if I had been gay. I thank God that this was never an issue in my case. But if it had been, I can only imagine what it might mean to have somebody at school with whom I could safely confide. When I voiced this opinion to Tyrell, explaining that not every parent would be as accepting as you or I, his anger prevented him from even responding to me. He continued in his dissertation as if I hadn't said anything at all. I then suggested that a great many kids do not come from families that offer unconditional love and support. Again, I was greeted with silence. I decided to let the matter drop, as I had said what I needed to say. It didn't endear me to my buddy Tyrell, but it needed to be said. Putting yourself in the other guy's place is not always an easy thing to do. But it is a quality I truly respect and admire.

XXVII
Hey, is This Guy Crazy?

I have now heard it said many times (by many experts in the field) that one out of every four individuals in the United States suffers from some form of mental illness. When I first heard this rather alarming statistic, I was amazed and flabbergasted at the same time. How could twenty-five percent of the U.S. population possibly be afflicted with some version of mental illness? Surely the experts are blowing this number way out of proportion. As the years continue to roll by, however, I am now more inclined than ever to believe that this somber statistic may indeed be accurate. And if you are someone who hails from a family of four, I guess all you can do is hope that it isn't you.

I guess it is accurate to say that my turbulent relationship with Dad varied on a day-to-day, week-to-week, or month-to-month basis. A report of good school grades or a good showing at the judo school would temporarily ease tensions. Problems at school or a less than successful showing at the judo school would bring them swirling right back. And of course, the ups and downs of Dad's job stress entered into the equation most profoundly as well. There were also those times when we had absolutely no idea what was going on in Dad's world. He certainly didn't tell us what he was thinking or feeling. All we knew was that he was in a foul mood, and it was best to steer way clear of him in any way possible. Even my mom took this approach on many such occasions.

One day my family was driving somewhere with Uncle Bennie and Aunt Doris. It's likely that we were carpooling to meet with the suburban cousins, but I can't really recall. It was decided that Benny and Doris would pick us up in their car, and Benny would do the driving. I sat up front (in the middle) between Benny and Doris, while the rest of my family (Mom, Dad, and Mack) occupied the back seat. Though Benny had driven to our neighborhood many times, my father seemed quite preoccupied with Benny's knowledge of the street geography. "Give Benny directions," Dad uttered to me. Though I was fairly sure that Benny knew his way around, I asked him if he needed my directions. Benny quickly replied that he was fine, so I relayed his response back to Dad. Immediately upon doing so, Dad's reply was "I Said, Give Benny Directions."

Sensing that Dad was in one of his wonderful moods, I proceeded to give Benny street-by-street directions (even though there seemed little point). "Make a left on Bay 50th Street," I instructed my uncle. At the end of the street, we stopped for a light. I then pointed out to Benny the entrance ramp to the Belt Parkway going north. I asked him if he saw where I was indicating, and my uncle confirmed that he understood the route perfectly. We then proceeded to the northbound entrance ramp, and from there Benny was good to go. He was actually good to go without my help, but that was neither here nor there. In any case, I had done my duty by giving Benny the requisite directions (or so I believed). And in fact, we had navigated the city streets perfectly and were now well on our way.

From the expression that still permeated my father's face, however, it was clear that he was still not satisfied. He grumbled to my mom about my failure to carry out his directive, while making no bones about how unhappy he was. By this point, my dad's angst was also beginning to make my aunt and uncle quite uncomfortable. In trying to assuage the situation, Benny asked Dad what was wrong. My father angrily replied that he wanted me to give directions and I failed to do it. In perhaps a combination of trying to protect me, while also easing the tension of the moment, Benny assured my dad that I had given him the necessary directions. And what's more, we were headed the right way and all was well. "E" for effort on Benny's part, but all was definitely not well as far as Dad was concerned.

More griping and grumbling from the back seat then ensued. This time I think my mom tried to settle him down, but she was even less successful than Benny. "I wanted him to give Benny directions," Dad continued. I'm not sure what Mom's reply was, but what shortly followed was an explosive return burst. In a voice that could have been heard ten cars away, Dad yelled *"Well He's Not Doing It!"* By this point everyone in the car was uneasy, and the trip was quickly becoming most unpleasant. "He was giving me directions," Benny implored. But Dad was just not having any of it. He remained silent for the remainder of the drive, despite Benny and Doris' attempts to keep things as convivial as possible.

Of course, my aunt and uncle were quite well acquainted with my father's often unpredictable mood swings. From my perspective, however, my best efforts to provide Benny with accurate and timely road directions had resulted in failure. And as such, I was the focus of Dad's wrath for the remainder of that day. I don't think any of us had a pleasant time when we eventually got to wherever we were going, and the return car ride was mostly a quiet and tense one. One of those days where the only good part was when we were safely back home.

For the life of me, I can't recall why Dad was in such a state that day. I don't think there was any obvious reason. But as was often the case, we weren't always privy to the unsettling things that were occupying his mind. Had my brother found himself in that front middle seat of the car that day, he probably would have borne the brunt instead of me. And there certainly were those days when our roles were reversed. But on this occasion, it was my turn. A question of simply being too close to a ticking time bomb.

Unfortunately, these situations presented themselves all too frequently back in those days. The best you could do was to ride it out (no pun intended) in whatever manner you could. Having a very thick skin was also a definite advantage. I must admit that my brother Mack had a much greater capacity than I to shield himself from the effects of Dad's frequent onslaughts. During a similar fit of rage (this time directed at Mack), Dad angrily denounced to my mom, "If I had a gun, I'd shoot the bastard." I can't recall the horrible offense that Mack must have committed to warrant such an extreme response, but suffice to say it wasn't worthy of swift execution.

The fact of the matter was that Mack and I were actually pretty good kids. I was in the "Special Progress" program at my junior high school, while Mack went about his scholastic duties with a fair amount of diligence. We participated in our extracurricular sports activities, while also studying the guitar, violin, and piano. Aside from the usual stupid things that kids sometimes did, I'd say my parents dodged the bullet and then some. Yeah, we'd skip school every once in a while, and even fail a class on rare occasion. And there was always the occasional fib, but in the grand scheme, I think most parents would have been very proud.

We never had any run-ins with the law, we never ran with the wrong crowd, and we certainly never did anything of a criminal nature. And even though we attended high school back in the mid-seventies, we were among the few students who didn't imbibe in marijuana. In fact, throughout our entire lives, neither of us has ever even smoked a cigarette. We respected our parents, relatives, and teachers, and did our best to get along within our community. I'm not trying to paint us as the perfect kids. But James Dean, Charles Manson, or Al Capone, clearly we were not.

Perhaps the most frightening part of living with Dad during these early teenage years was his totally unpredictable volatility. Like a Ferrari, his countenance could go from zero to a hundred miles an hour in no time at all. One second he'd seem calm and reasonable, the next he'd be off on some frantic tirade.

During the time my brother was receiving his driving instruction, Dad would often ask him if he wanted to drive us to the judo school. My brother must have been pretty darned excited at the prospect of driving a car, as he always agreed to get behind the wheel. Why he did so I'll never know, as my father was always extremely critical and often quite insulting. On one such afternoon, Mack approached the judo school and began perusing the neighborhood in search of a parking space.

I'll never forget this day, as it was the one where I was certain that my dad had finally gone completely off the rails. I don't mean that he was just in his usual rare form. On this day I was absolutely convinced that he was now undergoing a full-on psychotic break. Of course, at the time I had no idea what a psychotic break actually looked like. We'd occasionally hear stories about people suddenly going nuts, but we certainly had no practical experience in this area. I guess that's what made this moment so utterly terrifying. We'd certainly seen Dad get close to the edge on a number of occasions, but this time I was convinced that he would go careening completely off the cliff. And as I say, it seemed to come out of nowhere. But when it came, it came with the intensity of a major heart attack.

Things had been relatively quiet before Mack began searching for a place to park. Suddenly the somewhat calm mood of the car was completely shattered by the sound of my father screaming. "*Estupeedo Wallapalucci, Wallapalucci Estupeedo! Estupeedo Wallapalucci, Wallapalucci Estupeedo!*" It was as if a raving madman (of Latino or Italian descent) had suddenly inhabited the body of my father, while enveloping the entire passenger section of the car. What did these strange new words even mean? And why were they suddenly being shouted at ten thousand decibels? It was like a scene out of *The Exorcist*. One moment you're looking at a sweet innocent little girl, then suddenly she turns into Satin right before your eyes. Though Dad's head didn't actually rotate three hundred and sixty degrees, it was the same chilling feeling. Who was this lunatic shouting these unrecognizable words? Was Dad even still in there anymore? The Estupeedo Wallapalucci chanting continued for what seemed like an eternity.

I don't know if Dad was intending to scare the living bejesus out of us. But if that had been his intention, he certainly accomplished it. To think that your parent is truly exiting his or her mind is a terrifying experience. Especially if you've seen that parent go AWOL on so many previous occasions. Like Fred Sanford staggering around with his hands clutched to his heart and exclaiming "Oh Elizabeth, this is the big one. I'm coming to join you." On this day I was convinced that my father was indeed having the "big one." So what do you do when your father suddenly begins screaming in tongues at a level to wake the dead? You do what Mack and I did. You do absolutely nothing. You just sit there in silence, hoping that this psychotic episode will eventually burn itself out. And you hope that when it does, things can somehow find their way back to a relative normal.

So we sat there in silence, hoping the situation would escalate no further. With Dad's final blast of "Estupeedo Wallapalucci," he then added the words, *"You missed a spot right in front of the judo school."* Apparently, my father had spotted a prime parking spot that Mack had failed to see. As crazy as it sounds, this insane tirade was all on account of a parking space.

You might wonder how anyone could get so incensed about something so trivial. And to a rational mind, a parking space is indeed quite a trivial matter. Certainly not a thing worth elevating one's blood pressure over. But my father often did not act in a rational manner. This is why his erratic behavior was so alarming. You never knew what was going to set him off. And since you had no clue as to what might be plaguing him at any given time, there was often no way to predict the onset of these explosive outbursts.

Although I wasn't experienced or old enough to realize it at the time, I'm sure his fits of temper often had little to do with those of us who bore the brunt of them. And though it didn't happen often, every once in a while he'd apologize for his inappropriate behavior. Of course, by then the damage was already done, and our relationship would just grow that much more distant.

I doubt he ever realized the deleterious effect he was having on his family, but I do think he was sometimes aware of how hurtful he could be. I'm not sure how much it bothered him, but I am sure he realized that a gap was forming within his family. Although I wasn't there to see it, toward the end of his life he gathered together those of his family who were on hand. To be sure, it was a small gathering at that point, as there really wasn't much family left by then.

As for me, I wasn't present because I was the only one that didn't live in Arizona. I would have liked to have been on hand, however, as he so publicly apologized for being what he termed a "ballbuster." His actual words were, "I know I was a real ballbuster at times, but I never meant it." Hard to know how I would have responded to such a statement, had I actually been on hand to experience it. Perhaps it's best that I wasn't. But in my heart of hearts, I really do believe that he never meant it. I think he was just a man who was dealing with more than his share of demons. And insofar as that is concerned, I think he probably did the best he could.

XXVIII
Bruno Was a Sensitive Soul

Our high school Orchestra teacher (Mr. Godunov) had a sneaky habit of combining our group efforts, with putting one of us on the spot every now and then. Between movements of Haydn, Bach, or Beethoven, he'd ask one of us to play a series of highly technical ascending and descending scales. To non-orchestral instrument players, I know this probably doesn't mean much. To those of us who have ever donned a fiddle bow, however, suffice to say it's no small feat.

Progressing all the way up the neck of a violin involves a heck of a lot of finesse, as well as a fair bit of skill. There are a lot of notes involved in this process, and the neck of a violin is only about ten inches long to begin with. So as your fingers begin to move up the neck of the fiddle, those notes start to get closer and closer together. And as they do, the margin for error begins to disappear rapidly. To help you reach these elusive notes, it also becomes necessary to achieve "third, fourth, and fifth positions." These "positions" involve moving the left hand up the neck accordingly such that the desired notes are within reach. As one might imagine, achieving the higher positions on a violin takes some doing.

Long story short, if your fingers don't land on these notes rather precisely, you're going to give people one hell of a headache. Not to mention looking pretty foolish in front of twenty-five or thirty of your fellow orchestra buddies. Suffice to say that this little exercise was a good way of separating the men from the boys.

As Mr. Godunov doled out this directive in a rather indiscriminate manner, we had no idea when our time would come. He also didn't assign this task to everyone, so why he would honor only some of us (and not others), was another question for the ages.

I recall one day when it suddenly became poor Bruno's turn. Bruno was a sensitive soul with a great heart for music. His main instrument of choice was an unusual one for a Brooklyn dude, but he was one heck of a five-string banjo player. Being a bit of a hippie, perhaps his eclectic tastes in music were the result of his upbringing. As most orchestras don't indulge in Bluegrass style music, however, Bruno's role in our little high school ensemble was as a member of the "second violin" section.

It should be noted that "second violins" are usually not quite as adept as "first violins," though both groups are equally necessary to a full orchestra. In any case, it's a fair bet that Bruno didn't go home and practice his violin scales every night. My guess is that picking out the Foggy Mountain Breakdown on the banjo was a lot more fun. So when he was called upon to deliver the two-octave chromatic scales one afternoon, he seemed a bit uncomfortable and out of his element. Trouper that he was, however, he proceeded to give it the old "high-school try."

Everyone loved good-ole Bruno, so we all listened with anticipation and understanding. Alas, this poor sensitive creature quickly began to falter. It was like watching one of those Olympic figure skaters trying to navigate a difficult program filled with precarious jumps and spins. Though your heart went out to the brave participant, and as much as you wished them great success, you knew it was simply not going to happen. A clunker note here, an ear-shattering squeak there, and Bruno was in real trouble.

As the sounds coming from Bruno's violin became more and more suspect, Mr. Godunov's patience began to evaporate. Phrases like, "Try that one again," or "Wrong note Bruno," "No, no," "Back up and start that one over," began to emanate from our esteemed orchestra teacher. And with each criticism, Mr. Godunov's tone took on an angrier and more impatient countenance. We all watched in horror as our overly sensitive pal could no longer bear the strain. We could almost see a tear in his eye as he pleaded with Mr. Godunov to stop yelling at him.

I don't for a moment wish to suggest that our orchestra teacher was an evil man. In fact, he was usually quite upbeat and jovial. I do believe, however, that reducing Bruno to tears gave him an increased credibility among his students. So while he probably didn't set out to ruin poor Bruno's day, I think he took a certain pride in putting the fear of God into the rest of us. If it could happen to Bruno, then it could surely happen to any of us. Best to brush up on those scales a bit in our off hours, lest we suffer a similar fate.

Fortunately for me, I was a bit more serious on the fiddle than Bruno, and my practice sessions usually involved some technical scale work. Perhaps that's why I was quickly promoted to "first violin" shortly after joining the orchestra. While I'd sometimes be amused with an English class or two, I must admit that most of my high school curriculum was of little interest to me. But music always came fairly easy, thus I always looked forward to orchestra class. And while it wasn't my desire to be the center of attention with regard to the "solo scale" exercise, it didn't particularly worry me either. If and when the time came, I was confident that I'd get through it just fine.

In retrospect, playing the violin in high school was one of the few things that actually infused confidence into my persona. At a time when I was too terrified to even approach my teachers (or engage with most of my fellow students for that matter), I knew that I could always play the violin or the guitar. And though that didn't account for much in History, Science, Foreign Language, or Math class, it certainly came in handy during Orchestra time.

As far as "solo scale" time was concerned, in fact, my day eventually arrived. From out of nowhere Mr. G. looked at me one afternoon and said, "Gary, play the chromatic scales in two octaves both up and down." Not sure Bruno was still among us at that point, but he sure would have been proud. With little fanfare, I nodded okay to Mr. G. and proceeded about the task. With amazing proficiency, I slowly and methodically worked my way all the way up the scales. I then began my slow descent back down toward the bottom. With all due modesty, I was even surprising myself with the skill and dexterity that seemed to be flowing from my fingers.

I think I had one or two descending scales remaining before I finally hit a "clunker." Up to that point, however, I had been skating a perfect program. People were looking at me in amazement (including ole Godunov himself). When I finally stumbled damned near the end, I was more frustrated with myself than Mr. G. possibly could have been.

The best way I can describe the scene at that moment is a reference to the old Schaffer Beer commercial back in the sixties and seventies. The one where the new guy is asked to climb up on the barrel and sing the Schaffer Beer jingle in front of all his co-workers. Of course, the point is to humiliate and humble the newbie in front of all his peers. In the old Schaffer commercial, however, the new guy actually turns out to be an extraordinary singer. The entire crew is amazed and captivated as they listen to a rendition of the Schaffer jingle that will never again be duplicated. With unassuming respect, the new guy then turns to the foreman and asks, "How was that?" While still in shock, Mr. Foreman humbly replies, "That was good kid." I suppose I must have asked Mr. G., "Was that okay," after performing my scale rendition that afternoon. I seem to recall a look on his face that was very similar to the Schaffer Beer crew in the commercial. "That was good Gary," came his understated reply. I guess he felt no particular need to embellish.

John Dewey High School in Brooklyn, New York was termed an "experimental high school" when it was first established back in the early seventies. For me, I guess it was a failed experiment, as it provided much more freedom than I was prepared to handle. For one thing, Dewey was right across the street from our apartment building. That made going home and goofing off way too easy. Couple this with being painfully shy and not wanting to be around people anyway, and you've got quite the recipe for disaster.

To add fuel to the fire, Dewey had a rather forgiving grading system. As opposed to the traditional designations of A, B, C, D, and F, Dewey had only three grades, with two of them being somewhat ambiguous. "M" stood for Mastery, "MC" stood for Mastery w/Condition, and "R" stood for Retention for Reinforcement. While both the M and MC grades meant passing, there was quite a difference in the level of effort one had to put forth. A student who achieved a solid "M" was doing very good work and certainly achieving all the required expectations. While the "MC" was every bit as much the passing grade, it meant that you did not satisfy all the class requirements. In fact, it could very well mean that you skated by while putting forth the minimum amount of effort. And while your report card would reflect the MC designation, the grade would actually be entered into your high school transcript as an "M."

Naturally, if you put forth no effort at all, you'd come away with an "R." Though "Retention for Reinforcement" was a euphemism, this meant failure and the grade would not change on the school record. Granted, you really had to go some to come away with an "R," but I can surely attest that it was possible.

Being lazy and putting forth very little effort was indeed a slippery slope. There was a fine line sometimes between very little effort and simply not enough effort. And choosing not to attend class on too many occasions could certainly tip the scales. A student who's at least trying is one thing. But one that doesn't even bother showing up is quite another.

Unfortunately, I made the latter category on a number of occasions. For the first time in my school career, I was becoming a poor student. Though I was still able to skate by for most of my classes (while doing the bare minimum), I started failing courses in English, History, and even Spanish (a subject that I had always been quite good at). It wasn't that I lacked the ability or intelligence to pass these classes, it was simply that I didn't care. Instead of going to class, I'd head home and watch TV instead. I'd carefully observe the time, such that I didn't miss important events or classes that I actually enjoyed (such as Orchestra).

I'd try to keep a count on how many times I missed a particular class, and I'd try not to skip the class on consecutive days. On one occasion without realizing it, I skipped Spanish class about eight days in a row. Wondering what had happened to me, the teacher called one afternoon and I inadvertently answered the phone. This is your Spanish teacher Mrs. Gibson she announced. She asked why I hadn't been to class in eight days, probably thinking that I might have been deathly sick. The fact of the matter was that I felt just fine. I had just gotten out of the habit of attending her class.

Despite this, I told her that I had been sick and was planning to attend her class the very next day. I have no doubt that she didn't buy my story for even a second, but she was pleased that I'd be returning to class. As the woman had a kind heart, I didn't fail Mrs. Gibson's class that quarter. But others were not quite as forgiving, and I did indeed suffer the consequences from time to time. I didn't particularly enjoy being a bad student, but it did allow me to separate myself from the rest of the world. And at the time, that seemed more important.

One thing I did enjoy about high school (at least my high school) was the complete dissimilarity to junior high. As John Dewey was an experimental school, those who attended were there by choice. As such the students tended to be a bit more mature, and many seemed quite conscientious with regard to their studies. The "street thug" types that were so prevalent in junior high were all but gone, and the threat of getting trounced at a moment's notice also seemed negligible.

Another factor that probably weighed heavily was that Dewey did not offer competitive sports. We certainly had a physical education program, but all sports were strictly on an intramural basis. If you wanted the "jock" high school, you needed to go to Lafayette (a couple of train stops to the north). If your studies were the most important consideration, or if you wanted to pursue music or art, then Dewey was the place for you. It was also the place for you if you liked having your school right across the street from where you lived (as was the case for me). Though ultra-convenient, this was both a blessing and a curse (as I mentioned above). Had it been necessary to get on the train in order to head home, I probably would have logged more hours in class.

Another thing that struck me about Dewey was the abundance of girls. Of course, there would have been plenty at any high school, but Dewey certainly lacked for nothing in this area. In fact, it was impossible not to notice them sprawled out on the grassy campus lawns on warm Spring or Fall days.

The grounds directly surrounding the school building were quite attractive and offered a very comfortable respite between classes. On nice days, these grassy lawns featured wall-to-wall shapely and alluring female bodies. Everything a fifteen-year-old high school dude with raging hormones could possibly want for. One small problem, however. How the hell do you approach these strange creatures with all the curves. Some of them were getting a bit curvy back in junior high. But by now most of these gals had certainly shed their former prepubescent appearance. No doubt about it, they had turned into actual women right before our eyes.

Clearly, I was not the only one to have noticed. I also observed that many of these fine-looking gals were enjoying the company of some rather attentive and affectionate young men. I'd like to say that these young men were very much like my own self. And in many ways, I suppose they were. But as the Cowardly Lion proclaimed in The Wizard Of Oz, "What have they got that I ain't got?" *Courage!* "You can say that again."

Somehow these young men had courage, or more accurately, confidence. Where they got it or where it even came from, I had no idea. However they came to possess this elusive quality, it gave them an ease and comfort that I couldn't even imagine. For these fortunate folks, those grassy lawns of our high school campus must have been heaven on earth. To enjoy a cuddle with your favorite gal between classes on a warm spring day, or just enjoying the freedom of being young and relatively unencumbered. Having your whole future ahead of you, knowing you can accomplish anything you set your mind to. It is to weep.

XXIX
Whoa, Whoa, Whoa, Listen to the Music

When I turned sixteen my brother and I decided to check out a nightclub in Manhattan that we'd heard about on the radio. The drinking age in New York back then was eighteen. While Mack probably more than qualified, I was certainly still in the underage category. Fortunately, New York City nightclubs didn't worry so much about underage drinking at the time. As such, I rarely had a problem hanging out in these places. And in my defense, the point of going to a nightclub had little to do with drinking for me.

What drew us to O'Lunney's on mid-town Manhattan's east side, was that they featured live Country Music seven nights a week. Having migrated to New York all the way from Ireland, Hugh O'Lunney had a passion for this kind of music. His club, which featured authentic style live country music, was the first of its kind right in the heart of the Big Apple. As Mack and I were already hooked on the likes of Johnny Cash, Glen Campbell, Merle Haggard, Hank Williams, George Jones, Tom T Hall, Charlie Pride, and many others, O'Lunney's was a must visit.

What we experienced upon entering that little tavern that night was an absolute revelation. As we passed through a narrow bar area, a band was playing on a little stage nestled against the wall. Directly in front of the stage was a dance floor with a dining area just beyond. A polished and highly professional sound was emanating from the four young men who comprised the members of the band on this particular evening. There was a guy singing and playing the electric guitar. Another fellow played the drums, while a third member played electric bass.

The wildest and most fascinating of the four was the guy who played an instrument that resembled a highly mechanical stripped-down guitar. Moreover, this complex multi-component instrument seemed to be mounted atop a rectangular table. A bizarre looking contraption indeed, it was outfitted with vertical steel rods and a series of pedals at the bottom (toward the floor). There were also little metal levers that protruded down from the bottom of the table section. The man played this strange instrument by sliding a little steel bar (in his left hand) back and forth along the tops of the strings on the left side. At the same time, he plucked at the strings with finger picks mounted to his right hand. As if this wasn't enough to keep one occupied, he also pressed and released the little pedals at the bottom from time to time with his left foot. As for the little protruding levers coming from the bottom of the table, these he worked with his knees. This was accomplished while in a seated position.

Whatever he was doing to control the workings of that instrument, it was putting forth some of the coolest sounds I had ever heard in my life. I'd heard these kinds of sounds coming from the records that were played on the radio, but I had no idea that this was the contraption from which they emanated. I was soon to learn that this weird instrument was known as a pedal steel guitar. It was largely responsible for making country music sound the way it did back in that era. A smooth shifting and hauntingly whining sound that seemed to flow directly from the heart.

I certainly recognized many of the tunes being played, but one thing became clear pretty much right from the start. These guys were playing the songs even better than the folks who originally recorded them. What's more, they didn't set out to play the tunes exactly as they were recorded. Instead, they incorporated their own spin into the songs, thereby producing something that was uniquely their own.

There were moments when all four guys would sing at the same time, producing amazing harmonies I wouldn't have even thought possible. Perhaps best of all, they introduced me to tunes that I never would have heard on the radio (by artists I never would have discovered). Tunes that were amazing works of composition and expression, but were destined never to be radio-friendly. Though I didn't know it at the time, I was witnessing some of the finest musicianship I'd ever experience in my life. I don't know what these talented musicians were doing in New York City, but they could have given Nashville a run for its money any day.

This was to be the first of many such wonderful nights spent at O'Lunney's. It was as if you were entering another world when you stepped inside that little tavern. It was like experiencing an amazing high without even needing the drugs. And though I did have a couple of drinks on these nights, the effects were probably non-existent. Because I was only sixteen and quite poor, I would nurse those drinks for hours. There was also a cover charge to sit at a table, so the night did not come without a certain cost. Nevertheless, we escaped to O'Lunney's as often as possible, and I always exited with a new tune running through my head. Some of them would remain there for many years to come. And some of them, I would eventually record nearly forty years later.

It is the darndest thing about being a "First-Generation" musician. Having no one in the immediate family from which to draw, it becomes necessary to seek out more accomplished players anywhere you can find them. I am always envious when I hear or read stories about musicians who came from highly musical families. The uncles played and sang, the cousins played and sang, the brothers and sisters played and sang, Mom and Dad played and sang. Among musical types, there is no shortage of these examples.

And it's not just the fact that the entire family played and sang. It's the mentality that also presided. It's the fact that playing and singing were encouraged. Something to be proud of, and something that promoted family harmony (no pun intended). It wasn't feared or downplayed, and it was certainly never scorned. Perhaps I'm creating a certain Utopian fantasy in my head, about a perfect musical family that can always unite in this common theme. Not coming from any such background, however, I can only speculate as to such an upbringing.

One thing I do know, is that hanging out at O'Lunney's earned me a hundred times the education I ever received by going to high school. Not only did it teach me things that were of great interest, but they were also skills I could put to use immediately. While my parents certainly sent me for guitar and violin lessons throughout my childhood, no amount of these could ever teach you how to play in a band. And if the uncles, cousins, or siblings didn't play in bands, then it was going to be quite a challenge to acquire this unique skill.

By hanging out at O'Lunney's, however, I was privy to just this kind of education. I'd watch the many incredible guitar players that rotated through that little bar. I'd study the things they did and observe the little tricks that each one brought to the table. Then I'd go home and try to emulate these things on my own. When I'd hear someone play a phrase that absolutely blew me away, I'd often approach the player during one of his breaks. While complimenting the fellow profusely, I'd ask if he could please show me how that particular "lick" was played. In general, musicians love when people admire their playing, and are usually only too happy to show you their stuff.

After a while, I started bringing a little cassette tape recorder on my outings to O'Lunney's. (Of course, I did this on the sly). This proved infinitely helpful, as you can take in only so many mental notes on the spot. Once you had it on tape, however, you could back it up and listen as many times as it took. With enough repetition, you can learn just about anything.

It is important to note that we didn't have the benefit of the internet back then. Nowadays, there is a YouTube video for any instrumental phrase you can possibly think of. Want to know how James Burton played that part on the Elvis tune? Google it, and James himself probably has a video on it. (If not James himself, then one of his many admirers). But the internet hadn't even come along yet back in 1975, so you had to be a bit more creative.

I can't tell you how many "licks" and "tricks" I learned from those great O'Lunney's guitar pickers back then. But there's an old saying in music. If you're going to steal, steal from the best. And many of these guys truly qualified on that score. In fact, some of them have gone on to very successful careers as studio session men, backup band musicians for well-known performers, successful songwriters, or solo artists in their own right.

We ran into a guy at O'Lunney's one night that played about five or six different instruments. In addition, he was also an excellent singer. Larry Campbell played the pedal steel guitar, the lead electric guitar, the fiddle, as well as a couple of other things. His singing abilities also enabled him to perform both lead and harmony vocals. What was absolutely astounding about Larry was that he played all these instruments with extreme proficiency. He is probably one of the best pedal steel guitar and lead guitar players I've ever met. Some of his credits include long-standing member of "The Band" (with Levon Helm), backup band member to K.D. Lang, and studio work with Bob Dylan (just to note a few). He also tours under his own name and has earned quite a reputation in the business. (Look him up on the web and you'll see what I mean).

We met guys who played with Jackson Browne, Van Morrison, Carol King, Buck Owens, and James Taylor (as well as many others). There was another fellow (Buddy Miller) who went on to play in Emmylou Harris' band (as well as many other renowned groups). He is an astounding guitar player as well, and quite a good singer in his own right.

Then there was Gary Hayes. Gary was my age, but he was a hundred times the guitar player I was when I first heard him at age nineteen or so. This young virtuoso knew the intros, solo breaks, and endings to just about any country song that had ever come out of Nashville. As he was a wealth of guitar playing know-how, I can only imagine that he practiced this stuff ad infinitum. His expertise dazzled us with every tune he played. A phrase that is also used quite a bit in music, applies to Mr. Hayes. He's probably forgotten more stuff than I've ever learned.

Perhaps the player that impressed us most was a suave and sophisticated young fellow named Ray Gantik. Not only was Ray one of the most awesome musicians I've ever met, he was cool! Sporting a mustache and goatee, Ray was usually dressed to the nines. Talk about self-confidence, Ray was absolutely brimming with it. There wasn't a country, folk, or country-rock band in the entire New York Metropolitan area that wouldn't have wanted Ray as a member. If you look up the word "kick-ass" in the dictionary, there's a picture of Ray in the definition.

Here's what made Ray Gantik so "kick-ass." First of all, he was absolutely the greatest pedal steel guitar player I've ever heard. The variety of sounds that Ray could produce on that instrument was mind-boggling. One minute he was getting down and dirty to a George Jones or Hank Williams "honky-tonk" style tune, the next minute he was practically bringing you to tears while playing along on a love song. Then out of nowhere he'd go uptown and get your feet tapping to a jazz-swing improvisation. This guy had an instrumental bag of tricks that would have bogged down Santa's sleigh on Christmas Eve. And just when you thought you'd seen it all, he'd switch to the guitar where his prowess was no less astounding.

Ray was the "consummate musician." Whatever a tune needed, Ray could supply it. If that meant lending his voice to some high background vocals, or even assuming the lead vocal, Ray was your man. Ray was your man no matter what the tune called for. I imagine a good analogy can be made via the sporting world. If Ray were a football player, he could have played any position on the field. He could have thrown the sixty-yard touchdown pass (or caught it), ran for the vital first down, or just as easily kicked the winning field goal.

And like a star football player, Ray was a superstar "off the field" as well. Oh, how the ladies took to this guy. Though I never really got to know him that well, I have a feeling Ray didn't actually think of himself as being God's gift to the women. It was something he probably didn't have to think about at all. The simple fact was that Ray was God's gift to the women. At least that's how it always appeared to me. Ray went home with a different woman practically every other night. The ladies glommed on to him like bears to honey. There were nights when they would coax him from the bandstand (while he was playing), so they could dance with him. This didn't always sit well with the band leaders (as they were paying Ray to play). But his raw appeal to the fairer sex was undeniable. Ray went home with great-looking women even when there didn't appear to be any women left in the bar by closing time.

To say that I was in awe of this guy, would be a monumental understatement. But to also say that Ray presented a powerful influence on me, would be quite accurate as well. He was truly a "musician's musician," and I was determined to follow in his footsteps. Racking up the ladies like so many billiard balls, didn't seem like a bad way to go either. But if that part wasn't to be my destiny, I'd gladly settle for half of his musical ability.

174 Whataya Gonna Do?

Here's what a pedal steel guitar looks like:

XXX
Here's to Swimming with Bow-Legged Women

At the same time I was trying to bring my musical skills up to task, I also set about to tackle another of my earlier deficiencies. Though I was a pretty decent swimmer by now, it would be to my advantage to get certified by the American Red Cross. Now that I was trying to gain employment at my old summer camp, having "Senior Life Saving" and "Water Safety Instructor" credentials would put me in much greater steed.

So at age sixteen, I enrolled in the Senior Life Saving program at McBurney's YMCA in Manhattan. Led by a strapping young man named Tom Zajack, we practiced aquatic life-saving techniques twice a week for two solid months. Tom had us dragging our partners back and forth across that little pool for hours, as he introduced us to the "Cross-Chest Carry." Challenging stuff to be sure, but nothing we couldn't handle. And at the successful conclusion of the course, handshakes and certificates were issued all around. All seven or eight of us had passed, and we were now ready for the next big hurdle.

The following year a much larger group of us assembled (at a bigger pool in Manhattan) for the start of the Water Safety Instructor certification class. I was seventeen at this point and one of the younger members of the crowd. Of the forty to forty-five of us in attendance, most were in their low to mid-twenties. A few were even in their forties or fifties.

While Senior Life Saving had been a relative walk in the park, the mood quickly turned somber as we were introduced to Jesus Gonzalez. A slim and athletic fellow of about forty or so, Jesus had a "matter of fact" way of putting things that did not leave you with a warm and fuzzy. With a vastly receding hairline and a rather abrupt manner, Jesus was not one for mincing words. Immediately he warned us that this course would be difficult if not grueling, and that now would be a good time to pull out if we lacked the stomach for it. Though his words and manner were the essence of condescension, it was clear that this was of absolutely no concern to him. Truly, he was trying to weed out the dead wood right from the start. And if this meant blatantly insulting people, then be that as it may.

From the outset, Jesus did not believe that I was truly seventeen (which was the minimum enrollment age). In fact, he informed everyone reporting to be seventeen that they were obliged to bring a copy of their birth certificate to the next meeting. Jesus was one of those folks who didn't care if people liked him or not. He had a job to do, and by God, he'd get it done.

As the course commenced, it didn't take long to feel as if you were in Basic Training. Jesus certainly made good on his "grueling" threats, as he ran the program much like an Army drill sergeant. For several nights a week, we were in and out of that swimming pool for hours on end. Half the time we were working on advanced life-saving techniques, while the other half was spent honing our swimming strokes. And though this was to be the start of many such grueling weeks, Jesus offered no assurances at any time as to our eventual success. As it turned out, this was for very good reason.

By about the fourth or fifth week of the course, indeed some of the dead wood was beginning to weed. But in all fairness, not that many. I would say that most of us were indeed hearty souls, and we hung in with valor. By the time the training portion of the class was coming to an end, we felt like we'd been through a war. After all, the nice part about banging your head against the wall is the wonderful feeling you get when you stop. Unfortunately, we had now reached the point where the rubber met the road. The next several meetings would be devoted to testing, and this would ultimately determine success or failure. And did Jesus ease up and acknowledge our grand efforts and determination? If anything, he became an even bigger prick than when we started.

The testing was divided into two categories. The first was the five basic swimming strokes. This included: Crawl, Back Crawl, Breaststroke, Side Stroke, and Elementary Back Stroke. These strokes had to be performed slowly with extreme emphasis on technique. The first man to enter the water on test day number one was a particularly strong swimmer. As he displayed his superior Crawl Stroke, the young man gracefully glided through the water with the skill of a Michael Phelps. For two complete laps, we all admired the ease and power of his obvious aquatic athleticism. Surely this was a winning stroke, and this extremely able young man would pass with flying colors. Or so we were convinced.

As he exited the pool, however, Jesus Gonzalez began his assessment. "The arms are supposed to come straight over, and not across from the sides," Jesus explained. He also mentioned some additional points having to do with breathing and head movement. A hush fell over the crowd when Jesus finished by saying, "Therefore, this is not a passing stroke." I can't even describe the feeling of hopelessness that prevailed at this point. Most of us wished we had a Crawl Stroke as smooth and powerful as this young man, yet his efforts were for naught. If an awesome Crawl Stroke like that wasn't good enough, how in the hell would ours be?

To say that Gonzalez was critical, was like describing the Grand Canyon as a bit of a ditch. In fact, he continued to critique the rest of us in much the same manner throughout the remainder of the testing. And Oh. How the mood turned bleak. Strokes were failing left and right, and the participants were dropping like flies. And bear in mind, we hadn't even gotten to the actual life-saving portion yet. A general feeling of gloom and despair was raining down.

As for me, I was as terrified as everyone else. Don't ask me how I did it, but somehow I was able to pull a rabbit out of my hat. The Crawl Stroke had certainly never been my specialty. But as Jesus kept pointing out the issues, he kept giving me a chance to correct them. Suffice to say that I was probably the most astonished person in the room when he finally announced, "Believe it or not, I'm going to pass that stroke." I don't know what made him say it, but I certainly wasn't going to argue. I got out of the pool with complete bewilderment as to how my far less than perfect stroke was approved, while the poor fellow who went first had to settle for failure. I think it had more to do with bending to Jesus' will than anything else. As long as he knew that his word was law, he was a happy guy.

Having the Crawl Stroke under my belt (even by the narrowest of margins), I was able to get Gonzalez's signoff on the other four. Stepping carefully over all the dead bodies, I then prepared for the life-saving portion. Clearly, this was going to take a miracle, but at least I was still in the hunt. At this point, that was more than I could say for about a third of the group.

Needless to say, Gonzalez was no less critical during the life-saving portion of the testing. And for a good while, I was rolling. Things were actually starting to look rather positive until we came to one particular technique. And as aquatic life-saving skills go, I wouldn't have even labeled this one as all that troubling. Every time we practiced it on one another, it went off like clockwork. Here's how it worked. The trick was to rescue a swimmer who was in trouble and flailing around, but had not gone under. In this situation, the rescuer needs to cautiously approach from the front. At the right moment, you grab onto the victim's right wrist (as they're facing you) with your right hand. You then pull hard on the victim's wrist in both an upward and forward manner. This motion then turns the victim (a half turn) such that their back is now toward you. Before allowing them to wiggle away, you quickly reach across their body with your free arm. This arm then clamps across the victim's body, with the hand gripping at the armpit. Once you have them locked in (as such), you then tow them to shore using a modified Side Stroke.

Sounds good on paper, and while it worked fine in practice, Jesus Gonzalez wasn't going to make it easy. I must have yanked on his wrist six or eight different times, but there was no way on earth I was ever going to turn him around. He had a super annoying way of stiffening up his body such that it would simply not rotate. I'm not sure if this is something an actual drowning person might do, or if Jesus was just being his usual self. In either case, it was making the task impossible.

On one attempt I got him to rotate about a quarter of a turn. From there I tried to adjust my position, so as to turn him the rest of the way with my upper body. He saw that one coming, however, and made sure to wriggle completely out of my grasp. Exasperated and disheartened, I asked if he had any suggestions. I'm not sure if hollering "NEXT!" (to the participants who were still waiting to be tested) was his idea of a suggestion, but it did inform me that I was done.

The maneuver would thus go uncredited. And just like that, I joined the pile of dead bodies now littering the floor of that big pool area. Heartbreaking, to say the least. But I came as far (or further) than many of my fellow classmates. I truly had nothing to be ashamed of, though failure is never my preferred option.

Toward the end of the testing period, there arose one brave soul who confronted Jesus directly and publicly. I'd love to say that brave soul was me, but it most certainly wasn't. A bold young man in his mid-twenties spoke up and delivered the following message. "I'm noticing that at least fifty percent of the class is going to fail," he stated. "Is it the intention of the Red Cross to fail its students," the young man directed in a rather perturbed tone. The rest of us rose to attention in appreciation and admiration at the words of this brave young man. He alone had the gumption to put forth such a well-meaning and pertinent question to the man we were all beginning to despise.

The inquiry didn't faze Gonzalez in the least, as I'm sure he'd heard it many times before. "If the students aren't capable of performing the skills necessary in a satisfactory manner, then yes, it is the intention of the Red Cross to fail such students," came his straightforward retort. Two questions then arose in our minds. One was whether this guy actually had any friends. The other was how we were possibly going to get our Water Safety Instructor certification now that we washed out (so to speak) on the first attempt.

Fortunately for me, the answer came relatively quickly. Upon reporting for my second year of employment at my cherished summer camp, I informed Ham that my efforts to obtain a W.S.I. certificate during the winter had been unsuccessful. Unfazed, he quickly informed me that a class was taking place shortly at another camp nearby. Camp Susquehannock was a sports camp about thirty minutes driving time from Choconut. If I were to sign up now, I could get the class done in ten days.

I wasn't looking forward to another grueling swimming and life-saving regimen, but I guess Ham made me an offer I couldn't refuse. "Sign me up," I said. For ten consecutive evenings (starting at 6:00 pm and ending at 9:00), I drove Ham's little Volkswagen across lonely and desolate country roads to Camp Susquehannock. My first challenge was to actually find my way back and forth along those isolated and unlit roads (half the time in the dark of night). Bearing in mind that there was no such thing as cell phones or Google Maps back in those days, this was no small feat. Some of these roads were completely unmarked, and all were a challenge to even spot in the dead of night.

It also didn't help that no one ever bothered to fill up Ham's car with gas. So every time I got behind the wheel to embark on my Susquehannock journey, the damned thing was right near the empty mark. I was pressed for time on my first night of class, thus I decided to trust that there'd be enough fuel to get there and back. Bad decision as it turned out. I'd never completely run out of gas in a car before, but I assure you that it is not a pleasant experience. And when one is traversing over isolated country roads in the dead of night, it can be especially harrowing.

Thank goodness I had come to a halt only about a mile or so from my final destination. As such, I was then able to hot-foot it back to Choconut. Some of my co-counselors were waiting up for me, so I explained what had happened, and that we needed to retrieve the vehicle. With a few gallons of gasoline in tow, we hopped into the camp pickup truck and all was soon well again. Not an experience I ever wanted to repeat, however.

Though I kept expecting Jonathon Culp (or "Culpy," as he liked to be called) to be the reincarnation of Jesus Gonzalez, I'm happy to say that there was no resemblance whatsoever. Culpy was a darned nice guy and a pretty fair W.S.I. training instructor. There were only about eight of us this time around, and some of the group were counselors at Susquehannock. I imagined this might bode well, as Culpy would have to see these folks all summer whether they passed his class or not. And if he failed them, then hard feelings could certainly linger.

Still, he had us in that freezing lake for two or three hours every night. And make no mistake. With the absence of the daytime sun, those summer nights in northeastern Pennsylvania can get a bit brisk. Often chilled to the bone and sometimes shivering uncontrollably, I plodded on. And with my testicles sometimes seeking refuge in any warmer cavity of my groin that they could find, I toughed it out for the entirety of the course.

There were nights when I was so cold by the end of class, I struggled to regain my core temperature during the entire drive back to Choconut. Bundled up in my jacket, and with the little Volkswagen's heater going full blast, I shivered and sneezed all the way home. I was kind of skinny back then, and the cold seemed to permeate my body much more easily than that of my bulkier classmates. Two or three hours in a cold lake was definitely pushing it for me. As failure was simply not an option, I soldiered on and kept my complaints to myself.

On one particular evening, Culpy must have noticed how I was shivering while standing around in that frigid lake. The comment he made on this occasion has remained with me to this day. "It is important to keep in mind the comfort level of your students while they're in the water," he extolled. "You don't have to do anything about it, just keep it in mind," he laughingly concluded. Oh, what a kidder! If I hadn't been shivering uncontrollably at the time, I might have thought it was funny too. Ah well. As I say, Mr. Jonathon Culp was a heck of a nice guy, and at the end of the ten days, we had all passed with honors. What a "night and day" experience versus the horrors of Jesus Gonzalez.

With the W.S.I. certification finally in hand, I was a much more valued member of the Choconut counseling staff. In fact, I even got a raise that summer. Not only did it elevate my community standing at camp, but it also enabled me to snag some pretty cushy lifeguard gigs during the non-summer months back in New York City. Jobs that paid every bit as well as the more traditional fast food or supermarket gigs, but necessitated only that I sit on my backside while watching over a typically uncrowded pool. During my college days, these lifeguard gigs proved invaluable. They allowed me to sit there and study while getting paid at the same time. I guess the shivering and sneezing actually paid off.

XXXI
Sing Annette, Sing!

I know for a great many, high school is a magical time filled with milestones and exciting new adventures. Our very first romantic relationships are often formed in high school, and wonderful new friendships are forged as well. Not to mention that the mid-seventies was certainly a time for discovering the various substances that could either be smoked, snorted, or injected. I suppose by today's standards, things were probably pretty tame in this regard. The recreational drug of choice back then was marijuana, and it was everywhere. But from what I'm told, the pot of the seventies was nothing compared to the far more potent varieties of cannabis offered today. Be that as it may, if you were cool, you took a toke now and then just to be part of the group. If you declined, then you were either uncool or a nerd (or both).

    I guess some things never change. I wasn't cool back then, and I guess I'm still not. And though I certainly can't speak from experience, I'm certain that many young folks had their first sexual experience in high school. Although there were certainly communicable diseases back in the seventies, AIDS hadn't arrived on the scene yet. As long as a couple was conscientious about birth control, the ramifications of sex didn't seem nearly as scary back then. But if you were afraid to talk to girls, and you hung out on campus as little as possible anyway, this issue never really came up.

    I suppose the only excitement I can recall back in high school was when we were first trying to form a band. Though still very much lacking the necessary musical prowess, we had no shortage of high hopes and youthful enthusiasm. With my brother and I on guitars, and our crazy friend Howie tooting on a harmonica, we did our best to make a joyful noise. And who's kidding who, our rollicking version of *They Call It That Good Ole Mountain Dew* was a force to be reckoned with. Unfortunately, the rest of our repertoire consisted of *I'm A Lonesome Fugitive* by Merle Haggard and

Johnny Cash's *Folsom Prison Blues*. Hardly a setlist (and hardly a real band), but certainly good for about ten minutes.

From our extremely limited knowledge of putting a band together, we surmised that two additional elements were desperately needed. One was a drummer, and the other was a set of background singers. And as for these essential background singers, naturally they needed to be female. Looking back, perhaps it wasn't the female background singers we needed so much, but just the females themselves. Whichever the case, it gave us a legitimate reason to seek out and talk to some of the gals at school. And so we did. We popped in on some of the chorus classes being offered and made inquiries to see if any of the gals were interested in singing with our group. Lo and behold, we actually came away with three of them.

The first was a good-looking and talented young lady named Marie. Although she always had her serious boyfriend in tow, Marie was a very approachable gal indeed. She was warm and friendly and had a great enthusiasm for music. Though she didn't stay with us for long, it was always fun to run into her around campus. She also helped me to realize that girls weren't quite so scary. She had a very down to earth and extremely genuine personality. As such, she was very easy to talk to. She was also as smart as a whip.

The other two gals we met were Annette and Glenda. These two were good friends anyway, and the idea of singing in a group together very much intrigued them. Both freshman, Glenda was a bit on the "Rubenesque" side. Like Marie, she was a thoroughly nice and pleasant gal, also destined for good grades and a promising future.

Annette on the other hand was the epitome of the "bad girl" image. Though slim, pretty, and full of spunk, she tended to hang with the lower element that comprised the vast minority of John Dewey High School's student body. In fact, the two or three dudes whose company she seemed to prefer, struck me as a complete parody. In their attempt to emulate tough street guys, they came across as almost comical. Sporting leather jackets, white t-shirts, and gold jewelry, it was all but impossible to take them seriously.

Though I always got the impression that Annette was as bright as anyone else, she seemed determined to derail herself by hanging with undesirables and going out of her way to under-achieve. She also gave her parents quite a time, and plenty to be concerned about. Unlike me, who could usually manage to pull it together and achieve a passing grade (though expending very limited effort), Annette was not quite so successful. Her grades were a source of much concern, and her attitude at times was alarming (even by my standards). I don't know what might have been going on at home for her, but I often wondered why she was so disaffected (or why she was hanging out with those goofy derelicts).

It was not often that I was a step up from one of my fellow high school students, but such was the case with Annette. "Bad Girl" image or not, I was shocked to discover that Annette was actually quite shy. Perhaps that explained the persona she tried so hard to put forth. Bad Girl or not, she was a fan of Olivia Newton-John, and opted to sing one of her tunes in our group. So as to enable Annette to perform it with us, we did our best to learn Olivia's tune *"If You Love Me Let Me Know."* The song opened with a lengthy guitar solo (which culminates just before the start of the singing). I'll never forget the first time we all sat down to practice it. My brother picked out the notes of the guitar intro, while I strummed the chords. When this was accomplished, we waited with great anticipation for Annette's lead vocals. And we waited, and we waited, and we waited. And if we hadn't finally asked what was up, we'd be waiting still.

Turns out Annette wasn't accustomed to singing in a solo format, thus she was quickly overwhelmed by fear. So much so, that she was totally immobilized, and we couldn't get a single note out of her. We cranked up the intro once again, hoping she'd pull out of it, but again we were greeted with silence. My brother and I got lots of practice that afternoon playing that same intro portion of the tune, but never did we get to hear Annette utter a single phrase. In the end, we pretty much had to sing it for her, just so we could get through the tune. I must say, it was a vulnerable side of her that we hadn't anticipated.

As it turned out, Annette was the closest thing to a romantic relationship I'd ever have throughout my three-year high school journey. Her friend Glenda spilled the beans one afternoon by telling us that Annette had a major crush on me. Alas, our relationship was very short-lived. It consisted of snuggling on the couch in our apartment for about an hour one afternoon. After that, she pretty much went back to hanging out with her derelict pals. The one who claimed to be her boyfriend even pulled a knife on Howie and me one afternoon. This little incident was over almost as quickly as it started, with the comical thugs presenting far more bark than bite.

Not long after being introduced to our three new gal singers, we met Lenny Alderman. A tough, streetwise, and somewhat arrogant young man, Lenny was the drummer from band class. Why he agreed to play with us, I'll never know. He was into the usual rock groups of the time and had no affinity whatsoever for the music we wanted to play. Nevertheless, he teamed up with us for a brief time in high school, and we now had most of the trappings of an actual band. We still lacked for a bass player (an essential element indeed), but that didn't deter us in the least. At the time, we didn't really know what a bass guitar was anyway, or why it was such a key element. Indeed, there are times when ignorance is bliss.

Looking back, I think Lenny just saw it as an opportunity to show the girls what a "stud-muffin" he was. No matter what tune we were attempting to play, he'd always ask when his solo was coming up. Normally there were not a lot of drum solos in country tunes, but Lenny certainly fixed that. Hard to say if we were producing anything that even sounded like music, but we were certainly having a good time in the process.

Our unique ensemble now consisted of two guitars, harmonica, drums, and background vocals. I think we even inserted a Frankie Valli & The Four Seasons tune into the repertoire. All of this practice was in preparation for our big debut in the school cafeteria during "Dewey Day." Dewey Day was an all-school event that took place at the close of the quarter. All kinds of interesting activities took place all over the school grounds on this day, and students could choose to attend whichever ones they found most entertaining.

Our background singer gals showed up in coordinated outfits, while Lenny brought forth his entire drum kit. My brother and I unpacked our guitars and plugged them into our one amplifier, while Howie limbered up on his harmonica. Microphones were plugged into the makeshift cafeteria p.a. system, and we were ready to rock and roll.

There are only two things I remember about our actual performance that afternoon. One was that most of the audience cleared out sometime after the first or second tune. The other was the three or four girls that congregated right next to Lenny's drum set during his all-important solos. The rest is pretty much a blank. But I do recall that it was an exciting afternoon and we all got quite a kick out of it. And believe it or not, when her big moment finally arrived, Annette actually sang her tune!

XXXII
Girls, Girls, Girls

If you didn't come of age in a place like New York City back in the mid-seventies, it is understandably difficult to imagine growing up in a community where prostitution was rampant. From what I understand, my current home city of Seattle was quite the wild and wooly town round about the turn of the twentieth century as well. Back then Seattle was at the very heart of the western frontier, and brothels were quite the source of income and employment. While it's hard to think of mid-seventies New York City as a frontier, I imagine there was a similar spirit regarding "extracurricular male entertainment." I suppose the same could be said of Amsterdam's "Red Light" district, or similar places throughout the globe. At any rate, they don't call it the oldest profession for nothing.

Strolling the streets of Manhattan's "Times Square" district back in the day, one would almost certainly observe the blatant and bustling sex trade in all its glory. Scantily clad streetwalkers strutting back and forth while uttering crude invitations to male passersby. Storefronts featuring multicolored neon signs advertising "Girls, Girls, Girls." Small and dingy theatres sporting marquis announcing, "Live   Sex Shows."

There were the arcade joints where all manner of sex toys, magazines, and films were presented. Most of these also featured a large room with live naked women. As ridiculous and juvenile as it sounds, these gals could be privately viewed through steel windows that went up and down when quarters were placed in the appropriate slots. The bigger your stack of quarters, the more time you were allowed to gawk. A bit like Vegas slot machines, but with a different payoff. If you weren't from the big city, this environment must have seemed absolutely shocking. For those of us who grew up in it, however, it was just business as usual.

One holiday afternoon when I was about fifteen, my father and I hopped on the train for Manhattan. We were either shopping for a particular piece of sports gear, or perhaps a musical instrument. It had to be one of the two, as these were the only things my father and I ever shopped for in the big city. Perhaps Dad was a few paces ahead of me at one point, when all of a sudden I was directly confronted by a rather determined young lady. She looked to be in her early twenties and was not dressed in the usual "over the top" hooker getup. Except for her extremely forward manner, I wouldn't even have pegged her as a streetwalker.

As she stood directly in front of me, she boldly inquired, *"Do you want to go out?"* And to make matters worse, her boisterous inquiry was well within ear shod of Dad. Needless to say, at this particular moment, I had as much use for this gal as I did for a full set of hemorrhoids. I had no doubt that Dad overheard her question, even though he pretended otherwise. And since I was about fifteen or so at the time, the last thing I wanted him to discover was that I knew exactly what Ms. Lady of The Afternoon was referring to. After all, what possible experience with hookers could I have had up to that point. As far as my dad was concerned, I hadn't the foggiest notion of what she was talking about. And as such, I figured my best strategy was to simply play dumb.

So in answer to her question as to whether "I wanted to go out," I quickly replied, "I am out." My hope was that this naïve and clueless response would frustrate her to the point where she'd look for another (more eligible) customer. No such luck. To my witty retort, she replied, *"You know what I mean."*

With Dad still within audible range, my attempts to feign innocence were proving difficult. As Ms. Working Gal showed no sign of moving on, I replied, "Yes, I know what you mean." I guess if subtle had been her specialty, she probably would have gotten into a different line of work.

Frustrated by my efforts to remain coy, she barked, *"Well?!"*

To this, I offered, "Well, what?" By now she was becoming noticeably angry, but defeat was simply not in her milieu.

In a voice that could be heard up and down the entire street, she then bellowed *"Do you want to go out?!"* At least there was no pretending that Dad wasn't in on the exchange at this point. She had determination. I'll certainly give her that. What answer could I possibly offer now? You guessed it. "No thanks, I'm already out." And with that, she finally stormed off. Hard to imagine what she was expecting. I suppose I could have asked Dad to excuse me for about twenty minutes. And by the way, can I borrow a twenty? I guess stranger things have probably happened.

But like the lure of the Siren's Song, the appeal of affordable and readily available sex was not lost on many teenage boys. It wasn't lost on the male population in general, but for those of us who were yet to experience the real thing, it could be downright irresistible. So as a preview to one of our Saturday night O'Lunney's evenings, the three of us (Howie,

Mack, and I) cruised up and down Times Square in search of lurid adventure.

The "Red-Light" district was doing a brisk business on this particular evening, but we soon landed upon a cozy establishment that seemed promising. When one has never before been to a house of ill-repute, it can be daunting. For one thing, you never really know if you're going to have your first sexual experience, or if you'll be taken out back and beaten to a pulp. And if it was the latter, what recourse would you have. Good luck explaining to the cops that you were beaten and robbed at a place where you shouldn't have been in the first place.

That risk aside, I also had financial concerns. None of us were rich by any means, and blowing all our dough at the whore house would preclude the rest of our planned evening at O'Lunney's. Clearly, we couldn't just throw caution to the wind in complete pursuit of our sexual desires. To do so would have meant a very short evening indeed. I was thus understandably concerned when we were each asked to pony up fifteen bucks just for the whore-house entry fee.

The fifteen smackers got us a gal and a room, but it was clearly stated that additional charges would be assessed for actual "services rendered." The extent of the services was to be negotiated. Naturally, the more extensive the "services," the lighter our wallets would be in the end. As my goal was to part with as little money as possible throughout this experience, I made sure to negotiate carefully. Indeed, some of the more exotic services would have drained my cash good and proper, so I settled for the bottom of the line package. For an additional fifteen bucks, I was to be the recipient of my very first hand-job. Not nearly as exciting as most of the other options, but I figured it would bring me to the same end. My gal wasn't too thrilled about my low-cost selection, but now I'd have enough dough for O'Lunney's when this moment of passion had passed.

Looking back, I guess I made a wise choice. When the young lady's hand was finally upon me, I ejaculated in approximately twelve seconds (give or take). And despite its extreme brevity, I still thought it was a pretty thrilling experience. Even better, nobody took me out back and beat me to a pulp. And through my frugality, I guess I wound up practicing safe sex that night. On a cost basis, I'm thinking I gave my young lady something to smile about after all. The way I figure it, twelve seconds is about 0.0033 hours. Having spent a total of $30.00 for 0.0033 hours work, I figure she was working for upwards of $9,000.00 per hour (give or take). Not bad work if you can get it.

On a more serious note, I suppose that night set the hook (so to speak). Now that I knew the option was out there, it was all too easy to repeat the process on a steadier basis. The fact of the matter was that I was making some pretty poor choices at the time. Choices that were born of a low self-esteem and a general lack of confidence. All in all, I'd say I probably visited similar establishments about eight or ten times before the novelty finally wore off. And on each occasion, I knew it wasn't the right or healthy thing to do, but in those days lust always seemed to win out over logic.

As I say, I was making poor decisions. Thank God I never caught some hideous disease. Or even more humiliating, I never got rounded up during a random police raid (which the city police force sometimes conducted). Every now and again (just to show the public that the city actually gave a damn), these joints would be raided, and pictures of the "Johns" would then appear in the newspaper. Can you imagine having to explain that one to Mom and Dad (not to mention your entire local community). In the end, I suppose I was very fortunate to emerge from this destructive "phase" relatively unscathed. It's not a part of my life that I'm particularly proud of, but I am happy to say that it came and went fairly quickly.

XXXIII
I Don't Mean the Weather is Wonderful

I graduated from John Dewey High School in June of our nation's bicentennial year (1976). Unlike graduation from junior high school three years prior, I can't recall if I even attended the ceremony. As high school made no real impression on me one way or the other, it's quite possible that I skipped it entirely.

The only reason I remember my junior high school graduation so vividly is because our principal (whom everyone genuinely loathed), was publicly humiliated during the ceremony. His non-caring and callous manner when dealing with the issue of students racing for the lunchroom was the primary reason he was so despised. In fact, the students had quite a valid reason for high-tailing it to the cafeteria at top speed. If you didn't get there in a big hurry, you found yourself in a very long and slow-moving lunch line. As lunch period only lasted for thirty minutes, you'd barely have five minutes to eat by the time you finally got your food.

But our lovely junior high principal never bothered to investigate this situation. Instead, he hauled us all into the auditorium during lunch period one day, and proceeded to read us the riot act as to why we shouldn't race for the cafeteria. By the time he finished his dissertation, two things had occurred. The first was that we still only had about five or ten minutes to eat lunch that day. The second was that he no longer had a single friend among the entire student population.

The cafeteria was a bit like Disneyland before the advent of "Fast Pass." If you didn't run flat out to get in there ahead of everyone else, you were going to wait an hour and a half just to see The Country Bear Jamboree. So rather than mention anything to do with making the lunch line move a bit more efficiently, our good ole principal put the entire onus directly on the students. He warned that if we continued to race for the cafeteria, additional seminars in the auditorium (during lunchtime) would be held.

As it happened, our junior high school graduation took place on a particularly rainy and stormy day. It was windy and the rain was coming down in sheets. It was all we could do to get inside the building before becoming drenched (and in many cases, it was too late). A thoroughly rotten and nasty day to be sure. At last, we were all seated and the soggy ceremony finally commenced. It wasn't long before our lovely principal was introduced, and he proudly made his way across the stage.

In what I'm sure he thought would be an inspiring and thought-provoking speech, he began by saying "What a wonderful day this is." Of course, we knew he wasn't referring to the weather. But just as he said it, a lone voice in the crowd howled with laughter. At the sound of this, the rest of us unleashed belly laughs as well. Clearly, this unnerved Mr. Principal, so he chose to begin again. "What a wonderful day this is," he boldly reiterated. And once again, the lone voice howled (but even louder this time). Even the parents and relatives couldn't restrain themselves at that point, and uproarious laughter then filled the hall.

By now our lovely principal was really squirming, as he fought to contain this suddenly hostile atmosphere. Payback is a bear, as they say. Clearly, no one in the entire hall had forgotten that lunchroom disciplinary act, and this seemed a great time to express it. Mr. Principal made one last-ditch effort. "I don't mean the weather is wonderful," he implored. But before he could get any further, the gut-wrenching laughter was once again upon him. I'm sure that afternoon still haunts him to this day (if he's still among us), but many would say that he certainly had it coming. Anyway, that's why junior high school graduation sticks in my memory.

As for high school, I hadn't really forged any great bonds, nor had I made any great strides academically. The truth is that I got through it with mostly passing grades, and was able to graduate in good standing. If I looked over a list from the graduating class of 1976 today, I'd probably recognize about half a dozen names out of several hundred. And as I have a fantastic memory for most things past, that's really saying something about my high school experience. Ah well, onward and upward.

XXXIV
Oh, How Funny

For reasons that I've already explained, humor has always been a very important component of my persona. It was a way to be recognized and set apart in a crowd. It was also a way to obtain acceptance in a world where I didn't often feel very accepted. Or maybe it just made me feel better about myself, as I did seem to have the ability to make people laugh. In the adult years, humor can be a very attractive and inviting quality when casting our net upon the female pool. As this pool can get quite crowded at times, a sense of humor can make our net more alluring than many of the others. In any case, it was always important for me to maintain a well-established sense of humor. And as long as it didn't hurt anyone, why not?

It has also been my experience that most people do in fact appreciate someone with a sense of humor. Look at most dating website posts, and this seems quite apparent. Among other things, everyone seems to state that they're looking for someone with a sense of humor. Over the years, I met a great many gals on these dating websites. And quite a few that were looking for someone with a sense of humor. I don't know why so many of these women noted this quality, as a great many of them wouldn't have recognized a joke if it jumped up and bit them on the hindquarters.

When you say something that is meant to be funny, the response should not be, "That was like a joke, right?" In this situation, I'd usually reply, "Yes, it was very much like a joke, only without the laughter part." Naturally, this would be followed by a puzzled and confused look on the face of the woman I was seeking to entertain. But by then, you probably knew that was coming. Perhaps my favorite non-laughter response to my attempted jocularity came from my ex-wife's best friend. She'd analyze my comment for a couple of seconds, then with a big smile on her face she'd reply, "Oh, how funny." No actual laughter, just "Oh, how funny." Whenever she did this, my only thought was that it couldn't have been all that funny if she had the wherewithal to sit back and say, "Oh how funny."

192 Whataya Gonna Do?

At least she didn't respond by saying, "That was like a joke, right?

I spent a goodly amount of time in music stores as a teenager, and on one such occasion, I was with my friend Howie. As a preamble to this little tale, I need to put forth a bit of technical information. There was a certain kind of amplifier back in the seventies known as a "Leslie." Those of us of a certain age may recall the organ music that was played in ice skating rinks at that time. This very unique pulsating organ sound was generated by using this highly specialized Leslie amplifier. Though I was never an organist, I knew that Leslies were not cheap. In fact, highly specialized sound amplification equipment seldom is.

As Howie and I entered the store, we could not help but overhear two young men talking to the salesman with great concern and desperation in their voices. Apparently, their Leslie amplifier had recently crapped out, and they had an important gig to play that night (perhaps at an ice-skating rink). The men frantically asked if the music store guy could help them out by letting them rent a Leslie while their unit was being repaired. While the salesman was most sympathetic, the store simply did not have a Leslie it could rent. Seeing as how they were quite expensive; it was not a unit that anyone would have just lying around. The salesman explained that it would probably take at least a few days to get a hold of a Leslie, if it was even possible at all. Of course by then, it would be too late for the gig. And it must have been a darned good gig because these fellas seemed heartbroken at the thought of giving it up.

As we listened further, Howie suddenly blurted out, "Hey Gary, Don't you have a Leslie?" Although I owned a regular electric guitar amplifier at the time, Howie didn't realize that this was a far cry from a Leslie. When he very loudly posed the question, however, we immediately captured the attention of the two young men. In an instant they were filled with hope, as they waited for my reply with great anticipation. With the question still hanging in the air (and in a sad and solemn voice) I instantly replied, "I Don't Even Have a Barbara."

Though my callous and flippant retort was right off the cuff, you would have sworn that Howie and I had scripted this little routine. My little quip had come to me just that quickly. And just as quickly, everyone including the salesman nearly fell to the floor laughing. Perhaps it was the deadpan and instantaneous way in which the line was delivered, but my entire audience was instantly in stitches. Given the moment, I guess it was a pretty entertaining response. For these two guys to put aside the seriousness of their situation (and the financial loss that it was threatening), I guess it had to be funny. Naturally, I got a kick out of bringing such levity to such a stressful situation, while also bringing a smile to these two very anxious young men. I sincerely doubt they were able to come up with a Leslie by the night of their gig, but I do hope they found a suitable alternative.

Camp Choconut also provided me with a wealth of comical opportunities. And as a seasoned "Chain Yanker" (following proudly in my Uncle Benny's footsteps), what better chain to yank than someone who is intensely serious most of the time. Case in point, Mr. Alan Cumbati (formerly of Africa's Ivory Cost). Through the counselor exchange program, we were blessed to work with interesting young men from all over the world. And for one particular summer, this included a seriously intense young African man named Alan Cumbati.

In terms of intensity settings, Alan had two. "A Hundred and Fifty Percent," and "Off." From the moment we met Mr. Cumbati, we knew he'd be a most interesting study. During our first preliminary counselor's meeting that summer, Alan informed us that "beatings" were the disciplinary method of choice in his homeland. Naturally, I took the opportunity to throw gas on the fire and proclaimed that beatings were also our number one tool of discipline here at camp. Ham didn't find my sense of humor very engaging at that moment. He calmly assured Alan that there were many other effective ways of approaching disciplinary situations, and that we didn't resort to beatings here in America. (Apparently, lawsuits weren't that prevalent on the Ivory Coast). Though Alan seemed quite skeptical, he accepted Ham's advice at face value.

As the weeks went by, he settled into camp life well enough, and there were no reports of any disciplinary beatings. Nevertheless, it was easy to spot Alan's ongoing somber countenance. He just seemed to feel things more compassionately than the rest of us. Whatever the issue, if he was with the program, it was as though his life depended on it. And if his goal was to win you over, he would either succeed or die trying. In other words, Alan was a big fish just waiting to be hooked. Guys like Alan are typically the easiest to provoke. They also provide the maximum entertainment value for the least amount of effort. The only caveat with guys like Alan is that you have to be very careful not to push them beyond the edge. These folks have the capability of "going off" big time, and that would not be in keeping with my policy of "Do No Harm." As long as you knew when to throttle back, however, you could have oodles of fun playing Alan like a prized mackerel.

One day he and I (and one or two others) had a day-off together. As was the customary way to begin a Camp Choconut day-off, we headed to the coin laundry in the nearby town right after breakfast. Getting the laundry done in the morning left the entire afternoon and evening open to fun and frolicking. For fun and frolicking, however, it was necessary to have some cash. Though Alan was a bit light on this particular day, he did possess a check he'd drawn from our camp secretary just before heading out.

Normally the little bank just a few doors away from the laundromat would have been very happy to cash Alan's check. Upon quick observation, however, I noted that it was closed for some obscure holiday (that only banks would observe). And much to Alan's downfall, he failed to make the same observation. When it came time to convert his check into actual cash, I sensed an opportunity about to present itself. When he suggested that we head over to the bank, the game was quickly afoot.

In a casual but serious tone I said, "Alan, I don't think the bank will cash your check." He quickly shot me his usual intense glare, while explaining that they had done it for him before. And as such, he was certain they'd do it again for him now. But once again I cautioned, "Alan, I really don't think they'll cash that check for you." And with that, the hook was set. Alan's face twisted up and his nostrils began to flare. With raised voice, he vehemently declared, "Yes dey vill. Dey vill." Now it was just a question of slowly reeling him in. "Allan, I'm pretty darned sure they won't," I once again egged. By now Alan was screaming as though somebody was getting attacked, "*Dey vill, dey vill!!*" And once again, in the calmest voice I could muster, "Alan, I'm quite certain they won't."

By now he was in serious danger of throwing a coronary. His next couple of "dey vills," alerted the entire laundromat, and were enough to wake the dead. The expression on his face reflected a tortured soul who was absolutely ready to go medieval. With everyone in the vicinity now fearing for their safety, my face finally descended into a grin. And with that, he finally saw the light. With restored logic and a remarkable new sense of calm, he then looked up at me and said, "De bank's closed?" I nonchalantly replied, "Yup." I don't know how long it took for Alan's blood pressure to return to normal, but I was convinced that this wasn't the first time he'd been taken for such a ride. Nor, I was equally convinced, would it be the last.

XXXV
Quite the Dichotomy

Owing to my "stellar" performance in high school (having graduated in about the 28th percentile), I was accepted into Kingsborough Community College. The operative words here are "Community College" and "Accepted," as community colleges were obliged to accept anyone. Kingsborough was actually last on my list of college choices, but the more renowned and prestigious four-year city universities wanted nothing to do with me. Given my record of extreme academic mediocrity in high school, I can't say I really blamed them.

Though it was a somewhat auspicious beginning, Kingsborough turned out to be a very decent institution. During my two-year tenure, I discovered that they were building up the campus like crazy in preparation for converting to a full four-year university. I attended several classes in the new "Quad" building, which was ultra-modern and very sleek. It even featured a number of first-rate art studios complete with wrap-around observation deck. While waiting for my science class to begin one day, I decided to check out that observation deck.

As I gazed down upon the circle of young aspiring artists below, I noticed that they were painting the image of a nude lady who was posing in the center of the room. As a young and nubile naked woman was the last thing I was expecting to see at that moment, I was naturally quite taken aback. While I certainly got a kick out of the beautiful naked model, I also observed how the students were all hard at work honing their artistry skills. I was fascinated by how each artist's easel portrayed such a unique rendering of the same subject.

Alas, it was time to head downstairs for my science class. As I did so, I passed one of the art professors on the way. He gave me a rather suspicious look when he saw me, clearly imagining that I was up to no good. He quickly turned and said, "Hey, Don't be hanging around up here." My first reaction was that of getting caught with my hand in the cookie jar.

By the time I got downstairs, however, I reconsidered. For one thing, I had no idea there'd be a nude lady model present. And for another, it was an observation deck after all. And if they didn't anticipate people observing, why build it to begin with.

Kingsborough was among the dozen or more colleges within the City University of New York City college system (CUNY, as it was known). And though it might be very difficult to conceive, these colleges had always been free to all residents of New York City. Imagine a high-quality university education for a meager activity fee and the cost of textbooks. Unfortunately, 1977 was not New York City's most lucrative year. The city was in danger of going bankrupt at that time, and state government officials were desperately seeking any and all options for remaining afloat. There was even talk of selling Shea Stadium (where the New York Mets played), but no buyers came forward.

Long story short, the year that I entered the City University College System was the first year that New York started charging tuition for their CUNY colleges. We knew it was coming, but we all wondered with great trepidation what level of tuition would actually be imposed. What price do you put on something that had been free for so long? The short answer to that question was one thousand dollars per semester. Two semesters comprised the school year, thus an annual bill of two thousand dollars per year became the new norm.

Today that sounds like chump-change, but bear in mind that we're talking about the late seventies. And from my perspective at that time, two thousand dollars a year was an astronomical amount of money. I gained that perspective from the standpoint that I was the one that was going to have to pay it. With my brother and I both in college at the same time, Mom and Dad made it quite clear that all tuition expenses would have to be our responsibility. To this day, I hold no ill feelings about this. I know darned well that they would have paid it if they had that kind of money. But an extra four thousand bucks a year for two kids in college was simply not within their budget. As I mentioned earlier, they brought in about twenty thousand dollars a year between the two of them. Siphoning off twenty percent of that (even for such a noble cause) would have been out of the question.

With a newfound perspective on the economics of a college education, I must say that my attitude toward school took on a whole new meaning. Now that I was paying for the privilege of being there, it made infinite sense to attend class on a regular basis. Two things were becoming quite clear at this point. The first was that attending school was no longer my legal responsibility. The second was that the job of going to school was a low-paying one indeed. One might say that it was even a volunteer gig.

Clearly, it was now time to get serious. If I truly didn't want to be there, then the best plan would be to bail and look for an actual paying job. Although my prior lack of scholastic enthusiasm did give rise to a certain degree of laziness, I now decided to put this in the past. I had now graduated into the big leagues, and it was time to either "extricate" or get off the pot.

So with concentrated professionalism, I went about the usual core requirements of an eventual four-year degree program. I took the required classes, did what was asked of me, and completed them while earning respectable grades. I was, however, beginning to notice a prominent dichotomy among Kingsborough's student population. For some reason, there was a considerable constituency that seemed to hang around the cafeteria and lounge areas for extended periods. To my view, it seemed like these folks spent more time eating lunch, socializing, and playing pinball than they did going to class. If they awarded degrees for these activities, then these students would have graduated with honors.

I don't know how much things have changed since then, but a little current research yields some pretty interesting information. According to the National Center for Education Statistics, only thirteen percent of community college students graduate in two years. Within three years, approximately twenty-two percent of these students graduate, and within four years, the rate stands at twenty-nine percent. Needless to say, there are a bunch of folks that don't graduate at all. With no desire to spend any more time in community college than was absolutely necessary, I managed to achieve the more elusive two-year graduation statistic.

It begs the question, however, as to what these non-graduating students were even doing in college. Was all the socializing just an effort to meet the right romantic mate? Was it just a way to earn free lunches for two years (if one's income qualified?) Or was it merely a question of getting their parents off their backs? I really don't know, but chalk it up to the many things that cause me to scratch my head on an ongoing basis.

Along the way, there were several students who told me that the thought of graduating in two years was extremely naïve. And if you hang around the cafeteria and pinball machines most of the time, I suppose it is. But I also suspect that these same non-productive students were not actually footing the bill for their education. New York City had some pretty generous educational programs at the time. These served to benefit those whose family incomes were below a certain level (or for families who "reported" that their incomes were below a certain level). My buddy Howie not only received a complete pass on the school tuition, but he also collected additional cash for expenses while going to school (not to mention the free lunches).

While we can debate the merits of such programs ad infinitum, might it be possible that some people attended community college for reasons not pertaining to education? I guess there will always be those who know how to "work the system." And while I've heard community college sometimes described as one big "Come As You Are Party," I'd have to say that my experience at Kingsborough was rather productive. In any case, it was time to roll up my sleeves and get down to business. In the grand tally of good decisions, I was now up to one in a row.

Round about this time, I met the first of two people who were to become lifelong friends. I first became acquainted with Rod Emmons through an ad my brother and I placed in The Village Voice (a popular New York newspaper for aspiring artists and musicians). Not only was it time to get serious about college, but the time had also come to step it up with regard to my musical journey. The goal here was to put together a real band that could perform in the local clubs while earning some actual income.

Though Rod came to us as a bass player (which we sorely needed), his musical talents were vast. He played several other instruments as well, he was a terrific singer, as well as a remarkable songwriter. In fact, Rod was probably one of the best songwriters I've ever met. I was quite often awed by his ability to sit down and formulate lyrics and melodies in his head at any given moment. In my mind, he was right up there with the likes of Bob Dylan, only with a much better voice. The variety of tunes he came up with never ceased to amaze me, as he could navigate between musical genres with ease.

Sporting long unkempt hair and a scraggly beard, Rod was the very essence of a true musical soul. What was even more remarkable was that he loved many of the same artists that we too enjoyed. Trying to find people in New York who even listened to country music back in the seventies was hard enough, but a guy who knew the words to just about every Johnny Cash tune in creation was a rare bird indeed. As the character Red from The Shawshank Redemption would say, "Of course, we got along famously." Our friendship was just about instantaneous, and we quickly set about to start making some music.

Just one small problem, however. And that problem came in the form of Rod's gregarious wife Linda. And to be completely honest, there was actually nothing small about it. Though I will admit that Linda had a big heart for music as well, unfortunately, that is where her list of credentials ended. Not long after we hooked up with Rod, it was quickly brought to our attention that Linda wanted to be the band's drummer. She did, in fact, possess an entire drum kit that was permanently assembled in the living room of their Brooklyn apartment. Realizing that this new development could be fraught with danger, we agreed to give her a listen (though no promises were offered).

The best metaphor I can come up with for Linda's drumming would be like trying to play chess without first learning the rules of the game. Just as the various chess pieces have specific and very individual functions, so do the components of a drum kit. And unlike a lot of other instruments, it can be extremely perilous to completely make up your own rules when it comes to drumming. While I've seen many amazing musicians who were self-taught on a wide variety of instruments, there are some basic components of drumming that cannot be ignored. One could also say it's like knowing where to locate the gas pedal, the brake, and the steering wheel, before attempting to operate a motor vehicle. Sure, you might be able to make it up as you go along, but you might also kill yourself in the process.

So it would be a gross understatement to say that Linda's drumming left much to be desired. It would probably be more accurate to say that she had absolutely no idea what she was doing, and sounded terrible. And considering that she'd had a couple of drum teachers along the way (or so she said), this was indeed puzzling. It was impossible to believe that any drummer worth his salt could have taught her to play in the way that she did. What Linda lacked in technical proficiency, however, she more than made up for in sheer Chutzpah. (For those not familiar with the Yiddish, substitute the words gall, audacity, brashness, etc). In any case, "Houston, we had a problem."

One day the rubber finally met the road, and we had to render a decision as to Linda's role in our little ensemble. The decision we reached was the obvious one, but how to tell her in a way where she wouldn't get her feelings hurt. Her feelings notwithstanding, it was more a question as to how the rejection would translate into her husband's future plans. In the kindest intonations my brother and I could muster, we informed her that it simply wasn't going to work out. In addition to thanking her for her interest, we reminded her that we very much intended to continue our association with Rod.

Realizing that things were clearly not going her way, Linda's devious mind sprang into action. She then requested a private meeting with her husband. Rod had the look of a man who was about to be executed, but he could hardly ignore his wife's request. The two quickly adjourned to the bedroom, while Mack and I awaited their return with trepidation. It didn't take a degree in behavioral psychology to surmise what was being discussed behind that closed bedroom door. And when the two emerged about five minutes later, the verdict was quickly announced. Simply stated, without Linda, there would be no Rod. Losing Rod would have been absolutely grievous, as Linda was quite well aware. So, by means of extortion, I guess we now had a drummer.

With three of us trying to produce actual musical sounds, and Linda hopelessly walloping away on the drums, we then set out to conquer New York City's nightclub scene. And although we weren't exactly producing the world's sweetest musical sounds, we did manage to get a bunch of second-rate gigs. We were lucky to pull down twenty bucks a man in these dive bars, but a gig was a gig. We also had our share of nights when these gigs barely produced any income at all. Oddly enough, it kept us out of trouble while affording us an opportunity to build an actual repertoire. In time we learned to tune Linda out (in much the same way a chopper pilot no longer hears the whirring of his own propellers).

By far our favorite and most memorable recurring gig was The Deerhead Tavern. A particularly seedy and dirt-infested establishment, The Deerhead Tavern was nestled into the Bay Ridge section of Brooklyn. There were quite a few clubs in this somewhat trendy neighborhood, including some that were actually cool and exciting places to hang out. Unfortunately, The Deerhead Tavern was not among them.

With a clientele that always appeared only slightly north of destitute, and an atmosphere that featured a haze of thick cigarette smoke, there were few things (if any) about the Deerhead that could be described as cool. Least of all was its owner, a burned-out and pock-marked drunkard named Larry. I never knew his actual last name, so I used to refer to him as Larry Deerhead. Brother Larry had two favorite expressions. The first was "Get That Fiddle Goin," which he usually rendered at the top of his lungs, and typically while he was absolutely soused. Though the fiddle usually did stir up the inmates quite a bit, it required a significant amount of energy on my part to "get it going." Larry seemed to think that my fiddle had a little switch on it that would simply jumpstart the instrument to life. In truth, he wasn't paying me nearly enough to "get that fiddle going" as often as he demanded to hear it.

His other favorite expression was, "We had a bad night tonight, so I'm gonna need to pay you guys less." We heard these words just about as often as the ones pertaining to the fiddle. I guess my earlier statement about Larry having two favorite expressions wasn't quite accurate. He actually had three. The third one was, "You're fired." The first time we got the ax from dear ole Larry was when I asked him for more money one evening after he'd had a good night. As he had docked us so many times for his bad nights, I figured a little bonus once in a while (when the train finally did come in) was only fair.

Larry and I had an interesting relationship. Most of the time we couldn't decide whether we actually got along, or if we couldn't stand each other. Of the four of us in the group, however, somehow I was the only one who wasn't afraid to stand up to the guy. Perhaps I just didn't care all that much about the possible repercussions. And though Larry never would have admitted it, I think he respected me for it. Following one of his usual drunken "Get That Fiddle Goin" raves, I quickly and calmly told him to "Shut up." Between the look on Larry's face and those of my fellow bandmates, I'm not sure who was the more astonished.

While my buddies broke out in restrained laughter, Larry pretended to be offended by my complete lack of respect. As I say, we had a sort of love/hate relationship. Inwardly, I think he was laughing too. So when I asked him for more money after he'd had a good night, he acted like I had wounded him to the core. "You're fired. Don't come back here no more. That's it. You hurt me." For a guy who always looked like he had just gone ten rounds with George Foreman, he sure got hurt easily. Before we were through with Larry and The Deerhead Tavern, he probably fired us at least four or five times. It wasn't too many years later that this charming little watering-hole became a hardware store. We never saw or heard from Mr. Deerhead again. There were many other such gigs during this time, though none quite as colorful as The Deerhead Tavern.

No matter what your current life goal may be, it either moves forward or ceases to be. In our attempts to move the band forward, we began bringing a tape recorder to our gigs. The idea was to provide us with a good hard look at the way things were really sounding. Although we anticipated a few minor holes in the damn, what we heard was more reminiscent of New Orleans during Hurricane Katrina. You can replace a piston or two when some of the engine parts begin to wear, but what we had here was clearly a train wreck. It's one thing to be critical of one's efforts, but this was downright painful. I'm not saying that we three guys were the most accomplished players at this juncture (far from it), but what was emanating from Linda's drum kit was absolutely excruciating. If we ever wanted to graduate from places like The Deerhead, something was going to have to give. Undeniably, it was time to part company with our group's only female member. But as the wicked witch expertly stated in the Wizard Of Oz, these things must be done "delicately."

Rod was now clearly situated between a rock and a hard spot. He knew the change was inevitable but had no desire to face the unmitigated fallout that would surely result. As such, I suppose the unscrupulous plan Mack and I came up with relieved him of the burden. Our best version of "delicate" in this case, meant putting forth a blatant fabrication to both Linda and Rod. We concocted a story of having met a crazy Australian drummer named Justin. Courtesy once again of The Village Voice, that element of the story was actually true.

Though a certifiable lunatic, Justin was an excellent drummer and quite keen to join the band. The only question was how to make the switch without causing irreparable damage to Rod and Linda's marriage. The story we posed was that our new friend Justin had connections with one of the nicer Manhattan nightclubs. And by assembling a band, he could surely get us a gig or two at this club. To make it worth his while, of course, he would have to be the group's drummer. And I suppose that was as good a story as any. Regardless of whether it really made sense, and despite the dubious look on Linda's face, they actually bought it. In Rod's case, I think he just wanted it to make sense. Suffice to say that Linda was not a happy camper, but at least she didn't implode (not while we were present at any rate).

And with Justin now heading up the rhythm section, our musical journey began to take on a far more serious turn. The sounds that were now coming from the tape recorder became far less offensive, as things were finally beginning to take shape. With a more polished and professional sound, we were now able to approach some of the nicer New York clubs. Not only were these establishments far less intimidating than the Deerhead Tavern, but they also offered a bit more in the way of compensation. In essence, we were now entering the "big leagues" with regard to the New York City nightclub scene. This is also not to suggest a pathway to riches by any means, but at least things were now moving in the right direction.

During these years, we traversed the entire New York metropolitan area while disseminating our unique brand of musical entertainment. With show biz becoming an ever-increasing function of my life, various changes began to occur. The first was that my parent's concern for my future increased exponentially. A few extra bucks for playing music on the weekends was one thing, but an ever-increasing possibility of making it a career was quite another. The second was that Rod and Linda's marriage did crumble about a year or so following Justin's arrival.

Though Linda's unsolicited departure from the band was by no means a minor factor, it turned out that the two were having major-league issues way before that. The way in which they departed, however, was truly one for the books. Though she managed to keep it mostly under wraps toward the beginning of our association, Linda's selfish and mercenary tendencies had been quite well established. About six months prior to their actual separation, she told Rod that she now wanted to have an "Open" marriage. Though no one would ever have labeled Rod an "In The Box" kind of guy, there was no way he was ever going to interpret "Open Marriage" as a positive thing. Despite all his eccentricities (and there were many), he was a one-woman man through and through. As such, even the request for such a flamboyant arrangement was extremely distasteful.

Even more devastating was the accurate realization that his wife already had someone in mind concerning this new relationship format. For all we knew, she might have been well along in the process by this point. In any case, there was no way Rod was ever going to get on board with the terms Linda was now proposing. This left him with two very difficult choices. He could either grin and bear it, or he could tell Linda exactly where to go. The former might have kept her around a little longer, but at the risk of getting an ulcer. The latter would have meant foregoing his long-term marriage (and all the unpleasantness that divorce entails).

With neither choice being a clear winner, he initially opted to let Linda have her way. During this time we were treated to graphic and lurid stories of Linda's various liaisons, courtesy of our bass playing buddy. When I'd ask how in the world he knew about these things, he'd simply reply, "She tells me." Apparently, in "Linda Land" it was okay to do whatever she liked, as long as there was full disclosure with regard to her husband. In today's world, I believe this is known as Polyamory (a term I take to mean, having one's cake and eating it too).

Though he tried to make light of it, poor Rod was in hell. When she finally split for good, it was certainly for the best. From what I understand, Linda has been enjoying the single life ever since. As for Rod, he remarried several years after Linda's departure. Though he has suffered some tremendous setbacks over the years (most notably with regard to his health), this second marriage survives to   this day.

By now my life was becoming quite the dichotomy. After graduating from Kingsborough, I then moved on to a four-year university in pursuit of a bachelor's degree. At the same time, I was playing music three or four nights a week. I also had a lifeguard gig at a Manhattan health club on Saturday and Sunday mornings. And if that wasn't enough, Rod and I also started a little moving company for short-timers and apartment hoppers who were relocating on a budget. Oddly enough, that's how I met my first wife. But I'll get to that in time.

My selection for a four-year university was The College of Staten Island. Not quite sure why I made this particular choice, as Brooklyn College was closer and didn't require crossing a toll bridge every day. Not to mention it also had a better reputation. Be that as it may, most people are quite taken aback when I tell them that my undergraduate degree was in Biochemistry. I can certainly understand their reaction, as I'm often quite perplexed when I think back on it as well. The key was that my parents were still hoping to crank out a professional of some sort, and preferably within the health field. Truth be known, they were hoping for a doctor. As the pinnacle of society, docs were highly respected and most often quite well to do. And while I pose no argument to these beliefs, there was no way on God's green earth I was ever going to pursue such a career path. But that was the reason I wound up in a scientific curriculum, for which I had no propensity whatsoever.

On the other hand, nobody could have accused me of choosing coursework that wasn't challenging. Recently a friend of mine boasted that his degree in literature was among the most demanding curriculums one could pursue. While not wishing to minimize his collegiate efforts in any way, I think reading books and writing essays would have been a walk in the park (compared to the heavy-duty stuff I had to grapple with). I harken back to the many hours of absolute misery while trying to unravel complex calculus equations. (And by the way, the only time you'll ever use this stuff is if you either become an engineer or a calculus professor). Or trying to memorize large organic molecular structures in order to regurgitate them come test time.

And for a whole new level of pain and anguish, try dealing with the concepts of "enthalpy" and "entropy" while entering the world of Physical Chemistry ("P-Chem" as it was affectionately known). I had heard of colleges printing up tee shirts that read "I Survived P-Chem." I had to chuckle one day when our Biochemistry professor kept coming up with solutions to problems at the end of the chapter, and his answers differed each time from those printed in the text. If the professor couldn't even come up with the correct answer, how in the heck were we expected to? Still, it was funny to see the confused expression that came over him each time he was told that his answer didn't agree with the book. I don't think he got a single one right that afternoon. (Or perhaps it was the author of the book who didn't get a single one right. I guess we'll never know).

If I had to put a label on my time as a college undergraduate, I'd simply call it "Paying My Dues." I was simply doing what was expected of me, while at the same time carrying on the pretense of preparing for a medical career. I don't know if anyone ever got into medical school with a straight "C" average, but by the time I achieved my Bachelor's in Biochemistry, I was carrying a GPA of 2.3. Worthy of medical school? I think not. But not bad for a guy whose aptitude for science was probably right up there with Moe, Larry, and Curley.

Despite one's propensity (or the lack thereof) for the subject matter at hand, there are always people who influence us greatly when we cross their paths during our college journey. One such individual for me was Professor James Ostrom. A slim and understated gentleman in his mid-thirties, Professor Ostrom sported both an academic style beard and a photographic memory. Until that point, I'd never actually met anyone with this latter trait. Of course, I was later to learn that a photographic memory was practically a prerequisite for the study of Organic Chemistry.

About sixty of us filed into the big lecture hall for our first meeting with James Ostrom. Even though most of us had never met the man before, there was an indefinable quality about him that was immediately impressive. Though he was a humble organic chemistry professor (working at a non-descript Staten Island university), he somehow seemed larger than life. Quickly going to work with chalk and movable whiteboards, he presented us with a dizzying assortment of new material on that first day of class. After about three hours of this torture, he finally figured we'd had enough. Before adjourning for the day, he announced that we'd have our first quiz at the start of our next meeting. With brain overload and giant migraines, we all filed out quietly and with great relief.

True to his word, the good professor had his quiz questions already outlined on the whiteboards as we entered the great hall for class number two. "Take out a piece of paper and complete the answers to the questions on the board," he politely instructed. "When you're done, please place your paper in the stack on my desk." When we had completed the task, we each approached Professor Ostrom's desk and placed our paper on top of the growing pile. The remainder of the class proceeded much like our first session. We were to experience Professor Ostrom's true magic at the very start of class number three.

Upon observing that his students were all present and accounted for, he then proceeded to hand our test papers back to us one by one. I'm not saying that he read off the name at the top of each page, in order to locate the appropriate student with a raised hand. I'm saying that he looked down at the name on the paper, then silently and methodically handed the paper to the appropriate student. After just two classes, this man had somehow managed to learn the first and last names of about sixty students.

I was somewhat relieved to see the look of awe that spread quickly throughout the entire population of our organic chemistry class that afternoon. Nice to know that it wasn't just me. Throughout the group there were scattered rumblings of "How in the world does he know my name?" After completing two sessions, Professor Ostrom had accomplished this act of Voodoo simply by observing sixty names on sixty different pieces of paper, and then matching them to the appropriate sixty faces. Is it any wonder that complex organic molecules and deeply involved chemical reactions were things that he could easily commit to memory?

While his genius was undeniable, James Ostrom was also a very fair professor as well as a darned nice guy. I logged several visits to his office during those two grueling semesters of organic chemistry. On each occasion he was very polite, extremely patient, and always eager to help.

Whataya Gonna Do?

He even arranged for me to take a final exam on one occasion when I was too sick to attend the original test date. Though he had achieved superstar status as far as we were concerned, he was actually a very decent, kind, and modest person.

I consider myself very fortunate to have come on to this man's radar. I looked him up a few years ago through the magic of the internet. He had worked his way up the academic ladder to become chairman of the chemistry department at The College Of Staten Island. In an e-mail, I reminded him of his student memorization trick so many years ago. The one that had made such a huge impression on all of us. His humble reply was that there was no way he could perform such a trick nowadays. If I was a betting man, however, I think it would be foolish to wager against him.

XXXVI
The Men Are All Downstairs Doing What?

While I don't remember a great deal of organic chemistry these days, I will say this. People are like "molecules." If you put a bunch of them into a vessel of a certain size, seal it prior to placing some heat under it, you'll note that the people inside will start moving around more and more quickly. The more heat, the faster they'll go. And as they start to ricochet all throughout the vessel, it's only a question of time before they start clanging into one another.

This is only a metaphor of course, but it also happens to be an excellent segue back into the world of music and bars. For what is a bar, if not just a large vessel where people collect. The heat is provided by our need for love and companionship, while the clanging together is what happens when we finally do make a connection. So it stands to reason that the more vessels into which we climb, and with heat as a constant, the more "clanging" that will occur. And although I would never claim to be any "Ray Gantik" (you may recall my music playing hero), and with all due humility, I probably experienced my share of clanging. But aside from the brief moments of jubilation that these trysts provided, what mostly remains is a rather modest collection of amusing cocktail party anecdotes.

Included among those that linger in my memory, is the young gal I met one night while playing a gig way out on Long Island. I'd been chatting with her during our breaks, so it was only natural to ask for her phone number at the end of the night. When we hooked up a few days later, I was somewhat surprised to learn that she'd been disowned by her parents. As such, she was residing at the home of an unmarried uncle. Oddly enough, she was still in contact with her parents, who did not live far from the uncle. What she did to be extricated from the family home, I could only imagine.

Though definitely a wayward soul, she certainly didn't strike me in any way as evil. I can't say the same about the uncle, however, whom I actually met on a couple of occasions. What's more, the house he and his young niece occupied didn't seem nearly big enough to afford the requisite amount of privacy for such an arrangement. Be that as it may, I went out with this young lady (whose name I can no longer recall) about three or four times. I believe our last meeting took place on the night she invited me to spend Thanksgiving with her and her family. Though a little voice told me that there were strange things afoot, who was I to turn down a free Thanksgiving dinner.

With a fresh bottle of wine in tow, I headed to the home of the family where my date was no longer welcome to reside. The gang was all present (somewhat) when I rang the doorbell. As I was greeted by a smiling lady who introduced herself as Mom, I entered upon a home filled with the voices and smells of your typical large family Thanksgiving soiree. Additional introductions then followed as several more women emerged from the kitchen. I greeted them all in my usual polite manner, while at the same time wondering why I didn't see any of the men.

After the usual opening banter, I casually asked what the men were up to. Mom's reply came in a voice that was quite natural and absolutely unguarded. "The men are all downstairs watching _____." I inserted a blank space here because my brain automatically filled in the word "football." After all, isn't that what men usually watch on Thanksgiving Day? As it turned out, however, football wasn't the word with which Mom ended her sentence. While already heading for the basement, my brain finally finished transcribing the actual word she spoke. One of those times when you can't help but hope that you simply heard it wrong. No such luck. When I questioned what I hoped was hearing loss on my part, Mom quickly reasserted that "The men were all downstairs watching porn." Darn it, that's what I thought she said. In an effort to make light, I joked that I'd just as soon hang with the women for now.

No doubt about it, this was a new one. Combined with the interesting living arrangements (visa vi my young lady and the older uncle), all sorts of "interesting" thoughts entered into my brain. None of them were very comforting, but before long the sound of tromping feet sounded from below. Soon after, the men all filed into the main part of the house. More introductions were made, and a very pleasant dinner was had. At the end of the night, I thanked my hosts while executing a graceful departure. I was saddened by my experience on this night, and I hoped that more sinister things weren't taking place. I can't say what became of this young lady, as there were no more dates to follow.

I met "Puppet Gal" way out on Long Island as well. If you're beginning to suspect that weird things went on way out on Long Island back then, you could very well be right. I really don't have a big enough sample size to confirm. After finishing up our first set at this elegant joint, I headed off to the restroom to complete the final step of the beer rental process. On my way back, I passed a woman sitting alone at a table, with a very curious item attached to her left hand. Upon closer inspection, I could see that she was actually holding and displaying a puppet. Yeah, a puppet. Now why in the world a woman would come to a bar and sit at a table holding a puppet, I couldn't imagine. Yet there it was. And for that matter, who carries a puppet around anywhere? And even if you did own a puppet (or puppets), would you really want to display them to strangers at a pub?

Naturally, curiosity got the better of me, causing me to stop dead in my tracks at puppet gal's table. I then asked her the burning question that anyone in my position would have asked given these circumstances. "Hey, what's with the puppet," I innocently questioned. The young lady was only too happy to begin what was to become a lengthy conversation. I cannot remember for the life of me the explanation she offered for bringing Mr. Puppet along, but our ensuing conversations spanned the remainder of my gig that night. I politely excused myself each time I had to return to the bandstand, but we quickly took up the conversation again during the remainder of my breaks that evening.

Though the answer to the primary question will always remain a mystery, the fact was that Mr. Puppet was a pretty effective ice breaker. And in this regard, I will admit that it worked very nicely. At one point while I was playing, I recall Puppet Gal conversing with a fellow she obviously knew. The two talked for a while, and Puppet Gal later told me that this fellow was a colleague at the hospital where she worked. He was going through a rough patch with his significant other and was looking for a shoulder to cry on. While she did provide him with her shoulder, it was also quite obvious that she certainly wasn't volunteering any other body parts to help him get past his grief. Instead, she seemed quite intent on resuming her conversations with me.

When the night was drawing to a close, and we were packing up our gear, puppet gal made her way up to the stage. She then sidled up to me and asked if I'd be interested in coming back home with her for some leftover spaghetti. She told me she was a nurse at a nearby hospital and lived fairly close by. A flattering invitation to be sure, as I was pretty certain that "desert" would follow the spaghetti. Under normal circumstances, I would have been only too happy to oblige. At the time, however, I was already dating the woman who was to become my first wife. In addition to that, I was also the band's driver that night, which would have made the logistics very tricky indeed. So, in the end, I thanked her for the invite but told her that my girlfriend would probably not approve.

Upon reflection, she probably thought I'd been leading her on. As our conversation that evening was a lot of fun, this never even occurred to me. And had I really wanted to pursue the opportunity, I could probably have made good use of the Long Island Railroad to get back home. Though the relationship with my girlfriend (who did become my first wife) fizzled out rather quickly, I've never regretted my decision regarding Puppet Gal. Hmmm.

Though I also had to give myself low marks in the "appropriate" category regarding Kathleen, I must say that she was a thoroughly nice lady. Like a lot of folks, she was a bit lonely and was eager for companionship. Though probably a good fifteen years my senior, I made her acquaintance one night during an O'Lunney's gig. She was there with a friend, and I got to chatting with these two delightful ladies during one of my breaks. Kathleen thought of her gal pal as being very adept at meeting men. At one point during our three-way conversation, she implored her friend to allow her to meet a nice guy for a change (thereby assuming the friend already had her sights set on me).

Not being accustomed to having women compete for my attention, I remember feeling quite flattered at Kathleen's comment. The gal pal soon acquiesced, leaving Kathleen and me to get better acquainted. She lived on Manhattan's upper west side, in a neighborhood that was affectionately known as Hell's Kitchen. A cozy one floor walkup apartment, in what used to be a pretty dicey area.

As it turned out, Kathleen worked in the theatre district. As a result, I was treated to several wonderful Broadway productions such as *Children Of A Lesser God* and *Your Arm's Too Short To Box With God*. Upon returning from our evenings out, the companionship we enjoyed took on a far more intimate nature. I guess I'd have to say that Kathleen was my real introduction to sex. Though I was certainly an eager participant, sexual intimacy held a special place in Kathleen's realm. It was something she enjoyed thoroughly, and without any pretense to the contrary. She displayed an unbridled passion that would elude me even throughout my two marriages.

In describing this fairly short-lived triste, however, I do not for a moment wish to indicate that Kathleen was indiscriminate concerning her intimate dealings with men. We got along quite well, and it was obvious that a chemistry was definitely present. I thought highly of her at the time, and I still do. Our time together was fun, and the physical aspect was amazing. The fact that we both needed to move on at some point, however, was a foregone conclusion.

Perhaps what I remember most about Kathleen was her little

daughter (whose name I wish I could remember). She was probably about four or five at the time and an absolute sweetheart. This little girl stole my heart one night when she insisted to her mother that I sing her a song before bed. Though this was a first for me, I happily sat by her and delivered my (never to be famous) version of "Sneaky Snake." For those not familiar, it's a really cool song about a snake that loves root beer. Kathleen's daughter was absolutely delighted at the conclusion of my performance, as she drifted into dreamland.

Several years later I happened to be in Kathleen's neighborhood and decided to drop in. (I now know that this practice is very heavily frowned upon on the west coast. But back east it's actually pretty common). I was in luck that night, as she and her daughter were at home. We visited for a while and caught up on each other's lives. It was nice to see them both again. At one point her daughter entered the living room where Kathleen and I were talking. I hardly recognized her as she had grown considerably. Much to my surprise, she walked right up to me and asked if I remembered singing her that tune about the snake. I hadn't thought about that in years, but of course, it came back to me in a flash. My gosh, the things kids remember. You never know what kind of impression you're going to make on them. My heart absolutely swelled to know that she had remembered that tune all those years later. Google it when you have time (Sneaky Snake by Tom T. Hall). You'll be glad you did!

Another memorable individual from this period (though not nearly so delightful) was "Evil Violet." Of course, she didn't start out being "Evil" Violet. By the time our association terminated, however, the title was well earned. I believe we first met Evil Violet also while doing a gig at O'Lunney's one night. As it was her usual style to befriend the guys in the band, Violet acquainted herself quickly and easily. Though we probably didn't speak for long on that first occasion, we soon ran into her again at a club in Queens (the borough in which she resided). It was there that my association with her began to expand. When I asked for her phone number, she instead jotted down mine, and promised to call me. Apparently, she didn't have a phone at the time, which I suppose should have been my first clue. (Bear in mind this was 1980 or so, and everyone had a regular hard-wired phone back then). Be that as it may, she wasted no time in giving me a ring, and so it began.

Though it was undeniably exciting in the beginning (as most new relationships are), it didn't take long before Violet's true self began to emerge. It has been my experience in life that most people are basically honest. There are many notable exceptions, of course, and I've certainly run into my share. By and large, however, I'd have to say that most folks are pretty straight up and down. Violet was my first encounter with someone who defied this rule to the utmost. In Violet, I had met my first "quintessential/perennial liar." Even forty years later (as I write this now) I have only met one other individual that even comes close to Violet. When it came to stretching the truth, Violet elevated it to an art form.

As the comedian, Jerry Seinfeld once pondered, do our pants really spontaneously combust when we far exceed our lying quota? After all, the expression "Liar, liar, pants on fire" had to come from somewhere. Though there is no shortage of fibs being put forth in this world, I have never once heard a report of spontaneous trouser combustion. But like so many other destructive behaviors, a life of perpetual untruths is a slippery slope indeed.

As children, we are sometimes taken to telling lies to get what we want or to avoid some sort of retribution. Nothing unusual about that, but most of us outgrow it as we mature. And even as adults, we are sometimes prone to the occasional "white lie" every now and then. But even these convenient untruths are mostly to avoid hurting other people's feelings. As an outside salesman back in my younger days, I was reminded that there are two excellent reasons for always telling the truth. The first has to do with the moral implications. The second, however, is by far the more practical. In fact, putting forth a plethora of lies necessitates having to remember a great many details. The more lies, the more details to recall. Over time it simply becomes impossible to remember what you said or to whom. By contrast, the truth is easy to remember. You'll never get tripped up by telling the truth, as the real facts will be easiest to recall, and will always make the most sense.

Perhaps even more burdensome than having to remember all those fabrications is the snowball effect that lying seems to have. What might seem like a fairly harmless untruth, can quickly gain considerable momentum. Information is then added to supplement the story, and it's a downhill spiral from there. And while that very first lie may have been difficult to render, continued practice brings added skill. Now you're not only better at it, but you're more comfortable with the process. Taken to extremes, you then start lying in situations that don't even require it. It becomes a game of sorts. How long can I keep this going before someone catches on?

What I find absolutely mind-boggling about perennial liars is their unmitigated belief that they are so much smarter than the rest of us. Never does it occur to them that many of us didn't just fall off a turnip truck. Perhaps this is rooted in arrogance, or maybe it's simply a form of denial. I've even seen cases where the fibber can actually take it to the point where he or she begins to believe it themselves. This harkens me back to another Seinfeld reference. When Jerry consults his friend George as to how to beat a lie detector machine, George offers the following advice:

"It's not a lie if you truly believe it."

Like anything, there are probably some good rules of thumb for lying. If you want to tell your boss why you were late for work, it's best to make up one excuse and be done with it. If you don't do it too often, the boss might well believe that you got stuck in traffic. Your credibility goes out the window, however, if you say you got caught in traffic, and then got a flat tire. When lying, less is definitely more. But even for the more skilled and seasoned fibbers, getting caught is a foregone conclusion. It's a bit like Las Vegas. The more time you spend gambling, the greater the odds of losing. Eventually, one lie will conflict with another, or the details simply don't gel, and you're busted.

With regard to Evil Violet, I'd have to say that she was the "Hannibal Lector" of lying. She went about it seamlessly, and with no resulting change whatsoever to her pulse or heartbeat. Not that her stories always made imminent sense, it was just that she made it look so effortless. In fact, she was a lousy liar. But you had to admire her creativity. And Whoa Ho, the yarn that woman could spin!

One night she showed up unexpectedly at our gig in Queens with bruises on her face. We weren't expecting her that night, as she reported having alternative plans. Surprised by her entrance and shocked to see her battered appearance, we immediately asked what had happened. Violet replied that she had been mugged. But not just mugged, however. While taking the subway to meet us, she had been mugged and raped. We listened with horror as Violet explained that the crime had been perpetrated by three guys. More specifically, three "black" guys. (In making this distinction, I am not intending to sound racist in any way. I simply believe that this was an attempt on Violet's part to add shock value to her story).

New York was a rough and tumble city back then, and to be sure, these kinds of things did happen on occasion. And though we expressed the appropriate empathy and concern, several things just weren't adding up right from the start. If you were really the victim of such a brutal and devastating attack, wouldn't your first stop be the police station? And would you really continue on to the pub for a night of socializing after such a traumatic turn of events? And for someone who had just endured such a horrible crime, would you really be so calm and unfazed?

Violet reported the incident to us in much the same way someone might describe getting caught in a rainstorm with no umbrella. In fact, she hadn't been to the police, nor did she intend to file a report. And let us not forget, this was Evil Violet we were dealing with. By now her proclivity for putting forth tall tales was becoming the stuff of legends. "You buying any of this?" I later posed to Rod. "Not for a second," came his expedient reply.

No doubt there had been an incident. There was certainly no faking those bruises. My guess is that the actual events prior to her appearance at our gig that night were far less dramatic than the story Violet put forth. To this day, however, I would pay a king's ransom to know what really did happen.

Violet was also the type that got bored fairly quickly. Our whirlwind romance lasted approximately six months. And for the last couple, she did her best to transition over to Rod. This put a strain on our friendship for a little while, before Violet eventually moved on to greener pastures. About a year or so later, I found out that she had gotten married. The woman had an uncanny ability to meet a man and get married in practically no time at all. She'd done it on a number of occasions. More power to her. I know nothing else of Evil Violet, nor am I curious. The Evil Violet story, however, was quite indicative of the fact that I was still making poor choices. Unfortunately, I was still a few years away from breaking with this pattern.

XXXVII
If Bob Dies, Do You Want His Job?

Meanwhile back in the other significant corner of my world, I was still slogging along with my scientific studies. As I already mentioned, my undergraduate major was Biochemistry. And by no means was this simply a matter of jotting down complex molecular formulae while sitting in a big lecture hall. A goodly amount of it involved actual chemicals, test tubes, and Bunsen burners, in an effort to create the stuff we were scribbling down on paper. This joyous and more hands-on portion of the coursework was known as the "Lab."

I'll never forget my first day of Organic Chem. Lab. We were each assigned a dedicated equipment drawer where we would find all our needed glassware and assorted laboratory apparatus. We were then told to examine the contents of our drawer, making sure that all items were accounted for and in good working order. Upon perusing the contents of my drawer, I quickly discovered some disconcerting facts. Although it was possible that the glassware was all present and accounted for, the state of said glassware was far from its original condition. A good friend of mine (whom I was yet to meet) would have described it as "A Do It Yourself Sand Kit." While every other student's drawer was nicely equipped with a wide array of fully functional scientific glass components, everything that had once been glass in my drawer, had been reduced to a large pile of rubble. It was as if someone had taken a sledgehammer to it.

As this kind of equipment tends not to be cheap, I of course reported my findings to the lab professor as quickly as possible (lest he think that I was the delinquent who smashed it). While inquiring as to why I was the recipient of the "Booby Drawer," I was told that it must have been used by a student who failed during the previous semester. So while everyone else was calmly inventorying their equipment, I was frantically trying to plead my case for a complete set of new glassware. This took a great deal of convincing, as the powers that be took a very dim view of having to issue new equipment for any reason. And no matter how little sense it made, they seemed determined to hold me responsible. Perhaps finally convinced that I was not the perpetrator of such a heinous act of random laboratory vandalism, they begrudgingly opened up the vault and issued me a new set of glassware.

When we were finally all squared away, a new lab supervisor entered and immediately addressed the class. Perhaps in her low to mid-thirties, and with a hard expression on her face, she commenced speaking to us as if we were in the second grade. "If you break any of your glassware, you will be expected to pay for it," she began. "If any of your equipment should turn up missing, you will be held accountable for it," and on and on she pontificated for the next twenty minutes. To hear her give this degrading speech, one could not help thinking that a little power may have gone directly to her head.

She spoke as if we had access to plutonium and were planning to sell it to the Russians. Either that, or we simply enjoyed breaking glassware. Apparently, Ms. Hardnose had forgotten that we had all paid a significant lab fee prior to the start of the course. Much to his credit, there was one bold soul among us who pointed this out to her. "Shouldn't our lab fee take care of any accidents that might occur with regard to the odd piece of glassware," he politely inquired. "The lab fee doesn't handle glassware breakage," she quickly barked. To this day I couldn't tell you why it didn't cover broken glass, or what it actually did cover for that matter. It was an explanation similar to the one I got many years later when my tires weren't covered as part of my BMW lease.

I should mention that chemical laboratory work is by no means a speedy process. The projects were divided into lengthy segments, often spanning a period of several weeks. It was during one of these laborious sessions (during the making of polystyrene), that I was to learn a very valuable lesson about keeping a calm head in the face of disaster.

Having already spent the better part of two weeks working feverishly on my polystyrene preparation, I was finally ready to pour the entire liquid chemical soup mixture into the "Separatory Funnel." For those not familiar, a separatory funnel resembles a compact wine decanter turned upside down. A "stop-cock" is installed at the bottom to either initiate or terminate the flow of liquid from the vessel. With the stopcock positioned straight up and down, the liquid flows out freely. Turned sideways, all the liquid remains inside the vessel. Pretty straightforward. The importance of having the stopcock in the closed position when you first pour the liquid mixture into the funnel, however, cannot be overstated. Although this sounds like common sense, it's actually a pretty easy thing to overlook.

As I cheerfully poured my magical mixture into the separatory funnel, I failed to notice that the stopcock was in fact in the open position. Determined to pour the liquid carefully to avoid any possibility of spillage, I didn't witness the contents rapidly escaping out the bottom. By the time I finally did react, there was a huge puddle on the granite benchtop, and absolutely nothing left in the separatory funnel. I was immediately hit with a large wave of panic, as three weeks of intense effort had now been reduced to a worthless puddle on the bench before me.

Thoughts of intense despair then followed as I contemplated the miserable thought of having to start all over again. This would not only have put me way behind the eight-ball, but it could also have resulted in my failing to complete the course. At that moment I had a sickening feeling in my gut, as things were now looking pretty bleak. Perhaps these are the moments in our lives that really test our metal. It would have been all too easy to give in to panic and despair (or to start smashing glassware), but instead my brain suddenly kicked into gear.

I decided to approach the situation from a calm and logical perspective. Surely, there must be a way out of this jam. Some means by which to resurrect this grim situation, such that all would not be lost. Then it hit me. A "Squeeze Bottle." That might just do the trick. In any case, it was certainly worth a try. A squeeze bottle is a small plastic container with a screw-on lid. A long narrow spout juts out from the side pointing downward. This allows the liquid to stream out when the container is squeezed (thus the name). But what if the squeeze bottle was empty, I pondered. By first squeezing the empty bottle, would it then suck liquid back into the container if the little spout was submerged in the puddle?

Having little to lose at this point, I gave it a shot. To my delight, the squeeze bottle actually started sucking up the puddle atop the bench. And with each suck, more and more of the liquid began filling the bottle. Suddenly I started feeling as though I might not have to throw myself in front of a train after all. I squeezed and squeezed until I had sucked up as much of the liquid puddle as possible. At that point, I finally returned the soup mixture to the separatory funnel (this time making damn sure that the stopcock was closed). Fool me once, you know how that goes. Though I couldn't suck up the entire puddle, I did capture enough to complete the experiment. For some reason, it never did turn into polystyrene. By then, however, that wasn't a "make it or break it." The experiment had been completed, and that was the important part. I would live to tell the tale.

I never forgot this little chem lab mishap, as it did indeed teach me a valuable life lesson. Sometimes things can look very grim, and life can seem absolutely hopeless. If we keep a calm head, however, very often we can weather the storm. Perhaps another good lesson is to always check the "stop-cocks" in our lives before we carelessly pour ourselves into new situations. It took me a total of five and a half years to get through that rigorous undergraduate program, but at last, the system finally spit me out the other end.

If there's one thing I'll never forget about academia, it's the feeling that absolutely overcame me when I finally reached the finish line. I was taking my very last final for a class known as Quantitative Chemistry. Suddenly, it occurred to me. Upon handing in my exam paper, this would be my final obligation as a student. When you've been going to school all your life, it's impossible to imagine a time when you'd actually be done. And all of a sudden, that time was now upon me.

There were only about eight of us in Professor Wildman's Quantitative Chemistry class that semester, so we took the exam in his office. Upon reviewing my answers, and being satisfied that it wasn't going to get any better than it was, I approached the good professor's desk. While handing him my completed exam I announced, "This now concludes my final responsibility to the world of academia." As I had taken his class somewhat out of sequence, Professor Wildman looked at me a bit askance. He then reeled off the names of the classes that usually remained at this stage. I simply replied, "Been there, done that." At that point, he smiled while offering his hearty congratulations. And with that, I strode out of his office and exited the College of Staten Island for the last time.

As any university graduate will probably attest, the feeling at this point is surreal. Many years later I was still having dreams that I hadn't actually finished. These nightmares even included having to return for the completion of my studies. They were the kind of dreams where you thanked your lucky stars upon awakening.

Unfortunately, most of us don't get to enjoy this feeling of euphoria for long. All too soon the reality of now having to look for a job quickly becomes the next order of business. This now brings me to the second individual who was destined to become a life-long friend, as well as a valued mentor.

I met Norm Bestrum in 1982, as a result of answering a blind box ad in The New York Times. Though job seeking has changed quite a bit over the years (from a technological standpoint), the underlying principle is still the same. Fire as many arrows into the air as possible, and eventually one will hit its mark. Right from the outset of my interview, it was clear that Norm and I shared a similar sense of humor. A stout and high-spirited man of German ancestry, he sported both a handlebar mustache, as well as a keen sense of sartorial splendor. And though I wasn't exactly sure of his reasoning at the time, he was quite intrigued by my extra-curricular musical activities.

Although Norm was a married man (and quite happily by his own account), he had a very interesting concept of fidelity. In his dictionary, it meant having as many affairs with as many interesting and exciting women as he could find, just so long as his wife didn't know what he was up to. That somewhat liberal definition was a bit of a head-scratcher for me, thus it was an aspect of the man which I did not share. Nevertheless, it made for some pretty colorful stories around the Bunsen burner. Looking back, I think I got the job for two primary reasons. The first was because we got along so well. Secondly, I think Norm secretly harbored the hope that my musical exploits would increase his own sexual prospects. As mine was not to ask why, I gratefully accepted his offer of employment.

Putting his less endearing exploits aside, Norm was one of the most intelligent and knowledgeable people I've ever met. Though trained in a scientific discipline, his expertise extended to a vast array of subjects. With an easy manner and a startling vocabulary, Norm expressed himself well both verbally and in written form. He had the unique ability to disseminate technical information such that it was easily understandable. For this reason, the company sent him all over the world to consult with key customers and vendors. His greatest attributes, however, were that he was real and genuine. And if you approached him in like manner, you'd quickly get beyond the surface level, to the point where there is true connection. Rarely have I been able to reach such a point with most folks I've run into in my life. With Norm, however, it happened quickly and quite naturally.

To say that Norm tended toward the blunt was akin to saying that Jack The Ripper was prone to violence. When there was something that needed to be stated, he had an unparalleled ability to bypass all the usual social graces. The company had an outside salesman at the time who was based out of Los Angeles. His sales territory was quite expansive and included a good part of the western United States. Although only in his mid-thirties, Bobbie Feller was the unfortunate recipient of a weak heart. Quite unbeknownst to me, Bob had already suffered a couple of heart attacks in his young life. The news that he was now experiencing a major cardiac event, was at this moment sweeping through the company like wildfire.

As Bob was three thousand miles away, however, his prognosis was very much a mystery. All we knew was that it was a major event, and his life now hung in the balance. I hadn't seen Norm since the news of Bob's condition started filtering in on this day, but at one point he finally reemerged with great urgency. In a voice as serious as (well, a heart attack), Norm's first words to me were the following. "If Bob dies, do you want his job?" Instantly I recoiled with repulsion. I thought, what a cruel and insensitive thing to say at such a dire time like this. I stammered a bit while trying to find my voice, then summoned the following: "Yeah, I'll take it."

Norm's callous manner aside, it occurred to me that I certainly wasn't the deciding factor as to whether Bob would live or die. In fact, I had no influence over the outcome whatsoever. In my defense, however, I will truthfully say that I did not want Bob to die. I did want his job, but certainly not that way. But if it was the end of the line for Bob, then life would have to go on, and who better to take over than me. Happily, Bob lived and kept his job (at least for a couple more years). Ironically, he was fired not long after I moved on from the company. Though I lost contact with him many years ago, I'm happy to say that all indications suggest (at the time of this writing) that Bob is still with us today.

One thing about Norm that you could always rely on, was that he would give you an honest answer if you truly wanted one. He had no issue with letting you know what was on his mind, even if his thoughts weren't necessarily warm and fuzzy. Though I would never describe him as cruel, he was certainly not one to pull his punches or sugarcoat anything. If I showed up for work smelling like the cat's litter box, he'd find a somewhat tactful way to let me know. The same could be said for any possible wardrobe abnormalities, or personal sensibility issues. If I had the audacity to arrive for work even five minutes late, I was assured of being greeted with the phrase, "Good Afternoon Gary." Although irritating, this quickly cured me of any future tendencies toward tardiness.

As I mentioned, the man was an excellent communicator. Much to his credit, it was Norm who first insisted that my stomach condition was indeed problematic and concerning. He was the only one who ever had the wherewithal to approach the matter head-on, and without fear of consequence. What's more, he was steadfast in his opinions as well as his recommendations. And if I had stubbornly clung to my assertion of gastrointestinal normality, I have no doubt he would have pursued the issue even to the detriment of our friendship. You don't meet many people like that in your life, so you need to hang on to them when you do. I had only known Norm a short time at this point, but we had already reached a level that I could never even imagine with anyone else, (even including my closest family members). With Norm, there was no topic of conversation that was too delicate, too sensitive, or too embarrassing to broach.

And speaking of issues, may I state unequivocally (and for the record), that I was one lousy chemist. I'd probably screw up the day's formulation about the same number of times I'd get it right. Given this dubious track record, we were actually productive only about fifty percent of the time (if that). The rest was a do-over. Had we not been such close friends, I have no doubt that Norm would have kicked me to the curb in relatively short order. The same could be said if I hadn't maintained an appropriate level of respect or concern for his professional criticism. I'm sure he would have felt bad about giving me the ax, but I'm sure that wouldn't have stopped him. And I must say, there were certainly times when he would have been quite justified in so doing. Given this, I'd have to add patience and forgiveness to his long list of admirable qualities.

As there was no mistaking my shortcomings as a chemist, it was Norm who first suggested that I might wish to pursue a career in sales. Though Bobbie Feller's rapidly degrading health didn't afford such an opportunity at the time, it planted the seed for the direction my career was soon to take. Little did I know at the time, that I would remain in contact with Norm Bestrum for the remainder of his life.

Back in his forties, and despite his many years of smoking, he bragged to me about the remarkable health of his lungs. Upon reaching his sixties, however, this was apparently no longer the case. He had also gained a considerable amount of weight after he and I parted company back in Brooklyn. In addition to his love of all things food-related, beer and whiskey were also comforts that he very much enjoyed. He used to tell me that he had no "off switch" when it came to food and drink. After eating an entire dinner, he'd happily oblige if someone asked him out for a slice of pizza. On one particular visit to Brooklyn, I was astounded at the sheer quantity of alcohol that Norm could put away, while still remaining on his feet and somewhat coherent. I guess you could say that he was a happy drunk, a pleasure to be around, and the life of the party. It is ironic, however, that his extreme concern for my health didn't always extend to that of his own.

While retired and living in Louisville, Kentucky, he experienced what seemed like severe back pain one afternoon. Though his wife insisted upon driving him to the hospital, Norm downplayed the issue, hoping the pain would subside. When it didn't, he decided to drive himself to the emergency room. An examination quickly revealed that he was actually having a major heart attack. Fortunately, his heart was stabilized, and normal cardiac function was restored. Had he arrived at the hospital even thirty minutes later, however, the doc assured him that he would have been fitted for a body bag.

Very often smokers will say that they'd rather die happy than have to give up something that gives them so much pleasure. Just as often, however, they'll cling to life with everything they've got if the prospect of death becomes all too real. Toward the latter part of his life, I think he did give up the smokes and the booze. I believe he also shed quite a bit of weight. Too little too late perhaps.

A couple of years ago, a letter showed up in the mail one day with a return address marked "Ms. Sandra Bestrum." This caught my eye immediately, as it represented a departure from the couple's normal written correspondence. It had always been Sandra's style to write a form letter at Christmas time, to everyone the couple was close to (and there were a great many). This being the case, one letter to all was the practical approach. As these Christmas "form" letters always noted a return address of Norm & Sandra Bestrum, my heart raced when I noticed the revised format. Though I hoped my suspicions were misplaced, I proceeded to open the letter with more than a little trepidation. Sure enough, Sandra informed us with deep regret, that Norm had recently passed away. Evidently, he had been fighting a lengthy battle with heart disease.

Though the news surprised me little, it rocked my world, nonetheless. Norm was one of those people whom you couldn't imagine life without. A man whose life impacted so many others in such a powerful way. I owe my frankness and openness in large part to Norm, as well as my ability to approach new situations with enthusiasm and adventure. I miss him terribly to this day, and often find myself thinking that I'd love to tell Norm about the thing that's currently going on in my life. I'd love to tell him that I'm writing this memoir. I'm sure that would have given him a chuckle, as well as a substantial feeling of pride.

Though I didn't give it much thought at the time, some of the work I did under Norm's employ was a bit on the dangerous side. We often worked with some pretty obnoxious chemicals. Substances of a particularly odoriferous nature that would completely permeate the entire room (not to mention your lungs). In a perfect world, these caustic remnants were removed via a powerful air filtration system known as a Cargo Care. When the Cargo Care was working, all was well in our little corner of the world. The chemically-laden air was quickly sucked out and replaced with clean and rejuvenating fresh air.

Though I will admit that the system worked quite well most of the time, it always seemed to falter during the hot summer months of July and August. And though it was never down for more than a few days at a time, life got pretty miserable in a big hurry on those hot and muggy New York City days when it refused to operate. If the door to our lab was propped open when I arrived for work in the morning, I knew it was going to be a long day. Norm would place a fan or two by the door, in the hope that this would draw some of the chemically saturated air out of the room. On these days it didn't take long before the environment turned lethal.

Of all the tasks for which I was responsible, the one I dreaded the most was working with the powdered red dye. If your goal was to take as many years off your life as possible, then this assignment was right up there with working in a coal mine. Among other things, the company manufactured specialized photographic films for the graphics arts industry. Since red was a desirable color for such films, the powdered red dye was needed to obtain this result. In order to mix well with the other components, however, the powder needed to be milled to an extremely fine consistency. Reduced to such a small particle size, the resulting red powder was actually lighter than air.

Imagine a large quantity of finely sifted flour, packed in a big round cardboard drum. Imagine prying the lid off and watching a cloud of flour dust waft high up into the air. Same scenario here, except that it was now a giant cloud of red dye. As being shrouded in this huge red mist was the anticipated result, a full-length lab coat was donned. Further protection also included a shower-style cap, mask, and goggles. In the end, none of this really helped all that much. To emerge unscathed after shoveling this toxic red dust into plastic bottles for a couple of hours would have required a full Haz-Mat suit.

Regardless of the level of preparation, the inevitable result was taking on the look of a creature from a low-budget horror flick. In fact, the red powder was so finely ground, it permeated right through your outerwear and directly through the pores of your skin. Despite wearing a mask, it got into your nasal passageways while also working its way into your throat. Without going into tremendous detail, you were expectorating and sneezing red for the rest of the day.

It was a truly miserable task in every regard, and the cleanup process that followed was no more glamorous. The only way to remove the red from your skin was to apply liberal amounts of Clorox bleach, followed by a generous hot water rinse. By the time your skin began to revert back to its original color, you felt as if you'd been through a car wash. (Not to mention the Herculean effort it took to clean the bench and floor around where you'd been working). Once all your soiled gear was shed, and you looked somewhat normal again, only then could you resume your less hazardous duties.

But looking clean again only served to provide a false sense of security. A quick check of your limbs about an hour later would reveal that your reddish glow had returned with a vengeance. The sad fact was that the dye had worked its way through your skin, and was slowly exiting through the body's natural processes. A few more Clorox wash and rinses were then necessary, followed by a good hot shower upon arriving back home after work.

This particular aspect of my job gave me an understanding of the conditions my dad's dad must have experienced while working in that ancient hat factory so many years ago. And if I'd continued doing this kind of work for an extended period of time, I'm sure I would have suffered the same fate as he. Fortunately, my other tasks weren't nearly so objectionable or life-threatening.

While on Norm's many sojourns to hop-nob with customers or dealers, he'd often leave me completely to my own devices. Though there were usually one or two quality control functions that needed attending to, this still left most of my workday up to me. Wondering how to occupy myself during one such period, I decided that the lab could use a major overhaul with regard to organization.

While Norm was many things, neat and tidy were not among his attributes. And although I'm sure he had a system, the room always seemed like the epitome of chaos to me. Our lab contained a beautiful and well-constructed steel-top bench. Located right in the middle of the room, this solid and infinitely useful table spanned about twenty feet from end to end. Over the years, however, Norm had piled so much crap on top of that bench, that barely four or five feet of it were actually usable. And of this space, it was even necessary at times to brush stuff aside. Thus, my first order of business (while currently on my own), was getting that table cleared away.

Slowly but surely, and over the course of three or four days, I began finding new homes for all the junk that had accumulated on that bench. I utilized shelves in ways that Norm had never conceived, and scrapped things that I was sure had no remaining value (of which there were many). My only regret is that I didn't take "before and after" pictures, as the net result was a complete transformation. Every once in a while a co-worker would pop in, either to drop something off or to ask a question. When they did, it was a lot of fun to see the look of astonishment that came upon their faces after observing such a complete metamorphosis. By the time I was done, there was about eighteen feet of usable space on that impressive bench (made even more impressive by the fact that you could now see the top of it).

Perhaps it's just as well that I didn't get to see the look on Norm's face when he returned from his trip (since he always arrived for work about an hour before I did). Though I'm sure he gave me high marks for initiative, I think he found my organizational capabilities a bit threatening. I had reset the bar as far as neat and tidy was concerned, and I'm not sure he really appreciated my having done so. He was accustomed to being the star of the show, and I think my efforts may have brought him down a rung or two. A small price to pay, however, for all that added bench space.

Although Norm would factor high among some of the most intelligent people I've ever met, the "entrepreneurial" gene was simply not a part of his DNA. For a man who really enjoyed showing women a good time, I found this to be somewhat of a contradiction. I would note the same perplexity with regard to his constant desire to be in charge, and in control of his own destiny. Had he opened his own "peanut stand," I have no doubt that both purposes would have been abundantly served. His income would easily have risen at least ten-fold (which certainly would have come in handy for the ladies), and there'd be no doubt that he was in command of his own destiny. Perhaps it was just a level of risk that he was never willing to accept. Whereas I was a born entrepreneur, for Norm it was enough just to be a big fish in a small pond.

The machinery at the company where Norm and I worked was both expansive and extremely impressive. No doubt, the cost to set up such a massive and complex chemical coating line, carried a daunting price tag indeed. Not to mention the cost of a factory in which to house it, and the many employees necessary to carry out the process.

Although Norm was very good with money (and building an impressive personal nest egg), an initial expense of this magnitude was certainly not within his grasp. Can't blame a guy for not starting his own industrial film company when startup costs were in the millions. Then one day the earth tilted a bit off its axis for me. While discussing one of the film products that the company proudly sold, Norm mentioned that it wasn't actually produced at our own facility. In trying to make sense of this seemingly bizarre statement, I asked where it was made. Norm's matter-of-fact response was that it was produced for us by Polaroid. This information struck me as even more confusing. "Polaroid makes some of our films," I inquired? He then explained that we provide them with the formula for this film, and they produce it for us. Ding, Ding, Ding! Loud bells were suddenly going off in my head.

Astounded by Norm's response, I then asked him if Polaroid would make film for anyone. "Sure, as long as certain minimum quantities were maintained," he then assured me. Two things then immediately occurred to me. The first was that Norm knew the formula for every product the company made by heart. And even if he didn't, he was certainly clever enough to create his own winning formulas. In fact, that's what he'd been doing for years as a research chemist with the company.

My second realization was that Norm's finances were certainly sufficient to cover the cost of any product that Polaroid would produce on his behalf. And not only did Polaroid produce the film, but they also packaged it into saleable tubes ready for immediate shipment. With a bit of negotiation, I have no doubt that they would have warehoused it for a time as well. Suddenly all the pieces of the puzzle were now in place. The only thing lacking was someone who possessed the wherewithal to take this potentially lucrative ball and run with it.

While all of this newfound knowledge was now rocking my world, Norm was perfectly content to go about his job in his normal "business as usual" style. Could he not see what I was seeing? Being someone of such advanced intellect, had he not arrived at these same conclusions long before I did? Did he not think himself capable? In the final analysis, perhaps he wasn't capable. You either have an entrepreneurial spirit or you don't. And as most people are not entrepreneurs, perhaps it's just a mindset that eludes the mast majority. If he'd gotten past the fear factor, however, I have no doubt that Norm would have made quite a go of it.

This part of the story wouldn't be complete without a goodly amount of irony. At the time I was first making these startling revelations, the company was experiencing some fast-approaching competition. Though I didn't know it at the time, the nickname given to us by our competitors was "The Sleeping Giant." In the same vein as I.B.M., our company was the first of its kind, having actually invented the industry. For that reason, it enjoyed total market share in the beginning. When the founder of the company reached his sunset years, however, he had a choice of three kids in which to hand over the reins. Not having much faith in either of the two sons, he instead chose his only daughter.

Having experienced the daughter's leadership during my short time at the company, I can only imagine what the two sons must have been like. Thus, it would not be an unfair statement to say that she merely dabbled in the company (at best). Preferring most of the time to play with her racehorses in New Jersey, most of us had never even met the woman. On the other hand, the competitors were extremely keen and seized upon any opportunities that came their way. And as the Sleeping Giant was currently in a snoring coma, our company was finding its market share rapidly eroding.

From being the long-held leader of the industry, it didn't take long before we were reduced to just another player. And still, the Giant slept. And herein lays the irony. Had he been of a mind, Norm could undoubtedly have snagged a few prized "Golden Eggs" of his own. I have little doubt that he would have elevated his financial status to heights he never would have dreamed possible. Instead, he settled for retiring in his fifties, albeit with about three million dollars in the bank. Perhaps there was method to his madness after all.

XXXVIII
The White Knight

I first met Mira Haberman as a result of the little moving company I set up in the transient and trendy Park Slope section of Brooklyn. She and her roommate Terri saw our flyers tacked up around the neighborhood and hired us to move some large filing cabinets from their apartment and into storage. New York had been hit by a blizzard at this time, and the whole city had come to a standstill for several days. There was little to no traffic on the streets, and the icy conditions even made walking around treacherous. As I was developing a tragic case of cabin fever, I convinced my moving partner (and fellow bandmate Rod) that today was the day for the filing cabinet job.

When we phoned, the two gals were astonished that we were willing to go ahead despite the perilous conditions. With more guts than brains, we slowly and carefully pulled our pickup truck up to the front of their apartment building. The place was an old brownstone, which of course had no elevator. Large steel filing cabinets are heavy enough as it is, but the gals also hadn't bothered to empty them of their contents. With each one probably weighing in at about three hundred pounds, moving them from one place to another was a formidable task indeed. Combined with the fact that the gals lived on the third floor, we were certainly going to earn our pay for this job.

The only saving grace here was that we were moving them down the stairs, and not up. Up the stairs probably would have been beyond our capability (not to mention foolhardy). By tilting the cabinets down onto their sides, and with both of us taking up a position at the bottom end, we were able to carefully slide them down the stairs (taking extreme care not to be crushed in the process). After about an hour and a half of exhaustively proceeding in this manner, we finally brought them all to the lobby of the building. Once out the door, the same process was necessary to get them down the concrete front steps of the building. This was ten times as perilous, however, as the outside steps were extremely slick from the ice.

After another forty-five minutes of sweat-drenched toil, we miraculously had them all positioned upright on the sidewalk in front of the building. By tilting the cabinets onto the tailgate, and with both of us lifting from the back with everything we had, we were finally able to heave them up and into the bed of the pickup truck. There were four filing cabinets in all, and the pickup truck could only fit two at a time. We, therefore, had to make two trips to the storage facility. As the roads were extremely treacherous, we proceeded at about five or ten miles an hour the whole way.

It was a fairly simple matter to unload the units once we arrived at the storage facility. And with the help of a hand truck, it was a straightforward task to maneuver them inside. All told, the job probably took us about four or five hours. The gals were more than happy to pay, however, as their objective had been satisfied. From our perspective, we made a few bucks on what would normally have been a pretty non-productive day. Even more miraculously, we did it without requiring a trip to the emergency room.

Four or five hours of transporting filing cabinets around in the snow, however, provided ample time for discussions. And by the end of the job, we'd had a number of them. I know it makes me sound old, but back in those days you actually met people by going out and doing things. There was no online dating back in 1982, for the simple reason that the internet hadn't been invented yet. Be that as it may, that is how I met the gal who would become my first wife.

Of her and her roommate, Mira was the older of the two. In fact, she was even a few years older than me. About five foot six or so, she had a thin figure and straight shoulder-length dark hair, which she arranged in a ponytail. Though she had an easy-going and friendly manner, there was a distinguishable slurring to her speech. I'm happy to say that this was in no way related to alcohol consumption. Instead, it was the result of having been born somewhat hard of hearing. With the use of hearing aids, however, she seemed quite easily able to navigate her way through normal verbal communications. I was later to learn that this was a bit of a false front. In reality, she missed quite a bit of everyday conversation, and often felt quite ill at ease in the "hearing world." Instead of appearing confused or asking for clarification, however, she'd mostly just smile and nod.

While Mira could be regarded as generally attractive, her roommate Terri was gorgeous. While a bit shorter than Mira, she sported the classic hourglass figure, as well as beautiful dark hair that always looked like she'd just come from the salon. With curves in all the right places and jaw-dropping feminine Irish facial features, Terri was a sight to behold. And though she dressed rather provocatively, she could have stopped traffic if she chose to adorn herself in a burlap sack. But despite her obvious good looks, she seemed quite unsure of herself and generally lacking in self-confidence. It was as if she was unaware of her obvious attributes and the effect they had on the male population.

Though she became somewhat interested in Rod for a brief time, as a general rule Terri's choice in men was abysmal. She would typically gravitate toward uneducated and dim-witted guys, with very little to offer and very few prospects. Some weren't even very nice to her but simply sized her up as an easy mark. Perhaps this lack of self-esteem could be attributed to the loss of her mother at a relatively early age, as well as a father who was clearly a hopeless alcoholic. Whatever the cause, it gave Terri a generally sad and somewhat tragic countenance.

Mira on the other hand didn't seem to lack for anything in terms of self-appreciation. Though I wouldn't say that she was brimming with self-esteem either, I would say that she regarded herself far more highly than did her younger roommate. In terms of her appeal to men, hers was an attitude that almost approached arrogance. As Mira liked to say, she had no trouble finding interested men and availing herself of their obvious attentions. Also a product of a very broken upbringing, her success in attracting males came from a well-rehearsed ability to depict herself as helpless. And while presenting oneself in such a manner is often a telltale sign of a poor self-image, it is an equally bad sign to be attracted by such a quality. And since I was still well in the stage of making bad choices, I chose to rescue this damsel who so obviously needed the help of a caring man.

Not only were the filing cabinets not the actual property of the two roommates, the same could be said of the remaining furniture that adorned their apartment. Except for a mattress or two, these furnishings belonged to a man they simply referred to as "Gilz" (at least I assumed Gilz was a man). In fact, "Gilz" turned out to be Harry Gilz, a friend who was currently subletting the apartment to the two gals. How this arrangement came to be, I have no idea. But I didn't ask questions like that back in those days. Some things were just better left unknown.

Another discovery I soon made was that the gals were about three or four months behind in their rent. When one of them couldn't come up with their half on a particular month, the other one just figured they didn't need to either. Apparently, this little routine formed a pattern, and before long the gals were in arrears big time. Why either of them couldn't come up with their half, was always a mystery to me. They both held down full-time jobs and didn't seem to have a lot of other expenses.

Mira did own a car, but it wasn't as though she ever spent much money on it. Having moved to Brooklyn from New Jersey, she never bothered to observe the formality (or the law) of converting her license plates over to her new state of residence. As such, she never had to pay the cost of registering the vehicle. As she didn't consider basic maintenance a necessity, there was no money spent on oil changes or tune-ups. And with a vehicle that wasn't officially registered in New York State anyway, why bother paying the hundreds of parking tickets that she accumulated while living in the city. How she was never pulled over (or impounded while parked on the street) during this time of extreme delinquency, I'll never know. Or how she never came downstairs one day to find a boot on her car, was of equal mystery.

But in a year when the average price of a brand-new car was about $6,200.00, she managed to rack up about twenty percent of that just in parking tickets. I suppose the law of averages would have sooner or later prevailed, and the long arm of justice would have come down on her eventually. Before it did, however, there came a knight who rode in on a great white steed. This valiant knight then gave her the money to pay off all those parking tickets (some 1,400 dollars or so, as I recall).

The White Knight (or "schmuck") as may have been a more accurate title in this case, was yours truly. I also insisted that she officially register the car in New York and obtain the necessary insurance. Though no easy sell, she begrudgingly complied. In the end, the White Night saved the helpless damsel from sure disaster. In so doing he restored her good standing in the community, thus making her a legal driving entity. As for the outstanding rent, I don't think it was ever actually paid. At least the White Knight wasn't that big of a schmuck. The two gals were eventually evicted, and the landlord was thrilled just to be rid of them.

Of course, I wasn't aware of the whole picture when I first made the decision to call Mira for a date. The rest of the story began to trickle in over time. Had I received full information from the start, I'd like to believe that even a schmuck like the White Knight would have bailed. For a good while toward the start of our relationship, it seemed like she owed money to everyone. There is a good reason that men and women check out their potential partner's credit before embarking upon a serious relationship these days. It's not the most romantic of notions, but it is prudent and infinitely practical.

In addition to the New York State Department of Motor Vehicles, the Bureau of Parking Enforcement, and her landlord, she also owed hundreds of dollars to various family members. And if these debts were not enough, let's throw in the thousands of dollars she owed the government for student loans while attending college (which I'm sure were also never repaid). And these were the creditors I knew about. Doubtless, there were others.

To observe Mira for even a short time, would quickly reveal the reasons for her constant state of financial chaos. When it came to money, she was a child with no sense of restraint or responsibility. If she wanted something (and actually had some money at the time), she'd just buy it. After which, of course, she'd be broke again. And if she wanted the item badly enough (and didn't have the money), she'd simply borrow it from someone or buy it on credit. Thus the reason she owed money all over town.

Back in the eighties (and still very much like today), there were always predatory lenders that were more than willing to give people like Mira enough rope with which to hang themselves. In Mira's case, however, she never for a moment gave any thought to the eventual day of reckoning. Much like a child, she just figured someone would come along and take care of it. And for about three years or so, I was that someone (a. k.a. "The Schmuck and/or White Knight.")

Regarding my own financial status, I do not wish to indicate that I was well off in any way, shape, or form. I brought in a whopping $15K per year from my assistant chemist job working for Norm. Mira was a teacher with the New York City Board of Education, and actually made a bit more than I did at the time. Despite this, neither of us was destined for riches.

Unlike Mira, I always maintained an innate responsibility when it came to personal finance. As such, the task of managing our finances always fell to me. When she and I procured our own apartment (not long after she was ousted from the one she and Terri shared), our landlord was paid on the first of each and every month. And this was even considering that we lived in one of the more expensive sections of Brooklyn. Had Mira not insisted that we remain in trendy Park Slope, we could easily have pared a couple hundred bucks off our monthly rent tab.

Perhaps for the first time in her adult life, she was now living debt-free (save for the student loans). She no longer had to dodge the landlord (or any of her other creditors), or live with the fear of having her car impounded on any given day. And from my perspective, herein lies the most incredible aspect of the woman. You might think that this newfound financial peace of mind would bring great joy and inner tranquility. You'd be tempted to think it, but you'd be wrong.

As we began to emerge from Mira's pool of red ink, and actually started to build some savings, she grew more and more uncomfortable. Astoundingly enough, being debt-free and having some money in the bank actually made her anxious and stressed. I'm sure those who study psychology and human behavior would have a perfectly reasonable explanation for this. To my mind, however, it made little to no sense. At times she would even go out of her way to sabotage our finances. After depositing my four-hundred dollar paycheck in the bank one afternoon, I noticed that two hundred of it had been withdrawn the very next day. While trying not to throw a coronary upon seeing the new balance, I frantically asked Mira why she had withdrawn half my paycheck. She calmly replied that she used it to buy groceries.

Bearing in mind that twenty-five to thirty dollars would have easily bought an ample supply of groceries in 1982, I asked what kind of groceries cost two hundred bucks. "Cheese," she replied. "I bought some nice cheese." Though I don't recall, it must have been a case of imported Brie to warrant that kind of price tag. With tremendous restraint, I explained that this was something she just couldn't do. I reminded her that it was my responsibility to make sure the rent was paid, and that this kind of excessive spending was going to jeopardize my ability to get it done. "We're not rich," I explained. "You just can't do this kind of thing."

Sadly, I was filling the role of a parent in this case. An authority figure who had to reprimand their child concerning inappropriate or potentially dangerous behavior. I assure you that this did nothing for my peace of mind, as what husband wants to regard his wife as though she were a child. It certainly didn't sit well with her either, as it obviously brought back parental issues and thoughts of rebellion. After considering my comments for a minute or two, she then replied that "I was ruining her life." Obviously not my intention, but if fiscal responsibility was going to ruin her life, then so be it. At least it would be a long and debt-free one (at least while I was around).

Much like her estranged roommate, Mira's was also a very broken childhood. About six months or so before we got married, I had the pleasure of meeting her mom and dad. And when I say "pleasure," I mean that it was one of the most bizarre experiences of my life. To say that Mira and her dad enjoyed a particularly strange relationship, would be to understate it in the extreme. Thinking in terms of the relationship Norman Bates had with his mom would probably bring it more in line.

Except for their only daughter, the family still resided just outside Minneapolis, Minnesota (where they had grown up). While Mira migrated to New York in her early twenties to escape the brutal Minnesota winters, her two brothers chose to stay close to home. Though she attributed her east coast pilgrimage to the harsh Midwest weather, I got the feeling that she was also trying to get as far away from Dad as possible. There was something obviously going on between the two. Something that was blatantly amiss, but something that I was never really able to put my finger on. At least not then.

At the risk of offending all the perfectly wonderful folks who reside in the vast state of Minnesota, I'd have to say that some of the ones I met were among the oddest individuals with whom I've ever crossed paths. Case in point, Michael and Sonya Haberman, my first and very short-lived set of in-laws.

    Let me start by stating that Mr. Haberman never had any intention of attending his daughter's wedding. As that fateful day grew nearer and nearer, this fact became more and more clear. Although I could summon no obvious reason for it, there were widespread rumors among the family that Mom and Dad would not be in attendance. Though the tension between father and daughter was obvious, they still treated one another with a cordial familiarity. Nevertheless, it soon became clear that Michael and Sonya would be attending their daughter's wedding in spirit only.

    Though she tried not to show it, this angered Mira in no small way. The thought of Dad not being there to walk her down the aisle was a source of absolute panic and utter embarrassment. To be sure, it was certainly not a question of money. Michael was a high school principal back in Minnesota and had been for quite some time. I don't think Sonya worked, but I doubt she needed to. They lived in a big house in an affluent suburban neighborhood just outside Minneapolis. They drove a nice car, took nice vacations, all while building a sizable nest egg for themselves.

    As a compromise for not attending the wedding, they offered to visit us in New York several months before the nuptials. Why they were willing to come to New York to meet my family and me, and not for the actual wedding, remains one for the ages. Clearly, there was more going on here than met the eye. A lot more. In any case, Michael and Sonya's visit to New York was the first and only one we were ever privileged to experience.

    Besides meeting with my family, they also set aside time to visit Michael's sister and brother-in-law in Queens, as well as a set of cousins also in Brooklyn. Though the dinner at my parent's apartment was far and away the more memorable of the two evenings I spent with Mira's mom and dad, the dynamics with regard to their side of the family had its moments as well. The plan was for Michael and Sonya to treat his side of the family (as well as Mira and me) to a nice dinner in New York's famous Chinatown district. It was the "treating" part that gave the evening its special charm.

    Like most of us who were born and raised in New York City, I was well aware that the Chinese restaurants in this well-known district deal strictly in cash. Being from out of town, however, Michael was apparently not aware of this. That was his story, at any rate. After enjoying a very nice dinner indeed, good-ole Mikey slid his handy credit card alongside the bill. Upon doing so, the waiter politely informed him that cash payment was required. And wouldn't you know it, Michael hadn't anticipated the need for that kind of cash at a Chinese restaurant.

Though I don't recall the exact numbers, I'm guessing that the meal was probably about seventy or eighty bucks. Upon perusing his billfold that night, I don't think Michael was carrying even half that amount. So as much as he would have liked to, there just wasn't any way he could come up with the cash needed to pay the tab. Fortunately, good-ole Uncle Hiram (the brother-in-law) was indeed a practical man, and had left the house with ample cash in his pocket. Like it or not (and believe me, he didn't), Uncle Hiram got stuck with the check. Michael swore up and down that he'd pay Hiram back immediately upon returning home, but the look on Hiram's face was of one who had been down this bitter and frustrating road before. I couldn't tell you if he was ever reimbursed, but I can say that he certainly wasn't holding his breath until Michael's check arrived.

Naturally, there was much talk of our upcoming wedding plans during dinner, with the issue of Michael and Sonya's non-attendance eventually coming to the forefront. I don't recall any of the family specifically confronting Michael concerning his and Sonya's wedding plans (or the lack thereof), but my sense was that they all looked upon him as an odd duck in general. And knowing Michael as they did, this typically odd behavior did not seem out of character at all. Though their faces clearly conveyed confusion and bewilderment, they eventually resolved to take it in stride.

As I mentioned, the evening spent in the company of my mom and dad was surely one for the books. One of the interesting traits of my soon to become in-laws (and one that was shared by their daughter) was their blatant disregard for others. This was especially true when they considered the others to be unworthy. In short, they were probably a couple of the biggest snobs I had ever met. And while I would never say that my parents were the most socially graceful people in the world, compared to the Habermans they were practically Charles and Diana.

While my mom and dad went way out of their way to be gracious and hospitable, Michael and Sonya made it their mission to be rude and condescending. I'll never forget the six of us sitting in my folk's living room, trying to maintain a pleasant conversation. What discussions we could muster were strained and superficial at best, but a modest effort was still made. That is until Sonya would completely derail the dialog by asking her daughter a totally unrelated question any time the moment struck her. And it struck her multiple times throughout the evening.

When she did it the first time, we were pretty taken aback. Surely no one would intentionally be that rude or dismissive. Perhaps Sonya battled hearing issues, and her disruptions to the conversation were inadvertent. After all, you can give someone the benefit of the doubt the first time. By the third time, however, we knew that it wasn't a question of her hearing. In no uncertain terms, she was just letting my parents know that she held them in complete disregard.

Speaking of little regard, eventually the conversation got around to Michael and Sonya's plans to boycott the wedding. At this point, my father was becoming a bit more blunt in his dealings with this lovely couple now gracing his household. Michael's reply was simply that we shouldn't try to plan the wedding around his schedule. He was actually trying to convince us that his not attending would be easier for all concerned.

I can certainly say that it wasn't making anything easier for me. My soon-to-be wife couldn't deal with her dad's rigid intractability and was now blaming me for his "inability" to attend. At the time I had no idea how truly complicated this situation was. I guess it was far easier to blame me, than to try and deal with a parent who was acting in such an irrational manner. Mercifully, the evening finally came to an end and the Habermans eventually slithered out. I tried to console my father by saying that we'd probably never see these stuck-up idiots ever again, but he was understandably concerned.

In the end, Michael made good on his promise, and indeed he and Sonya skipped the wedding. It went off as well as could be expected, but the absence of the bride's parents was more than conspicuous. About a year into our marriage we both had some vacation time coming and contemplated how to spend it. Amazingly enough, the Habermans were adamant that we should come and visit them in Minnesota.

My wife, whom I now referred to as "Dopey" (though not to her face), was also dead set on a visit to Minneapolis. I realize now that it was because she was very close to her brothers (whom she didn't get to see very often), and probably had little to do with connecting with Mom and Dad. In any case, you can probably guess my reaction to Michael and Sonya's invitation. And though I would never voice such a clearly disdainful refusal in audible terms, my message came through loud and clear.

Though Mira informed me that turning down their invitation was tantamount to a cold slap in the face, I can't say that this concerned me terribly. I couldn't help thinking that skipping our wedding for no particular reason was tantamount to the same thing. We instead wound up taking a trip to Colorado, where Mira made certain that I had a thoroughly rotten time. Happy wife, happy life (as they say). As one could surmise, this ill-fated and poorly conceived marriage was well on its way to oblivion by now. At this point, I was learning some very hard lessons. Making life-changing decisions when one is not in a good place in life, is simply not a good decision.

Long after our ridiculous marriage terminated, I contemplated some of the things that had transpired between Mira and her father. I had heard a few stories during visits from her brothers, and slowly some of the pieces began falling into place. At one point the brothers mentioned how Dad would make "visits" to Mira's room at night when she was still a teenager. These visits seemed to conjure up bitter memories for her.

Though my own upbringing was far from ideal, I never realized what a sheltered life I had led. As such, I didn't give these "visitation" stories a great deal of thought at the time. I figured it was just typical growing-up issues between a father and a daughter. It was many years later when I finally realized that it was probably much more than that. Toward the last few months of our marriage, Mira spent some time with a therapist. This seemed a prudent step, as our marriage had been heading downhill in a big hurry. Once again, I was clueless as to why their discussions always seemed to gravitate toward issues with her father.

Following one particular session, she told me how the therapist was horrified by some of the things she revealed about the man. Though it would have been pointless to press her, she never let me in on the actual details. Though my brain would never have gone in such a dark direction back then, I can only imagine that the situation must have been pretty bleak.

Perhaps owing to these grim circumstances, Mira was a person that you could only get so close to. Once you got to a certain level, the wall would come down and no further details would be forthcoming. I guess relating such dark and painful information involves a tremendous amount of trust. A level of trust that certainly wasn't present in the relationship that she and I had. For all I know, it might not have been present in any of her relationships. Thus a very heavy burden to carry around.

There are so many times in life when ignorance is bliss. When things finally began clicking into place so many years later, I was truly saddened by the thought of Mira falling victim to the kind of domestic abuse I was now imagining. Whenever Michael's face and "phony-baloney" personality conjured in my head, it stirred fierce feelings of anger. I almost wished I could go back in time so that I could confront him in a way that he deserved.

To my mind, a father that would inflict this kind of pain and abuse on a child is one of the lowest forms of life on earth. I don't know what prompts these evil and damaged people to propagate, but I now know that this kind of thing happens much more than any of us would like to think. The only upshot here was the realization that Mira's behavior toward me was probably not personal. In fact, it probably had little to do with me at all. As such, I no longer look back upon her with anger. I see someone who was merely trying to survive in a world where she was dealt a pretty crappy hand.

Through the magic of the internet, I recently discovered that she wound up marrying the guy that she hooked up with just after she and I parted. As I said, she took great pride in her ability to attract men. Call him an opportunist perhaps, but he sized up our marital situation pretty quickly. He and Mira hooked up way before the ink was even dry on our divorce papers. Though their swift union didn't completely surprise me, I was quite taken aback to learn that they soon married and relocated to England (Edward's original place of birth). Apparently, a child also came along at some point. As far as I know, the two are still together to this day.

XXXIX
This is Like "Africa Hot"

By the ripe old age of twenty-two, I'd had more than my fill of New York City, and decided to pursue any possible avenue of escape.

One day during my tenure as Norm's lab assistant, I spotted a trade publication on his desk. In his absence, I looked it over and discovered a small "Classified" section toward the back of the magazine. A large industry distributor had placed a prominent ad, noting that they were looking for salespeople in all areas of the country. In keeping with Norm's advice, I could see no reason why I couldn't sell these kinds of products for a living. I then decided to test the waters and quickly fired off a resume to these folks.

As it turned out, they were indeed interested. So much so that they offered to fly me to Dallas to meet the branch manager for the southwestern region. I didn't know how thrilled I was at the prospect of setting up shop in Dallas, but at that point, I figured anyplace would be a step up from New York. One should be very careful when making assumptions like that.

Our particular industry was like a lot of specialized industries, in that everyone knew everyone. And quite unbeknownst to me, my prospective new employer had done some checking prior to whisking me out to Dallas. So much so that their checking actually came to the attention of my current employer. Naturally, I hadn't wanted to tip my hand as to my future plans, thus I was doing all of this on the Q.T. It wasn't long, however, until Norm got a call from one of our own sales reps, informing him that this prominent distributor was courting me. Though I hadn't planned on telling him what I was doing until the deal was a bit more firm, I now needed to come clean. While I don't think he was upset that I was looking to expand my horizons, I do believe he was disappointed that I didn't confide in him.

In any case, he was a very good sport about it and behaved with his usual degree of ultra-professionalism. As it turned out, this was much more than I could say for my prospective new employer. Had they acted with a bit more discretion (and not contacted one of my current company's own reps), the entire situation would probably have remained on the QT. In the end, my current employer figured I'd be a strong advocate for their products as a rep for the distributor in Texas. I was then given their blessing.

I have a very vivid memory of standing in the parking lot at my new employer's Dallas, TX branch while waiting for the branch manager to conclude a telephone call. It was summer and I distinctly recall thinking that I'd never before experienced heat to this extreme. My body was telling me that it was about a hundred degrees outside. In fact, the temperature that day was about a hundred and five. It put me in mind of the Neil Simon play *Biloxi Blues*, (which was made into a movie starring Mathew Broderick). While standing in formation for the first time upon arriving in Biloxi, Mississippi, Broderick's character remarks that "This isn't just hot, this is like Africa hot." That is exactly how I felt standing there in that Dallas parking lot on that stifling hot summer day.

My brother likes to say that there's a difference between a dry heat and a wet one. And up to a certain temperature, that may be so. Wet, dry, or somewhere in-between, as anyone that's ever endured temperatures north of a hundred degrees will tell you, it doesn't really matter much. It's the same level of misery. I also remember thinking that if it's going to be this hot all the time, I'm not sure how I'm going to survive living here. Surely this place must have a winter, I recall rationalizing. It can't possibly be like this all the time. And while trying to quash my genuine concern for the extreme climate, I donned my happy corporate face.

The branch manager and one of the sales reps then took me to lunch, where they proceeded to barrage me with questions as to my knowledge of the industry. Finally convinced that I wasn't just another pretty face, we returned to the branch to talk turkey. Although I'm now aware that it isn't legal to ask, part of the questioning concerned my marital status. There was also much concern as to whether my wife was on board with the change. I should mention that the details of my pending divorce were not something I bothered to share with my prospective new employer. "But of course," I replied. "She's very excited about the change of scene, and quite looking forward to this new venue," I further added. What was I supposed to say? Our marriage has been on the rocks ever since it began, and by now it was all over but the shouting? While this was the truth, I have no doubt that it would have gone over much like a pork chop at a bar mitzvah.

Satisfied with my highly "interpretive" answer, the branch manager then proceeded to make me an offer. Unlike in *The Godfather*, however, it wasn't one that I couldn't refuse. In fact, his offer left quite a bit to be desired. And if I had it to do all over again, I probably would have dismissed it out of hand. The salary was scant, while the rate of commission was also not worth writing home about. There were other conditions concerning the compensation package which also didn't sound entirely promising.

I was later to learn that this company's reputation was not all that highly regarded within the industry, and that turnover among the staff was extremely common. Last but certainly not least, Norm made it quite clear that I'd always have a place with him, no matter what the outcome of my meeting in Dallas. On the plus side, however, this distributor had an extensive line of equipment and supplies that were well suited to the industry. And with such an impressive product line, it was certainly possible to make a few bucks with this outfit (if one were willing to really hustle). In the end, I think it was my overwhelming desire to get out of New York that drove my decision. With much trepidation, I decided to accept the job and forge ahead to the next chapter of my life.

The three-day drive from New York to Dallas was a memorable one indeed. I decided to combine it with a bit of pleasure, and I camped out at every stop along the way. The first night landed me somewhere in Virginia, which had always been among my favorite destinations. I've always loved the lush green rolling hills of the Blue Ridge Mountains, thus this made for a very pleasant and picturesque first stop.

Less familiar to me was my second night's stop in Carthage, Tennessee. Located in the heart of the Smokey Mountains, this charming town is halfway between Knoxville and Nashville. The area just about took my breath away when I arrived at my destination. The camping facility I had chosen was surrounded by majestic and heavily forested mountains on three sides. All throughout the great Smokey Mountain Range (and directly adjoining the camping area), was a series of stunning tributaries. These beautiful lake-like bodies of water were isolated and absolutely pristine.

My timing couldn't have been better when I rolled in on this second evening. I still had about an hour or so before the sun went down over this majestic and awe-inspiring Appalachian mountain range. As I luxuriously and carelessly floated on my back in those warm and inviting waters, it occurred to me that I could stay in this place forever. It also dawned on me that this might be a far better place to settle than Dallas. In fact, the thought of pitching the Dallas job and trying to make a go of it here in Tennessee reverberated frequently in my head. From my current vantage point, I just couldn't imagine how it could get much better than this. And had I been a far more adventurous and risk-taking soul back then, I might never have left.

You just never know where life is going to take you sometimes. Quite often our destiny is simply the result of a geographical choice we make somewhere along the way. That old Robert Frost poem about "*Two Roads Diverging in a Wood*" comes to mind. "I took the one less traveled by, and that has made all the difference." Mr. Frost may have been disappointed by my choice, however, as I probably took the safer and more traveled one in this case.

I had about four thousand bucks in my pocket at the time. Though not a fortune by any means, back in 1984 I probably could have made it last at least six months. Surely it would be enough time to snag some form of employment, just to get myself up and going. And let's face it, I was a college graduate with a couple of years of work experience in a scientific discipline. With a bit of effort, I could probably have made a name for myself in this part of the country. In the end, however, safety and security won out. By the next morning, I was off to my final interim destination.

I arrived in Arkadelphia, Arkansas in the late afternoon with a very dubious expression on my face. Carthage, Tennessee or Martinsville, Virginia, it was not. One might say it was the complete opposite of those places. As opposed to hills or mountains, this part of Arkansas was flat, lifeless, and remarkably unattractive. And as I was destined to continue in this south-westerly direction, I couldn't help but wonder if the area around Dallas would be any more appealing. At that point, I also began to wonder if it was too late to head back to Tennessee. I spent a most unsettling evening while camping out in the Arkansas prairie that night, awaiting the final leg of the journey into Dallas.

If Dallas was any improvement over Arkansas, it was slight at best. Truth be told, I was really beginning to question the wisdom of this entire enterprise. Aside from the requisite culture shock that a native New Yorker was bound to experience in this part of the world, Dallas held some unique characteristics back in 1985. The city was anticipating a large influx (due to the availability of jobs), but the onslaught had not yet arrived. Houses, condos, and apartments had been constructed in mass, but remained largely vacant in advance of future residents.

The same could be said of other commercial enterprises. I signed up at a beautiful new health club at one point, and was the only member present on more than one occasion. Imagine having the run of a colossal new health club and being the only member in attendance. On one such occasion, I showed up at the racquetball challenge court in the late afternoon. I then waited in vain for over half an hour for someone to play with. When another human being failed to surface, I finally gave up in disgust and went home. Had I gone to the pub instead, I'm sure there would have been lots of people to talk to. With regard to exercise, I was noticing a prevailing philosophy in this region. To a great many, it seemed that opening the pop-top on a beer can qualified. And although I don't mean to dump on Texans during the mid-eighties, there were other prevailing attitudes that I also found rather hard to take.

I'd always thought of New York as being a very racist place. Had I instead grown up in Manhattan (and not the heavily blue-collar boroughs), I'm sure I would have seen things quite differently. Nevertheless, I'd never heard the "N" word spoken more times than during my two-year tenure in Dallas. As an educated and intelligent individual, I found this extremely offensive. It was as if I was now surrounded by a large population who had never finished fighting the Civil War.

I'll never forget a particular exchange I had the misfortune to witness when a vendor treated me to lunch one day. A rather upscale and uniquely southern-looking establishment, Barney Olefields featured a lavish buffet, as well as seasoned African American waiters sporting old-style serving attire. The scene was like something out of *Gone With The Wind*. An unassuming and respectful African American man in a fancy white frock soon approached to take our drink order. My hosts were well familiar with this stately gentleman and quickly greeted him by name. "Hello George. How are you today," they inquired. "Ohh, jus fine sur," came George's dignified reply. "Can I get you fine gentlemen yo usual cocktails," he then queried. "That would be great," my hosts returned.

For reasons that I can't remember for the life of me, the conversation with George somehow turned to the car my hosts were driving on that day. Upon being asked whether he noted the car, George replied, "Ohh yes sur, and a fine automobile it is sur." I viewed this rather surreal exchange with extreme disbelief. I was thinking that this is normally the point at which Rod Serling would step out to let us know that another episode of *The Twilight Zone* had just begun. Did George really act like this when he wasn't waiting tables, or was it just a way to get better tips? Though I said nothing, it was a very embarrassing spectacle indeed. I couldn't believe that people were still carrying on in this manner in 1985.

Putting all this recent upheaval and unanticipated culture shock into perspective, I had utilized my long westward pilgrimage to take stock of my vastly changing circumstances. I was now taking up residence in the suburban community of Grapevine, TX (some twenty miles north of Dallas). Though technically still a married man, I entertained few thoughts of ever rejoining Mira. By now the wheels of divorce were turning, and it was simply a matter of time before I'd be a free agent once again. With regard to my new Texas colleagues, however, my wife would soon be joining me when all was wrapped up in New York. Naturally, that couldn't have been any farther from reality.

244 *Whataya Gonna Do?*

There was a really nice Mexican restaurant in Grapevine, and on one particularly pleasant evening, I ducked in there for a relaxing dinner. In addition to good food and cocktails, the place also featured a lovely courtyard out back where you could dine al fresco. On this particular evening, there was a band playing in that courtyard, which made it all the more inviting. The music was good, the food was good, and the beer was delightful on this most agreeable evening.

I remember thinking that it was nice to be free of all that marital stress I left behind in New York. Sitting in that little cantina that night, while sipping on a beer and enjoying the music, I settled into a wonderful state of peace and serenity. For the first time since fleeing my old life, I started to believe that things might be okay. That it would be alright to be on my own again, and with a whole new life ahead of me. The beer and margaritas were flowing, the music was playing, couples were dancing, and I was at peace with the world for the first time in a long time.

And as I contemplated all of this, I noticed a couple of nice-looking gals entering the courtyard. I even contemplated asking one of them to dance, but wondered if a guy who was still technically married had a right to be flirting with women. I didn't have to ask myself this question for long, as the younger of the two gals suddenly approached my table and asked me. I accepted her invitation without hesitation. We danced, then we talked, then we danced some more. By the time I knew it, we had danced and talked right up till closing time.

Technically married or not technically married, I knew I didn't want the night to end there. At that point, her friend reappeared to ask if she still needed a ride home. Though I was quite rusty with regard to picking up women in bars, I figured this was my "now or never" moment. I turned to my young lady and told her that I'd be very happy to drive her home. At that point, a suspicious look quickly enveloped her face, and she smiled nervously. "Oh no. No, No, No," she replied while shaking her head. And with that, she said goodnight and quickly headed off. On the one hand, I was somewhat relieved that my decision to dive back into the single world didn't have to take place on that particular night. But if we're being honest, I'd have to say that I was far more disappointed that things didn't get more passionate with the pretty cantina gal.

When I look back, I often wonder about the significance of that evening. Had things gone in a different direction, it could well have been a turning point. Perhaps it would have brought a new sense of confidence regarding my appeal to the ladies. No doubt it also might have been a source of closure with regard to my failed marriage. More importantly, it might have given me the strength to realize that the single life is not such a dreaded thing after all. And that waiting for the right person was a much better idea than just settling for the first one that came along. To state it in more global terms, it's better to make good decisions instead of bad ones. But to make good decisions, one has to feel genuinely good about themselves. I wasn't quite there yet.

XL
Meet the Neighbors

My new neighbors in that Dallas apartment complex all seemed to have one thing in common. The place where they were from far outshone the place they were now. None of them seemed very happy that they somehow wound up in this particular part of the world. They griped continuously about the lack of hills and greenery, the dry and hot weather, and the flat lifeless landscape. Not that they didn't have a point, but the fact of the matter was that they were where they were. I wondered why they couldn't just stop griping and make the best of it. I guess that's the advantage of being from a place you're dying to leave. Any place seems like an improvement (at least in the short term).

Take the case of discontented couple number one, Matt and Billie Hailey. I don't recall from where Billie originally hailed, but Matt was from Birmingham, Alabama. You never met a fellow in your life who was more proud to be from Birmingham, Alabama than was Matt Hailey. He talked about the place like it was heaven on earth. And woe to him that his company transferred him to their miserable Dallas, TX branch. If only he could have remained in Birmingham, he would have been the happiest guy on the face of the earth. Damned his bad luck, but he was now doomed to live this portion of his life in this God-forsaken region.

Matt expressed this sentiment so many times that it got old in a big hurry. As for me, I was pretty excited about starting over in a new place. Matt was bringing me down. Aside from his constant issue with Dallas, he was the kind of guy who talked your ear off (and always about himself). "I'm doing this, I've done that, I think this, I think that." On and on with no break. In fact, when Matt began pontificating, you quickly became trapped with little chance of escape. As there was no opportunity to get a word in, you simply had to hang in there as best you could, while trying to summon any possible excuse to make your exit.

I seriously wondered if Matt had any notion as to how people felt when he cornered them for hours on end while subjecting them to his endless ramblings. We were neighbors, however, so I tried to be as cordial as possible. His wife, on the other hand, was a thoroughly wonderful and altogether pleasant person. Genuine as the day is long, ultra-friendly, and extremely personable, you could not help but take to Billie.

It was certainly no secret that Matt enjoyed a drink or two after work, and his drink of choice was George Dickel Whiskey. I'd almost always see him sipping his whiskey on the rocks in the late afternoon when his day's work was done. And if you happened to be coming along, he was certainly more than happy to offer you one as well. Matt had an interesting way of asking Billie to refill his glass when it became empty. He'd thrust his outstretched arm toward her with the whiskey glass in his hand, while snapping his fingers in rapid succession. Why Billie put up with this I could not say, but she knew it was the signal to provide her husband with a refill. She came running every time he stretched and snapped. I think they both thought it was funny.

Not being a whiskey man at that time, I'd usually sip a can of beer while he extolled his great tales. The beer was the only thing that enabled me to stand there listening to Matt drone on endlessly. When I had finally downed my one can, I'd make my excuse and head back home. I never really understood the true extent of Matt's drinking until the couple invited me to dinner one night. The thought of being in close confines with Matt for an extended period of time was a daunting prospect indeed, but I figured Billie would be pleasant company. And what the heck, it was a free spaghetti dinner.

As it turned out, I needn't have worried about being driven insane by Matt's monotonous droning. By the time dinner was ready, Matt had already passed out in his recliner chair. I don't know how many whiskeys it took to put Matt's lights out that night, but the guy was completely unconscious. He never made it to dinner. When Billie was serving up the grub, I asked if we should rouse Matt to the table. She very calmly told me it was best to just leave him there. He'd rouse himself eventually, and the spaghetti would be saved as leftovers if he eventually wanted it. To me, this seemed a very strange way to live, but Billie was quite familiar with the routine by now. The two of us enjoyed our spaghetti dinner with Matt snoring conspicuously from the living room. I conversed a bit with Billie after the meal, then thanked her for the grub and a pleasant evening. Matt was never conscious again until the next morning.

The drinking was just one of several intimate details I was to discover about Matt and his relationship with his wife. The second aspect came as a result of a disastrous plane crash that occurred at the Dallas/Fort Worth Airport that year. Many people will probably remember this tragic incident where wind shear caused the plane to completely miss the runway in a failed attempt to land safely. It was a horrible crash with serious loss of life. Long story short, Billie was convinced that this was indeed Matt's return flight from his latest business trip to Florida. As part of his job, Matt was often flying back and forth to Lakeland, Florida. This plane had taken off from Fort Lauderdale, with Los Angeles as its final destination. It made one stop in Dallas, which was why it was chosen to be Matt's flight.

For reasons that I don't recall, but luckily enough for Matt, he wound up rescheduling to a later flight. Needless to say, when Billie discovered that Matt was actually not on the ill-fated one, she was absolutely overcome with relief and joy. In fact, her immediate plan was to show her husband just how happy she was to have him home and safe. Suffice to say that her passions were probably running pretty high at that point.

Somewhere around 10:00 that evening, Matt came running over to my apartment with a look of restrained alarm. He was desperately in need of help, as Billie was apparently getting ready to destroy their apartment with a fireplace implement. Perhaps my presence interrupted her frantic outburst, but she quickly got into her car in an effort to seek refuge in a calmer environment. At the same time, I noted Matt sitting alone on his patio with a look of complete misery on his face. Though I wasn't sure if he truly wished to confide in me, I nonetheless took a seat next to him.

It didn't take long to discover the source of his wife's unhappiness. Billie's efforts to initiate intimacy that evening had been met with rejection. Much like Matt's frequent passing out before dinner, this was not a new experience for her. The difference was that she had finally reached the end of her rope. It took a near-death experience to get her there, but she had no doubt arrived at that point. I'm not sure if all the drinking was causing Matt's lack of libido, or the lack of libido was the reason for the drinking. In any case, Matt's solution was simply to decline his wife's sexual advances. As I didn't get the feeling that he was all that comfortable talking about it, I didn't press for specifics. Clearly, the proper husband and wife communication was not taking place, and feelings had reached a critical mass.

I got the final details of their colorful dissolution from a few of our other neighbors. As Matt's company housed several of its employees at that same apartment complex, the list also included Matt's boss. I had met Dan several times and thought he was an entertaining and rather personable fellow. So did Billie. Suffice to say that there was interest on both sides. And as luck would have it, Dan was the guy who decided when and how often Matt needed to be in Lakeland, Florida. And wouldn't you know it, all of a sudden he needed to be there a lot?

It wasn't hard to observe how Billie's good cheer returned in direct proportion to Matt's absences. And while the rest of us surely had our suspicions, given the circumstances, it was hard to find too much fault with Billie. Matt caught on before too long, and the two eventually went their separate ways. I was also to learn that Matt had found my own marital situation quite amusing, most notably the part where Mira took up with Edward (the Brit). What is that expression about people who live in glass houses?

Discontented couple number two was Beau and Janet Smith. They had arrived from northern California (up in the Bay Area). Beau was an aspiring (but yet unlicensed) electrician, who was thankful for the many construction opportunities that Dallas had to offer. While still in his early to mid-thirties, Beau sported the classic male horseshoe hair loss pattern. This was accompanied by a short and neatly trimmed black mustache. Not quite six feet tall and with a stocky physique, he was well equipped for the physical challenges that his labor-intensive job posed. With a happy-go-lucky attitude and a perennial smile, Beau was one of the most jovial and laid-back guys I've ever met.

His wife Janet was the quintessential opposite. Over the past four or five years, she had gained considerable weight. This was obviously something that made her quite self-conscious. Prior to the added girth, however, I have no doubt that she was quite the attractive specimen. I don't recall what kind of work she did, but I'm fairly sure it was office related and clerical in nature. What made Janet truly memorable, however, was the level of pleasure that she derived by making Beau's life as miserable as possible. And toward that end, she was extremely proficient.

To this day I've never met anyone quite like Janet. No matter how much good cheer Beau would bring to the table, she'd do her best to reverse his mood. She'd continue to poke and prod at him until finally succeeding in starting a massive argument. And despite Beau's firmest resolve, he was powerless to evade his wife's constant abuse. In the end, she'd always succeed in turning him into a miserable wreck. For some inexplicable reason, this was her life's goal. It was the kind of marriage you'd observe even for a short time and wonder how in the world these two people could stay together.

One day Beau came running over to my apartment in the early evening with a frantic look on his face. He quickly blurted out that Janet was acting very bizarre. Of course, I wondered how this differed from any other time. On this occasion, however, she was babbling on incoherently with a wild look in her eyes. Except for the expression on Beau's face, my first inclination was, what else is new? Upon quick observation, however, this particular episode was way beyond her usual escapades. She was extremely animated and was having considerable trouble even remaining standing. Beau was frantic as he suspected that she had taken some kind of pills. By the look of things, I was inclined to agree.

    At that point, the two of us hoisted her up and deposited her into Beau's Ford Bronco. While he drove to the Emergency Room of Grapevine Hospital, I stayed and searched their apartment for any signs of empty pill bottles. In fact, I found quite a few when I inspected the bathroom trash. I threw them in my jacket pocket and quickly headed for the hospital to join Beau. I don't recall what kind of drugs they were, or if Janet had even taken them. Whatever she did ingest that evening, however, she was quite fortunate that it wasn't anything life-threatening. Thankfully, it was also not necessary to pump her stomach or perform any similar radical procedures. By the next day, she was back to her old self, albeit quite a bit more humble. She even apologized to me for being such a pain in the neck the night before.

    Though it took a while, the two eventually split. Amazingly enough, they had been married for over ten years. By no means was Beau a saint, but he surely didn't deserve a boat anchor like Janet. I was actually very glad to hear that he was finally rid of her, as I knew he had no chance of happiness as long as she was around. I have no idea what became of my ole buddy Beau, but I'd like to think that his positive spirit and jocular manner enabled him to land in a good place.

    As long as I was now grappling with some major life changes, I figured it was about time to embark upon another one that was probably long overdue. In an effort to kill two birds with one stone, I had asked our divorce attorney if she also handled name changes. Though I will admit that part of the discomfort I felt for my given last name was due to its extreme ethnicity, there was a broader and more accurate explanation.

    Though there is absolutely nothing wrong with the last name of Silverstein, I never really felt that it suited me. For one thing, I'd gotten very comfortable with the stage name I adopted while playing music in New York. My actual middle name was Floyd; thus Gary Floyd was a name I took to right from the start. To my mind, it seemed to represent the person into which I was developing. Gary Floyd was a name that didn't invite assumption or pre-judgment. As such, it made no hint or reference to the past. It represented a new and unique entity, which seemed entirely appropriate for someone who was so eagerly seeking to reinvent himself. It was indeed a very welcome change, and it filled me with a deep sense of promise. A fresh start, so to speak. And having now arrived at such a vital crossroads, what could be more appropriate than that? The requisite legal paperwork was then drawn up, and all was signed off. Just like that, I was a new man. Well, almost.

At that time, the law concerning name changes in Texas required that you go before a judge and explain your reasons. Merely a formality I was told, nonetheless, it was necessary to get the official seal of approval from His Honor. What actually transpired during my brief court appearance that day still gives me a chuckle.

Before entering the courtroom my attorney advised that I was to remain quiet during the proceedings and to let her do all the talking. As I was paying for her services and expertise, I was more than happy to comply. She had typed up a perfectly plausible and well-written explanation in advance and was prepared to deliver it upon the judge's request. After some brief opening statements as to our purpose in court on this day, the judge then directed his inquiry directly to me. "So, why do you want to change your name, Mr. Silverstein," His Honor posed? As my attorney specifically informed me that she would be doing all the talking, I calmly turned to her with complete confidence. And as if her previous directive had never been spoken, she then replied, "Gary, tell the judge why you want to change your name."

And this woman did this kind of work for a living. "Are you freaking kidding me," I now silently pondered. Fortunately, I had the presence of mind to tell my wonderful and highly knowledgeable attorney that I thought she had actually summarized it quite well. At that point, she took the hint and read the contents of her summary to the judge. His honor considered the response for about two seconds, then turned to me and smiled. "Alright, Mr. Floyd. So done." And with that, I was official.

If my father ever had an issue with my name change, he never said so. I've now been Gary Floyd for a lot longer than I was Gary Silverstein. As for my upbringing and official ethnicity, I've never made any mystery of it. And even if I wanted to, it would be a hard thing to conceal, as I constantly draw from my vast repertoire of colorful Yiddish expressions. "Oy," such wonderful expressions!

XLI
I Saw You on the TV

Speaking of Dad once again, it occurs to me that I have two good memories of my father. When he passed away in 2014, my brother asked me to recite some good and positive stories about him (for a video journal that he was preparing). After thoroughly wracking my brain, I came up with the better of my two good memories. I sincerely wish I had more than two, but here is the one I wish to present.

    No one would ever have called me lazy during the early part of my twenties. Having earned a Water Safety Instructor certificate during the summer when I was seventeen, I snagged a cushy weekend lifeguard gig in Brooklyn at a Jewish health club. After that, a similarly cushy gig at a spa in midtown Manhattan. Both jobs required only that I show up and sit at my little table for the duration of the daily swim hours.

    In addition to the lifeguarding, I was also making a little bit of money doing gigs with the band. Courtesy of our crazy drummer's wife (who worked for an advertising agency), we snagged a one-time gig playing on the street one Sunday afternoon. The gig was part of an effort to promote the opening of Yankees manager Billy Martin's new western wear shop. So that weekend's itinerary looked about like this. A gig at the regular Manhattan nightclub on Friday night, bright and early Saturday morning for my lifeguard job, a gig at the same Manhattan club on Saturday night, bright and early Sunday morning at the lifeguard table, street gig in front of Billy Martin's western wear shop on Sunday afternoon (followed by a private gathering also for the Billy Martin opening), and lastly the Sunday night gig at the Manhattan night club. All told, I took in about $500.00 that weekend. Considering we're talking about 1980 or so, that weekend was a slammer.

    As it happened, the Billy Martin western wear thing was a big deal. Anything that Billy Martin did back then was news, so the network television crews were out in mass that day in order to capture it. While my buddy Rod and I were pickin and grinnin, people kept running over to us saying the TV news crews were on hand. So we played our hearts out and mugged for the cameras that afternoon, giving it little thought as the day progressed.

Our evening gig went well, and it was probably about two or three in the morning when I finally made it home. Even though I'd arrive back home totally exhausted after these late sessions, it was my habit to prepare a "midnight snack" before going to bed. Sometimes I'd even break out the pots and pans to prepare my moonlight meal, albeit I'd try to do it as quietly as possible. After all, Mom and Dad were fast asleep down the hall, and I didn't want to risk waking them. Years later I would learn that it wasn't actually the racket I was making in the kitchen that woke them up, but the aroma of the dish I was preparing.

I don't remember if I was actually cooking something elaborate on this particular night, or just fixing a sandwich. All of a sudden, however, out of the corner of my eye I noticed my dad coming into the kitchen. My immediate thought was that his confronting me at two or three in the morning on a Sunday night couldn't possibly be good. Obviously, he was upset about something, most likely having been rudely awakened in the dead of the night by my inconsiderate kitchen rattling. With humble apology at the ready, I prepared for his approach.

Instead of an angry accusation, however, I was absolutely flabbergasted when his face suddenly broke into a smile. I'm not sure if this worried me more than a galled expression, but in a startlingly proud voice he simply said, "I saw you on the TV tonight." As it was the last thing I actually expected him to say, it took me a few seconds to collect myself. I replied that I was glad he saw me, as we had been told that the TV camera crews were on hand. Again he said, *"Yeah, I saw you on the TV."* And with that, he slowly sauntered back to bed.

Suffice to say that Dad was in no way a "night owl." He must have willed himself to stay up until I got home that night. I know that couldn't have been easy for him, and for that reason, I was quite touched. It was the first and last time I was ever on network television, but it provided me with one of the few fond memories I have of Dad. I truly wish there were more.

XLII
Mr. Two Face

At the ripe old age of twenty-six, there were some definite changes on the horizon. Although the dissolution of my marriage was now a done deal, I was now at odds with my current employer, and I was getting good and sick of Dallas. Clearly, it was time to clean house. Next order of business, find a new job (and find it in a place where I might actually like to live).

At first, I believed this task would be quickly achieved. While still working for Norm, I met a man who worked for another industry distributor. A similar operation as the company in Texas, but much better run and with a much better industry reputation. The fellow that I had met back in Brooklyn was an important man with this Los Angeles based distributor, and had a fair amount of influence with the top brass. Coupled with Norm's recommendation, it seemed I was a shoo-in for a post that was now vacant in the San Francisco Bay area. And although I was indeed on a very short list of applicants, I was soon to find out that my new friend and benefactor had more than one face.

Though my territory would be the "Bay Area," the William B. Dorsett Company was actually headquartered in Los Angeles. As I'd soon be working for these folks, I figured it would be a good idea to meet the top guys as soon as possible. And as luck would have it, the biggest industry trade show of the year was coming up shortly in Indianapolis.

Upon perusing my handy United States Atlas, I discovered that the driving time from Dallas to Indianapolis was about thirteen hours. I had nothing much to do at the time anyway, as I had parted ways with my Dallas employer by then. After what the branch manager said to me, I simply found it impossible to continue working for him any longer. He said, "You're fired." In all honesty, there was never a job I regretted losing less than that one. It actually came as a tremendous relief, and I never sweated it for a moment. And when the entire outfit went out of business only a couple of years later, it came as a surprise to no one.

At any rate, I packed a bag, jumped in the car, and headed off to

256 Whataya Gonna Do?

Indiana. As it turned out, this was probably one of the wisest decisions I've ever made. I strolled into the Screen Printing Association (SPA) Show on the opening day and headed directly for the William B. Dorsett booth. Almost immediately upon arriving, I met Mr. Gregory Dorsett himself. Gregg had taken over the company from his father (William), who had started it somewhere back in the 1940s. William was an old man by then, and Gregg had assumed the reins about twenty years prior.

Somewhere in his late fifties, I found Gregg to be a most personable, easy-going, and very friendly individual. Upon introducing myself, he extended a very warm greeting. He then acknowledged that he'd heard my name bandied about in connection with the Bay area post. Gregg made a very positive impression on me right from the start. He was a "no-b.s." kind of guy and seemed as genuine as the day is long. Looking back, I'm fairly certain I made a very similar impression on him. During our brief conversation, he kept looking around in search of his partner. Tim Jameson was the Vice President of the company and was pretty much responsible for the day-to-day operations. As such, Gregg was very much hoping that I'd be able to meet Tim, whose input as to my future would no doubt be of importance.

I could probably write an entire book on Tim Jameson, as he was one of the most influential and driven businessmen I've ever met in my life. As such, he was also one of the busiest. Apparently, he was already buzzing around the floor of the show like a hornet at the time. Luckily, he happened by the booth toward the tail end of my conversation with Gregg. When he did so, Gregg quickly snagged him and said, "This is Gary Floyd from Texas. He's the one we were thinking about for the Bay area territory."

Though Tim had very little time before he needed to be somewhere else, he smiled warmly and told me that he also knew who I was. I guess you could say that he conducted one of the quickest interviews of all time. His only question was, "Would you rather work in the San Francisco area or in L.A.?" Since I was still thinking about the Bay area territory at that moment, I answered that this would be my preference. Just to hedge my bet, however, I also told him that I was extremely flexible. And with that, he said "Okay," before quickly heading off. I thanked Gregg for his time and told him it had been a pleasure. I then utilized my remaining time in Indianapolis to take in the rest of the show.

During the long drive back to Dallas, I enjoyed a feeling of genuine accomplishment. I drove with the pride and confidence of a man who had just secured his next place of employment. I was excited at the prospect of moving to San Francisco, as I've always heard that it was a wonderful city. As I strolled triumphantly into my Dallas apartment, I noticed the green light flashing on my answering machine. (For the younger folks who may never have experienced a telephone answering machine, this of course meant that there were phone messages). After listening to one or two that weren't particularly important, the voice of the two-faced rep (the guy in charge of getting me the Bay Area job) came on the line. "I know I promised you the job" he began, "but there's been a change and I filled it with someone else." He wished me good luck in my search, and quickly signed off.

So much for the feeling of accomplishment and triumph. As you can imagine, this was not exactly the news I wanted to hear immediately upon my return. Ah well. Nothing is ever a done deal until it is. I was later to learn that Mr. Two Face had indeed given the job to someone else. But not just anyone else. He gave it to his nephew. Seems to me that expression about blood being thicker than water may apply here. Life is so full of irony. In the end, the nephew actually held the job for about a month or so. During that time he snagged what he thought was an even better job, and soon exited the company completely.

All of this was neither here nor there, as it turned out. Not long after Mr. Two Face's phone message, I received a call from Tim Jameson. He was every bit as succinct on the telephone as he was in person. "There's a job available in L.A. Do you want it?" "Yes," I replied. And with that, I was back in my car again. This time it was the start of my journey to Los Angeles.

I arrived the day before my meetings with Tim and Gregg and set myself up at the Comfort Inn in Glendale. Early the following morning I made my way to the Harbor Freeway and headed the twenty miles or so south to Gardena. The headquarters of the William B. Dorsett Company was a busy place indeed. Though not massive by any means, the office area contained about twenty desks with people hard at work and phones ringing constantly.

Toward the back were the private offices of the company's top officials including Tim and Gregg, as well as a company controller. An accounting area separated off to the left into a smaller room, also toward the rear. Just beyond this accounting area (and further toward the left) was another room where accounting functions were also being carried out. This room had an entirely different look than the first one. To step into this room was to be transported back in time about fifty years. Men wearing plain white dress shirts and black slacks (while also sporting visors), toiled with antediluvian office machines that looked like they should have been in a museum.

My favorites were the large adding machines with the old-fashioned "typewriter-style" buttons, and the large crank on the right side. The worker's fingers danced quickly and expertly all over those keys, "chick, chick, chick, chick." Then the crank was activated with a large mechanical Clang. At that point, the big roll of paper advanced, and the rapid "chick, chick, chick, chick" would begin again. Though computers for office use were indeed making their way into smaller companies by this point, this room contained nary a one. Even the desks were of old-style wooden construction, with ink blotters and fountain pens. Another experience where I expected to see Rod Serling.

    As he was now back in his own domain, Tim greeted me much more casually and with far greater purpose. This is not to say that people weren't constantly popping into his office, or that he wasn't continually being barraged with phone calls, but clearly his purpose was to spend some time orienting me as to my role in the organization. As he escorted me from desk to desk making introductions, the crew was mostly polite, congenial, and professional. That is until we got to the desk of the office manager, Ms. Marcia DeLuca.

    For some reason, this middle-aged lady had an attitude about a mile long, with a chip on her shoulder to match. I don't think I've ever been greeted with such cold and callous indifference. "This is Gary Floyd. He's going to be a new sales rep," Tim proudly announced. At first, Marcia pretended that she was too busy to even have heard what Tim just said. The look on her face portrayed that it wasn't all that important to her anyway. As I stood there waiting for her Royal Highness to acknowledge my presence, I wondered why she was going so far out of her way to make me feel unwelcome. Even Tim seemed a bit embarrassed by her behavior. After much hemming and hawing, she finally turned toward us. With a great deal of effort, she then uttered, "Yeah, alright. Fine." Clearly, Ms. DeLuca couldn't care less about my joining the company and wished to make this quite clear right from the start. Oh well, there's always one.

    After all the introductions had been made, and a tour of the facility was conducted, we returned to Tim's office to discuss my moving plans and official first day of work. Although Tim offered to pay for a moving company to pack up all my Dallas possessions and transport them to L.A., I politely explained that it would probably be easier to return to Dallas and handle things myself. Although his offer was quite genuine, I'm sure his underlying purpose was to get me up and going in L.A. as quickly as possible.

    It was all a new adventure for me at that point anyway, and I didn't mind having to make another round-trip drive between Dallas and L.A. That would give me some time to mull the whole business over anyway, which seemed a better plan than immediate and total immersion. By the time it was all said and done, I believe I arrived for work in L.A. two weeks later.

XLIII
So What Made This Guy a Bad Husband?

When I first rolled into my new apartment complex in Van Nuys at about 7:00 at night, I wondered how in the world I was going to single-handedly unpack all my worldly possessions from the back of my Toyota pickup truck. As I stood pondering, a pleasant looking young man happened to emerge from the front gate of the building. Upon spotting me standing at the rear of a fully loaded pickup truck, he quickly introduced himself and asked if I could use some help. His name was Whooton (I can't be certain of the spelling), and he was the very first Iranian person I'd ever met.

A thin and athletic fellow approximately my own age, he wore studious looking glasses and was dressed in jeans and a casual button-down shirt. Quite taken aback by his unsolicited and completely unexpected offer, I accepted with much appreciation. As we transported my belongings for the next hour or so, Whooton explained to me that he and his wife had lived in the apartment complex for a year or so. It was obvious to me that he was an educated man, and that helping out a fellow apartment dweller was an innate part of his character. I'm not sure how long he'd been living in the U.S., but his English was excellent, showing only trace elements of his former Iranian upbringing.

After we finished moving all my worldly goods, he introduced me to his wife (whose name I can no longer recall), and I believe they offered me a cup of tea. His wife was every bit as nice and personable as he was. Though I offered, they certainly would take no money from me for the moving efforts. The three of us hit it off instantly and we remained friends throughout the remainder of my time at that apartment complex.

My arrival in L.A. was in late December of 1985 (just prior to the New Year). When New Year's Eve quickly rolled around, I knew almost no one except for my two new Iranian friends. There were parties going on in many of the apartments all around me, and I could hear music and revelry coming from all sides. That night I prepared dinner for myself and relaxed into my soft white rocker recliner chair while watching TV. I was feeling quite out of sorts being in yet another strange new place and not really knowing a soul. I don't know what time it was when I conked out in my chair that New Year's Eve, but I must have been out for quite a while.

When I ran into Whooton the next day, he told me he'd come down to invite me over, but noticed I was fast asleep in my chair. I had to chuckle, as there was no doubt I had been dead to the world. I was quite touched, however, that they were thinking of me. Unfortunately, I lost track of Mr. and Ms. Whooton when I left the apartment to buy a condo a couple of years later. Thoroughly nice folks and I'll never forget their kindness and friendship.

Aside from getting acclimated to work, I made it a priority to get out and meet some new folks. I got hold of the local San Fernando Valley newspaper and noticed an ongoing classical music event that took place at a private residence on Saturday nights. I believe the lady (who hosted this weekly event at her home) charged five bucks a head, which included snacks and wine. Not only was it a good time, but the musicianship was often excellent.

About twenty chairs were set up in a large living room which also housed a grand piano. The style of music varied on a week-to-week basis. One night could feature a solo performer on the piano, while other times it was a chamber group or even a gypsy style guitar band. In addition to the main performance, there was a social hour (or two) where we could just mix and mingle with one another. One of the women (who was a regular in the group) would often play the piano, and the rest of us would gather round and sing along. For a guy who was new in town and didn't know anyone, it was a good time and a great way to meet some new folks. Not to mention that many of these new folks were ladies.

On my first evening with this group (which wasn't long after I arrived in L.A). I met a young lady named Evyonne. Though about five or six years my senior, Evyonne was very friendly and a lot of fun to talk to. As it turned out, her marital situation was not that different from my own. At the age of thirty-three or so, she was currently in the process of getting divorced. She had been with her husband for about thirteen years and was now claiming irreconcilable differences. Evyonne was quite good-looking and had a pretty decent figure. Shoulder length brown hair complemented her smooth features, and a welcoming smile usually adorned her face. She also had an engaging sense of humor and loved to laugh. Needless to say, she captured my attention. As it turned out, she was a close friend of the gal that played the piano. Following the group meeting that night, Evyonne and I went for a drink. We talked and laughed for another hour or two before exchanging phone numbers and saying goodnight. Before parting ways, however, I was treated to quite the romantic kiss. It had been a good night indeed.

For the next six months, I was getting everything from a relationship that my marriage had failed to provide. Evyonne was always good company. We did exciting things together and got along just famously. As far as the physical part was concerned, let's just say that it was everything I could have wanted and then some. As my buddy here in Seattle likes to say, that blinking red light of desperation on my forehead had finally been extinguished (thanks to Evyonne).

I know it's a very male philosophy, but I recall walking into my health club and thinking how envious all these other guys would be if they knew what kind of sex life I was now enjoying. Perhaps it's also the philosophy of your typical single male in their twenties, thirties, or forties. Call it shallow or juvenile, but a great sex life does put a certain spring in your step. I'm sure this is quite true for the ladies as well, though society often dictates a certain discretion with regard to the fairer sex.

As with all relationships, everything is wonderful and exciting in the beginning. Your new partner seems absolutely perfect and all is bliss. After a few months tick by, however, slowly but surely you start to see some of the stuff that lies just below the outer veneer. If you're lucky, these more inner components are just the typical everyday traits and feelings with which we all grapple. Those annoying little imperfections and experiential baggage that serve only to make us human.

If we're not so lucky, however, then what lies below the surface needs to be examined with great care. At first glance, some of these things may seem irrelevant or unimportant, especially if we're caught up in the excitement of the relationship. Even so, it is wise to note them for future reference. At some point down the line, they may indeed be valuable clues as to behavior that may prove problematic.

One such red flag that popped up along the way with Evyonne involved a visit to her mother's house. Her parents had been divorced for a number of years and this was to be my introduction to Mom. Not long after entering this very typical suburban L.A. "ranch-style" home, I noticed an unsightly collection of old wooden boards, nails, sawdust, and other debris scattered in a large pile on the way to the living room. The ceiling just above was in shambles and this section of the house was in complete disarray. Mom was friendly enough as she introduced herself and showed us around, seeming completely oblivious to the unmitigated mess that was plainly evident.

I have met my share of people who were embarrassed if a piece of furniture in their home hadn't been dusted, a section of the carpet seemed worn, or if a bed hadn't been made. I've seen these people apologize profusely for such minor household imperfections. But here was Evyonne's mom playing host to her daughter (as well as her daughter's new boyfriend), without a care in the world as to the chaotic state of her home. Naturally, I didn't say anything about it while Mom was present. But on the way home in the car, I asked Evyonne what was up with the big pile of junk near the living room. In addition to being extremely non-photogenic, I'm sure it also didn't make for a very healthy environment.

Evyonne replied that the house had been like that for the last ten or fifteen years. Absolutely astonished, I said, "You mean to tell me she's been living like that for ten or fifteen years?" Evyonne explained that Mom had begun a remodeling project all those years ago, but never bothered to complete it. Making all possible allowances for the fact that the remodeling money could have dried up, or any number of other circumstances that may have occurred, it was still hard to get a beat on this situation. Even if things were tight, and the completion of the remodel was out of the question, at no time could she possibly have just cleaned up the mess? In ten or fifteen years she couldn't have invested an hour or two to throw out the old boards, clear away the debris, and vacuum up the floor?

I wondered if instead, she was preserving it as some kind of a shrine. A shrine to what, I couldn't say. Perhaps to the end of her marriage or to a happy home. Or perhaps it represented a point of immobilization. A situation that was simply too grim to face, thus a complete denial of its existence. In any case, it left me wondering if this woman was in some sort of crisis. The big ugly pile of rubbish seemed an obvious cry for help. A cry that seemed to go unanswered. A woman who was remodeling while living in ruins, with no foreseeable end in sight.

Though Evyonne complained bitterly and frequently about her soon-to-be ex-husband John, I must admit I was at a loss to understand just what crime (or crimes) he had committed. He worked hard, was an expert in his field, and brought home a very respectable paycheck. He seemed a devoted family man and spent quality time with his wife and son. He certainly wasn't the philandering type and didn't seem to have any harmful vices of any kind.

According to Evyonne, everything John attempted, he achieved with excellence. He wasn't abusive in any manner and was liked by everyone whose path he crossed. I've never received such excellent references from a wife who was so adamant about dumping her husband. In fact, the only thing John ever seemed guilty of was being too darned perfect. I've heard a lot of rotten stories about a lot of rotten spouses in my day, but John always sounded like the model husband. And let us keep in mind that the source of my opinion came from the wife that couldn't wait to be shed of him. There was no doubt that Evyonne wanted out, but her reasoning simply wasn't adding up.

And just because John wasn't the philandering type, this was not to say that Evyonne was of similar spirit. Perhaps the most concerning aspect of the woman came when she described the affairs that she'd had while married to John. (Yes "affairs," meaning more than one). Bearing in mind that Evyonne and I were dating at the time, these stories were of considerable import to me.

Though her infidelity bothered me, I was determined to give her the benefit of the doubt. I had just gotten out of a very unfulfilling marriage myself. And as such, I was certainly aware that there is often much reason to seek love and affection elsewhere when you're not getting it at home. So I asked if she started having the affairs when the marriage began going downhill. And though I had to respect her honest reply, I was shocked to hear that she was having them even when times were good. Once again, this just didn't compute. I thought of her poor shlub husband at that point, who probably wasn't even aware of his wife's cheating ways.

I've never been much of a poker player, so I'm sure that the disappointment must have shone clearly on my face. There are things you can live with (and possibly work around), and then there are game-changers. This was clearly the latter. To this day I have never had to face the situation of finding out that my beloved partner had been unfaithful. I thank God for that, as I'm sure it would be a terrible blow for me. Evyonne deduced my attitude on this subject immediately, and it was the beginning of the end for us. Although we continued to date for another month or two, she eventually went on to greener pastures in the form of an old boyfriend. And much like the case with Mira, she married the ex-bough not long after we parted company. And also just like Mira, I believe the two are still married to this day.

In the final analysis, I'm not sure whether Evyonne constituted a good decision or a bad one. Our brief association gave me some much needed comfort and confidence, but it was hard when it ended. In her mind, it was to be nothing more than a transitional relationship right from the start (much like the three or four others she'd had before I came along). Perhaps if I had held it in similar regard, things would have been a lot easier for me.

This experience did serve to teach me a valuable lesson about myself, however. Apparently, I wasn't the kind of person who was capable of casual and intentionally short-term relationships. Not that there is anything wrong with this particular modus operandi, but it is important that both parties are on board with the concept. In real life, I think this is actually quite rare. More often than not there's the one who's treating it casually, and the one who's getting much more heavily invested. As such, the latter party usually feels manipulated and exits with hurt feelings. To avoid similar pitfalls in the future, I would need to vet my potential partners a bit more thoroughly. It was a hard lesson at the time, but perhaps it was the start of better decisions to come.

XLIV
The Joanne Sessions

About my new job, suffice to say that I wasn't exactly bursting from the starting gate. As is very typical of an outside sales job, we had monthly quotas to meet. Unfortunately, I was getting off to a rather slow start. The company believed that a salesman's income should be the direct result of his or her own efforts. In other words, if we sold a lot of stuff we'd make decent money. If we didn't sell much, we probably didn't have much of a future with the company.

For the first time in my sales career, I received almost no salary at all. I was given a $350.00 per month car allowance, and the company paid for half of my auto insurance. They also picked up fifty percent of my total gasoline tab, and happily reimbursed me for any meals with clients. Other than that, my income was based solely on commission. I received 3% on everything I sold.

For the first three or four months, I probably didn't even make enough to cover state and federal taxes. I knew that they probably wouldn't have kept me on the payroll (such as it was) for too long, were this to continue. As such, these first several months were an anxious time indeed. Fortunately, I began to hit my stride around month number five or so, and things started to take off nicely from there. Unlike the Dallas company, I was not penalized for the beginning months when I fell short of quota. This enabled me to gather a goodly amount of momentum.

I would say that the most fun I've ever had as a salesperson was when the "Gerber 4B" was introduced into the marketplace. The Gerber 4B was a compact computerized machine that electronically produced signage and graphics for advertising and promotional purposes. Slightly larger than an IBM typewriter, the 4B sat on a desk or countertop. It featured a keyboard and small LED screen at the front, with steel rollers that supported the vinyl material at the back. The leading end of the vinyl was fed into the mid-section via sprockets, where it advanced in accordance with the pace of the machine. The operator entered the design that was to be produced into the 4B's memory via the keyboard.

There were controls for changing the font size, the actual fonts themselves, some special effects (italics, underlining, etc)., and some basic alignment characteristics. A thin and very precisely machined knife blade was positioned just above the vinyl material. As the vinyl quickly advanced through the machine, the knife blade would bob up and down while maneuvering from side to side. This enabled the 4B to make very quick and precise cuts to the vinyl, thus producing elements of all shapes and sizes.

Although extremely primitive by today's standards, this unit was revolutionary back in 1986. It was the first such machine of its kind, and it took the industry by storm. Before the Gerber 4B came along, it was very typical for a sign shop to have a number of skilled workers cutting large sheets of material completely by hand. These people were practically artists and possessed a level of accuracy and precision that was startling. Not only did they have to cut the letters and shapes to exactly the right size and with extreme precision, but they had to do it with such consistency that the end result was perfectly congruent.

As skilled tradesmen, however, they were also paid in accordance with their expertise. Worst of all for the shop owners, they took lunch breaks, went home at the end of their eight-hour shift, incurred occasional sick days, and took vacations every now and then. The Gerber 4B had no such requirements. And best of all, it was no longer necessary to hire skilled tradesmen.

Anyone could program a Gerber 4B and it would produce perfect results every time. You could even program it at the end of the day, and it would run during the evening while you weren't even there. Compact enough to easily fit into the trunk of a car, and with a starting price tag of ten grand, it was a salesmen's dream come true. As long as you vetted the customer properly, all you had to do was plop it on a convenient bench or table and turn it on. At the conclusion of just such a quick and dirty demonstration, it was fun to see the look of astonishment and sheer joy settle on the customer's face. More often than not, they would tell me to leave it right where it was, and they'd rustle up the ten grand somehow.

The Gerber 4B was a game-changer, and all the sign producers knew it. And if your competitor down the street bought one, you damn well better get one too if you had any hope of competing with him. It was the first and only time I've even been involved in an industry where technology was about to change the old ways forever. Not only was it a wonderful feeling to have a product that turned people's heads so dramatically, but it also didn't hurt my bank account either. With the Gerber 4B in my arsenal, I could typically count on an extra thirty to forty grand a month in sales (over and above everything else I sold).

Unfortunately, the Gerber party was over almost as quickly as it began. While I was a thoroughly happy camper, my boss was not nearly as enthusiastic. Like most money-making ventures, there's always a hitch. The Gerber Corporation had a nasty habit of setting up multiple dealers within each geographical territory. And in the Los Angeles area, it didn't take long before I was competing with several other players for the 4B business. This made the customers happy because competition among the dealers resulted in deep discounts for them. It also made Gerber very happy since more and more machines were being sold. It made the dealers very unhappy, however, as we were all suddenly thrust into a price war in order to maintain control of market share. Gerber knew that this would weed out some of the smaller dealers, but as long as they continued to sell machines, they couldn't have cared less. My bosses quickly said the hell with it, however. And just like that, we were out of the Gerber business. Ah, but it was fun while it lasted.

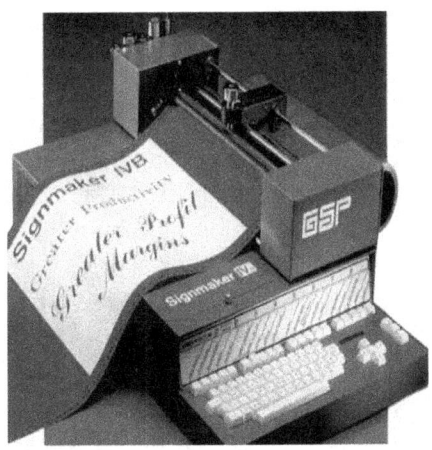

I was finally beginning to relax a bit, as business was now looking up and my income prospects were becoming more and more favorable. It was at this point that I made one of the best decisions of my entire life.

I met Joanne Bergman at a two-day workshop she was giving on self-improvement. Though I wasn't aware at the time, this was how therapists rustled up quite a bit of their business. A high-spirited woman in her early to mid-fifties, Joanne had a natural ability to make people feel comfortable and at ease. I think this was due to the fact that she also came across as extremely real and genuine. Among her many talents was the ability to take the time to truly listen to what you had to say. Then and only then would she render any advice or opinions. And more often than not, when she finally did offer counsel, it made a great deal of sense.

Perhaps her greatest virtue was the sheer joy she derived in knowing that she was truly helping you. She was not afraid to tell you what she was really thinking, even if it wasn't exactly what you wanted to hear. But in not pulling her punches or sugarcoating her message, she was never unkind. There was something that just emanated from this woman such that you knew she always had your best interests at heart. And if her counsel resulted in a marked improvement to your life, she was absolutely over the moon.

Upon establishing a weekly counseling session with Joanne, it didn't take long for me to trust her implicitly. Every week I looked forward to my time with her, and every week she gave me something new to think about. I always left her office in a much better mood than I had upon arrival, and with a much brighter outlook toward the future.

One of the most valuable tools that Joanne bestowed upon me was the proper way to approach interpersonal conflict. While most people shy away from confrontation altogether, Joanne taught me that it could be dealt with in a positive light. And as conflict is pretty much a guarantee in life, this is a useful skill indeed.

It's not easy to go from someone who avoids confrontation at any cost, to someone willing to approach it head-on. With the right tools in your arsenal, however, it's amazing how your level of confidence will rise to the challenge. And as it turns out, the technique is actually quite simple. The key is to approach the issue from the standpoint of personal feelings. It starts with a simple statement beginning with, "I feel _____." The blank is filled in with whatever emotion the person's comments or actions are having on you. As an example, "I feel devalued when I reach out to a new co-worker, and I don't feel acknowledged in return." Or "I feel angry when my opinions don't seem to be taken into account."

While no system is full-proof, it's much harder to argue with the way someone is feeling, as opposed to having been accused of wrongdoing. In the first example above, it's very tempting to accuse your co-worker of having treated you with malice and disregard. "I introduced myself as one colleague to another, and you completely disregarded me." Worded that way, you can almost certainly expect an angry retort and probable hard feelings. And the statement, "You completely disregarded me" is both inflammatory as well as easily arguable.

On the other hand, "I feel devalued" is a very hard statement with which to argue or disagree. If you feel "devalued" or you feel "angry," how can I possibly argue that you don't feel that way? At any rate, this approach makes your antagonist stand up and take notice. After all, life frequently presents those who try to exercise power through intimidation. Stating your feelings is a great way to show them that you are not intimidated. It also helps get your point across without the need for accusation or harsh judgment. You are also far more likely to receive an apology when the person with whom you are in conflict doesn't feel threatened. It works with co-workers, it works with spouses or significant others, and it works with friends. Does it work all the time? Of course not. If someone is determined to rant and rave, they'll always find an excuse. But for a great many cases, it's a wonderful skill to have. And few folks will ever fault you for trying it. In fact, they probably won't even realize you're doing it.

Naturally, Joanne tried to get me to put this new skill to use as often as possible. As my father usually provided all manner of conflict, this was a prime testing ground. Upon returning from a life-changing vacation to Italy, I was very excited to tell my parents what I had experienced during my two weeks in this enchanting country. An upcoming trip to visit the family in Arizona quickly provided just such an opportunity. As I was enthusiastically extolling the virtues of Venice, Florence, Tuscany, and the Cinque Terra, my dad suddenly and rather impatiently interrupted. "Hey, Gary. Why don't you ever talk about going back to New York?" Although it was very much beside the point, I've always enjoyed my occasional visits to New York as well. But clearly, New York City and Italy are vastly different experiences. More to the point, Dad's dismissive interruption made the definite impression that he was not the least bit interested in my European travels.

Italy was an absolute game-changer for me. I was completely enchanted by the terrain, the architecture, the art, the food, the culture, the music, and the Italian people. At some point in my life, I would probably even enjoy living in Italy. So you can imagine how the wind quickly evacuated from my sails when Dad cut me off in such an uncaring and abrupt manner. The incident left me with a somewhat hopeless feeling. I somehow imagined that talk of my Italian travels would put us on a better plane of understanding. I thought it would provide a much needed bridge to better communication between my father and me. As it turned out, it accomplished neither. If anything, it probably had the opposite effect. In the end, I think Dad interpreted my enthusiasm as boastful, thus his desire to end the conversation as swiftly as possible.

"Hope is a dangerous thing," once again recalling the words of Red in *The Shawshank Redemption*. It gets you thinking that there might be some possibility, then you're completely crushed when you're catapulted back into reality. Nevertheless, I decided to put Joanne's confrontation method to use in this case, as I felt it was necessary to tackle the issue head-on.

Confronting my father about anything was a risky undertaking, but by now I felt pretty confident about my new skills. I think the particular "feeling" I chose, in this case, was, "Sad. Our conversation about Italy left me feeling *sad*, as I think we missed the boat in terms of communication," I thoughtfully explained. With Joanne in mind, that was the best presentation I could come up with. (And personally, I thought it was a pretty good one). Though I don't remember much detail as to where the discussion went from there, I do recall that it did not end positively.

Taking nothing away from Joanne's vast expertise with regard to effective communication, my father was just a particularly challenging case. "What do you mean by missed the boat," he demanded. "Are you saying we're lousy parents?" he further accused. "No," I explained. "I'm saying the conversation left me feeling sad, as I think we missed the boat here."

Looking back, it's funny how Dad used the term "we" with regard to being bad parents. Actually, my mom listened very politely when I spoke about Italy. Never in a million years would she have interrupted with such a flippant response. Be that as it may, we made little progress that afternoon in trying to clear the air about the Italy discussion. In the end, we eventually retreated to our separate corners and let the issue drop. Clearly, no amount of conflict resolution (even from the most positive standpoint) was going to have much of an impact in this case. Much like Vegas or Wall Street, no system is full proof.

Though clearly not a winner in this case, there is certainly a sense of personal satisfaction and fulfillment one gets in just knowing that you tried. As opposed to simply ignoring the situation and letting things fester, you did your best to approach it head-on and in a positive manner. And what more can you do. In that sense, I guess you're a winner either way. The important thing was that Joanne was teaching me to make good decisions. And for the first time in my life, I was now steering in a strong and healthy direction.

I was soon to discover that good decisions beget more good decisions, just as success begets further success. I won't say that each and every subsequent decision was an absolute winner, but I would say that I now clearly understood the difference. And if I was about to make a bad decision, I now had the wisdom and the wherewithal to reverse course. I was discovering that the most important thing in life was to be able to look in the mirror every morning and say, "I like that guy." If I could do that, then I knew I was on the right track. From then on my decisions were based on exactly that criteria. How will it affect the way I feel about the guy I see in the mirror every morning? And from that perspective, the answer was usually pretty clear.

I have pondered many times the course of events that led me to a career as an outside salesman. Although most people would probably have regarded me as pleasant and courteous back in those days, there was still a large part of me that was quite introverted. Perhaps the key was that this was not by choice. In my heart of hearts, I saw myself as an outgoing and gregarious sort, someone who wasn't afraid to mix it up with anyone. At least that is what I aspired to. It was now becoming obvious that the only thing keeping me from attaining this goal was me.

As a little kid, I was outgoing and personable to a fault. Some of the stories of my early school days certainly bear that out. It wasn't until early adolescence that my personality train seemed to come to a screeching halt. But like most things in life, it all comes down to a simple choice. Just because past events had shaped me into someone who was afraid of everyone and everything, by no means did I need to maintain that perspective any longer.

I learned some very hard and valuable lessons from those dark days of painful shyness. I learned that being timid and afraid to approach people leads to a very lonely and isolated existence. Perhaps for a true introvert, this isn't a problem. But for someone who aspires to make genuine interpersonal connections, or establish a healthy sales career, it's a formidable barrier. In fact, in the world of corporate sales, being shy and afraid to approach others is a recipe for certain disaster. So in essence, my newfound career forced my hand with regard to tweaking my personality. And though I was one of the rare salespeople in my field who actually held a college degree, this was indeed the instrument that led to my new career. We never know where our education and experience will eventually take us, but the skills and tools we acquire along the way will often prove invaluable.

During those dark and deeply introverted days, I can tell you for certain that I didn't much appreciate the guy I saw in the mirror every morning. By stark contrast, the guy I see now is often the one telling jokes at a party. During social gatherings, he's regaling people with funny stories from the past. He's also quite willing to approach people he's never met before in a warm and friendly manner. He's even orchestrating his own get-togethers in order to build friendships. He's a warm and genuine guy, in whom people quickly trust and easily confide. And best of all, he's a guy who can quickly navigate beyond the surface level to establish relationships that are truly meaningful. Quite the metamorphosis, even if I do say so myself. And though I'll never cease to be a work in progress, I'm usually quite pleased when I now look at that guy in the mirror.

A long journey begins with a single step, and I believe that Joanne Bergman was the jumping off point for me. For this, I will always be in her debt. Even with the magic of the internet, I haven't been able to locate Joanne at the time of this writing. It is sad to contemplate the very real prospect that she may no longer be with us. She was about fifty-five or so during the time I knew her, and that was a little over thirty years ago at this point. No guarantees in life once we reach our mid-eighties, but I'd like to think she's still out there somewhere. Wherever she is, I have no doubt that she's bestowing warm and positive thoughts on all those fortunate enough to cross her path.

XLV
Enough Ethel Merman Tunes to Last a Lifetime

Of course, there were many people whose paths I crossed during the four years I was to remain in Los Angeles. And concerning the young ladies, my healthy decision-making skills were frequently put to the test. I bumped into Lila not long after I joined a local chapter of the Toastmasters organization. Lila was very bright and impressively educated, but there was something about her that suggested a lack of stability. Going out was actually her idea, thus I admired her forwardness. After the second date, however, that little voice was telling me not to pursue it from a romantic standpoint. We remained friends practically throughout the rest of my time in L.A., which was a perfectly acceptable outcome.

As it turned out, the little voice knew what it was talking about. A couple of years later, Lila wound up marrying another fellow from our Toastmaster group. Suffice to say, things did not go well. The stories of her comings and goings got more and more bizarre, and the couple disintegrated fairly quickly. During their brief tenure, they fought often and grew increasingly distant. Lila rotated through three or four different jobs during this time, while picking up about fifty pounds. In the end, I believe she moved out of the state in pursuit of yet another job (while their divorce was pending). I haven't heard from her since.

The Toastmaster group also produced Marsha. Part of the thinking behind joining this group was the prospect of meeting some eligible women. In that sense, I guess it was working. Marsha was about seven years older than me, which gave me cause for concern right from the start. Nevertheless, I decided to give it a shot. Although she was an extremely nice and genuine gal, she always portrayed a general lack of self-confidence. Given this trait, she picked a rather curious profession. Much like my own livelihood at the time, a realtor needs to personify confidence and self-esteem. Unfortunately, Marsha didn't put forth any such impression. Although she wasn't bad-looking by any stretch, her choice of attire always seemed to cast her in a disappointing light. Perhaps this was in accordance with her level of confidence, but one or two of those "Dress For Success" type books might have gone a long way.

The other "non-commanding" aspect of her personality was her voice. Wispy and a bit on the "mousey" side, it came across as almost apologetic. Not too long into our relationship (and for obvious reasons), Marsha informed me that she carried the Herpes virus. This came about as the result of a short-lived relationship with a man she described as a real jerk. Though I felt bad for her, I was obviously concerned about contracting a disease with such obvious and unpleasant ramifications. Although not fatal, Herpes posed an ongoing danger if you weren't constantly vigilant. In any case, it was a risk I was simply not willing to accept.

She took it pretty hard when I called it quits, but I knew it was the prudent choice. Marsha's real estate career hit the skids not long after, and her finances soon reached the point of crisis. Though we also remained friends throughout my entire L.A. journey, I lost track of her when I eventually moved on. By extreme coincidence, however, Marsha contacted me fairly recently completely out of the blue. After waitressing for a while just to keep the lights burning, she became a substitute teacher. From there she went on to a successful full-time teaching career. Though she never married or had any children, she currently enjoys a very happy and fulfilling retirement. I was delighted to discover that things had worked out in the end.

And just to give the ladies equal time, there were certainly one or two along the way who decided that I wasn't their particular cup of tea. I can recall having a goodly number of "friendly" dates. Dates that were polite and cordial, but didn't amount to anything at all.

In the case of "Dead Head" gal, we never actually got to the date part. For those not familiar, "Dead Head" folks are people who follow The Grateful Dead band almost everywhere they perform. Ms. Dead Head was introduced to me by yet another member of Toastmasters. During our telephone conversations, it quickly became clear that she was a very busy gal indeed. She'd agree to a date, but it would have to be about three or four months into the future. Although I thought this was bizarre and then some, we penciled each other in for about four months down the road. I think I did it mainly as an experiment. I wanted to see how long before our scheduled date it would take her to cancel.

As it turned out her cancellation call provided me with about a week's notice. Although I certainly wasn't holding my breath as to date night with Ms. Dead Head, the experiment was nonetheless entertaining. If you're truly interested in meeting someone, why in the world would you schedule a date so far in advance? I guess she had a full docket when it came to making those Grateful Dead concert dates. I hear she eventually hooked up with Jerry Garcia. Just kidding!

Another thing I did to keep the social fires going was to join a group called the Monday Night Maniacs. This group, consisting mostly of single thirty-somethings, formed as a result of a common membership to the United Methodist Church of Sherman Oaks. Though technically not associated with the church, I'm pretty sure the group's underlying mission was to introduce new members. As the name implied, we met on Monday nights, mostly for conversation and fellowship (whatever that actually means). We discussed all manner of topics, but would usually land somewhere in the neighborhood of Jesus and his teachings. This wasn't a subject with which I was very comfortable at the time, but I did enjoy meeting these colorful new folks.

There were the two Julies (who were best of friends), and for some reason enjoyed singing Ethel Merman tunes on an impromptu basis. Julie Mayor was the older of the two at about age thirty-three or so. Though a humble secretary, Ms. Mayor aspired to be a screenwriter. Her other aspiration was to seek out and marry a well-to-do "fifty-something" man. This second aspiration was in order to achieve the first one. Perhaps due to her extreme animation, I was never able to achieve a normal one-on-one conversation with Julie Mayor. My efforts seemed to have a disquieting effect on her, as she was far more comfortable in her own effervescent world.

Though equally as exuberant, Julie Farr was the more approachable of the two. Unlike her buddy, she was quite capable of relating on a one-on-one basis. At times she would even approach me to initiate conversation. Equally enamored with the entertainment industry (this was L.A. after all), Ms. Farr had already snagged a job as a production assistant on a TV show. I don't think she was getting rich by any means, but she certainly enjoyed her work. Julie Farr was quite a likable gal, especially when she wasn't directly in the company of Julie Mayor.

Another very charming member of the group was a young lady named Ellen. A very slim and attractive gal somewhere in her late twenties, she sported a short blond hairstyle and an ultra-friendly personality. Consistent with the two Julies, she also aspired to a career in show biz. At one point Ellen insisted that I join her in accompanying some of the youth on a weekend outing sponsored by the church. The purpose of this trip was to introduce these young teenagers to the philosophies of Christ and the Methodist church. Not that I knew much about either, but I thought it would give me an opportunity to get to know Ellen a bit better. As she seemed very eager for me to go, I figured who was I to decline such a polite and heartfelt invitation. And like I said, Ellen was kind of cute.

Among the seven or eight of us Monday Night Maniacs, I'd have to say that Ellen was by far the most "Christ-focused" member. During the youth trip, I watched with admiration one day, as she tried to explain her feelings about Jesus and religion to a particularly belligerent young man of about fifteen. Every time her unwilling pupil cracked wise with a question that showed his obvious disdain, she patiently hung in there while providing the best explanation she could summon. Though I must admit I really didn't get the whole Christ/Church thing at that time either, I had to give Ellen an "E" for effort. She believed in what she was doing and tried her best to make a positive impact on this rather distrustful and reticent young man.

Truth be told, I also found Ellen's fervent dedication to her faith a bit intimidating. Though I was soon to become a believer and a church member myself, that time had not yet come. When the second day of the trip rolled around, our cynical young man no longer wished to participate. This being the case, Ellen and I ventured off to a nearby beach where we spent a couple of very pleasant hours conversing and relaxing. I must say I was quite attracted to this kind and very genuine young lady, but the disparity concerning spirituality gave me pause. There was no way to shake the feeling that I'd eventually disappoint her with my lack of faith. On the other hand, she may well have accepted me simply for who I was. Hard to say, as we never pursued it any further.

There was Craig and his wife (whose name I can't recall). Craig was quite theatrical as well. The kind of guy who would have made an excellent game show host or sports announcer. I was told that the couple had divorced at one point, but later remarried. I've known very few people in my travels that have been able to make that work.

One of my favorite Maniacs was Joey Bartelli. Joey had joined the group with his girlfriend Lucinda. Although he made his living at the time as a representative for a cookware line, he was quite the guitar player and a very formidable singer/songwriter. Yet another member of the group that aspired to the limelight.

Our talented little group put on a variety show one Sunday night for the congregation, while also preparing a spaghetti dinner. It was a fun evening consisting of music, skits, and supper, all courtesy of us Maniacs. When asked what form of entertainment I wished to provide, I told them I'd be happy to play a couple of tunes on my fiddle. Joey joined me on the guitar for a version of *Boil The Cabbage*, and the audience was thrilled. Later on, he sang one of his original tunes. He performed it masterfully and I was quite impressed with both his musicianship and vocal ability. Some years later while listening to the "Cool Jazz" station here in Seattle, WA, the host announced that the next tune would be that of Joey Bartelli. He'd made it to the radio waves with a new album that he'd just released. I'm not sure how he's doing now, but I was awful proud of his accomplishment.

Perhaps the Maniac I got to know best was Shari Connelly. Shari was by far the friendliest and most down to earth member of the group. A divorcee in her mid to late thirties, her attitude always seemed a bit contrary to that of your typical churchgoer. Though she attended services regularly and certainly believed in the word, Shari had a naturally flirtatious manner.

Though I would never say she was stuck-up or overly proud, she was good-looking and definitely knew it. In fact, her looks gave her an air of confidence when it came to attracting the opposite sex. It certainly worked on me, and it wasn't long before I called to ask if she wanted to join me for a drink. She accepted without hesitation, and we hit it off pretty quickly. Although we had quite a good time when we got together, I quickly became aware of two pretty good size barriers with regard to forming a romantic partnership. One was that she was about eight years older than me. The other was that she had a young daughter. Given these factors, I planned to keep it friendly and strictly platonic. And though I presumed that she had come to the same conclusion, that proved to be a most incorrect assumption.

One afternoon Shari invited a bunch of us over to her apartment for her birthday brunch. The gathering consisted mainly of fellow Maniacs, including the two Julies (which is where I first heard the Ethel Merman routine). Shortly after all the guests had arrived, Shari asked me to go with her to the supermarket to pick up a few items she needed for the party. I was happy to oblige, so we piled into her broiling hot Volkswagen and headed for the store. On the way back, she turned to me and said that she'd been looking forward to being alone with me all day. As we'd been enjoying our wonderful platonic relationship, I was quite taken aback by her comment. Nevertheless, I put my arm around her and gave her a hug. I figured that was what platonic couples did. The hug then turned into a Hollywood-style romantic kiss, and things got quite passionate for a brief time.

Guests were waiting back at Shari's apartment, however, and it wouldn't do to abandon them. Feeling more than a bit confused, we headed back to the party. Despite getting my fill of Ethyl Merman tunes for the remainder of my lifetime, it was a fun couple of hours and the celebration passed quickly.

One by one the guests thanked their host while making their polite exit. Julie Farr and I were the last remaining guests, and before long Julie politely announced that she had to be going as well. Somehow the thought of being alone again with Shari now made me a bit uncomfortable. "Yup, I guess I'll head off too" I announced, while gallantly offering to walk Julie back to her car. My attempt at not being too obvious must have come off as transparent indeed, as Shari quickly confronted me upon Julie's departure. "Have I done something to make you mad," she implored. "No, not at all" I replied. "It's just that I'm confused. I had no idea you thought of me in that way," I explained.

While I was somewhat confident that my confession would dissuade her, it seemed to have the opposite effect. With her next comments, I quickly went from confused to dumbfounded. "I was hoping we'd become much better friends," she continued. And when I continued to feign ignorance, she was then determined to leave no room for doubt. With an alluring smile, she then confided, "I want to fuck you."

For the first time in my life, I knew how Dustin Hoffman's character must have felt when he encountered Mrs. Robinson. It wasn't that Shari was a married woman, but clearly, we weren't right for one another. It would have been nothing but a short physical tryst, and in the end, I was sure to be the loser. I'm not exactly sure how I extricated myself from the conversation that afternoon, but somehow we did agree to table it. Calmer heads prevailed when next the issue was broached, but I'm happy to say that things never went any further. As for Shari, she seemed to move on in a big hurry. I recall several very enthusiastic suitors during the remaining years of our acquaintance.

Last but certainly not least was the pastor of the Sherman Oaks United Methodist Church, Reverend Chaz Waterston. Chaz rarely attended our Monday Night Maniac meetings, but he would drop by every now and then. On one such evening in which we were graced with his presence, he regaled us with an eerie story that I will never forget.

Before describing this tale, I should say that Chaz was one of the most jovial, easy-going, and fun-loving forty-ish men I've ever met. During some of his more formative years, however, this was not always the case. He described for us a bleak time (in his not too distant past) when all seemed rather grim and hopeless. Knowing Chaz as I did, this was hard to imagine. Nevertheless, he suffered so badly during this dark time, that he made up his mind to take his own life. As his determination in this regard was absolutely steadfast, he planned the whole business out in detail.

After putting his affairs in order, he proceeded to write a note as a final statement to those he was leaving behind. During the course of preparing this grim missive, he received a most unexpected phone call. Determining that it couldn't hurt to answer it, he suddenly found himself in contact with an old, old female school chum. This woman had tracked him down on a whim and chose that particular moment to give him a shout. According to Chaz, this was Divine Intervention. He and his old school lady pal happily spoke for hours, while reminiscing about old times and current ones as well. The conversation went so well that the woman invited him for a drink that same night. As it turned out she lived fairly close by.

Bearing in mind that Chaz's immediate plans for that evening involved blowing his brains out with a handgun, this completely unanticipated blast from the past was quite the turn of events. Chaz now proceeded to the part of the story that truly made my hair stand on end. When the woman asked if he wanted to get together that night, his mind took the following course. He figured he could always blow his brains out after the reunion with his old gal pal, so what difference would a few extra hours make. And so, the two got together for a thoroughly pleasant and very exciting evening. While I'm fairly certain that the topic of Chaz's original plan for that evening never came up during their conversation, I do recall him saying what a wonderful time they had.

I can only imagine that somewhere during the course of this most unexpected reunion, Chaz decided to give life another shot (no pun intended). I guess sometimes in life, timing is everything. Either that or indeed it was Divine Intervention. Call it what you like. If the woman had called even a half-hour later (or chose not to call at all), the story might have had a very different ending.

As it turned out Chaz went on to lead a very happy and fulfilling life, and I have no doubt that he continues to do so to this day. Though the old gal pal didn't turn out to be a permanent connection, he met a wonderful lady at a shopping mall one day. The two fell madly in love and were married not long after. Chaz has influenced countless people in his work as a pastor and derives a tremendous amount of pleasure and fulfillment in so doing. Personally, I always thought he was one hell of a guy. (I suppose in Reverend Waterston's case, he'd be one "heck" of a guy.) Not only didn't Chaz come to an untimely end, but he factors prominently into my life as you will see shortly.

XLVI
Music/Making a Living?

Though my love life wasn't exactly rolling at the conclusion of my first year in L.A., things were going fairly well on a professional level. My efforts in pounding the pavement were beginning to produce dividends, and the sales were starting to mount up. This made both my boss (Tim Jameson) and me pretty happy.

Of all the professional business people I have met in my day, I'd have to say that Tim was by far the most driven. Though many came to the company before him (including some who still worked there), none were able to establish the predominance that Tim achieved. Being in his mentorship for even a short time, it was not hard to see why this was so. In short, Tim would do whatever it took to establish a successful situation. If that meant waking up at four o'clock in the morning in order to meet me at a customer's place in the San Fernando Valley at eight, then that's what he would do. Tim lived all the way down in Orange County. A morning jaunt up my way in the horrendous L.A. traffic could easily take more than two and a half hours.

I was told that his zeal for business often usurped his time with family, but I guess that's what you do if you're determined to rise to the top. Being in the man's presence and experiencing his energy was truly invigorating. It was also fun to see the impact that he made on the customers, many of whom felt honored just to receive a personal visit from him.

Tim was a wealth of knowledge in the particular niche that he carved out for the company. Our claim to fame was a fully automated line of Japanese-made printing equipment that was among the fastest and most productive in the industry. Largely through Tim's efforts, our customers quickly became well aware of this. So much so, that they were willing to part with up to $150,000 for the privilege of owning such a high-end line of equipment. And let us not forget that this was back in the late eighties. I shudder to think what these machines must cost now.

While Tim claimed that he had specially trained salespeople for this elite equipment line, the truth of the matter was that opportunity abounded for any of us with "boots on the ground." If we were able to steer any of our clients in this direction, Tim knew darned well that he'd have to compensate us for it. During my tenure, I introduced several of these high-end printing lines within my customer base. And each time I did, I was compensated handsomely. Not only was it a most lucrative business model, but unlike the Gerber 4B Signmaker machine, my company indeed had an exclusive on this line of equipment. Naturally, this arrangement was orchestrated by none other than Tim Jameson himself. The bottom line was that no one was going to beat us to the punch simply by offering a cheaper price. As I said, there was a reason that Tim rose to the top.

Although I was building a pretty respectable career as a sales guy, the comfort of furthering my bank account was dragging me further and further afield from my love of music. One must realize, however, that being a musician is very much like being an alcoholic. Perhaps it is no coincidence that a lot of musicians are alcoholics. It's something that gets into your blood. Although a recovering alcoholic may think about booze less and less as the years roll by, somehow they're never completely free from the temptation. The same is true for music. You can put it down for years at a stretch, but there's a part of your brain that will always hold it in storage. And like the aroma of a good Scotch, those same old feelings of euphoria can be easily triggered.

I played some music for a brief time while living in Dallas, but certainly not in any kind of serious way. Now here in Los Angeles, I was playing even less. This was despite the fact that musical careers in this vast entertainment capital were being made everywhere I looked. And though my own career was clearly no longer heading in this direction, I'd get a wistful and depressed feeling whenever I ran into people who were still pursuing their musical passions. I'd go into a club and wonder why that wasn't me up on the bandstand. I'd attend a concert and wonder why I wasn't performing as part of the group. During these times I'd have to remind myself that I had purposefully chosen a less risky path. A path that was putting food on the table, a roof over my head, and propagating a net worth statement that was expanding nicely.

Still, it was hard not to be envious of the folks that were getting out there and doing what was truly in their hearts. The really amazing part was that many of these L.A. musicians couldn't hold a candle to the folks I met back in New York. Some of these west coast groups were actually scoring record deals, even though they probably wouldn't have made the first cut back in my old O'Lunney's stomping grounds. Many of these L.A. bands wouldn't have scored a fifty-dollar-a-night gig, let alone a record deal with a notable label. As they say about the Lottery, however, you've got to be in it to win it. Clearly, it was no longer my game, but that's not to say that the thought didn't plague me more than a little.

XLVII
Hey, You Can Meet Women by Going Skiing?

Courtesy of my Toastmaster friend Les, I decided for the first time in my life to take a shot at skiing. Les was a member of a rather upscale health spa in the San Fernando Valley called the Mid Valley Racquet Club. Though my own club was every bit as nice, I noted that Mid Valley's membership dues were about three times what I was paying. Be that as it may, Mid Valley was organizing a ski trip one winter at the Bear Mountain Ski Resort at Big Bear Lake. I decided to sign on as my buddy's guest.

The trip included the bus ride over and back, two nights of boarding at the resort itself, and two full days of fun on the slopes. Another of Les's buddies also joined us, and the three of us shared the one room. While Les and his pal were experts in the sport, I had never been on a pair of skis in my life. I was told, however, that this was of no consequence. The equipment could be easily rented at the facility, and lessons for beginners were readily available. And with that, I decided to take the plunge.

My friends informed me that skiing could get quite chilly, thus a warm ski jacket was an absolute must. Other essential items would include water-proof bib overalls, long john underwear, thick athletic socks, goggles, and sunglasses. It was becoming quite apparent that skiing could also be a rather pricey endeavor. A further investment for the ski rental, as well as the beginner lessons, was also forthcoming. Despite the mounting expense, I armed myself with all the necessary gear and set out for my very first ski adventure.

On day one Les and his pal showed me where the rental area was, then quickly ditched me in pursuit of their favorite black diamond runs. I didn't blame them a bit. As a complete beginner, I surely would have been a thorn in their side. Besides, I was plenty occupied with my first lesson, as well as the subsequent practice on the bunny slope for the remainder of that morning.

By the afternoon it was time for lesson number two. This involved a chairlift ride up the real mountain. Although our instructor chose a particularly easy run, looking down over that awe-inspiring snow-covered mountain left me quivering in my ski boots. "Okay folks, no reason to be scared," our seasoned instructor calmly advised. "Let's just form a line behind me and we're all going to ski down the trail nice and slow." I remember thinking that this guy must be absolutely out of his mind. To me, it seemed like we were on top of Mt. Everest with the trail sloping down at an incredible angle. Was he trying to kill us on our very first time out?

And just like that, our instructor slowly began to glide down the mountain while cutting a wide and sweeping side to side swath. It didn't take long to realize that this slow and calculated serpentine route allowed for a predictable and steady progression down the mountain. Perhaps this guy wasn't crazy after all. The group followed in slow succession, and amazingly enough, we all eventually reached the bottom. With nary a fatality or broken limb among us, we had all lived to tell the tale. Even better was that the original sense of terror had now been abated. We now realized that it was entirely possible to ski down the side of a huge mountain, albeit slowly and carefully.

With the lesson culminating about an hour or so after it began, our lives were now forever changed. I spent the rest of that first afternoon riding up and down the chairlift in an effort to navigate that same snow-covered peak. My first ski day had been an absolute game-changer. As the sun finally began to set on that awesome snow-covered landscape, I was a new man by the time I rejoined my two buddies.

The new ski jacket and long john underwear came in extremely handy on day number two. There was no sun on this day and the temperature had plummeted. Light icy rain accompanied the cloudy skies with intermittent gusty winds. This deterred the ski community not at all, as we were warm enough just as long as we kept moving.

I noticed that most people skied in pairs, thus the chairlifts were quickly loaded two by two. My buddies informed me that the proper etiquette for one person wishing to board the chairlift was to shout "single" when approaching the front of the line. This allows the other solo skiers to board the chairlift as a pair. This isn't an issue when the slopes aren't busy, but loading at least two people per chair is much quicker and far more efficient when the facility is going full steam.

Not wishing to throw a monkey wrench into the machinery, I hollered "single" several times before heading up to the same trail as the previous day. I shared my chair with various people during these rides, at the same time enjoying some polite conversation. On my third or fourth chairlift ride that morning, I was joined by a young lady in white ski attire. Though I couldn't see much of her face (seeing as how it was mostly covered by goggles and a woolen ski hat), I could tell that she was tall and possessing of a rather slim figure. She had a very friendly and outgoing personality, and we talked during the entire time on the chair. By the time we reached the top of the mountain, it was quite clear that we were both very much beginner skiers. When she suggested that we ski together, I was more than happy to oblige.

I was very relieved to see that she was indeed quite the novice, as the two of us exchanged numerous face plants on our various jaunts down the slopes. It was clear that we enjoyed each other's company much beyond that of just plummeting down the mountain together. Her name was Caroline, and just like me, she had also come to the Big Bear Ski Resort with two buddies. Her friends were Louisa and Tyrell, a married couple living in one of southern California's beach communities. Louisa was Caroline's oldest friend, as the two had met as kids growing up in the San Fernando Valley.

Both Louisa and Tyrell were excellent skiers. The difference between Caroline's buddies and mine, however, was that Louisa and Tyrell had no intention of ditching their long-time friend despite the huge disparity in skill level. As such, Caroline was absolutely delighted to let them know that they were now free to go about as they wished. She had met someone of her own ability and was perfectly content to ski with her newfound companion. Needless to say, Louisa and Tyrell were also pleased with this sudden turn of events. They wasted no time heading over to their favorite black diamond runs, where they could truly test out their death-defying skills. A win-win, you might say. Caroline was delighted that she was no longer holding her friends back, the friends were delighted to be skiing in accordance with their abilities, and I certainly wasn't complaining either. We spent the remainder of that morning skiing together as true beginners and having a thoroughly wonderful time.

I thought about taking our time together to the next level when I received what I interpreted to be a telling sign. Caroline explained to me that she and her pals had a lunch date at 1:00. In order to join them, she'd have to break off shortly before then. While I waited for her to forward me an invitation to this luncheon, no such offer came. At that point, I figured I probably shouldn't push it, so I told her that would be fine. Before parting ways, however, she asked if I wanted to continue skiing together after lunch. Hmm. No offer to join her for lunch, but an offer to ski together again afterward? Perhaps I was just overanalyzing the situation, but I took it to mean that she wasn't looking to get involved on too personal a level. If indeed I did want to rejoin her after lunch, the deal was that we'd meet at

288 Whataya Gonna Do?

Chairlift #13 at two o'clock.

Figuring I had little to lose, I headed over to the meeting point at the designated time and found her eagerly awaiting me. We picked up right where we had left off, skiing and talking for the remainder of the afternoon. As the five o'clock hour approached, I once again wrestled with the decision of asking for her phone number. We did have a wonderful time together, but perhaps people wind up skiing together all the time. Perhaps it's just what people do at these places, and I shouldn't make too big of a deal over it. In the end, I told her that it had been a lot of fun, but I needed to get going.

As I headed off to rejoin my group, that little voice inside me was saying that I had just blown a pretty good opportunity. I'd love to say that the little voice made me turn around and come to my senses, but it didn't happen that way. "Stupid, stupid, stupid," is what I kept saying to myself on the long bus ride home. Not only that, but I had caught quite the chill out there on the slopes during that second afternoon. I spent most of the return bus trip sneezing while trying to sleep.

During our conversations that day (between face plants), Caroline had told me where she lived and many other personal bits of information. She told me about her relationship with Louisa and Tyrell, and how those friendships evolved. Apparently, she also told me what she did for a living and where she worked. Though I don't doubt it for a moment, I had absolutely no recollection of her mentioning her job or place of employment. As for me, I explained about Les and the Mid Valley Racquet Club. I told her that I had been Les's guest, which is how the ski trip came about for me. I'm sure I also mentioned being an outside sales rep for a company based in Gardena, as well as many other personal odds and ends.

As it turned out, we lived about fifteen minutes from each other in the San Fernando Valley (even though we met at a ski resort many miles away). Though I'd been a major league boob at the end of our time together that weekend, the wheels of fate were turning.

Unbeknownst to me, Caroline was absolutely crushed when I failed to ask for her phone number at the end of that fateful afternoon. When she returned to work the following Monday, she immediately went into full-blown detective mode. Had my memory been firing on all cylinders, I would easily have recalled that she worked as a Human Resources assistant at Sherman Oaks Hospital. This being her occupation, however, she was quite good at sleuthing people out while obtaining pertinent information.

Remembering that the ski trip was sponsored by the Mid Valley Racquet Club, she put in a call. When a friendly male voice answered, Caroline explained that she was trying to get some information on the ski trip that took place over the weekend. Though this very friendly fellow was all too happy to help, he politely explained that he was not authorized to give out any information concerning the club's members. At Caroline's insistence, and with great trepidation, however, he did confirm that a member named Les took part in the trip. I guess Caroline must have pulled out all the stops at that point, as she explained the true reason for her call. She then pleaded with the health club fellow to see if Les registered a guest on the trip named Gary. Also with great reticence, the young man confirmed this information as well. By the time Caroline asked him for my phone number, he must have just figured "In for a penny, in for a pound." And with that, she now had a way to get back in touch with me if she chose to do so.

I believe it was Tuesday evening when I saw the red light blinking on my answering machine. A somewhat nervous but very pleasant sounding female voice then came across my machine. "This is Caroline. You may recall that we met skiing this past weekend. Could you please give me a call if you have a chance?" Of course I recalled, but I was startled to receive her message. I had no idea how she managed to contact me, as I was sure I didn't leave her nearly enough information to track me down.

As George W. Bush tried so hard to say one day, "Fool me once, shame on you. Fool me twice, shame on me." I had magically been given a second chance, and I wasn't about to let it slide through my fingers this time. I immediately returned her call. When she quickly came on the line, I asked, "If this is *the* Caroline." When I asked how in the world she had gotten my number, she replied that it was a long story. Not leaving anything to chance, I asked if she wanted to get together. "Yes," she replied. "That was kinda the idea." I figured the detective story would make good conversation for our first actual date.

Our actual first date took place the following Saturday afternoon at a popular lunch spot not far from where we both lived. As I had little idea as to what Caroline actually looked like, I was understandably a bit apprehensive. When a fairly attractive and very friendly young lady soon introduced herself, however, I breathed a heavy sigh of relief. As I remembered from our ski expedition, she was tall and slender. Without neck warmer, goggles, and ski hat, I could now see that she had long curly brown hair and a very pretty face.

Though she was dressed casually, her outfit was attractive and certainly well-coordinated. It immediately occurred to me that she had put some time and thought into this process. I wish I could say the same as to my own appearance that afternoon. Aside from her extremely genuine and friendly personality, what impressed me most was the warm and affectionate hug that immediately accompanied her greeting. I was not someone who easily and quickly hugged back in those days, so this physical exchange made quite an impression.

    Most first dates are challenging enough as it is, but Caroline's embrace was completely disarming. The effect was to totally dispel my feelings of uneasiness and tension. Initially, I suppose we talked about skiing and how she succeeded in tracking me down thereafter. The Herculean effort she put forth on that score was also pretty inspiring. After that, we easily moved on to a variety of other topics. With so much to communicate, our roughly two-hour lunch seemed to go by in a whirl. As we were drawing to a close, Caroline mentioned that she had plans to visit her buddy's art exhibition immediately following our lunch date. As neither of us wanted the date to end, she asked if I'd like to join her for that. I told her that would be great, except that I had plans to meet with my Toastmaster pals later that afternoon at the zoo. Apparently, her buddy's exhibition wasn't going to take that long and there would be ample time before my zoo appointment. Long story shorter, our date pretty much lasted for the rest of that day and well into the evening.

    As promised, the art showing was fairly brief, after which time Caroline was delighted to accompany me to the zoo. The Toastmaster gang was immediately impressed with this lively and attractive gal with the engaging and outgoing personality. I distinctly remember receiving many congratulatory comments that afternoon. Most notable was the one I got from Les Robertson. Les was the Mid Valley Racquet Club member responsible for my initial meeting with Caroline during that fateful ski trip. In Les's mind, if anybody was going to hook up with a snow bunny that weekend, it should have been him. While I can't fault his thinking, he did hang out with his other male pal throughout most of the trip. Had he stood at the base of the chairlift all afternoon shouting "Single," he might have had better luck. As for me, if I'd known that you could meet women skiing, I would have taken up the sport long ago.

    Our date officially transitioned into the evening when we decided to have dinner at a Thai restaurant following our time at the zoo. I'd never had Thai food before, and when we ordered "Chicken on Fire," the bird was truly presented at our table in flames. I'm sure this was just for effect, but once extinguished, it was actually quite good. And speaking of flames, there was certainly one building between Caroline and me.

    Upon entering Joanne's office for my next therapy appointment, I told her I had a story that she was really going to like. As I knew she'd be genuinely excited, I baited her just a bit so as to pique her curiosity to the utmost. I said, "This is a story that's going to make you truly glad you decided to become a therapist. This story is absolutely going to make your day, probably even your week," I further taunted. After that, I resolutely sat back for a few moments while saying nothing. Finally deciding that I had her complete and unwavering attention, I slowly regaled my tale of falling in love with the mysterious yet captivating young lady from the ski slopes.

True to form, Joanne was absolutely beseeched with pleasure and delight. I could just see her laying out this sublime story of professional success to her family, friends, and colleagues in the days and weeks that followed. And why not? As far as I'm concerned she had every right to claim responsibility for my extreme good fortune. She put me on the road to good decision making, and deciding to take a whack at a completely new and previously unexplored activity was right up there.

A Short Tribute To Michael Phelps

Over the last several years I've seen commercials featuring the great gold medal swimmer Michael Phelps. While he's endorsed many commercial products including cell phones and swimwear, I very much admire his testimonials concerning counseling and therapy. I've known many people over the years who probably would have benefited greatly from counseling, but were far too embarrassed to pursue such a valuable resource. It saddens me to think that seeking professional counsel is still a stigma among many. I can only imagine that there are a number of prevailing reasons that this is so. As far as men are concerned, we're taught to be strong, self-reliant, and unflappable. Asking for someone's help is considered weak and unmanly. The comical case of men stubbornly refusing to ask for directions when they're hopelessly lost, is a classic metaphor. Rather than admit we need help, we'll drive around for hours in a state of total disorientation. I've seen men take a nasty fall, then refuse all manner of help while bleeding and hobbling about. When asked if they're okay, the inevitable answer is "I'm fine." In fact, "I'm fine" is a pretty good catch-all response to just about anything a man is ever asked. We could be walking around in complete turmoil, with no end of personal stress looming all around us. But when asked how we're doing, we're always doing "Just fine."

But the simple fact is that we're not always just fine. As a buddy of mine likes to say, life sometimes hands us a complete gut punch. From out of nowhere a giant fist slams into our abdomen leaving us writhing and gasping for breath. Over the years I've seen men deal with this giant fist in a number of unhealthy and non-productive ways. One example are the ones who simply choose to ignore it. Their way of dealing with the problem is to put on as convincing a display of stoicism as they can muster. You'll never see any emotion bubble up, as they power their way through the crisis. Perhaps convincing others that they're not in pain will also convince themselves. To quote Woody Allen in the movie Annie Hall, "I don't get angry, I just grow a tumor." I've seen men climb into a whiskey bottle until their sorrows have been sufficiently drowned. Worse still (as in the case of my long-lost cousin Harris), are the ones who unexpectedly blow their brains out one day when things become too painful. Apparently, these methods are far more manly than seeking therapy. As such, I am very grateful to Michael Phelps for his heartfelt testimony of a life that was spiraling out of control. If a man who holds the record for gold medals in swimming can admit that counseling brought him back from the brink, then maybe it is a manly thing to do. Maybe it's not so bad to ask for help every now and then. As for me, I am well acquainted with the power of therapy, and the transforming effect it can have on our lives. While it shouldn't be used as a crutch for life's everyday ups and downs, it's certainly there when the genuine gut punches come along. And thank you Mr. Phelps for so eloquently pointing this out.

A Brief Word About Hugging

I mentioned just above that I was not a "hugger" by nature. Perhaps this was a remnant from my days of distancing from people whose very presence represented danger. I never really thought too much about it until my non-hugging ways were suddenly brought to the forefront one day. Prior to meeting Caroline, I played softball on Sundays with some of my church pals. Though I knew it would never develop into anything serious, I briefly dated a gal who played on our team. She was quite friendly with the pastor and his wife, and one afternoon they invited us over for lunch. The pastor's wife was quite a warm and affectionate individual and immediately gave my then-girlfriend a nice big hug. When she attempted to do the same with me, she could immediately sense my body begin to stiffen and recoil. Though I certainly didn't react this way by conscious thought, the woman took it rather personally. So much so that she loudly proclaimed, "This man doesn't hug, does he?" Looking back, I suppose I could have construed her comment as a rather harsh personal criticism. For whatever reason, however, I chose not to take it that way. For one thing, the woman seemed far too nice for me to regard her in a bad light. For another, she seemed genuinely hurt when her affections were not returned in kind. In any case, I took it as a wake-up call and an opportunity for growth. It was a defining moment, as I decided then and there that I didn't want to be someone who couldn't (or wouldn't) hug.

    And as it turned out, it was a relatively easy thing to fix. From then on I practiced my hugging skills at every opportunity that presented itself. And every time I tried it; my efforts were always met with success. Well, almost always. I hugged my old camp director (Ham) one time, and he acted like he was going to die. As he was always an odd duck anyway, I didn't count that one. The more I hugged, the more natural and comfortable it became. Like anything else, practice makes perfect. After a while, I didn't restrict myself to hugging only women. Lo and behold, men like to be hugged too (even by other men). These days my guy buddies and I hug all the time, usually at the culmination of our get-togethers. Not bad for a guy who was once a staunch "non-hugger." To look at us, you'd think we were a bunch of women. And that's just fine by me.

XLVIII
The Wedding Scene

I guess you'd have to say that I was starting to make a pretty decent life for myself in L.A. It was the late eighties, and I was pulling in about sixty thousand bucks a year with my sales job. While that certainly didn't qualify me for lifestyles of the rich and famous, it was a pretty decent living for the time. It enabled me to bail out of the shoddy apartment I'd been in for the first six months, in favor of purchasing a two-bedroom condo in a new development. Though I really had to finagle to qualify for a home loan at that time, it turned out to be a very good investment. I had formed a nice circle of friends, I now had a comfortable place to call home, the job was paying off, and my relationship with Caroline was getting quite serious. For the first time in a long time, the road ahead seemed optimistic and filled with endless possibility.

    Caroline and I were married on December the sixteenth of nineteen eighty-nine. The ceremony took place at Caroline's childhood Methodist Church in Sherman Oaks. Though it was a bit brisk when we took our wedding photos that morning, the southern California sun quickly rose to its usual prominence. And who should be presiding over our nuptials on this most auspicious occasion? But of course, it was the Reverend Chaz Waterston (whom I so dramatically detailed earlier on). Trouper that he was, Chaz was only too happy to brave the horrendous L.A. traffic all the way from his new home in Santa Barbara. As a man whose indomitable spirit enabled him to pull himself back from the brink, I was very proud to have him officiate on this most joyous occasion.

    I'll never forget the overwhelming emotion I felt when looking over the crowd gathered in that little church on this monumental day. To me, it seemed the culmination of all that had been accomplished in an effort to define who I truly was. While all decked out in their Sunday finest, our impressive group looked on with great pride. Both sets of parents were joyously on hand (mine having flown in just for the occasion). Each of our grandmothers also proudly stood in attendance, as did our respective brothers and their families. I was also honored by the presence of my old friend Norm, who made himself available all the way from New York. Of course, there was a good assortment of cousins, aunts, and uncles as well (mainly from Caroline's side). Even Tim Jameson managed to free up that morning, making the trip from way down in Costa Mesa.

Needless to say, the friendship contingent certainly included Louisa and Tyrell (without whose influence Caroline and I probably never would have met). My Toastmaster pal Les was also on hand, as the same could be said of him. My other Toastmaster buddies also made up a goodly complement, with several comprising the actual wedding party. Indeed, it was an extremely humbling feeling standing at the alter that day. Looking out at all those proud and reverent faces, while listening to the Reverend Waterston recite those sacred marriage vows, is a memory that will never fade.

Our honeymoon was indeed a tribute to the way our relationship had originally begun. We spent it skiing in the gorgeous town of Jackson, Wyoming. Two things stick with me about our time in this jaw-dropping ski resort. One was the feeling of getting off the plane and experiencing the sting of a fourteen-degree day. While it took a day or two to acclimate to this rather extreme temperature, we were treated to many happy hours of shushing down the slopes of those exhilarating and pristine trails.

Far more pervasive than the cold temperatures, however, was a sudden and unanticipated barrage of adolescent southern California kids who quickly arrived on the scene. When they showed up round about the second evening during our stay, this unruly mob seemed to completely take over our lovely mountain-side hotel. Obviously, the product of well-to-do parents, these loud and obtrusive youngsters made themselves right at home. While endearing themselves to no one, for several days they robbed us of the much-needed bliss and tranquility which we were seeking.

Needless to say, I was as put out as anyone else regarding the presence of this most unwelcome gathering. Owing to the geographical background of my new wife, however, my thoughts concerning members of southern California's youth were somewhat frowned upon. Nevertheless, I was quite tickled upon arriving back at the hotel round about day four. Upon noticing that the undesirables no longer seemed present, I commented to Caroline that the California kids appeared to be gone. A woman in the lobby overheard my comment. Immediately she turned to me before loudly exclaiming, "Thank God." Amen sister!

XLIX
Meet the Parents

I'll never forget the first time I met Caroline's parents, Len and Roberta Bosworth. I can't recall whether it was Thanksgiving or Christmas, but I distinctly recall being asked if I ate ham. As they weren't planning to cook a ham in the first place, I found the question a rather curious one. No doubt Caroline had mentioned my ethnicity, and I suppose they were testing to see just how "Jewish" I was. Not that it would have been a problem had I been devout, but I guess they were just curious as to who their daughter's new young man really was. At that point in my life, I was probably about as Jewish as they were, so the topic never really arose again.

Curiously enough, my parents probed me along similar lines when they found out I had met a nice Christian gal. "How do her parents feel about Jews," my father pointedly inquired. It probably didn't help when I replied, "They usually shoot them on site, but I'm sure they'd make an exception in this case." Suffice to say that I really didn't think long and hard about issues of ethnicity when choosing friends or potential mates. I prefer to think of people as individuals.

In describing Caroline's dad, I'd have to say that Len was the kind of guy who'd give you the shirt right off his back. The very definition of an extrovert, he was gracious and hospitable to a fault. He clearly welcomed me into his home with open arms, while doing his best to make me feel as comfortable as possible. A man of solid stature, his boisterous tones could be heard from every corner of the house. His manner truly revealed his deep satisfaction and pride regarding his daughter's choice of a mate. As for me, I was proud to be introduced to a man of such genuineness and sincerity. His wife Roberta shared many of these same endearing qualities while representing her husband's exact compliment. Where he was boisterous, she was calm and a bit reserved. Where he was quick to voice his opinions, she was well-ordered and systematic. And when her husband's emotions ran high, she was a calming force.

Both Len and Roberta had obtained their bachelor's degrees as adults, working by day and attending school at night. As such, they each achieved a fair amount of success in their chosen fields. This was very inspirational to me, as they both grew up in rather humble circumstances (much like me). A product of Illinois farming communities, Len and Roberta had clearly pulled themselves up by their own bootstraps. While most of their relatives achieved a high school education at best (and never moved far from home), Len and Roberta had carved out a very nice upper-middle-class existence as respected members of L.A.'s business community. You had to admire them for their internal motivation and self-driven metabolism.

Perhaps I should have regarded it as an omen, but my introduction to their beloved family cocker spaniel was a rather rude one. Pixie was certainly getting on in years, but I was later informed that her unpredictable disposition had been a trait right from the start. As it turned out, I could have used that information a bit sooner.

While a few of us were sprawled out on the living room floor watching Pixie jaunting about playfully, I reached over to give her head a little pat. Her attack came out of nowhere and was far swifter than I could possibly have imagined. I had absolutely no time to react before I felt the little dog's sharp teeth break through the skin just above the jaw on the right side of my face. I'm not sure I had ever been the victim of a dog bite before, so my first reaction was that of absolute shock. Once that quickly dissipated, I was blatantly aware of just how painful a dog bite can be. Even a little dog is capable of tremendous bite strength, and my face now ached from the force of those tiny jaws. In addition, I was now bleeding on the right side where the sharp front teeth had penetrated.

To my new father-in-law's credit, he rushed in and immediately grabbed up the little varmint. Though he was clearly enraged, he showed tremendous restraint in not pounding the animal's head in right then and there. I must admit to being a bit torn at that moment (and I'm not just referring to my face). Part of me wanted to see the daylights beaten out of that rotten mutt, but of course, there was also the part that wanted to show the family what a kind and understanding person I was. Though a voice inside of me was screaming, "If you don't kick that miserable mutt's teeth in right now, I'd be very happy to do it for you," I assured the folks that I was fine, and all was well.

Obviously, all was not well, as it took some time for the bleeding to stop and my face to cease throbbing. Still, there was a greater mission here. It was the first meeting with the folks and there was a lot more at stake than my temporary injuries. Both Len and Roberta apologized to a fare thee well, so I decided it was best to let the matter drop. The remainder of my visit that day was both pleasant and non-eventful. While you can't blame an animal for an uneven and somewhat volatile temperament, it did bother me that no one thought to mention it right from the start. Perhaps it was a source of embarrassment for the family, but an ounce of prevention might have worked wonders in this case.

L
Gone to the Dogs

I suppose things have a way of evening out in the end. I wound up having a few embarrassing moments of my own when I adopted a canine companion not long after I moved into the condo. As I've always believed that we'll never have a shortage of animals that need homes, I took a trip to a nearby dog and cat shelter.

The inside of the facility was comprised of a long line of cages, with each enclosure housing two or three dogs. While strolling down the line, I noticed a cage that contained only one occupant. A forty to fifty-pound German Shepherd/Golden Retriever mix was lying down rather placidly toward the rear of the cage. Upon seeing me approach, he slowly and methodically arose and repositioned himself at the front of the cage where I was standing. Though certainly not overly demonstrative, the dog somehow considered it his duty to regard my presence. I was somewhat struck by this, while also wondering why this particular dog had no roommates.

As the line of cages was arranged in the middle of the floor, it was possible to walk around them in a complete circle. When I had circled back to the lone dog, he was still positioned at the front of the cage where I last left him. As I once again approached (this time from the back of the cage), this very respectful canine repeated his prior gesture. Upon noting my arrival, he once again methodically arose and calmly placed himself in a heap directly in front of me.

Once could certainly be considered a coincidence, but twice was too significant to ignore. I located one of the keepers and asked if she knew why this polite and respectful young dog was in a cage all by himself. Her explanation was that "He must be vicious." I turned back to look at the dog for a moment, then replied "Him?" "Oh yes, he must be vicious," came her repeated assertion. I don't claim to be any kind of expert on dogs, but there was no way in the world that this one was vicious. I looked at the woman and said, "I don't believe that for a second." With a look of disdain, she summarily dismissed me and headed off.

Upon entering the lone dog's cage, he quickly became delirious with excitement. The animal's entire countenance seemed to express overwhelming joy and gratitude. I suspect he didn't get too many visitors with the unwarranted reputation that he had somehow earned. A few minutes inside his cage was enough to convince me that this dog didn't have a mean bone in his body. It was when I actually took possession of him that I got the actual story of his lone confinement. Turns out that he was an unneutered male among a house full of females. He'd been placed in a cage by himself as a means of keeping him separate and apart from the surrounding females.

Talk about having the cards stacked against you. Not only did he not have a proper home, but he was labeled a deviant in a place where unwanted animals had no future. No wonder he was grateful when I entered his cell that day. Upon leading him out of the shelter and into the parking lot, there was no doubt that he wanted to get away from that place as quickly as possible. He practically dragged me out the door as he desperately sought to discover which car was mine. When he was convinced that we'd be departing in my red Toyota Camry, he dove into the back seat as if his life depended on it. And I suppose it did. I quickly named him "Larson" after a sea captain in one of my favorite Jack London stories (The Sea Wolf). As the character's full name was Wolf Larson, I figured this would be a fine tribute to my new energetic and high-spirited companion.

While he was one of the most loving and gentle animals I've ever encountered, we certainly did have our moments every now and then. I could find absolutely no explanation as to why he absolutely hated the UPS guy. Perhaps it was something about the brown uniform. Our affable UPS courier, however, was a perfectly nice fellow and held no disregard toward Larson whatsoever. If anything, he was a bit fearful of dogs in general. Probably seen way too many along his route. Perhaps it was his caution that alerted the dog, but Larson's reaction to this most unassuming fellow was unlike any other that I ever observed. He seemed to know whenever Mr. UPS was about, even without actually spotting him. It was uncanny.

Larson's unique reaction never failed to alert me when our humble courier was nearby. (Well, almost never). During our walk one day we strolled past the UPS truck, which was parked alongside the curb. Upon spotting it, Larson immediately went into his growling routine, despite the fact that the driver wasn't even inside. As I tugged on the leash to lead him away, Larson's eyes frantically searched the vehicle for his hated nemesis. The truck's engine was silent in its parked state, yet the dog knew perfectly well to whom it belonged. It was probably best that our timid courier was not about at that moment, but Larson's reaction to all things UPS never ceased to amaze me.

A friend of mine purchased a unit in my same condo complex. One day she telephoned to say that she was coming over. When the doorbell rang several minutes later, I naturally assumed that she had arrived. Unfortunately, I misinterpreted Larson's angry response for his excited one. Thinking my gal pal was standing on the other side of the door, I eagerly opened it without a care in the world.

As Larson and my condo friend were quite well acquainted, I knew their reunion would be a joyful one. Wouldn't you know that the UPS guy picked that exact moment to deliver a package? By the time I knew what was happening, Larson was out the door like a shot. A look of sheer terror instantly enveloped the poor man's face, as he threw aside his packages and fled for his life. It was quite a scene watching the UPS man sprinting desperately around our little condo swimming pool, with the menacing dog in hot pursuit. Naturally, I joined the chase as well, in the hope of corralling Larson before he caught up to the fleeing UPS guy. In the end, Mr. UPS jumped into the pool in a final attempt to escape his angry canine pursuer. It was at this point that I was finally able to snatch Larson by the collar and haul him back inside the condo.

Watching this scene unfold was an absolute nightmare. In my heart of hearts, I didn't think Larson would actually attack the poor man even if he did catch up to him. But as the surprise attack on the right side of my face (from my in-law's Cocker Spaniel) reminded me, you can never really be certain when it comes to animals. I helped our soggy UPS fellow out of the pool and apologized profusely (just as my future in-laws had done when I had been on the receiving end). Fortunately, there was no real damage done, aside from the fact that the UPS guy needed a dry uniform. Believe it or not, the man actually apologized to me when he got out of the pool. Apparently, he was still holding onto the package that he originally meant to deliver. Looking like he had just fought a war, he bravely looked up and said, "I'm sorry. Your package got wet."

"No problem," I replied. Somehow we had all dodged the bullet that day, but I knew darned well that things could have ended on a much worse note. I never opened the door again before making absolutely sure I knew who it was.

Aside from our most unfortunate UPS fellow, Larson's friendly and loving manner was known far and wide throughout my entire social circle. I even had a neighbor that would grab him for a walk once in a while (unbeknownst to me), when I hadn't even gotten home yet. He was also the biggest coward on the face of the earth when it came to visiting the vet. From the moment I hoisted him up on that little metal examining table, his entire body would begin to tremble pitifully. When the exam was over, he needed no help whatsoever in getting down.

One of the most amazing behaviors I've ever seen him exhibit was when I acquired a tiny newborn kitten one day. Unfortunately, the kitten was taken from Mom far too soon and didn't fare well in the end. During the short time I had him, however, he was convinced that Larson was his mommy. This confused and frustrated the dog thoroughly, as the kitten constantly tried to climb on top of him. Having convinced Larson that his behavior toward the tiny kitten was being scrutinized thoroughly by yours truly, he desperately tried to devise a peaceful means of keeping the pesky feline at bay.

One day while keeping an extremely watchful eye, I observed in amazement as Larson gently and carefully picked up the tiny kitten by the scruff of the neck. I stood transfixed while watching this large and powerful dog gently transporting the helpless kitten. With clear concern for the safety of the tiny creature, Larson then traversed the entire distance of the living room. At that point, he slowly and cautiously placed it back down again. Of course, I was concerned by the nature of the action itself, but something in Larson's manner assured me that he meant no harm.

How a powerful dog with large canine teeth had learned to transport a helpless kitten with such care, was absolutely beyond me. It was obvious that the kitten was no worse for the wear, as he immediately made a beeline back to the dog once back on his feet. And once again, Larson very patiently picked him up and placed him back on the other side of the room. This went on about three or four times before I finally decided to set the cat up in a separate room. Here was a dog that easily could have crushed the life out of this highly vulnerable kitten, but instead chose to be loving and gentle. I suppose it was a good thing the cat wasn't wearing a UPS uniform.

I'll say one thing about dogs. Some of them can be extremely clever. Larson knew darned well that he wasn't allowed on the couch, but that fact wasn't about to alter his choice of sleep venue. As I would often observe that my sofa was coated with dog hair in the morning, I decided to investigate the situation. If I was particularly quiet upon rising, I could catch him still blissfully stretched out on the couch without a care in the world. Once busted, he'd quickly jump down with a most embarrassed and guilty look on his face. The sly hound waited for me to head off to bed, then made himself comfortable on the sofa when the coast was clear. If that isn't intelligence, I don't know what is.

Larson and I shared one another's company for the next eleven years. He had a long and happy life. For a dog who didn't seem to have much of a future right from the start, I am very proud of that. It absolutely broke my heart when it became necessary to put him down. It was one of the hardest things I've ever had to endure. I swore right then and there that I'd never go through that again. To date, I've never had another dog, nor do I plan to.

LI
No Such Thing as PMS

I've heard many people describe their "dating" years as a fun and exciting time in their lives. They look back with a wistful gleam in their eye, as they recall these years of youthful glory. And though I certainly experienced a wide range of dating adventures during my time in L.A. (and back in New York), I would never say that these were the good ole days. I recall my father frequently waxing nostalgic about the successes and joy he obtained back in his single days. I suspect, however, that when you've been married for a very long time, one tends to look back on the footloose days with rose colored glasses.

One of his most memorable quotes concerning this subject was, "Guys like me, used to walk into the joint and walk out with a broad." When he'd recite this quote in the presence of my mom, she'd always remind him that the proper term for a girl was not "broad." Putting my dad's many idiosyncrasies aside, I would have to admit that he was a darned good dancer. Thus I don't doubt for a second that some of the ladies were indeed receptive to his charms. On the other hand, it has always been my experience that people tend to act in their own best interests. If the single life was that appealing, then one has to wonder why you would ever pull up stakes and get married.

One day when my father trotted out this famous quote (for the four hundredth time), I decided to ask him that very question. "I guess I just wanted the convenience," came his swaggering reply. For a guy who enjoyed such tremendous success with the ladies, however, I would think that being married would be decidedly inconvenient. Perhaps those glorious single days weren't really so glorious after all. And perhaps he would have changed his tune in a big hurry if it ever became necessary for him to revert back to those days.

Not long after I arrived in L.A., I joined a divorce seminar group. I was still smarting from the breakup of my previous three-year marriage, thus I figured that some group therapy on this issue would be most beneficial. Though the group was open to both men and women, the only other male participant was the group leader. Aside from him, our ensemble consisted of seven women and me. These gals ranged in age from thirty to sixty-five, so I got a pretty representative sampling across the different age brackets. Our fearless leader was a spirited and rather opinionated fellow in his early forties named Ron. And while I didn't always agree with his perspective on the various topics, I'd have to say that he ran a thoroughly organized and very well thought out program.

Ron was going through a rather difficult divorce himself at the time, so he knew from whence he spoke. He certainly surprised the heck out of me (and the seven women) one day, when he staunchly proclaimed that there was no such thing as PMS. Though the gals wanted to thoroughly flog him for making this most callous comment, Ron never backed off for a moment. Though the ladies were good and peeved (as they had every right to be), Ron made it abundantly clear that nothing was going to change his mind on this subject. Though I had to admire his tenacity, I certainly also noted his lack of sensitivity (especially considering the bulk of his audience). Still, there's something to be said for stating what you believe and sticking to it.

On another occasion, he regaled us with a story about a woman who decided not to avail herself of his attentions. Though he was once again adamant in his view, I must say that I clearly understood this particular young lady's point of view. Right from the start, it was clearly not a relationship that was destined to have any kind of long-term future. Ron's take was that she was putting way too much emphasis on the future, as it was "just dating." The young lady, on the other hand, didn't want to waste her time with someone when there was clearly no long-term objective.

While both could easily build an adequate case for themselves, clearly they were of very different mindsets. As such, perhaps Ron should have realized that not everyone is going to share his opinion on "dating simply for the sake of dating." I understood the gal's perspective very well, for I too don't believe in entering upon relationships for no particular purpose. As I have met many people in my travels who do, I would maintain that there is absolutely nothing wrong with this. As far as I'm concerned, both perspectives are just fine, as long as both parties are on the same page. Much like the great PMS debate, however, Ron stuck to his position like grim death. Realizing Ron's propensity for intractability, the ladies were usually pretty quick to forgive.

An enlightening perspective on this subject comes from my wonderful grandmother. Back in her day, the young folks were brought together via dances that were held in their various communities. On one such occasion, a man of rather limited vertical stature asked her for a dance. Grandma turned the poor man down flat, as she was not about to dance with a fellow she'd have to look down upon. While I could never understand why height is of such concern to so many, it was obviously a deal-breaker for my grandmother. I probed as to why she didn't dance with the man just for the sake of dancing. "Oh no," she replied. "Since he was so short, I didn't want it to lead to anything." Though her reasoning seemed rather superficial to me, the common thread was the concern for the future. And if this was the way that folks hooked up in those days, then perhaps she had a point. In any case, you don't argue with your grandmother. As everyone knows, grandmothers are extremely wise! (Let's not count the fact that there is absolutely no scientific basis for waiting an hour to go back into the water after you've eaten). But that's a whole other discussion.

We had many interesting and entertaining discussions during the course of that divorce seminar group (and there were certainly times when I actually agreed with Ron). One thing I learned beyond a shadow of a doubt, however, was that men and women are not so very different when it comes to the things that really matter. We may go about it in vastly different ways, but in the end, we're all just seeking love and acceptance.

LII
Houston, We Have a Problem

As is typically the case when two people are so thoroughly smitten, it was absolute bliss when Caroline and I entered into the bonds of holy matrimony. Per one of my father-in-law's favorite jokes, she was so surprised when I asked, that she nearly fell out of bed. Ironically enough, that's how I actually did ask. That aside, you might say I was on a roll. Good decisions were bringing good results, and I was convinced that I had now reached the pinnacle of good decision-making. Unlike the first time around, I had now gotten married for all the right reasons. I knew this in my heart and soul. Caroline was very loving and truly cared about me. She was easy on the eyes, not to mention highly intelligent. She had a very positive outlook on life and always found the joy in everyday situations. She was practical to a fault, with her feet planted firmly on the ground. Considering my first marital experience, these wonderful qualities cannot be overstated.

But as wonderful as our prospective new partners are (and Caroline was certainly right up there), there are always certain differences that need to be considered. I was very adventurous and often chose the road less traveled. Caroline was somewhat risk-averse and usually opted for safety and security. Music was a very important part of my persona, and I was still planning to exercise my craft in one way or another. Caroline took a far milder interest in music and didn't really understand the heartbeat of a true musician.

As safety and security would suggest, she was content to work for large organizations in a very traditional role. In my heart of hearts, I think I always knew that I was destined for a life of entrepreneurship. I was extremely dubious with regard to children at the beginning, while she definitely dreamed of a family. While I was growing increasingly disenchanted with L.A., Caroline had been born and raised there. Had I not posed serious thoughts of leaving, it wouldn't have occurred to her for a second. Despite these disparities, however, we seemed to have far more items in common. As such, we got along just famously and had a lot of fun together.

Some compromises are easy, some are more difficult, and some are agonizing. Then there are the ones that are absolute showstoppers. Perhaps an easy one was getting her to shift more of her financial portfolio into stocks (as opposed to safer vehicles), seeing as how we were still fairly young. Getting me to the point of starting a family was probably a far more difficult one. Trickier still was convincing her that a move to the Pacific Northwest would be to her benefit. But as newly married couples often do, we poked and prodded each other along, while making choices that weren't always comfortable. Other than the child issue, I'd have to admit that I probably yanked her out of her comfort zone much more often than vice versa. My adventurous, risk-taking ways were simply not a part of her genetic makeup. Be that as it may, we managed to navigate these occasional uncharted waters, while maintaining a happy and healthy relationship.

As it turned out, however, there was one compromise I was called upon to make, that was absolutely beyond my ability to accept. It was one of those things that I realized right from the beginning but unwisely chose to set aside. "Houston, we have a problem." This was my thought the very first time our relationship was "consummated." That first sexual experience was exciting because it was all so brand new. At the same time, however, I realized that we had very different needs in this area.

As was my usual pattern in those days, a second round of lovemaking would usually follow the first, after an appropriate intermission consisting of intimate pillow talk and cuddle time. When round two got underway, the level of intensity was usually a notch or two higher than that of round one. I daresay that this pattern would sometimes repeat itself in the form of round three (although this could be proceeded by a bite to eat). With the culmination of this closing escapade, we could then collapse into a state of blissful exhaustion. I'm not suggesting that my style was good, bad, or indifferent, nor am I trying to bill myself alongside Rudolph Valentino. The point is simply that Caroline had very different expectations when it came to the physical.

Putting all the sordid details aside, I made what was undoubtedly a very poor decision at this early juncture. I decided to put my own preferences aside, for fear of opening up what might be a very large can of worms. And in this way, I set a very unhealthy precedent concerning the fate of our sex life. As her patterns were far less energetic than that of my own, I'm not sure she could have changed even if she had wanted to. Realizing this, I accepted her modus operandi, thus making a compromise that would plague me throughout the remainder of our marriage.

Of course, there were times when her way was just fine. But more often than not, it left me wanting and feeling largely unfulfilled. Another disturbing pattern began to emerge as the years ticked by. If I wanted intimacy, I was going to have to pay strict observance to the "ten o'clock rule." Not that she was imposing this rule to be dictatorial per se, but apparently her body was not capable of performing sexually beyond the hour of ten. At that point, she was simply too tired, and sex was going to have to wait until the following day. As she often explained, it was something with which she had no control. And in the lives of two active working people, it's amazing how quickly ten o'clock can roll around.

This most difficult and frustrating situation left me with a number of options, none of which was a particular winner. Of course, I could try my best to initiate before the hour of ten, but this was not always practical. And as the weeks would proceed merrily on, the option I chose most often was to satisfy myself on the downstairs sofa while she was fast asleep in the upstairs bedroom. I often exercised the same option in the morning while in the shower. Naturally, it was only a matter of time before these most unfulfilling alternatives became quite vexing. What was the point of being a married man if I had to "take matters into my own hands" on such a frequent basis? Yet most of the time, this had become the norm.

Of course another option was to simply confront her openly and honestly, thus bringing the issue front and center. But this prospect was also fraught with peril. For one thing, she could take it as an assault on her character and become angry or defensive. In this event, we'd now have two big problems. We'd still have the original sex issue, but now she'd be harboring anger as well. It's also possible that she'd be shocked and very hurt to hear that I was not fulfilled in that way. Once again, a second problem would rise to the surface.

Another alternative was to pursue an extramarital affair in order to fill the gap. Also not a great option for several reasons. For one thing, I'm just not made that way. Once again, there's that part about having to look yourself in the mirror every morning. And if she ever found out (which she probably would have), it would almost certainly bring down the entire house of cards. As I say, no clear winner regarding any of the above choices.

Believe it or not, I plodded on in this way for the first eleven years of our marriage. No doubt I was carrying around a lot of unresolved anger, and no doubt this was having quite a deleterious effect on our relationship. The turning point finally came when I had to take a business trip to Las

Whataya Gonna Do?

Vegas. During the day I attended an industry trade show in the hope of drumming up business for the manufacturer's rep company I was endeavoring to start. With such a singular purpose in mind, my thoughts were consumed with talking to as many people and handing out as many cards and flyers as possible. As anyone who's ever worked a trade show will tell you, it can be an absolute whirlwind right up to five o'clock in the afternoon (when show hours finally conclude). There could also be drinks or dinner to follow in a further effort to woo prospective clients. By the end of the day, all that walking, talking, and schmoozing usually leaves one absolutely exhausted. By the time you get back to your hotel room, all you want to do is collapse and decompress. This decompression is an absolute necessity, as it's not unusual to feel extremely "keyed-up" after an entire day of working a trade show.

Unfortunately, the options for relaxation in a Las Vegas hotel are often not the most healthy or wholesome. Even ruling out the unique (and intimate) fraternization opportunities that such a place has to offer, this still leaves an unlimited number of alcoholic options. There are bars conveniently located just about everywhere, not to mention a goodly assortment of booze readily available right there in the room. And if drinking is not necessarily your vice of choice, then the handy TV remote control offers a countless assortment of viewing possibilities. And let's face it, your mind is already being bombarded by the plethora of exotic and scantily clad "Vegas women" that are paraded in front of you no matter which direction you take. So is it any wonder that your television viewing choices may wander toward the more "Adult" selections? Seeing how this is a far safer alternative than any of the more "one on one" choices available, this was the alternative I chose on this particular evening.

In retrospect, I was probably better off getting soused. Observing those extremely graphic sexual depictions only served to reinforce what I wasn't getting back home. By my third self-induced orgasm that evening, I had arrived at a landmark decision. I could no longer continue to keep this under wraps. Though I was fully aware that there would be some degree of unpleasant fallout, I knew darned well that I could no longer continue to ignore the problem. I made up my mind right then and there that I'd confront it honestly and directly on the first night of my return.

Though attitudes have changed considerably over time, there is still much debate as to the wisdom and propriety of sex prior to marriage. And although many people might regard sexual incompatibility as a rather superficial reason for opting out of a relationship, I would have to conclude that it shouldn't be too easily dismissed. After all, it reared its ugly head in both of my marriages thus far, and in both cases, it caused considerable distress.

In the case of my current marriage to Caroline, we did have sex prior to wedlock. Although I disregarded the compatibility issue in favor of the good stuff that was also present, it did give me a fairly accurate portrayal of what was to come. The problem was that I should have listened to the little voice that was trying to warn me as to the oncoming danger. If couples abstain from sex before marriage, however, there is a very real chance of being completely blindsided if it turns out to be an issue. If it crops up beforehand, at least there's time to confront it before permanent plans are put into effect. In any case, it was clear that I had reached a definite crossroads, and that it was now time to confront the elephant in the room. I had no idea how this very sobering discussion would go, but I must admit that the decision to act decisively brought a much-needed sense of relief.

The conversation that took place upon my return was both sobering, as well as highly emotional. Looking back, I believe Caroline thought I was initially heading in the direction of wanting out of the marriage. When the actual subject of our discussion became apparent, she was only slightly less concerned. Though I can't recall my actual words, I laid it out in a rather straightforward manner (though making every attempt not to be accusatory).

With hurt enveloping her entire persona, Caroline listened in shock and disbelief. Oddly enough, she had been totally unaware that a problem of this nature and magnitude had gotten between us. And for this, I take full responsibility. After all, I had kept it under wraps for quite a long time. When I was through explaining things from my perspective, only then did she reply. With great sadness and complete disbelief, she implored, "You mean I've been disappointing you for all this time?" And as long as we were being completely open and honest, there could be only one answer to that question. I sadly replied, "Yes, I'm afraid so."

Though we agreed to earnestly work through this most distressing and difficult issue, I'd have to say that it marked the beginning of the end for us. With regard to the physical part of our relationship, we were simply two very different people. Try as we might, there was just no way to fill such an expansive gap. One of life's stubborn conundrums that was sadly unfixable. For the next fourteen years, however, we did everything we could to work things out.

LIII
Enter, the Pacific Northwest

Despite the minor Cocker Spaniel snafu, my relationship with the in-laws had become quite strong. While the conventional wisdom would have advocated a non-threatening "stay the course" sort of approach, I once again opted for the road less traveled. Though Los Angeles, California was my third place of residence, I guess I always knew right from the start that it wouldn't be my last.

My biggest complaint by far was the air quality (or lack thereof). As an outside salesman before cell phones had come into being, it was necessary to find handy outdoor phone booths (several times a day), from which I could call in to the office. Upon receiving my messages, I often needed to spend another hour or so getting back to the clients who had been trying to reach me. It was therefore possible to log quite a bit of phone booth time during any given day.

During one such session, I suddenly became aware that I was coughing incessantly. Upon concluding the call, I wracked my brain as to the reason for this fit of coughing. I had left home perfectly healthy that day and had no traces whatsoever of any respiratory symptoms. Why then was I expectorating to beat the band? I looked out over the hills for a moment before quickly coming to the following conclusion. I couldn't see the hills. I knew that there were hills in the direction I was surveying, but my eyes detected only a thick brownish/greyish layer of smog. Suddenly it dawned on me that this was what I was breathing.

As a non-native of southern California, my delicate system simply wasn't used to this. It was as if every breath deprived you of a little more oxygen. The more you tried to breathe, the more it left your lungs wanting. And the more it made me cough. With this realization sadly noted, I quickly returned to the safety of my car's filtered air conditioning system. I frequented no further outdoor phone booths for the remainder of that day.

In much the same way that my parents objected to Orlando,

Florida's extremely touristy atmosphere, I was also having issues with the show biz ambiance of L.A. While not everyone dreamed of a "Hollywood" existence, there were certainly an awful lot of Angelinos who did. Folks who were doing anything they could just to survive while aspiring to careers as actors, screenwriters, models, dancers, singers, musicians, you name it. This phenomenon creates a certain ambiance that is not always welcome among those who are just trying to maintain a normal (non-showbiz) lifestyle. Once again, this might not be something a native would even notice. For me, however, it seemed quite contrived and distractingly surreal. I also noted that the children in L.A. wanted to grow up far too quickly. I surmised that this was due to the trappings of a luxurious lifestyle that was evident all around them. Combined with a ridiculous cost of living, and the complete absence of seasons, my desire to jump ship after four years was building steadily.

Despite my well-founded reasoning, the decision to move was an extremely tough sell with regard to my new bride. As I mentioned, she was born and raised in L.A. and knew of no place else. Her parents and brother lived there, as well as a number of long-term friends. Last but not least, she also had a pretty decent job. Despite numerous well-meaning warnings not to take the L.A. girl out of L.A., my determination won out in the end. And even though she was consumed with trepidation, I think even Caroline realized that there were better places to raise a family than L.A.

Though I offered to join her in breaking the news to Mom and Dad, she wisely preferred to handle it herself. I was about to steal their only daughter out from under them. Clearly, this would not make them happy, nor would it stand me in great stead. My acceptance with the new in-laws was about to be severely tested.

The decision to elect Seattle as our new home came about for two reasons. The first was that I had visited the city some years earlier and recalled that it was a nice place. The second reason was that Seattle would at least keep us on the west coast. This would assure a fairly convenient plane route for family visits back and forth. Somehow I imagined that this would soften the blow for both Caroline and her folks. To seal the deal, however, I agreed to hang around for one last Christmas in L.A. I figured this was a small concession, as it would perhaps provide the family with some degree of closure prior to our departure. And what the heck, one more L.A. Christmas with Santa sweating bullets in his little red shorts wasn't going to kill me.

The forlorn looks on the faces of Caroline's mom and dad the day we headed out is something I'll never forget. Though they bore it with extreme grace, I'm sure the pain and sadness weighed heavily upon them. For that matter, the gravity of the situation took a toll on my new bride as well. As I say, in many respects we were very different people. As this was now my third major relocation, I suppose I was becoming an old hand with regard to major venue changes. This particular sojourn, however, was far and away the most speculative and risky one I had ever attempted.

For the first time, I was moving to a place where I didn't have a job already lined up. Unlike the moves to Dallas and Los Angeles, however, this time I was armed with forty thousand dollars in cash. Even though Seattle is not a particularly inexpensive place to live, that amount would surely tide us over until we got on our feet once again. While having a preordained job already in the pipeline brings a definite feeling of security, it also delivered me to places where I didn't really want to be. This time I simply decided to put the job on the back burner and set up shop in a place I was going to like. As far as our careers were concerned, we were going to let the chips fall where they may.

As I quickly became aware, I had a great deal of incentive to like Seattle. Not long before we left L.A., Caroline explained in no uncertain terms that this was the last relocation I'd be allowed to make. As I was transporting her light-years beyond the boundaries of her comfort zone, I figured this too was an equitable trade.

One thing we did line up while still back in L.A. was a rental house in the city of Edmonds. This lovely place is about eighteen miles north of downtown Seattle. It features a charming city center with a vibrant retail community. From much of Edmonds, it's also a fairly short walk to the picturesque Puget Sound (a walk we took on many an evening).

Though it was a wonderful place to live, the Edmonds house we chose had certainly seen its share of use. Built sometime back in the 1960s, it was a single-story "rambler style" brick design. While older houses can certainly have their charm, our landlady never once considered making any improvements to her aging home. The first evidence of this came when I tried to plug the power chord of my computer into the wall outlet. Amazingly enough, there wasn't a single outlet in the house that could accommodate a three-prong (grounded) plug. In order to power up my computer, I had to use one of those antiquated "three-prong to two-prong" adapter devices. I'd have to conclude that this third (ground) prong is fairly important, as my computer never ran right again. I have no doubt that the house's ancient wiring dealt a death blow to my faithful and trusted Tandy 1000 computer.

In addition to the wiring, the pipes creaked and groaned whenever water was circulated. It was a sound that reminded me of whales communicating in the deep ocean. All of the carpeting and vinyl had certainly seen better days, while the kitchen floor slanted significantly. The place was also badly in need of a new roof, as there were several leaks all throughout the house. It was even necessary to keep a bucket strategically located in the living room on rainy days. The windows were also original. They were of the wooden single-paned "cantilever style" that was popular back in the sixties (when security was not so much at issue). As such, they were a burglar's delight as there was no way to lock them. None of these windows contained screens, so there was also no way to keep out any pesky flying insects.

Perhaps the most concerning feature of the home was the back door. It contained no deadbolt lock as such, just the simple thumb-turn that is part of the doorknob itself. Though hardly adequate, this served as the only means of securing the rear portal. After a few months, however, we were shocked to learn that even this crude locking device didn't function the way it was supposed to. The bottom line was that the rear door was never actually locked at any time. Any thief who spotted this place didn't even need the agility to break in through the window. He could have easily entered just by walking in through the back door. Fortunately, in the year or so we spent in this humble dwelling, we never encountered any incidents of burglary. Perhaps the thieves just figured there couldn't possibly be anything of value inside such a neglected house.

One afternoon during the weekend there came a knock on the door. We were greeted by a friendly and pleasant looking fellow approximately in his mid-thirties. He told us his name was Paul, and he had been the tenant in this house prior to our arrival. Curiously, he was carrying what looked like one of those fairly inexpensive fluorescent light fixtures that could be purchased at the home store for about fifteen bucks. When asked what we could do for him, he replied that he was returning the light fixture at the request of his former landlady. Paul had apparently availed himself of this fixture when he left, and its absence had somehow become conspicuous. How our landlady ever noticed it was gone, I'll never know. Paul had liberated it from a giant stack of junk that was strewn all throughout the upper section of the garage. Apparently, she had some kind of a system for this organized chaos. In any case, she noticed the cheap and flimsy fixture was missing, and requested its immediate return. As my dad used to say, "If you're going to steal, steal a million dollars. Don't steal twenty bucks."

I have never understood (nor will I ever understand) people who litter their backyards with great collections of junk. A quick walkthrough of this "jungle-like" area behind the house turned up such items as old tires, piles of wire fencing (as well as other assorted and rusted building materials), various hub caps and other useless auto parts, as well as a full collection of dilapidated major household appliances. Is it really so difficult to dispense with these items in a timely manner via junk collection or drop-off facilities? And does it not affect one's pride in the least to have these retched eye soars strewn all throughout the back yard of your house?

There are all manner of collection facilities that will happily take old and useless metal appliances (free of charge), as well as transfer stations that will accept just about anything else for a nominal fee. Our landlady was far from poor and could easily have availed herself of these options. Instead, she chose to scatter them indiscriminately throughout her backyard. It would have been an interesting experiment to pull out one of those rusted and deteriorated washing machines back there, just to see if she would have noticed that too.

Our plan was to buy a house once we arrived in Seattle, so we didn't actually figure on being in the Edmonds rental for all that long. Thus the reason we were so willing to put up with all those deficiencies. As it turned out, however, Seattle was enjoying a tremendous boom back in 1990. People from all over the country were discovering what must have seemed like a paradise here in the Pacific Northwest. Houses were still relatively cheap, the air quality was good, jobs were plentiful, and the area itself had much to offer.

Among the great influx were an enormous number of Californians drawn by the vast improvement in air quality, the availability of jobs, as well as the affordability of real estate. This stirred up quite a bit of controversy back in the day, as many high-priced California homes were rapidly being converted into cash. These funds were then used to buy up much cheaper (and far more elaborate) homes here in Seattle. Not only were these notorious Californians buying up houses right from under the noses of long time Seattle natives, but they were also driving up the cost of real estate in a big way. The bottom line was that there was lots of money chasing after a limited supply of houses during this period.

From the perspective of a typical native Seattleite (doing all they could just to scrape together a down payment), it's not hard to see from whence the California prejudice came. In any case, this made purchasing a home quite a challenge back in 1990. By the time it was all said and done, we wound up staying in that rickety Edmonds house for more than a year. When we finally did move on, it was just as well. The landlady informed us that she had a son returning to the area, and now needed to reclaim the house. Though I suppose she was kicking us out, I'd have to say that we certainly weren't too broken up about it. (Which is more than we could say for the house).

As anyone that's ever looked for a house during a boom period will probably attest, it tends to bring out the worst in many people. There is real power at play whenever everybody wants what you have. This being the case, why should you part with it without exacting as big an ounce of flesh as possible. While I suppose this is just human nature, I was shocked at the length that some people took when it came to house negotiations.

While searching in an area some thirty-five miles north of downtown Seattle, we signed a deal to purchase a two-story home that was just beginning construction. We met with the builder himself and hammered out a deal with the aid of our trusted realtor. At the end of the meeting, we agreed to purchase the home for $108K. All necessary paperwork was signed, and handshakes were exchanged all around. The builder confidently informed us that he'd have the house ready in three months. As we were still safely tucked away in Edmonds at the time, this seemed entirely workable.

As the months began to drag on, however, it was becoming more and more apparent that the house would not be ready within the promised timeframe. That's another thing about a housing boom. It creates lots of delays in terms of "permitting" and assorted other bureaucratic red tape. As the saying goes, "Beggars can't be choosers," so we waited patiently.

About a month or so after completion was originally promised, we were summoned to an emergency meeting with our realtor. In a matter-of-fact tone, he informed us that the builder now wanted to cancel our deal. With all the time that had passed, and with the housing market still booming, he now realized that the house could be sold at a higher price. Canceling our deal would allow him to do just that. Never mind that the delay was through no fault of ours, and never mind that we signed paperwork and shook hands. Buried in the documents somewhere was a clause that gave him the right to pull out of the deal if it didn't come to fruition by a specified date. It didn't stipulate any terms or conditions as to why the deal couldn't close in a timely way. It simply gave the seller the option of backing out if he so chose.

How you promise somebody you'll build them a house within a certain time frame, then cancel the deal when you fail to live up to your own promise (and knowing you're doing it simply because you want to make more money), is absolutely beyond me. But this was the tack that many Seattle builders were taking during this time. When I directly confronted this particular builder, he simply replied that he was not a charitable organization. In other words, the delays and their corresponding cost increases were subtracting from his bottom line. With home values going up steadily, why then should he settle for making less.

As I say, these extraordinary conditions were bringing out the worst in many people. Believe it or not, this insidious builder offered to reinstate our contract for an additional six thousand dollars. Same exact house with the exact same features, now six thousand dollars more. At that point, we told him exactly what he could do with his house.

LIV
A Sunset Industry

As it turned out, employment came rather quickly for me in this initial stage of life in Seattle. With the help of a competent headhunter, I hooked up with a company that sold offset "duplicator style" printing machines. As I'd been associated with the printing industry both in New York and L.A., it seemed a good fit. My assignment was to peddle these offset printing machines within a specified territory located well south of downtown Seattle.

As I was soon to discover, there were a couple of major hurdles that I needed to clear. The first was that my knowledge of "offset printing" was rather cursory at best. Though I was acquainted with the very basics, the equipment was actually quite a bit different than that of my former branch of the printing industry. While some of my previous knowledge transferred over, there was much to learn about these new machines (and the offset industry in general).

In a very real sense, I was starting over again from the very beginning. This was disconcerting, as I had built up a formidable knowledge base within my previous field of printing machinery. It's hard to go from sounding like an expert, to feeling at a loss when questions are posed and technical information is needed. I guess this is why many people do not stray far from their original area of expertise. While they quite often migrate from company to company, they mostly stay within their respective industries.

The second hurdle had to do with the "south end" territory to which I was assigned. My first clue as to the viability of this territory should have come from one of the reps who had been with the company for several years. This particular fellow actually resided within the south end territory. As opposed to working these accounts from his very convenient locale, however, he instead chose to take a circuitous (and expensive) ferry ride every day in order to work one of the downtown Seattle territories. It didn't take long for me to understand his rationale.

This particular downtown territory included Boeing, which just happened to be the company's biggest customer. In addition to the aircraft giant, there were other noteworthy accounts in this most lucrative territory as well. The accounts of note in my territory tended to have names such as "Harry's Printing & Iron Works," or "Joe's Used Cars & Quick Printing." To be fair, my territory did include a large pickle and canned food operation in Tacoma. And though the pickle folks did purchase a sizable piece of our equipment during my tenure, the remainder of my accounts were far less appetizing. The fact of the matter was that the company had chosen to largely ignore this less prized territory over the years. While the reason for that was obvious, it allowed the competitors to gain a pretty sizable foothold.

I'll never forget a conversation I had with one particular small print shop owner. His chief complaint with regard to buying my machine was that he had amassed quite a stockpile of parts for our competitor's machines. As a result, he had kept these aging machines running for quite a number of years. Each time one of his old machines would break down (which they frequently did), he'd effect repairs via his vast collection of replacement parts. In fact, he fancied himself quite the tinkerer of old offset printing duplicators.

Had he been someone who repaired printing machines for a living, I probably would have gone right along with him in terms of his rationale. As someone who made a living via printing, however, I wondered why he took so much pride in constantly repairing his equipment. While keeping this particular thought to myself, I posed the following scenario. I explained that a new piece of equipment purchased from us would include a service agreement. At the first sign of trouble, we'd immediately dispatch a service technician to remedy the problem. This agreement covered parts as well. Not only would he no longer have to crawl around for hours on his hands and knees to fix his ancient machinery, but any replacement parts needed for our machine would also be provided at no additional cost.

And now for the sixty-four thousand dollar question. Considering what I had just told him, "Why then is it important that you have a closet full of our competitor's parts?" At the conclusion of my query, the man's face went completely blank as he grew strangely silent. It reminded me of a very rudimentary computer chess program I owned many years ago. Whenever you made a really good move, the opposing king's crown would start to blink for quite a few seconds. That's how I knew I had made an extremely valid point with this print shop fellow. The man was absolutely stymied as to a suitable response to my question. Unfortunately, being right is not always the same as getting the sale. As opposed to shaking my hand and telling me that we had a deal, he simply chose never to talk to me again. Deep down I guess he knew that I was making sense. Damned if that meant he had to admit it, however.

Working at this printing equipment company gave me a very clear understanding of what is meant by the term "Sunset Industry." Indeed the sun was rapidly setting on the folks who manufactured this kind of equipment. As one of the oldest "trades" in the world, the offset printing industry was now transforming in accordance with the highly computerized and digital age. Where an expert "tradesman" was once needed, technology was now making it possible to produce excellent quality printing with a few simple computer keystrokes. Old style offset duplicators were rapidly becoming a thing of the past, replaced by sleek and "space-age" looking digital copiers. I got quite a chuckle one day while flying out of the Vancouver, BC airport. For some reason, they had set up a little museum with various kinds of industrial equipment from the past. I remember remarking to my wife, "Holy cow, I have customers who still use that stuff."

My boss was the kind of guy who didn't like to lose an argument. The subject matter may have long ceased to be important (or even relevant), but he'd continue the argument ad infinitum just for the sake of asserting his authority. On one such occasion, I witnessed a lengthy and spirited altercation between him and one of the other salesmen. The two parties each had a different read on a situation concerning a customer and a pending sale. The rest of us couldn't help but overhear this heated debate that seemed to go on for about an hour.

Valid points were made on both sides. Then they were restated by both sides. Then they were restated again, and again, and again. Though it was clearly not my place, I eventually informed the two that they had been going around and around on the same points for quite some time. Perhaps they should just agree to disagree at this juncture. For my money, there was no doubt that the young rep knew the customer a lot better than the boss did. After all, this whole deal came about through numerous visits to the customer's shop. In truth, the boss had little to do with the day-to-day interactions between the customers and the sales guys. In the end, and much to the boss's dismay, I believe the rep went with his own thinking. I couldn't tell you how it all worked out, as I was long gone before it ever resolved.

At one point, however, I found myself in a very similar debate with Mr. Boss Man. I had just sold a machine to one of our south-end customers (a sale that would have gone to the competitor had I not been around). All newly installed machines needed to be calibrated, which was a function of the service technician installing the machine. To perform an accurate calibration, however, a metal printing plate was needed.

There are typically three different kinds of printing plates that can be used in these types of machines. The metal plates are the most durable and stable, and therefore the most expensive. Plastic plates are cheaper but less durable. At the bottom are the paper plates. These are far and away the cheapest, but can only be used once before being discarded.

Suffice to say that my customer didn't use metal plates, and therefore didn't actually own any. To rectify this, Mr. "Had To Be Right" insisted that I sell them a box of metal plates (so that the calibration could be performed adequately). A box of one hundred metal printing plates carried a price tag in excess of two hundred dollars. In essence, the boss was insisting that I clip the customer for over two hundred bucks, for an entire complement of metal plates that they would certainly never use (save for the one needed for the calibration). Please bear in mind that this was a customer who just spent thirteen thousand dollars for one of our machines (in a territory where we would usually lose out to our chief competitor).

In much the same manner as my fellow sales rep, I simply told the boss that I wasn't about to do that. Why on earth would we want to alienate a brand new customer who chose to favor us with a most unexpected (but very welcome) order. I watched as steam shot from the boss's ears when I reasserted my position. Even so, I remained steadfast. What he was telling me to do seemed ludicrous and was probably coming from his own superiors. He was just going to have to relay my message to the folks upstairs.

Sometimes common sense needs to rule out. In the end, we didn't sell the customer an expensive and needless box of metal printing plates. They were happy with their purchase, and we made a new "South-end" friend. A job well done, I'd say. The service tech laughed when I told him about the argument with the boss. He was well acquainted with the politics of the company. He told me not to worry about it, as he always carried some extra metal plates with him for just such a situation.

I met a very colorful character while with this outfit. Though Ed was pushing sixty at the time, he was quite fit and most energetic. With a stately head of silver-grey hair and a perennially cheerful demeanor, he was one of the few sales reps at the company who didn't smoke. His voice was that of a television news reporter, and his witty sense of humor was always at the ready. Ed was a natural born salesman who could maintain an easy rapport with anyone. I rode with him a couple of times when I first came on board, and it was quite clear that his customers both liked and trusted him. His knowledge of the offset printing industry was vast, as his last post had been as a plant manager at a large print shop. Ed clearly knew his stuff, and his winning personality afforded him a great deal of success in the sales arena.

Naturally, our compensation package was designed to reward the sales reps in a manner commensurate with their individual level of accomplishment. In short, the higher the revenues generated, the greater the sales commission rate. As an example, a salesman who sold $25,000 worth of machinery in a given month might be compensated at a rate of 3%. By contrast, if the rep sold $50,000 in a given month, he might be compensated at a rate of 5%. This tipping point with regard to total monthly revenues generated was known as "Break-Point." As the commission rate was quite a bit higher, Break-Point was something to which every rep aspired. At one point I asked Ed how often he would achieve Break-Point. He replied that he'd been achieving it every month ever since the program was initiated.

There was no doubt that Ed was an excellent salesman. One of the main reasons he always reached Break-Point, however, was due to a machine simply known as the "3985." Without going into needless industry specifics, the 3985 offered major printing benefits at a very reasonable cost. It was also a very high-quality machine that was easy to operate, while displaying very few (if any) flaws. The customers loved it because it was both extremely versatile and very economical. The salesmen loved it because it was $40,000 and easy to sell. Since it was also a machine that our company sold exclusively, there was no pressure to offer discounts due to competition. A "win, win, win," you might say. Except for one small detail.

Despite the fact that our printing machines were mostly built at the company's massive plant in Chicago, the 3985 was not actually manufactured by our company. In fact, we sold it through an exclusive partnership with a Japanese firm. And although it was an amazing machine, the profit margin for this Japanese import was far more modest than the equipment built under our own roof. With the sun continuing to set on the already declining printing industry, and demand for our own machines dwindling in general, the company was becoming far less enthusiastic about a product that wasn't emanating from its own factory.

So the company did what it was very fond of doing. It decided to tweak the compensation package in accordance with current conditions. In fact, on one particular "tweak," a rather large chunk of change wound up bypassing my own pocket. When I mentioned my consternation to Ed at that time, he dismissed me out of hand. His exact words were "I'm trying to stay positive Gary." Fair enough.

Then came the fateful sales meeting bringing word of the next revision to the compensation package. "From now on, the 3985 will no longer count toward Break-Point," Mr. Argumentative announced. With that, Ed went into a tizzy. As I looked over at him, he was scribbling madly into a notebook while furiously cranking out figures on his calculator. At the same time, he was muttering discouragingly to the rep sitting just to his right. Clearly "Mr. Positive" was now quite perturbed.

At the end of the meeting, I approached him to see what had gotten his back up so badly. With a deeply troubled look on his face, he replied "Do you know how much money I would have lost if the 3985 had not counted toward Break-Point?" Apparently, this is what he'd been frantically calculating at the announcement during the meeting. He then further lamented, "Do you know how much money I'm going to lose without the 3985 from this point on?" I replied, "I don't know Ed, but I'm trying to stay positive." Payback is a bear.

My own sales were not exactly setting the world on fire, and I was getting very tired of peddling products for a living in general. Though I moved on a short time later, it turned out that Ed didn't hang around much longer either. The 3985 had taken the spring out of his step permanently. He wound up purchasing his own print shop, which is probably what he did best anyway.

In the meantime, my new wife was not getting a big kick out of her change of venue. During these first six months or so she was a fish out of water. Her job search was proving quite a bit more challenging than mine had been. In a state of temporary unemployment, she suddenly found herself with lots of time on her hands. As productivity is her natural modus operandi, her world seemed to be spiraling down around her.

With no family or friends nearby with whom to easily commiserate, she sank into a rare episode of depression. As someone who still professes to live in her own self-created "joy bubble," her equilibrium had been totally shattered. Had things continued in this way, our marriage would probably have been a short one. Being the educated, experienced and resourceful individual she is, however, new career opportunities eventually began to trickle in. A temp job here, a contract gig there, and eventually an offer or two of full-time employment.

While I wouldn't say the new job instantly made her as happy as a pig in slop, it certainly went a long way in terms of curing the "displacement blues." As a productive member of the working world once again, equilibrium was restored and the future now offered something to look forward to. And Boy Oh Boy, did her mood improve.

Though I'm not sure she'd agree with me, I think it's a good idea to reinvent yourself every once in a while. Often in life, we have no idea just how much strength we possess until it becomes necessary to call on it. I'm not saying that we should go out of our way to make our lives as difficult as possible, but breaking out of our comfort zone every now and then can be a very useful thing.

Though it is natural to fear change, I've often found that most change is for the good. It may not seem that way at the time, especially when the change is forced upon us, but the net results are usually positive. And for reasons that I will make abundantly clear in the chapters to follow, my wife's relocation to Seattle proved extremely beneficial in the end.

Caroline's mood was further enhanced when we began a new search for a house, this time in a location twenty miles or so south of downtown Seattle. As I mentioned above, looking for a home during a "boom" time is like heading for the Klondike when the first discoveries of gold are being reported. Any place that even had a stick planted in the ground had already been sold. I'll never forget being driven through a huge development where new houses were springing from the ground like weeds. "Which of these places are for sale," I eagerly asked our realtor. "None of them," came her expedient reply.

As we continued on, she eventually rolled to a stop in front of a large lot that was completely bare. We were then given a set of diagrams showing various house configurations and plans, then told that this would be the next section developed. If indeed we were serious about purchasing a home, then we should pick from the half dozen or so designs, and put down some money as quickly as possible. Once our financing was in place, it would then simply be a question of hurry up and wait.

So that is what we did. And we waited, and we waited, and we waited. When it was finally time to sign the papers, I wrote what had then been the largest check I'd ever scribbled. Twenty-nine thousand dollars. It was a happy day indeed, though I now had a great understanding of the term "House Poor." A total price tag of $129,000 seemed outrageous to friends, family, and well-wishers at the time. Four or five years later, however, no one thought that was expensive in the least. When I finally sold the place about thirty years later, its value had more than tripled. Sometimes it's a good idea to hang tough even in a boom period.

LV
Some Pretty Fishy Jobs

Following my departure from the offset printing industry, my own career began to flounder (Ha, ha). One thing I was sure of, was that I didn't want to sell things for a living anymore. Though it served a definite purpose, it was never my natural habitat. Talk about getting out of your comfort zone, however, it made me a much more outgoing and gregarious person. In essence, it was excellent training for what was to be my eventual calling.

In the meantime, however, I was discovering just how challenging it was to change careers in midstream. When I decided to take another crack at a scientific occupation, I learned that life proceeds in a forward direction only. My attempt to recreate the carefree days of working for a dear friend in a chemical research lab was a dismal failure.

I got hired on by a company that tested soil samples by means of high-tech laboratory instrumentation. As I had never really worked with this kind of equipment in the past, the learning curve was steep. Additionally, the workflow was so frantic that there really wasn't a great deal of time to be brought up to speed. By the time I finally got the hang of the instruments, the company was just about ready to give up on me. Basically, the job was to run the samples through as quickly as possible, while hoping the results didn't turn up anything troubling. And even if they did, the veterans knew how to deal with these kinds of issues. There were "shortcuts" that could be performed in order to keep things moving and problems off the radar. These tactics weren't always ethical (or even legal), but they did keep your productivity on track.

Like anything that's slightly "off the grid," the trick was to make it seem like you didn't do anything out of the ordinary. I was taught several of these tricks while working for these soil analysis folks. Even so, my throughput was constantly lagging. As such, my hours got longer and longer with few tangible results. In the end, I was fired for performing one of the "shortcuts" on a sample that was undoubtedly laced with some ungodly component. It was another one of those jobs where getting canned came as a tremendous relief. It was obviously the wrong direction for me, and the sooner it ended, the better.

Wondering how I was going to keep the mortgage company happy, I then embarked upon a number of temp assignments and short-term contract work. The money wasn't great, but some of the jobs were actually pretty interesting. Of course, I got on better in some places than in others, but I met a lot of interesting folks in a variety of fields. Most of all, it gave me something to do while at the same time keeping the lights burning.

One of the more interesting assignments was a large food processing manufacturer that churned out mass quantities of cake, muffin, and pancake mixes. The state of the art machinery that this company utilized was impressive and then some. Tanks containing all the necessary dry ingredients (flour, sugar, flavoring, etc). were positioned throughout this colossal production facility. These tanks fed their respective contents into a massive central mixing unit via large vacuum conduits. The amount and order of each tank's material were determined and monitored by a highly sophisticated and extremely specialized computer system. Programs for each of the company's dry baked goods products were stored in the computer's memory, to be called upon whenever the schedule dictated.

In addition to the central production area, there were also a number of modern kitchen facilities where the products were prepared for quality control purposes. If you happened upon one of these QC kitchens after a batch had been put through its paces, you could pretty much be assured of something tasty to go with your morning or afternoon coffee. In fact, if you didn't exercise a little self-control, this job could be pretty hazardous to your waistline.

Aside from the sophistication of the operation itself, several additional items impressed me about this company. Though they employed hundreds of workers (of which I was merely a temp), I had an opportunity to meet the CEO not long after I started. Not only did he address me by name, but he also commented that he had heard some good things about the work I was doing. I came to discover that he was a very hands-on kind of guy, and often provided his employees with very sincere and well-placed compliments. I was quite taken that he chose to do this in my case.

The other thing that impressed me was that they bought me an expensive chair immediately after I assumed my assignment. I wouldn't have said that the existing chairs were necessarily all that thrashed (I'd certainly seen worse in my travels), but they wanted to make sure I was comfortable. That they would invest several hundred dollars on a chair for a temp, spoke volumes. It was a shame that I couldn't swing a permanent post with this outfit. My extremely early work schedule, however, afforded me a great deal of time in the afternoon for scheduling job interviews. It was a good gig.

Though the money was pretty decent, the assignment at the large Seattle insurance company was not a good gig. I was filling in for a woman in the purchasing department who was getting ready to have a baby. After taking a couple of weeks to bring me up to speed, her plan was to take a minimum amount of time off in preparation for the birth. According to her, the baby would be born on a Friday, and she'd be back to work the following Monday. I didn't even know this was possible (let alone healthy). Despite my skepticism, however, she insisted that it was a viable plan. If everything went like clockwork, it wasn't going to be a very long temp assignment anyway.

As it turned out, I never got to find out whether things proceeded according to schedule or not. During the course of my training, I was instructed as to the manner in which printed materials (mainly insurance forms) were procured. My very pregnant trainer embarked upon a deal to purchase a large quantity of these forms from a trusted printing house. I nodded in agreement as she explained that purchasing the forms in a higher quantity afforded us much better pricing. She then informed me that the company utilized an outside storage facility to house all this printed material. With the heavy volume discounts, however, it was worth it to pay the added storage fees. On this point, I could only take her word for it. In any case, I was still more or less with the program. I had a little more trouble with her next message.

Apparently, the company was just about to change its name, and correspondingly revise its logo. In fact, this change was going to be made public very shortly. In a half-joking manner, the woman commented that these newly purchased forms would probably be antiquated not long after they arrived at the storage warehouse. In other words, this massive quantity of outdated printed material was destined to be housed in the storage facility for the remainder of time. And all the while, racking up charges that would continue in perpetuity. And we were buying this large quantity to save money?

As I began to scratch my head, I seriously pondered the wisdom of this plan. In as polite and professional a manner as I could muster, I suggested to my learned colleague that this might not be the best way to go. Though she didn't exactly disagree, she simply replied that it was the way the company was used to doing things.

At the extreme risk of breaking through political lines, I advised that we should perhaps adopt a different strategy in this case. Perhaps a plan that was more in keeping with the current circumstances. As might be expected, my advice was not met with a great deal of enthusiasm. Quite the contrary, in fact. The next day I was summarily terminated. No doubt my crime was "Rocking the Boat." Oh well, it was going to be a quick assignment anyway. Turned out, it was even quicker than I imagined.

From the standpoint of absolutely ridiculous short-term postings, the fish chemical company is one of my all-time favorites. This one was actually supposed to be a full-time permanent job, but I think I was kidding myself right from the start. The first red flag was when the boss resolutely refused to finalize my salary during the phone call when he offered me the job. Had I not been thoroughly in need of employment at the time, I would have politely declined. Another disconcerting discussion point was his request that I start the workday at seven-thirty. Not that I minded getting up early, but this company was not exactly right around the corner from where I lived. In fact, it was a most inconvenient location even during the best of times. In short, it was one hell of a commute.

With regard to my salary, the boss also had no desire to discuss it even when I actually began working there. In fact, he didn't make himself available much in general. I was quickly taken under the wing of his second in command (a sort of General Manager), who introduced me to the daily operations of the job. And no, the General Manager had no interest in discussing my salary either.

Apparently, we were in the business of making chemical products for the fish farming industry. That should have been my next clue. At the time I had no inkling as to the dubious reputation that this industry had garnered. I was later to learn in no small detail that fish farming can be an absolute nightmare where the environment is concerned. That having been said, I was now in charge of procuring all the chemical materials and equipment necessary for the manufacture of these highly questionable products.

To give you an idea of the nature of this business, it is sometimes necessary to introduce what's known as a "Piscicide" into the waters of the fish farming environment. As the name implies, this deadly chemical kills everything that swims in these large holding tanks. To be honest, I'm not really sure why this is done, other than to rid the environment of possible disease and harmful organisms. Perhaps in this way, the farms can be restocked with fresh and healthy inhabitants. Again, this is only my guess. In any case, I'm thinking that most environmentalists would have a serious issue with intentionally destroying large populations of marine life. Or for that manner, breeding certain fish species in such a way so as to promote an unhealthy environment in the first place.

As it turned out, I worked for about a week and a half for this crazy outfit without ever finalizing my actual salary. A middle-aged lady came in one day claiming to be the boss's partner, and I finally had a chance to broach the issue with her. At the end of our discussion, she told me the matter would now be taken under advisement, and that they'd be getting back to me shortly. I guess "shortly" is relative, as I never heard from her (or ever saw her) again.

One day I was given a list of chemicals that needed to be obtained, so I telephoned the recommended supplier. When I finished running through the list of what was needed, there was a pause on the other end. When the man's voice returned after several seconds, he demanded to know why I was purchasing these items. I explained that I had not been on the job very long and was simply given a list of items that were needed. With his next statement, it was quite clear that he didn't believe me for a second. In a directed and accusatory tone, he replied *"If you're buying this stuff for Harold Smith, I guarantee you I'll find out about it."*

"I'm sorry," I politely explained, "But who is Harold Smith?"

Once again, the man didn't buy into my ignorance for a second. Again, he angrily repeated, "I'll find out."

I never even got the chance to ask our elusive president about this bizarre phone conversation. Not long after, the General Manager entered my office with a rather long face. "I'm afraid we're no longer in need of your services," he grimly announced. "We'll pay you for the two weeks that you were here, however."

"We never even determined my actual salary," I then reminded him. I must say I was totally bewildered. Was there never any real job here in the first place? Was this all an elaborate rouse just to get some unwholesome chemicals procured by someone who was absolutely clueless? Before I exited, I told one of the other employees what had just transpired. In a disgusted tone, he told me they did the exact same thing to the guy who came just before me. Somehow I always imagined the president of this company eventually doing time in some minimum security prison somewhere. Either that or hiding out in some remote country. The whole thing was pretty fishy right from the start. (Sorry)

While toiling throughout his career at the United States Post Office in midtown Manhattan, my dad used to tell this marvelously entertaining story about a former co-worker. At least it was marvelously entertaining the first couple of times he told it. After about the twenty-fifth time, however, not quite as marvelous or entertaining. But a pretty good story if you're hearing it for the first time.

Seems he had this colleague in the accounts payable department (where Dad was also stationed), who was pretty savvy when it came to creating opportunities for himself. Though he didn't have the world's most ethical outlook with regard to his job, you'd certainly have to give him high marks for initiative and creativity.

While I believe most people start out basically good, I am equally convinced that we all have a tipping point when it comes to financial opportunity. And if enough of these opportunities present themselves during our work-a-day lives, it's possible that even the straightest arrows can often be tempted to bend. And while we wrestle with some of these ethical dilemmas, let's throw into the mix the usual assortment of work-life catalysts. How well does the company treat us in general? Are we made to feel valued and appreciated? Are we paid at a level that seems fair and just? Do our bosses treat us like a human being, and not just a meaningless worker-bee? Suffice to say that all the conditions for a negative overview seemed to have been met in abundance at my dad's place of employment.

Now add to all of this agony and despair, the fact that New York City's main post office branch is absolutely colossal. And with size, often comes considerable confusion and anonymity. Thus an ideal environment for a disgruntled (yet highly astute employee) to create substantial opportunity for himself.

Though I have no way to know exactly how this shrewd fellow started down this larcenous track, I have a feeling it was a slow (or even accidental) progression. As a member of the accounts payable team, his job was to make sure certain the company's vendors got paid. And as it turns out, the United States Post Office is one of the country's biggest purchasers of goods and services. Therefore, there are always a lot of vendors that need to be paid.

As I don't like to presume that our man was a rotten scoundrel right from the get-go, let's give him the benefit of the doubt. Let's just assume that an honest mistake was made at some point. Perhaps he entered the wrong address when filling out the vendor information. Perhaps instead of the check going to the vendor, it incorrectly landed back in his lap. In any case, a light suddenly came on and a brilliant plan was hatched. In order to get these checks to start landing in his lap on a continual basis (and with his own name printed on them), all that was necessary was to create a few bogus companies.

Apparently, this is a very old trick that dates back to the origin of companies. It even has a clever name. It's called "Inventing Receivables." And so our man discovered this age-old scheme and started exploiting it with extreme prejudice. In much the same manner as Andy Dufrane and Warden Norton did it (in *The Shawshank Redemption*), I suspect that creating phony companies (who could then generate real invoices) was quite doable back in the sixties and seventies. "And oh how the money began to roll in." Once the "dummy vendors" were in place, it was simply a matter of kicking out the invoices and putting them through the system.

And who better to manage that, than our man in accounts payable.

What's truly remarkable about this story is how long this fellow was able to keep this bogus enterprise going. And this was despite the fact that he constantly bragged about it to his fellow department mates. If my father knew what he was up to, I'm sure the rest of his cohorts did as well.

The tale is not without its share of irony, however. The man's zest for getting the company's vendors paid on such a timely basis prompted his supervisor to offer him a promotion. Imagine the boss's shock when his subordinate refused the promotion with extreme indignation. After all, a promotion at that point in this man's career would have meant a substantial pay cut. To my knowledge, our post office "entrepreneur" was never caught and worked his way up to a very comfortable retirement. Score a big one if you're on the team of "sticking it to the man."

If you're of a mind, there are so many ways to wrangle an extra buck for yourself while at work, it's hard to even imagine. And the more expansive the company or organization, the greater the possibility. Through another of my recurring temp assignments, I got hired on by a rapidly expanding computer mail-order reseller. This company treated its employees like dirt even if you were the chief financial officer. (There had been about a half dozen of these, even in the two years or so I worked there).

Despite the lack of respect, it was indeed an interesting job. I learned a great deal about the computer industry during this time. And as always, I met of bunch of interesting people along the way. Much like most merchants within the on-line shopping community, this company had very liberal "return" policies regarding products that did not perform to customer expectations.

The "Single In-line Memory Modules" (typically referred to as SIMMS) were particularly troublesome when it came to returned merchandise. Depending on their strength and capacity, these small memory chips could be quite pricy. Placing a new set of them in one's computer, however, could speed up the machine's processor significantly. As people generally want faster computers, these memory modules were always in high demand.

When these chips were returned, it was mostly because they didn't make the customer's computer as fast as they would have liked. This being the case, I suspect that there were actually very few modules that contained any mechanical or electrical defects whatsoever. Nevertheless, the so-called "defective" SIMMS were collected, and refunds to the customers were issued. The modules were then temporarily stored at the company's "Returns Warehouse" (pending eventual shipment back to the vendor). And owing to their very compact size, a great deal of them could be stored in a relatively small space.

There was a very easy-going, yet extremely capable fellow named Robert overseeing the Returns Warehouse at that time. Everybody liked Robert, as he was such an affable and pleasant fellow. In fact, the folks who worked directly under him thought he was a great boss. From my dealings with the man, I do not doubt that he was. Unfortunately, and very sadly, Robert developed a serious heart condition about six months before I left the company.

I was very shocked when he walked through our purchasing department one day. This vital fifty-five-year-old man with a fairly athletic build had lost about fifty pounds. Suddenly he was looking tired and extremely gaunt. My heart went out to him, as it was abundantly clear that his health was failing rapidly. Not long after that, Robert took a leave of absence, and that was the last any of us ever saw of him. Word on the street was that he needed a new heart, but I have no idea whether or not that ever came to pass.

Upon his departure, the company (in its infinite wisdom) decided that they no longer needed someone to directly oversee the Returns Warehouse. To the rest of us, however, this seemed like leaving the door to the hen house wide open, so that the neighborhood foxes could come and go at will. The fox, in this case, turned out to be one of my fellow purchasing associates.

Sara joined our department from a more specialized post, where she enjoyed a fair amount of autonomy. Though the rest of us were content with desks set up in an open environment, Sara walled herself off with an arrangement of fabric office dividers (that she took from her previous location). Though she stuck out much like a sore thumb in our department, this odd configuration didn't make her feel conspicuous in the least. In fact, she enjoyed the curious attention that it brought.

Most of the time she remained fairly aloof, but news of her pending marriage was something she wasn't shy about disseminating. Although she wasn't getting rich working for this miserly computer outfit, and her betrothed was by no means a man of great wealth either, her wedding was a grand affair indeed. At a cost well in excess of $150,000, I imagine the couple were married in grand style.

A short time after the nuptials, Sara was conspicuously absent from our weekly purchasing meeting. Not long after we sat down in the conference room, our manager explained that Sara would not be working here anymore. In fact, she was under investigation for the theft of about three hundred thousand dollars worth of SIMMS chips. Though it was obviously a serious matter for the leadership of the company, it was very hard for the rest of us to keep a straight face. To avoid paying Robert's replacement about forty thousand a year, the company was now mourning the theft of a far greater sum. Last we all heard; Sara was on the run (probably with her new husband in tow). I'm not sure if the authorities ever caught up with her or not. As my father might have remarked, however, at least she didn't steel twenty bucks.

LVI
My Best Day

Putting aside most of life's usual monumental moments, it's interesting to ask people to describe their "Best Day." By summarily dismissing your wedding day, the day your partner proposed (or the day you met), your graduation day or the birth of your kids, it's not a question a lot of people can answer quickly or definitively. As for me, I can answer it with little hesitation.

One weekend during my early college days, I was anticipating a visit from my old summer camp buddy who lived in Philadelphia. Hank was planning to come down to Brooklyn on Friday night and spend the weekend. As he was quite the musical individual in his own right, our big plan was to introduce him to our favorite Manhattan nightclub (O'Lunney's) on Saturday night. My brother and I had discovered that a new band would be performing that evening, and we were well acquainted with three out of the four of its members. These three guys were absolute superstars. To this day they remain some of the best musicians I have ever met in my life.

Listening to these musical geniuses play together was always an absolute thrill for me, so naturally, we were pretty stoked as the weekend approached. Though I was not familiar with the group's fourth member, suffice to say that he was right up there with his bandmates. And while the other three were about ten years my senior, this new guy was right about my age. Though we were on equal footing age-wise, that was most definitely where the similarity ended.

Clearly, this young fellow was a hundred times the guitar player that I was. As such, we were captivated right from the group's very first note. It is not sufficient to say that these guys were absolutely incredible, as it goes well beyond that point. They were simply the best band I'd ever heard or am ever likely to hear.

It never ceases to amaze me what four highly accomplished musicians can sound like when they combine forces. Suffice to say, the result is far greater than the sum of the parts. What most people don't realize when they hear a band playing, is that it's not just a case of four or five guys joining together to play the same song. By contrast, four or five guys playing the same tune together, by no means constitutes a "band." In the worst case, it can even constitute a fiasco.

A genuine band can be more closely compared to a submarine crew or a squadron of fighter pilots. A group of highly trained individuals that have honed their unique skills for years, and are now working together like cogs in a finely tuned and well-ordered machine. At peak capacity these highly specialized human components mesh with one another with great precision, thus creating output that is both highly efficient, as well as extremely effective. A lean, mean fighting machine in the case of submarine and airborne squadrons. But a euphonious triumph in the case of a musical band. The same can be said of the converse. A submarine or airborne squadron that doesn't mesh together with precision is destined to crash and burn. The same level of disaster will also befall a band whose members do not mesh.

These four guys (who called themselves "Paydirt") were absolutely at the top of their game. The music they cranked out that night took me to new and vastly unanticipated heights. It was a high that couldn't possibly be achieved even through the most potent of narcotics. In fact, this was my drug of choice. And considering that I've only had two or three nights like this over the course of my lifetime, the effect is even more powerful.

Distracted only by the occasional sipping of our beers, the three of us sat absolutely transfixed for four solid hours. And when the evening was concluded, my life had reached a point of radical transformation. From that point on, I would never hear music the same way again. So putting aside all of life's usual milestones, I have a very obvious answer to the question of my "best day."

Back in the late seventies, bands that were not "signed" by major recording labels didn't crank out CDs like so many loaves of bread (as they do now). Recording an album was an expensive proposition back then. And if you were not signed by a major recording label, the only way to accomplish it was to foot the recording studio bill yourself. In those days this could carry a price tag anywhere between ten and twenty-five thousand dollars. In today's dollars, forget it.

As the cost to build your own lavish music-making facility was in the millions, "affordable recording" was rather an oxymoron during this time. I mention these details because our superstar band played a particular tune on that extremely memorable Saturday evening. One that stayed in my head for many years to come. Sadly, this group didn't stay together for very long, so the chances of ever hearing that song again were pretty much nil.

And try as I might, most of the lyrics (as well as the melody itself) were rapidly fading from memory with the passing of time. After a while, all I could recall was the melody of the chorus, with fragments of the lyrics therein.

He looks a little paunchy
He talks a little raunchy
But he loves her oh so gently
In his heavy-handed way.

Perhaps the tune stuck with me for so long because the group actually played it three times that night. Having already performed it twice, the young lady who wrote the song then entered the club. Noting her sudden presence, the band felt compelled to give it a third run-through.

As it turned out, the songwriter was a young lady named Susan Taylor. Ms. Taylor had been a member of a folk trio called the Pozo Seco Singers during the late sixties. Though this group barely missed breaking into the top forty with one of their tunes, they are noteworthy, nonetheless. This musical threesome (in addition to Ms. Taylor and a young man of little acclaim) included a fellow who went by the name of Donny Williams at that time. Those familiar with the country music scene of the seventies, eighties, and nineties will easily recall "Don Williams" as one of its true giants.

Following the dissolution of the Pozo Seco Singers, Don scored a solo contract in Nashville, where he strung together a nearly unparalleled collection of top 10 country hits. Why Susan Taylor decided to come to New York (as opposed to joining Don in Nashville) I'll never know, but suffice to say that she came nowhere near the success of her former singing partner. Despite Ms. Taylor sinking into relative obscurity, her song continued to live on in my memory.

By the time I'd been in my Seattle home for about ten years, I decided to construct a simple recording studio of my own. By this point, recording technology had progressed to where it could actually be done quite affordably. As I now had instruments strewn all about the house, I dreamed of one day having an all-inclusive "music room," where everything would be accessible and ready to go at all times. As my wife was getting pretty tired of a house bursting at the seams with instruments and musical gear, adding on a "music room/man cave" was not a particularly tough sell. As we were on decent financial footing at that point, six months and about thirty thousand dollars later, my dream had become a reality.

For the first time in my life, I now had about two hundred square feet set aside entirely for the purpose of making music. Within this space resided my entire collection of instruments, amplifiers, and other sound gear, as well as a rapidly expanding collection of recording instrumentation. With a complete drum kit in one corner, three or four amplifiers strategically scattered about, a p.a. system mounted atop various bookcases, and all manner of acoustic and electric instruments hanging from the walls, it didn't take long to fill the space.

Though the room was "well equipped" to say the least, it was quite manageable from the standpoint of getting from one instrument to another. There was even a rocker/recliner chair where I could sit back and listen to my creations as they were coming together. As I was now "armed and dangerous," I decided that my first recording project would include all those tunes that I've most loved throughout the years. And of course, this collection would not be complete without that amazing Susan Taylor song that I heard back at O'Lunney's so many years ago.

Though it's often used for frivolous purposes, the internet is one of the greatest inventions of our time. Via a quick Google search, I was able to locate Ms. Taylor without too much difficulty. Though a member of the vast "independent" recording community, she remained an active participant in the folk and country genres. She no longer went by the name Susan Taylor, however. Over the years, she morphed into the simple title of "Pie." (I recall from the New York days that she named her group "Taylor Pie.")

Having set up in a Nashville suburb, she was delighted to receive an e-mail from someone who remembered her tunes from way back in the New York days. After reminding her that we had met at O'Lunney's all those years ago, I inquired as to the tune I had kept in my head for more than thirty years.

She quickly informed me that the tune to which I referred was called *Doreen In The Diner*. And in fact, she was sure she had a demo of it stashed somewhere in her home (probably on an ancient cassette tape). I was elated upon hearing this, and I told her I'd be eternally grateful if she'd send it to me. She wrote back to say that she was getting ready to fly back east to attend to her ailing mom. When she returned, however, she'd do her best to scare up the tape and send it on to me. I thanked her profusely and told her that it would be both an honor and a thrill to record her tune.

I thought it best not to mention that she really wasn't all that gracious when we'd first met back at O'Lunney's all those years ago. In fact, I thought she came off as rather conceited and snooty. At this point in her life, however, she seemed to have put those past proclivities well behind her. Perhaps convinced that she was no longer destined for a life of country stardom, she became a very humble and down-to-earth person. In any case, I was overjoyed when a package with a Nashville return address arrived about a month later. Indeed it contained an old cassette tape, as well as a short hand-written note. "Here's the tune you asked me about," it read. "Please send me a copy of your recording when it's finished." It was one of the most joyous packages I'd ever received. I was off to the races!

Though I hadn't remembered any of the lyrics to the verses (or even the tune that went with them), I did recall the style in which the song was performed. That is to say, I remembered the basic rhythm and the way in which the verses and the chorus were blended. I also recalled how the tune modulated to a higher key, while radically changing rhythms to emphasize the final verse. Of course, all these things came tripping back as I listened to the various versions on that old demo tape. And naturally, it reminded me of that wonderful night back at O'Lunney's when I'd heard it performed by Paydirt for the first time.

"Doreen In The Diner" became the first of many tunes I'd record over the next five years in my newly commissioned Federal Way, WA home studio. To get it done, however, I had to hire a drummer, as well as recruit the services of my bass playing buddy from church. I also sought help from another friend and fellow church band member, a gal who had the voice of an angel. An aspiring country singer herself, Jamie absolutely sealed the tune with her gorgeous background vocals. As for me, I supplied the lead vocals, acoustic and electric guitars, pedal steel, and fiddle.

Truly a labor of love, "Doreen" came out sounding just great. Not only did it give me a thrill to put the finishing touches on this thirty-year cycle, I think it unquestionably put a smile on Susan Taylor's face as well. It's a great feeling when people remember your tunes, especially when they take the time to record them themselves. And since none of us were planning to make any money in the process, the joy of creating something wonderful and unique is its own reward. Here are the complete lyrics to "Doreen In The Diner." My version can be heard via YouTube.

Doreen In The Diner
(https://www.youtube.com/watch?v=cRLMt7uzj9s)

Doreen in the diner, with a chicken salad smile.
Worked for Jo and Eddy to support her only child.
Her nights were filled with table talk
and ten-cent country songs.
But short order strangers who could only eat and run.

He came from out of nowhere, in the middle of the night.
Beckoned to the diner buy a blinking neon light.
The tattoo on his forearm said that he was homeward bound.
And she looked him over closely as she laid his coffee down.

Whataya Gonna Do?

He looked a little paunchy
He talked a little raunchy
But she can't keep from smiling
at the things he had to say.
Her heart's a little dusty.
Her kiss a little rusty.
But he loves her oh so gently,
in his heavy-handed way.

He shipped out on a tanker
when the fillin' station failed.
And for seven years he rode the waves
like his daddy rode the rails.
And he told her salty stories
'bout the people from his past.
Took her mind off greasy spoons
and donuts under glass.

She was looking all of forty in her morning light.
And he couldn't help but notice
how they looked so much alike.
But he left her sleeping soundly on a trip around the horn.
And she'd be there waitin' tables
till he worked his way back home.

He looked a little paunchy
He talked a little raunchy
But she can't keep from smiling
at the things he had to say.
Her heart's a little dusty.
Her kiss a little rusty.
But he loves her oh so gently,
in his heavy-handed way.
Her kiss a little rusty.
But he loves her oh so gently,
in his heavy-handed way.
Doreen he loves you
in his heavy-handed way.

LVII
Life Sometimes Hands Us a "Do-over"

Upon entering my thirties, I got a wild and crazy idea one day. As it turned out, I thank God for this off-the-wall inspiration, the results of which shaped my future in ways that I couldn't possibly have imagined. The thought suddenly occurred to me that I had never really given my education a fair shake. True, I did tough it out back in my early twenties with a Biochemistry curriculum, for which I had absolutely no propensity. And true, my efforts were eventually rewarded with the completion of an honest to God "Bachelor of Science" degree. The plain fact was, however, that I never really applied myself to a field of study for which I had a genuine interest. The whole science thing came about through my parent's most adamant wish that I'd go on to become a doctor. While this had been their dream, I can tell you with extreme certainty that it was never mine.

The fact of the matter is that very few young people truly know what they want to do for a living when the college years suddenly approach. To the ones who were always certain that they wanted to be a doctor, or a lawyer, or a teacher, or an accountant, I take my hat off to them. Like the vast majority of us, however, I had no idea what the future held in store career-wise. And registering for college did nothing to change that fact.

Those interminable undergraduate years were simply an obligation that I needed to fulfill. It was my job at that time, thus simply a matter of paying my dues. For if you truly want to test your metal as a young person, try becoming familiar with complex concepts and formulae for which your brain is ill-configured. Even now I chuckle aloud at the memory of my calculus professor literally ripping my test paper out of my hands when the completion time had expired. There was no way in the world my brain was going to process those convoluted differential equations in the time allotted, yet that was the expectation. I'm not sure if that arrogant educator ever realized how close he actually came to getting slugged that afternoon, but I am grateful that I was able to hold my temper.

Getting back to the wild and crazy idea, I had reached a point where I realized that life sometimes hands us a "do-over." And if we are fortunate enough to be granted such a rare opportunity, then we should certainly grab the ball and run with it. I have always been critical of my father for his many complaints as to the injustice of life, while making little attempt to reshape it in his own image. And while it's probably best to learn from a good example, it is equally possible to learn from a negative one. With these things in mind, my moment of truth had surely arrived. I realized that it was now within my power to change what lay ahead.

At the still formative age of thirty-one, I had most definitely reached a major-league crossroads. One direction was to give my education another shot, possibly creating a plethora of new adventures and opportunities. The other was to take a similarly passive approach, much like the one my father typically preferred. But to choose such an apathetic direction at so critical a juncture now seemed unthinkable. When you got right down to it, it's probably fair to say that I made the only real choice. As a young and determined thirty-something, I was now heading back to school.

Rather than fill me with dread, however (as it did in the undergraduate days), this time it gave me a sense of excitement and exhilaration. I had always enjoyed business and finance (investments in particular), thus setting my sights on a Master of Business Administration curriculum seemed an invigorating prospect. This new adventure would certainly not come without considerable sacrifice, but what worthwhile endeavor ever does.

There was still the matter of making a living, so my education would have to take the form of evening classes. For four nights a week, I'd be going to work during the day and heading off to school in the evening. And even when I was back at home, the lion's share of this time would be used for studying and participating in group projects. And let's not forget the formidable cost of graduate education. By the time the curriculum was completed, I'd be looking at a twenty-three thousand dollar bill. Add to that the cost of books and fees, and it adds up to a bunch of money. A bunch of money that I surely didn't have lying around at the time. As the saying goes, "If it was easy, everyone would do it."

I should also point out that it was no easy matter to get accepted into an MBA program at one of Seattle's accredited private universities. As several prominent administrators were quick to point out, they did have their standards. And getting accepted into the program with a 2.3 (undergraduate) grade point average wasn't exactly an easy sell. There is irony everywhere, but the simple fact was that I could easily have maintained a 4.0 undergraduate GPA if I had chosen to major in music. This was a subject for which I'd never received a grade of less than an "A." (I chose a music class whenever I needed an "elective.") In fact, many of my music professors were quite perplexed to discover that it wasn't my major. I'd explain to them that having food to eat and a roof over my head were things I considered important. Most of them would chuckle at this. The fact of the matter was, however, that a 4.0 in any discipline would surely have paved the way to a master's curriculum.

Though I tried to explain that Biochemistry was a particularly challenging course of study, I made little impact on the academic powers that be. Fortunately, I got a boost from a favorable result on my Graduate Management Admissions Test. The "GMAT" (as it is more commonly known) is an exam that all prospective MBA candidates are required to take. Similar to the SATs (which are taken at the high school level), the GMAT is a combination of mathematics and reading comprehension. I'm not sure if they are any more demanding than the SATs, but suffice to say that they are challenging just the same.

To bone up for this all-important exam, I signed up for a GMAT preparation class. As it turned out, this was also an excellent decision. Though we poured through many previous years of GMAT exams, the most important thing I learned was proper test-taking skills (with an emphasis on relaxation techniques). One very common reason for lower than ideal test scores is that people get nervous and forget things that they actually know. In short, some people are just not very good test-takers. With regard to this community, I was a solid member. The GMAT prep class included invaluable breathing exercises meant to calm the nerves and focus one's resolve. Bottom line, it worked.

With trembling hands, I opened the letter from the college board that arrived in the mail a couple of weeks later. Sure enough, I scored a 540 on the GMAT, an impressive result indeed. Though I tried not to flaunt it, this even exceeded the score my wife obtained when she had taken the test back in her college days. Be that as it may, it served to bolster my argument concerning the lackluster GPA of my undergraduate science days. Not long after, I was officially accepted into Seattle Pacific University's MBA program. Talk about your "do-overs," a proud moment to be sure.

Attending grad school is a bit like going to the health club. It's easy to find all kinds of excuses to avoid it, but once you get there, it's actually pretty easy to get into the flow. Just like pumping iron or attending a SPIN class, there's a certain synergy that kicks in when you sit down in a graduate-level classroom. These folks are all here for the same reasons that you are, they have all reached the same point in life, and are equally determined to further their careers. Perhaps my wild and crazy pursuit of an advanced degree wasn't so preposterous after all. Of course, this sudden infusion of adrenaline doesn't last that long, but it's certainly enough to get you off the starting blocks. And like running a marathon, it simply becomes a matter of gritting your teeth, while hunkering down for the long haul. And while I suspect that most marathon runners wouldn't describe each and every mile as fun, I would say they find the experience exhilarating in the aggregate.

I would describe my graduate educational journey in much the same manner. I relished the moments of downhill coasting when it came to Finance, Marketing, and Entrepreneurial courses. By contrast, I endured side-splitting cramps while attempting to conquer even the basics of Accounting. After completing this particular requirement, I am convinced that Accounting was invented solely to assuage the most anal-retentive of individuals. How could anyone actually believe in a system where every dollar balances out perfectly in the end? This was simply a concept that my brain refused to grasp. Ours is an imperfect world. As such, how on earth could everything possibly balance out with such precision? Be that as it may, I suffered through it.

While massaging my agonizing accounting cramps, I actually scored an A-minus in my final accounting class. To be sure, it was indeed a very charitable A-minus, but my professor (who was a particularly nice guy) enjoyed the paper I wrote on the subject of "Mark to Market Accounting." Perhaps he just enjoyed the title, "Mark to Market Accounting – A bean counter's dream come true, or his worst nightmare." I wasn't above charity, however, and accepted the good grade with grace and humility. To this day I couldn't "account" if my life depended on it. I can tell you all about present and future value, compounded interest rates, and return on investment, but I'd be hopeless if ever asked to prepare an income statement or balance sheet. Thank God there are anal-retentive accountants for that sort of thing.

Grad school turned out to be a three-and-a-half-year venture. During that time, my life was no longer my own. My non-classroom hours were spent pouring through textbooks and boning up for exams and projects. The most time-consuming were the group projects that were assigned by the majority of our professors. The thinking was that our careers would require functioning well within a group environment, thus these group projects would provide the perfect training. I'll never forget having to extradite myself from a bluegrass festival one Sunday afternoon, just to meet up with my finance group. It's quite a feeling having to suddenly shift gears from relaxation and revelry to a stark return to the grindstone. My fault, however, for trying to squeeze in a little fun while in the throes of an MBA program. As per our marathon analogy, a bit like taking a small breather, only to find that valuable ground has been lost.

And speaking of time, had I not switched to becoming a full-time student in my last year, the program would have stretched on for quite a bit longer. My wife and I decided that it would be best for me to quit work for a year so that I could complete the program as swiftly as possible. It was a bold move to be sure, but it got the job done. And like our metaphorical marathon runner who finally collapses across the finish line in a state of absolute exhaustion, the successful completion of my MBA degree was a similarly monumental moment.

It was a celebration on so many levels. The most important of which was the feeling that I was finally beginning to live life on my own terms. I was now free to pursue a livelihood that truly represented my interests and talents. The fact that I was the first one in my family to achieve such an academic landmark wasn't bad either. Ironically, I turned out to be the only one in my immediate family to receive a college degree of any kind. As someone who never really took school all that seriously in the formative years, I found this quite the paradox.

But there was one more period to be placed at the end of this sentence. My undergraduate Biochemistry degree was awarded to a guy named Gary Silverstein (the name to which I was born). My newly awarded Master of Business Administration degree would be presented to a man named Gary Floyd. A very fitting tribute to an individual who was so bound and determined to reinvent himself. The very stately-looking diploma from Seattle Pacific University hangs ceremoniously over my desk as I write this memoir. It is a symbol of what can be accomplished when one is focused and determined. And it remains one of my proudest achievements to this day.

Our day of commencement was a grand affair. With two hundred or so graduating students all donned in cap and gown, and thousands of very proud family members on hand, the great university auditorium buzzed with self-generated energy. Before the presentation of diplomas, we listened intently to the heartfelt and inspirational speeches of the various faculty members and university heads.

Our keynote speaker for this most auspicious occasion was the reverend Lloyd John Ogilvie. Up till that point, I had never heard of Mr. Ogilvie. Apparently, he was a Presbyterian minister who served as Chaplain of the United States Senate from the 104th through 108th Congresses. Though most of us didn't know him from a hole in the wall, his words were extremely inspirational and thoroughly engaging. Some years later, I was intrigued to note that he was called upon to deliver the opening prayer throughout the Clinton impeachment hearings. It was during this time that Mr. Ogilvie became a great source of material for television's late-night talk show hosts. Mr. Leno and Mr. Letterman (as well as many others) seemed to feel that the good reverend was somewhat lacking for a sense of humor. Whether this was true or not, it made for a goodly amount of late-night comedy. Of course, it didn't help when Mr. Ogilvie fired back angrily at being belittled on late-night television. Any wonder that the Lloyd John Ogilvie jokes increased at that point. I guess he truly didn't have much of a sense of humor. As it happens, Reverend Ogilvie passed on only a year ago (2019) at the age of eighty-nine.

When all the speeches had been made, the great procession of students then commenced. And as the proud congregation of graduates slowly made their way onto the stage, the long sought-after diplomas were prominently disseminated. Throughout the great auditorium, there were many shouts of encouragement from loving and supportive friends and family members. I got a particular kick out of hearing one group burst forth with, "*Way to go, Grandma!*"

As for me, both sets of parents had flown in just for the occasion (mine from AZ and my wife's, from Los Angeles). My wife's brother and his family also made the trip from L.A., and our good friends from Portland were in attendance as well. You might say I had quite a group on hand. And why not. After all, how many times in life do you graduate with a master's degree. Sadly, my brother and his family were not in attendance. For reasons that I can't even recall, we weren't getting along well at the time. The animosity had somehow reached a level where my brother fervently believed that I had gotten this degree just to spite him. I'm pleased to say that we've long since settled these differences, but the thought that he wasn't there to celebrate with me, is a source of sadness to this day.

My day of commencement also righted another very old wrong. You recall how I mourned the forfeiture of a limousine ride way back when I was a kid during our family vacation. I was taking no such chances this time around. I personally hired a limousine way in advance of commencement day, and I booked it for the entire afternoon and evening. We'd all be arriving at the ceremony in grand style, and chauffeured to a fine seafood restaurant thereafter. Finally, at the end of the evening, we'd all be ushered back home as though we were truly important folks. It took a long time to right this wrong, but I must say it was sweet (even though it was a warm summer, and the limo's air conditioner was on the fritz). It was also a wonderful feeling when I finally paid off all those student loans about ten years later.

LVIII
It is a Very Important Role in Which We Are Privileged to Endeavor

Following the euphoria of completing my MBA program, two things then occurred to me. The first was that I'd finally have a personal life again. The second was that I now needed to look for yet another new job. And not just any job, but one that was worthy of my newly enhanced education. When an offer came to join the purchasing team at MultiCare Hospital in Tacoma, I was ambivalent, to say the least. The human resource gal who called to make the offer, actually seemed embarrassed when she revealed how much the job paid. Suffice to say, I couldn't blame her for feeling that way. Given the professional nature of such a position, the salary was appalling, to say the least. I even had to ask her to repeat it, just to make sure I'd actually heard it correctly. Unfortunately, there was nothing wrong with my hearing.

About the only positive the job offered (aside from not having to look for work anymore), was a cushy fifteen-minute commute from my home. While every fiber of my being told me to continue my job search, by the end of the conversation I had foolishly agreed to accept the post. It was one of those moments where you knew you were making the wrong decision, yet you proceeded as if you didn't hear the sirens going off all around you. As we all know, looking for a job is not one of life's pleasures. I suppose the idea of being gainfully employed simply won out over the prospect of a long and possibly arduous job search. Fortunately, it didn't take long to realize that I had indeed made a most unwise choice. My brief time with this organization, however, was not without notable incident.

As it turned out, I had been offered the job as a result of my experience purchasing computer equipment and accessories. I was now in charge of purchasing these items for the entire hospital. To be entirely accurate, my responsibilities had more to do with pushing paperwork at the behest of the hospital's I.T. department. In addition to telling me exactly what to buy, the folks at I.T. had also negotiated a pricing schedule with the various suppliers. In essence, my boss had hired an MBA to purchase computer equipment from predetermined suppliers at predetermined prices. Why she needed an MBA for such a mindless task, I'll never know. Perhaps she just liked the thought of having one working under her.

Of course, nothing was preventing me from trying to negotiate even better pricing and payment terms from these various computer vendors. And being armed and dangerous (with my newly acquired educational status), that is exactly what I set out to do. I also advised various department heads (who would sometimes take it upon themselves to purchase computer equipment), when I thought that better deals could be had. As most of these individuals made no claim to be purchasing specialists, my advice was usually well-received. Most of my suggestions were born of simple business and finance concepts. These included asking for discounts when paying upfront, making sure that return policies were in place if items didn't perform as expected, etc. These things made imminent sense but were often overlooked by folks with more of a clinical mindset. As such, they usually thanked me for my diligence and concern.

I received a very different response, however, when I first met the hospital's Director of Information Technology. Phil was obviously very proud of his most prestigious post and wore his title like a badge of honor. Unfortunately, at the time I was blissfully unaware of the kingdoms and empires that are often formed within large organizations such as this. When Phil inquired as to whether I had noticed how much computer equipment was being purchased, there were indeed a great variety of politically correct responses from which I could have drawn.

Looking back all these years later, I can now easily construct a perfectly suitable reply. Something on the order of, "Yes, it is a very important role in which we are privileged to endeavor." That might have been laying it on a bit thick, but you get the gist. My actual reply, however, was designed to let our esteemed I.T. leader know that he was dealing with an equally devoted and qualified professional. "I am gaining an appreciation for the volume of computer equipment that is being purchased," I replied. I then inquired as to whether he had noticed my efforts to minimize these costs at every opportunity.

And with that, the man's face assembled into an unmistakable scowl. "How are you doing that?" he demanded. Sensing his sudden and unexpected agitation, I simply replied that I was using the usual tricks of the trade (or words to that effect). My folksy wit was not appreciated, however. With no change to his sudden harsh expression, he simply extolled that I should just purchase what I was told, and not concern myself with anything else. He then assured me that his group had already secured the best possible pricing, as well as the most advantageous terms. In short, just buy the stuff and shut up.

What I didn't mention to our esteemed I.T. Director at that moment, was that I didn't spend three and half years getting an M.B.A. to simply buy the stuff and shut up. As the warden in Cool Hand Luke would have put it, *"What we have here is a failure to communicate."* Not even one month into the job and I had already made a powerful enemy. Clearly, my earlier instincts about this post were proving most accurate.

Suffice to say that if I was the type to "Just buy the stuff and shut up," I probably would never have thought to write this book. The fact of the matter is, however, that there is one distinct advantage to having a job for which you are decidedly ill-suited. The plus is that you certainly wouldn't lose too much sleep if such a job were lost. So despite Phil's threatening pontifications, I set out to impact the hospital's bottom line in as positive a manner as I could. And when I was able to obtain better pricing and terms than he and his illustrious subordinates, he took it as a personal affront. To Phil, this was a deep source of embarrassment and humiliation. To my mind, we were all on the same team and working for the good of the organization. In a land of kingdoms and empires, however, I quickly became a cancer that needed to be quickly excised.

Perhaps the final straw for Phil was an order he personally placed toward the end of the fiscal year. Apparently, there was some money left in his sizable annual budget, and he was on a quest to utilize it (whether he needed the equipment or not). To leave the money dangling, however, was to risk having said budget trimmed in the following fiscal year. Not wishing to have his kingdom diminished in any possible way, he quickly purchased two novel copy machines (that had just been introduced into the marketplace), whose reputation in the industry was yet to be established. In so doing, we were probably the first organization to utilize these brand-new and unique copiers. Seemingly oblivious to the fact that he was throwing the copier company a tremendous bone, and despite the hospital paying cash upfront for these pricy machines, Phil was perfectly content with paying the full list price.

I only received the details of his extravagant purchase several days after the deal had already been consummated. In orchestrating his dealings, he saw to it that I was completely out of the loop (save for filing the paperwork on the back end). Naturally, I was incensed when I finally had a chance to look things over. I then took the paperwork into my boss's office and asked if this deal made any sense to her. Feigning ignorance, she also seemed puzzled as to the pricing and terms Phil had hastily hammered out. In truth, I'm sure my boss was well aware of Phil's actions. If I was a betting man, I'd even stake a claim that she and Phil stood to profit nicely from some "under the table" rebates they no doubt planned to split.

    Normally I wouldn't have adopted such a cynical attitude towards people's comings and goings, but these kinds of shady deals seemed to happen with some frequency at this particular organization. There was a well-established tale of a woman who headed up the hospital's in-house printing department. Rather than processing many of the jobs in the hospital's own well-equipped facility, she instead farmed them out to a particular commercial printing company (who rewarded her with a tidy percentage). The woman was eventually discovered and fired, but not before profiting handsomely from her ill-gotten gains.

    Be all this as it may, I immediately got on the phone with the copier company and demanded that we reopen negotiations concerning the terms and conditions of Phil's deal. I then threatened to cancel the order if they refused to do so. Mind you, I didn't know if this was within my authority, but the copier company had no way to ascertain this. I can only imagine the velocity at which the kimchi must have hit the fan at that point. Phones started going off both in the Purchasing and I.T. departments as if we were in the White House Situation Room. Though I was perfectly aware that my actions were in direct opposition to Phil's "Place the orders and shut up" directive, I was determined to put a halt to a deal that was obviously detrimental to the hospital's bottom line (not to mention my own sense of corporate responsibility).

    I never did hear from Phil directly, but I can only imagine the level of froth that no doubt formed over his seething muzzle. Before it was all over, I had gotten the copier folks to render a pretty sizable discount on the machines themselves, as well as an additional reduction for payment in advance. In short, I probably nixed the dough that was due to siphon directly into Phil's (and my boss's) pocket. (A fact that amuses me even to this day). Needless to say, it wasn't too much longer before I was officially handed my walking papers. As an example of my crimes, my boss pointed out that I had gotten coffee from the cafeteria while some folks were having a meeting in there. No doubt, a major breach of professional protocol. Once again, onward and upward.

LIX
Please, Not the Hobby Lobby!

Have you ever wondered why people in show business (or the arts) almost always seem to marry other people in show business? Or why they befriend or associate so predominantly with other show biz folks? With regard to actors, singers, dancers, and the like, we're tempted to believe that money plays a large part concerning the choice of a mate. Of course, not all of these show biz types make large sums of money, but I'm tempted to believe that there are many more factors at play here.

I once saw a television documentary about this sort of thing. One such example of a vastly successful show business wife (Jane Fonda), who was married to a politician (Tom Hayden), was specifically cited. When interviewed on the subject of whether money and fame play a role in the success of a marriage, Mr. Hayden was quick to point out that his wife's income was easily fifty times that of his own. Despite this tremendous disparity, however, he confidently described his marriage as being rock solid. Success, fame, and money need not get in the way of a loving and successful marriage, according to Mr. Hayden.

According to Mr. Google, however, Jane and Tom were married in 1973 and divorced in 1990. And although seventeen years is a goodly amount of time, the union ultimately dissolved. Jane's first marriage to a famous French film director only lasted eight years, while her much publicized split with cable television tycoon Ted Turner came after ten years. Given this history, it can certainly be argued that in all three cases Ms. Fonda chose men whose careers put them directly in the public spotlight.

So the question remains. Why is it that people whose careers make them such prominent public figures, choose partners of similar widespread notoriety? In our Jane and Tom example, Jane's income alone could have easily provided a life lived high on the hog. And with the advent of pre-nuptial agreements, her possible fears of economic loss could certainly have been assuaged if the marriage should fail. The question I'm pondering is whether money is really at the heart of these extremely "public" relationships. And to no small degree, perhaps it surely does play a part. If we are to put the financial aspects aside, however, I suspect that there may be a far more encompassing explanation.

Careers in the arts and entertainment world (or high-level political arena) involve a way of thinking that is clearly outside the box. It taps into an individual's creative energy, as well as a strong desire to be out front where one can "perform." It is a most unique set of characteristics that define this relatively small percentage of the population. These are the ones who truly desire to captivate and entertain others.

Except for the four years that I lived in Los Angeles; my experience is that the great majority of the population has no such desire to "perform." By contrast, one could say that those who do are somewhat rare. For these folks, it's a tight market for companionship indeed. And that's why they feel so "at home" when they meet someone of similar ilk. For only an entertainer can truly "get" another entertainer. It is a world they well understand and appreciate, even though most others don't "get" them. Outsiders can certainly be supportive, but they'll never really understand what is at the heart of the true artist or entertainer.

It is probably of equal difficulty to understand an artist's obsession with constantly honing his or her craft. To the layman, these folks must seem like stubborn and unmitigated "perfectionists." Why can't they simply see that what's "good" is good enough, and move on to more normal pursuits? Or from the perspective of the artist, why can't the rest of the population realize that "good" will never be good enough? To the outsider, this must border on insanity. To the artist, however, it is a way of life and makes imminent sense. What it adds up to in the end is that these two worlds can often be light-years apart.

During my recording days here in Seattle, I once repeated a particular drum part a total of fifty times. Then and only then was I satisfied that it was up to par. Part of the reason for this (aside from wanting to get it right), was that drumming was my least experienced musical skill. In fact, I had taken two-plus years of drum lessons at the Seattle Drum School, just so I could be my own drummer on these recordings. While well aware that this tune was requiring multiple drum takes, I had no idea I had topped out at fifty. I was quite taken aback upon observing the recording software, which had noted the number of "takes" (or tries) for this particular element.

The fact that I'd run through it fifty times, however, absolutely blew my mind. Any decent drummer would have gotten it on take number two or three (at the most). Nevertheless, I can only imagine what my wife must have been thinking as she listened to that same drum pattern time after time and day after day. I'm pretty sure that take number fifty came somewhere on the third day. Had I been married to an artist of similar mindset; I'm thinking she may have understood my need to get it right. Perhaps she would have realized that this particular drum track was pushing my meager percussive skills to the limit. It's also likely that she would have been impressed with the time and effort that I was putting into this tune. In reality, I must have driven my poor wife to drink with my endless efforts to affect the perfect drum accompaniment.

A pastor at a church we attended for several years, made what struck me as a similar observation one day while referring to his beloved spouse. Seems she really enjoyed frequenting craft stores. She was someone who got a tremendous kick out of creating things that she could fashion up from many of the items sold in these shops. This was her world, and she could spend quite a bit of time perusing the aisles of Michael's or Hobby Lobby. To her husband, however, this was his version of purgatory. It wasn't long after entering such a store before his back started to hurt, and he began feeling extremely fatigued. Why in the world was she taking so long to buy a couple of tubes of paint and a few sheets of poster board, my poor pastor friend bemoaned. Had it been him purchasing said items, he'd have been in and out of the place in about ten minutes. His wife, on the other hand, was taking what seemed an eternity.

While I'm certainly not saying that I would have enjoyed my time at the Hobby Lobby, I have no trouble understanding why this environment held such fascination for his extremely artistic wife. No doubt the store itself stirred her creative juices, and no doubt she was thoroughly energized within its confines. I also have a sneaky suspicion that deep down, she was hoping that her enthusiasm for the craft world would in some way rub off on him. From the telling of this story during his sermon, however, not so much.

Most of us will agree that it's important to have things in common with our partner or spouse. Similar philosophies and a shared love for common activities do indeed bode well for a long-term relationship. Feeling like you are genuinely understood, and truly appreciated for who you are, goes a long way as well. And in the world of artistic endeavors, who better to appreciate a true artist than someone of a similar artistic bent?

Perhaps it shouldn't have come as such a shock that my wife had absolutely no desire to hear the finished product of my "fifty drum-take" tune. Even so, it was hurtful when she claimed to lack the time to sit for the final rendition. Particularly deflating, especially in light of how much time and effort it took me to get it right. "I'm quite busy right now," she'd say. "Can I hear it tomorrow?" With hurt and anger in my voice, I'd retort: "It's a three-minute song for God-sakes. What are you doing that's so important, it can't allow for three minutes?"

In truth, she wasn't doing anything that couldn't easily withstand a three-minute break. The fact of the matter was that she had absolutely no interest. To this day, I can only speculate as to what caused her total disassociation with regard to my music. All I can say with certainty is that it really hurt at the time, not to mention that it was driving a goodly size wedge between us.

When Caroline and I first met, I had just finished writing a song called The Big Picture. I was delighted to learn that she played the piano, as the song sorely needed one. I'll never forget how much emphasis she put on learning my tune, thus preparing a suitable part when I recorded it shortly thereafter. Some years later she confided her total belief that the relationship would have derailed, had she not been willing or able to play the piano on my recording. Naturally, I was quite taken aback to hear this, as I surely wasn't basing the future of our relationship on her ability to play the piano. Nevertheless, she felt it was of vital importance, and poured her heart and soul into learning The Big Picture. I was quite touched at the time and very appreciative of the effort.

I was later to find out that Caroline was the kind of piano player that could stumble through the same tune for thirty years, while never seeming to master it. Canon In D Major was an excellent example of this, but it was the same for any piece I ever heard her play. Canon starts out fairly simple, but builds steadily as it goes along. Toward the latter sections, it gets quite a bit more technical, thus requiring a much greater level of proficiency and concentration.

Caroline's version would typically begin pleasantly enough, but toward the halfway mark it would always falter in the same places. And as the piece increased in terms of technical challenge, her efforts began to take on a very "choppy" feel. Lots of starts and stops would then ensue, with a plethora of sour notes thrown in for good measure. Undaunted, she would continue plodding her way through right on to the end. This was pretty much the way I heard her play it (and everything else) throughout the entirety of our twenty-five-year marriage. Being no stranger to the concept of musical instrument practice, it was very hard for me to understand why she was content to struggle with every tune over such an extended period of time.

Around year twenty or so, I could contain myself no longer. In an attempt to offer the kindest and most helpful form of constructive criticism, I posed the following. "Dear, I've been listening to you play that piece for a long time and if you wouldn't mind, I'd like to offer a word or two of advice." By way of reply, I noted a low grunt and an attitude of general dismissiveness. Given this lukewarm response, I'm sure it would have been better to withhold my well-meaning advice.

"It seems that you struggle with some of the passages in the latter part of the tune," I explained. "Perhaps it would be helpful if you highlighted these parts, and maybe spent about twenty minutes a day just going over these rough patches. Once these wrinkles are ironed out, I'm sure you'll have no trouble blasting through the entire piece. Best of all, you won't have to feel frustrated anymore when you get to the end."

I've heard it said that a husband should never try to teach his wife how to drive. There is a very good reason for this. The wife will always see her husband's advice and criticism as a deeply personal affront. It will end in a big argument, and both parties will wind up extremely unhappy. As I discovered upon rendering my well-meaning piano advice, the same is true with music.

From that day forward, Caroline never played the piano in my presence again. And she made no bones about explaining that this was due to my cruel, insensitive, and judgmental comments. Herein lies perhaps another clue as to why she had no interest in listening to any of my tunes. All I can say is that I would never have gotten that drum part right if I hadn't gone over it ad nauseum. Perhaps the key is that I absolutely needed that drum part to be rock solid. Anything less would have caused great frustration every time I listened to it.

To Caroline, just getting through Canon In D Major in its entirety was enough for her. It didn't matter if she was ever able to play it proficiently. And the fact that she would probably never get there was of no interest either. While she couldn't understand why I was being so critical, I couldn't surmise how she could be so unconcerned and complacent. Hard to say if there's room for compromise given these two greatly disparate philosophies, but the conundrum is certainly worth considering. Getting back to my comments about show biz or artist types hooking up with their own kind, it's interesting to ponder how this dynamic may have played out in my marriage. As I say, it often brought us light-years apart.

LX
Dear Zindagi

My marriage was weakening on several other key fronts. While it's important for couples to maintain their separate interests and activities, it is also necessary to share some common pursuits. And with us, these seemed to be getting more and more scarce. Sensing that we were drifting, I had suggested that we designate health club nights (or days), even though our workout routines differed significantly. Still, I figured the act of hitting the health club together, and perhaps stopping at Starbucks on the way back home would result in a shared feeling of camaraderie. This was quickly poo-poo'd on nights when Caroline didn't feel like going. "We don't exercise together anyway," she'd comment. "So why do we need to go together?"

I then suggested that we attend a weekly Bible Study together at the home of a couple we knew from church. (In fact, it was run by the gal who sang on my albums). We did this for several months before Caroline decided that it was eating up too much of her private time, (time that could have been used quietly reading her newspaper). We also tried attending some Meetup groups as a couple. Hard to say if this would have worked, as one of the groups quickly disbanded, while the other wasn't all that welcoming in the first place. In essence, all attempts to provide some together time were met with little success.

Perhaps one of the most telling moments was a movie night that ended with hurt feelings all around. Despite having left for the theatre at exactly the time that Caroline had requested, we wound up having to really hustle to make the start of the show. Sensing her angst, I was far less proficient with regard to my parking job that evening. Without blowing my own horn (no pun intended), I am one of the best parallel parkers I've ever met. On this particular evening, however, I screwed it up royally and ended up way too far from the sidewalk. Realizing that I now needed additional time to pull back out and repeat the process, Caroline's anxiety increased to a point where she soon became rather terse and somewhat insulting.

By the time the car was adequately parked, I had no desire whatsoever to continue our evening. My feelings were now hurt, and my only desire at the moment was to put some distance on the person who was hurtling verbal epithets at me. I began walking at a slow pace toward the movie theatre while Caroline charged ahead. From about fifty feet in front of me, she turned to ask if I could possibly walk any faster. I replied that I didn't think so. Despite the great disparity in our pace, we arrived at the theatre at about the same time. At this point, I noticed a decent-looking restaurant across the street. Neither of us had actually eaten dinner yet, and I pondered whether I should just let Caroline go to the movie while I enjoyed a leisurely evening meal. Of course, this would have sent a very negative message, but there didn't seem to be much chance of salvaging the evening at this point.

Deciding to try and push past my hurt feelings, we entered the theatre and quickly found a seat. As it turned out, there was no reason for Caroline's little meltdown back at the car. We actually got there with five or ten minutes to spare (and I mean before they even started the coming attractions). And as it also turned out, that was still plenty of time for Caroline to tell someone in a nearby seat that they needed to stop talking. This routine (which had been forming over the past few years) of telling people in movie theatres to shut up, was becoming quite tiring, as well as somewhat concerning.

While I would certainly agree that movie theatre attendees have become less and less concerned with politeness and etiquette in recent years, telling them to shut up on a continual basis can be an unsafe practice indeed (especially if you're the poor shlub husband who just happens to be in the general vicinity at the time). As we were filing out of the theatre on one such occasion, she admonished a couple for talking all throughout the movie. This couple laughed in her face while she spoke, while giving no credence to her words whosoever. When she asked me in total bewilderment as to why they found her message so funny, I had to explain that they were probably quite stoned. Though I am certainly no expert, my experience is that people who are stoned seem to find everything funny.

In any case, on the dubious movie night to which I am eluding, it would have been much better had I gone with the leisurely dinner idea. The movie was a rather serious expose about an abusive husband, whose alcoholic consumption had clearly gotten the better of him. At one point, the rotten dipsomaniac even hurled a full glass of whiskey at his wife's head from across the dinner table. As my own marital situation was rapidly devolving (although certainly never violent), the film was making me even more depressed than when I first entered the theatre. If I had wanted to see a story about a dysfunctional marriage, I could have just stayed home (and saved the thirty bucks or so it cost for the tickets).

Caroline used to describe herself as having no sense of perceptiveness. Although she said this on a somewhat frequent basis, it was impossible for me to believe that someone could have no perceptive instincts whatsoever. By contrast (and often sadly), I always seem to know what others are thinking and feeling. After the first fifteen years of our marriage, however, I had to admit that she was probably correct in her self-assessment. Why someone with no degree of perception would go into a field like Human Resources, I'll never know. Clearly, however, perceptive skills were not her strong suit.

Following this highly depressing movie (and given my already trampled feelings), she then suggested that we stop off for a bite to eat. While wondering what planet she might have been from at that point, I told her that I had no appetite whatsoever. And although I didn't say it out loud, I had absolutely no interest in spending any more time with her that evening (even if I were hungry). Our date night had been an unmitigated disaster, and there was no use in prolonging it any further. The nice thing about banging your head against the wall is that it feels really good when you stop.

I'd also have to say that a marriage is probably not on good footing when your spouse suddenly threatens to kill you. As I stated above, our union was never actually violent, but I was mystified when things took such a radical turn on one particular evening. I had often commented that Caroline was getting way too wrapped up in her laptop (and later on) with her smartphone. It is a condition that is all too common these days. The advent of smartphones has brought a level of separation to families that is unprecedented in my lifetime. While I do think the internet is a wonderful invention, it needs to be held in perspective. While it is now possible to be connected to work seven days a week and twenty-four hours a day, one has to wonder if this is really healthy.

On one particular Sunday evening (about 10 pm or so), I noticed Caroline busily inputting into her phone. From the duration of the activity, it was obvious that vast amounts of information were being communicated among the various parties. As I have always considered Sunday evening to be a last refuge of leisure before the new week kicks off, I found this fast and furious late-night exchange somewhat intrusive. I should also mention that it was taking place in our bedroom while I was trying to relax in front of the tube.

When I asked who she was emailing for half an hour at ten o'clock on a Sunday night, she replied that it was her team at work. "Your team at work are all emailing at ten o'clock on a Sunday night" I frustratingly inquired? "Oh yeah, they're all working," came Caroline's nonchalant reply.

Not attempting to minimize the crucial nature of this impromptu late-hour meeting, I inquired as to whether the problem could be dealt with first thing Monday morning. "Oh no," came her immediate reply. "The manager wants to have the solution on her desk when she arrives for work first thing." It was then that I wondered what people did in the days before the advent of technology that enabled 24/7 connectivity. Would the entire organization have come to a standstill if the issue were not resolved such that the solution was on the manager's desk first thing Monday morning?

Bearing in mind that Caroline was not a member of the White House senior staff (or a NORAD official who had just noticed a missile en route to the U.S.), I was of the mindset that it probably could have waited a few hours till morning. After all, unless somebody had totally snapped and was getting ready to go medieval, what Human Resource issue could be that critical? Nevertheless, the team all stood ready to conquer the situation right then and there. And conquer it they did. It also begs the question as to where you would stand (with regard to the team), if you blatantly chose to observe the waning hours of a Sunday evening as non-work time. Would you then be ostracized and ridiculed by the remaining group members, who are obviously of a far more "team player" mentality?

For some, this never-ending access to communication and technology is a temptation that is simply too great. Even if it doesn't involve work, there are always personal e-mails, texts, and tweets to read and compose (not to mention all manner of shopping, gaming, and social media opportunities). Like the lure of the Siren's Song, these enticements are much too powerful for many to resist. Taken to the extreme, it's as though the victim is no longer even present. Their body may still occupy the room, but like Elvis, their mind has totally left the building. It got to the point where Caroline and I couldn't even watch a movie or TV show at home anymore. In a flash, the phone or laptop would come out, and she'd be off in techno-land again.

Hindsight is a wonderful thing, as I now realize that a rational conversation concerning the use of technology in the house might have served us well. Instead, I eventually reached a point of total frustration. "One of these days I'm going to abscond with that laptop" (or words to that effect), I angrily stated in a half-serious manner one evening. By contrast, Caroline's response was calculated and decidedly cold-blooded. "If you do anything to my laptop, I'll kill you." This lethal declaration stopped me dead in my tracks (no pun intended). It took me several seconds to gather myself, as I was rendered speechless upon hearing her words.

By then we had been married for about twenty years, and in all that time I don't ever recall her making such a heinous statement. "You'll kill me," I asked? Still reeling from the threat, I inquired "How exactly would you do that?" I'm not really sure why the method was important to me at that moment. I guess I just wanted to gauge her level of earnestness, and to ascertain the length she would go to uphold such a threat. Though it was hard for me to imagine her physically carrying out such a thing, the tone of her voice and the look in her eyes made it equally difficult to dismiss.

In response to my question concerning her preferred method of execution, she muttered "I don't know," before quickly sauntering off. Suffice to say that some serious couples counseling may have been in order. The excessive use of technology never ceased to be a problem throughout the remainder of our marriage, but I can assure you that her laptop and smartphone never met with any foul play. At least not from me.

This discourse concerning my twenty-five-year marriage is by no means an attempt to convey that I was the perfect husband. In direct contrast, I can say with certainty that I was not. To my credit, however, I was never abusive or violent in any way. By the same token, I didn't drink to excess, nor did I indulge in recreational drugs. Having been raised in a home with a frequently abusive father, I learned never to say anything to a loved one that I couldn't possibly take back. Along life's journey, I also managed to avoid many of the other proclivities that serve to trip people up. I've never been into gambling, and I've always been very responsible about family finances. While I certainly thought about other women from time to time during our marriage (especially given the strained nature of our sex life), I never once acted upon these feelings.

So much for my plusses. Now for the minuses. Though I was extremely responsible with family finances and getting the bills paid, there was a time when I played much too fast and loose with regard to our taxes. I was running my own business at this point, and simply cut too many corners with regard to reporting the company's bottom line. It is certainly possible to carry the "risk-taker" philosophy a bit too far, and I simply got too cocky. The I.R.S. sought fit to audit us at one point, and the results were not pleasant. In addition to a painstaking and stressful audit, the bottom line was a bill from Uncle Sam in excess of a hundred thousand bucks.

By this point, we had damn near paid off our mortgage, so it was as if we were starting right from the beginning (from the standpoint of house debt). It was indeed a blow, but Jerry Seinfeld's metaphor of a tax audit being the I.R.S. equivalent of a full rectal exam is entirely correct. Not something you'd ever want to experience, but worse yet, definitely not something you'd wish on a spouse. It made for a tough time, but we got through it and lived to tell the tale.

While I'm not saying I'd ever want to go through that again, the irony is that it actually brought us closer by the time it was done. We had joined forces to fight a common enemy (the I.R.S.), and we were working as a team for the first time in a while. Perhaps needless to say, I never again played "loosie goosy" with regard to tax reporting. I had learned a valuable lesson, while thankful for the support of a loving and devoted spouse.

This particular transgression aside, my other faults included a lack of patience and forgiveness, as well as a tendency to be overly controlling. If I had to rate these things, I'd say that the forgiveness part would have come out on top. I've always struggled with this issue, probably owing to the poor relationship with my father. Possessing some of his negative qualities is a troubling thought indeed, but we are quite often the product of our upbringing.

Dad used to take great pride in the fact that he held grudges to the grave. It took me many years to realize that harboring anger and disdain only serves to poison ourselves. Unfortunately, I don't think my father ever reached that conclusion. Though it certainly played a part in the demise of my long-term marriage, the good news is that it's never too late to make positive changes. Though still a work in progress, I've come a very long way in the last ten years or so in terms of forgiveness.

With the issue of being overly controlling, I can say one thing about marriage that is unequivocal. It concerns an area with which men struggle far more than our feminine counterparts. Though we are a couple, it is extremely important to have our own people and our own interests.

There is an absolutely wonderful movie that came out in 2016 called Dear Zindagi. Written by a native of India (and filmed entirely in India), I wholeheartedly recommend this movie to anyone that wants to learn a thing or two about romantic relationships. The film centers around a young woman (Kaira) who is very troubled by her lack of ability to maintain a long-term and meaningful romantic relationship. By happenstance, she meets a rather unconventional and warm-hearted therapist named Jug. A man of age forty or so, Jug's life is far from perfect as well. The counseling he provides to Kaira, however, proves to be invaluable.

There is one section of the film that will always stand out in my mind. Kaira is obsessed with the notion of finding a "soul mate." By her definition, this is a man that will share her every passion, thought, and interest. A man who will be her "everything" because he will understand her so completely. Once she reveals this to Jug, however, he is absolutely dumbfounded. "Isn't that an awful lot of pressure to put on one person," he questions?

And with that one exchange, bells went off all throughout my head. That was exactly the trap I had fallen into with my marriage. I was expecting my wife to be all things. A best friend, a trusted confidant, a lover, a wife, a business partner, a fellow musician, everything. And indeed, that was entirely too much pressure to place on one person.

As Jug continues his counsel, he poses the question as to why a person can't have more than one soul mate. Of course, he is not suggesting that Kaira should maintain a romantic relationship with several men. He is merely stating that different people are needed to fill different roles. A spouse doesn't necessarily have to also serve as best friend, nor does he or she need to be a source of creative inspiration. By contrast, someone who provides us with creative energy doesn't have to be a person to whom we feel romantic. Different roles filled by varied individuals, but soul mates just the same.

This eventually made imminent sense to Kaira, as it now does to me. A relationship requires the participation of two "whole" people. When one or both individuals are wanting to be made whole by the other, the result can easily be a spouse that is overly controlling. And in my marriage to Caroline, that spouse was me.

Of course, control can be a "chicken or the egg" proposition to some degree as well. In the early days of the marriage (especially when we were new to Seattle), Caroline needed me a lot. She was away from her friends and family for the first time and lacked the familiarity of her career at this point in her life. Given these unfamiliar and extremely uncomfortable circumstances, it stands to reason that she clung to me most ardently. In a relatively short time, however, her career resurrected itself and she slowly began carving out a new life. As I said earlier, she found a strength within herself that she probably never realized she had. With this newfound inner strength came increased confidence, as well as a burgeoning sense of independence.

As the years rolled by, she seemed to need me less and less. Moreover, I often got the feeling that she much preferred the company of her friends, as opposed to that of my own. By the same token, I probably should have put more effort into developing my own new friendships. Be all this as it may, it's hard to determine which really came first. Did I become overly controlling because I felt her slipping away, and was determined to somehow reel her back in? Or was she simply feeling overwhelmed because I was relying on her too much, thus creating the need to seek separation? Perhaps it was a bit of both. Whatever forces were actually at play, it created a very stressful and unhealthy tug of war.

LXI
You're Coming to the Meeting

Following the sudden estrangement from my hospital purchasing post (and determined to return to the land of gainful employment), I rifled through the newspaper want ads. One day I spotted what seemed like a very promising post. A wholesale distributor of sign-making equipment and supplies was seeking a purchasing manager. As a guy who had peddled his share of Gerber Signmaker 4B machines back in the old screen-printing sales days, I was most intrigued. A brief telephone conversation with the company's president one evening certainly confirmed a mutual interest. Mr. Tom Leonard was very impressed that I had such intimate knowledge of his industry, and quickly suggested that I come for an interview. When I described my experience touting Gerber machines back in southern California, I was practically a shoo-in.

    Following a somewhat tense discussion concerning my starting salary, Mr. Leonard offered me the position several days later. Once again the money wasn't dazzling, but this time I was certain that there were interesting opportunities for growth down the road. Given my industry experience and newly achieved educational standing, I was overjoyed when Tom Leonard invited me to "Help him run his company." Surely, this was a position for which my much-garnered MBA status would be worthy. In short, I was fairly certain that I had found a new home.

    On day one of the job, however, I started to question that assertion. Although there was an unoccupied quasi office-like space toward the front of the building, I was relegated to a small cubicle among the company's telephone sales staff. Noisy and completely lacking in terms of privacy, I wondered how I was going to help "Run the company" from such a meager and humble location. Sensing that I may have been sold a bill of goods, I cautiously set upon the nuts and bolts of the job.

Whataya Gonna Do?

My second disillusionment came several weeks down the road. It came to my attention one day that Tom was setting up a meeting among the "company managers." As someone who was hired to "Help run the company," I surely assumed that this included me. Having not received an invite, however, I walked into Tom's office to inquire. When I asked him point-blank if this wasn't something I should be involved in, his reply was quick and dismissive. "This meeting doesn't have anything to do with purchasing," he simply stated. To my mind, this was surely not the point, but I chose not to engage him at that moment.

By this time, however, I had already mentioned to the company's General Manager that I was experiencing considerable confusion concerning my role in the organization. Tom's response (to the G.M). was to feign ignorance as to the source of my trepidation. Thus I decided to make this upcoming "management" meeting my "do or die" moment. If indeed I was sold a bill of goods, then it would be best to find out now, thus enabling me to move on quickly (and without any further resentment).

I must admit that this made for a rather tense morning, as I waited with great anticipation to see who the actual meeting participants would be. I was resolved, however, to hand in my resignation that very day if indeed I were not among them. As the so called "Company Managers" finally began to emerge, Tom immediately approached my cubicle. "You're coming to the meeting," he definitively stated. No doubt sensing that I was quite possibly nearing the end of my brief tenure, he quickly decided to make me the newest member of the "management team." Why somebody who was hired to "Help him run his company" wasn't already a member of this elite squad, I'll never understand. Nevertheless, I accepted his sudden and graceful promotion, thus proceeding to throw myself wholeheartedly into this new enterprise.

The other members of management were as follows. The General Manager (to whom I had appealed previously) was an outgoing and friendly fellow named Mitch Johnson. A former carpet salesman (of right around my own age), Mitch had a decidedly authoritative air. He seemed to be right at home directing twenty-somethings, who often required a frequent heavy hand.

Mitch always gave me the impression that he'd fit right in as a fast-food restaurant manager. I could easily have imagined his authoritative and "whip-cracking" style, sending high school-age employees scurrying all about. The result culminating in hundreds and hundreds of hamburgers coming off a Burger King oven conveyor. I'm not sure if Mitch ever actually worked in fast food, but he certainly would have been a natural. I found his genuinely friendly demeanor and impromptu sense of humor most disarming, thus he and I took to one another fairly quickly. Apparently,

Mitch had sold Tom some carpeting back in his previous life, which is how the two had met.

In addition to Mitch (and also right around my age) was the company's Marketing Manager, Al Cashman. Though quite a bit more cerebral than Mitch, Al had a quick wit and friendly demeanor as well. And also like Mitch, he became acquainted with Tom in a professional capacity. Impressed with Al's contract work as a freelance desktop publisher, he was then hired on permanently. His main function was to create a new and vastly improved product catalog. Once I was elevated to the status of company manager, Al and I also got along quite well.

To the boss, however, Al was much more than just a trusted employee. For that matter, the same could be said of Mitch. Their relationships spilled over way beyond the confines of work, and Tom regarded them both as close personal friends. The three would frequently get together on weekends, often spending time at Tom's Lake Washington home. Although my promotion certainly made me an important member of the team, it afforded me no such intimacy regarding my relationship with the boss. Perhaps this was because I came along as a result of a Seattle Times classified ad, and not during Tom's personal or professional wanderings. Hard to say, but I was definitely not a true insider when it came to anything beyond the company itself.

Last but certainly not least, there was Lila. Upon first contact with this early-fortyish woman, she seemed a perfectly likable and friendly sort. Fairly slim and generally attractive, she was a more than adequate bean counter. As such, she headed up the company's accounting and bookkeeping functions. Unfortunately, it didn't take long before another side of Lila began to emerge. In fact, it was right around the time that I was brought into the fold with regard to the company's management team. Whereas Mitch and Al welcomed me into their ranks with open arms, Lila quickly adopted an attitude of suspicion and distrust. She immediately set about to establish a hierarchy whereby she would outrank me upon this narrow but elite totem pole.

While I hadn't met that many women in my professional travels whom I would term a "Bully," Lila could most definitely be described in that manner. Confident in the knowledge that she would always emerge victoriously, she seemed to relish the opportunity for squabbles and dissension. She also seemed quite at home with leveling personal insults at co-workers, having accused me on several occasions of possessing extremely bad breath. On one such occasion, she even emphasized her point by waving her hands vigorously in front of her face, so as to "shoo" the offensive odor from her presence.

I must say that I often found her lack of basic sensitivity quite unnerving, but I did my best to maintain a positive and professional demeanor. Somewhere around the third halitosis accusation, however, I calmly but rather pointedly stated that I was sorry to have offended her delicate sensitivities. Though she got the point, she was not at all pleased at my decision to finally confront her in such a direct manner. No matter how many times I would directly challenge Lila's mean-spirited and ill-conceived remarks (albeit calmly and professionally), she'd resume her attacks only a short time later.

In all my previous experience with bullies, they almost always backed down the very first time they were stood up to. Not so with Lila. It was like doing battle with a bulldog. She might lick her wounds every now and then, but she always managed to come back even tougher the next time. The source of her strength seemed to reside in the knowledge that a confrontation with a relative newbie would result in the removal of such an adversary. And in that regard, I'd have to say that she was probably right. In fact, I was notified by Tom on several occasions that my career was largely dependent upon getting along with her. But to let an incident go unchecked was hazardous as well. This only served to provide her with additional fuel for future attacks. These cumbersome conditions made for a classic case of office politics, while often positioning me directly between a rock and a hard spot. And so the thrust and parry with Lila continued for pretty much the entire first year of my tenure.

Perhaps the creepiest aspect of the woman was her ability to suddenly shift gears at a moment's notice. The effect was to create a one-hundred-and-eighty-degree rotation of her personality. On these occasions when she wasn't criticizing my breath or attacking my professional capabilities, she'd act as though I was her dearest and most trusted friend. Truth be known, I was far more comfortable during the times when she was going for my throat. The "best friend" routine always made me feel like I was in a horror movie (waiting for the other shoe to drop).

During her "best friend" moments she'd often drop by my office to ask my advice on business, as well as personal matters. One day she even asked if I'd co-sign a note to help her purchase a car. My most uncomfortable instance was the afternoon she came by to discuss her sex life. Suffice to say, much more information than I needed. There eventually came a point where it became clear that Lila had most definitely missed her chance to send me packing. Her best bet at bumping me off certainly would have come during that first year. And indeed, there were some tense moments during that period. What she didn't count on, however, was that I would throw myself completely and unreservedly into the organization.

In addition to focusing my efforts on the company's inventory needs, I took a much wider view of the operation as a whole. I studied the way in which the warehouse was run and organized, while familiarizing myself with the entire product line. I also talked with equipment and supply vendors, while studying trade publications to better understand how the field of sign production was gravitating. In a relatively short time, I had not only gotten the lay of the land, but I had also gained a fairly wide understanding of the current state of the digital graphics industry. In short, I could now "talk the talk" and "walk the walk." In essence, I had become an industry insider.

And with regard to the company itself, my efforts to promote efficiency and cost savings were beginning to have a very positive impact on the bottom line. All this is to say that my departure was no longer imminent should further conflicts with Lila occur. Sensing this to be the case, she finally began to back off ever so slightly. Not long into my second year, the door completely slammed in her face when the current General Manager suddenly departed. It was at this point that I was quickly offered his job.

As I mentioned, Mitch Johnson was a very nice fellow indeed, but that was also his downfall. Though he had no trouble talking tough when the situation necessitated, the employees knew that he was a soft touch when it came to making the really hard and unpopular choices. As a smaller company of about thirty or so employees, an atmosphere of informality had been established. Unfortunately, this meant that many of the staff arrived for work at whatever time they found convenient. Although working hours were technically 8 AM till 5 PM (with an hour for lunch), many chose to disregard this relatively minor detail.

Many mornings would find me in my little cubicle, scratching my head as to why I was part of a fairly small contingency who actually began work promptly at eight. Of course, this observation hit me long before I became the company's General Manager, but it was still quite the curiosity. On some of these mornings, Mitch would see me at my desk and wander over to commiserate. Apparently, the situation was causing him considerable stress. With furrowed brow and disgusted expression, he'd lament his frustration as to why the employee's desks were only half-filled by the time eight-thirty had rolled around. Though it wasn't my responsibility at the time, I'd have to say that I was equally befuddled.

Determined to change this most undesirable circumstance, Mitch announced his intention to raise the issue most stringently at our next weekly company meeting. And raise it he did. "It is very important that all of you arrive for work on time," he stated gravely. "I cannot emphasize this concern greatly enough," he further admonished. Changing the course of a river is not an easy thing to do, however, thus the tardiness issue continued in much the same manner   as before.

Highly distressed that his words had fallen largely upon deaf ears, he then announced that a special meeting on this matter would be held. And with that, whisperings of concern then circulated among the staff. When half the employees were late to the "special meeting" (to discuss why people were arriving late for work), Mitch's frustration reached its climax. At that point, he was left with two very obvious (but equally unpleasant) choices. Get tough or get out. As I was eventually offered his job, it's not difficult to conclude which alternative he chose.

Yet even though Mitch had decided to leave, in actuality he wasn't really gone. At this point, there were great plans afoot. It was also at this stage that my exclusion from the inner circle (Tom, Mitch, and Al) began to reach a noticeable apex. While I am by no means the world's most business-savvy individual, I do possess a certain level of intuition. Mitch's sudden departure was explained merely as quick and unpredictable. In short, we were led to believe that the man had simply vanished into thin air. In my heart of hearts, however, I knew damned well that this was not so. Something was definitely up, and obviously, I was not supposed to know what it was.

Just to test the waters one day, I asked Tom if he had ever heard anything from Mitch following his unexpected departure. It wasn't the answer that I was mainly concerned with, but rather the look on Tom's face when he gave it. Although his actual words were brief and dismissive, his expression and body language spoke volumes. Ah, there was something afoot alright. That much was for certain, and equally obvious was that Mitch was a definite part of it.

Round about that same time, Tom began taking a number of weekend trips to Salt Lake City. Though he was as secretive about these as possible, his Utah destination was not hard to ascertain. There was a renowned manufacturer of high-quality sign-cutting equipment in Salt Lake City, so that mystery was easily solved. What I didn't know at the time was that this company was now in play, with Tom being a major contender for the role of primary stockholder. Obviously, I had underestimated the man, as I had no idea that he possessed the resources to acquire such an expansive operation.

In any case, Mitch's apparent departure was for relocation purposes. He was to be the point person for operations within this new and much larger Salt Lake City organization. A major boon for Mitch, as it killed two birds with one stone. No more having to stress out over the actions of unmotivated twenty-somethings, not to mention a healthy promotion to boot. Tom was a happy man too, as he eventually emerged as the new president of the Salt Lake City manufacturer.

By the time he decided to formally let me in on his actions, it was very much a foregone conclusion. Additionally, Al simply couldn't resist spilling the beans to me as to Mitch's new role in the organization. When he told me that Mitch wasn't really gone, it was also a simple matter of deduction. Still, the message was clear as to my place within Tom's scope. Al and Mitch were trusted inner circle members, while I clearly was not.

Considering how devoted I was to Tom's enterprise, the feeling of being on the outside looking in was painful indeed. I suppose I can't fault his thinking entirely, but it would have been interesting had I had ever revealed to him that Al was not as trustworthy with highly sensitive company information as he believed. As for Lila, there was no way Tom was ever going to endow her with any more information than she absolutely needed. By this time she had proven herself to be extremely high-maintenance, as well as a turncoat many times over.

In the end, it didn't take Mitch long to realize that Salt Lake City was no place for a non-Mormon. He soon tired of it, and within a few months, he was totally gone for real. As for Tom, he now set about expanding his entire operation. His immediate goal was to move the entire Utah manufacturing plant to his own backyard here in Seattle. As for me, in addition to the challenge of taking over the reins from Mitch, I was also about to enter a whole new phase of my life.

LXII
Not Even a Diagram of the Basic Parts

I took the day off on the 23rd of December 1996. It was a cold and rainy Monday, and my wife had been in labor at Saint Francis Hospital for what seemed like an eternity (especially to her). As Murphy's Law would dictate, the doc was scheduled to go on vacation at the exact time Caroline was due. We, therefore, made a most unwise decision. We chose to induce labor such that our daughter could be born a week earlier, thus having our trusted doc on hand to handle the birth.

Had we known two very important facts before making this most foolish decision, we surely would never have hastened the process. Fact number one is that birthing contractions can be ten times as intense (and painful) as those accompanying a normally occurring and non-induced birth. Fact number two is that the doc actually plays a relatively minor role with regard to the process as a whole. In reality, the nurses are a much more important factor. Their steadfast dedication is evident pretty much right up to the last moments. The only time the doc gets involved is at the very end when the baby is actually being delivered, or when there are any kind of complications. This is not to say that their role is merely incidental. It is to say, however, that a replacement doc would have been a far better alternative to the pain and suffering of being induced.

Be all of this as it may, when our daughter finally emerged it was as if the world stood still for just a few moments. Though I know it's a cliché, it is as if you are witnessing a true miracle. One of life's truly surreal moments that aligns your perspective and brings you completely into focus. A moment when you realize that life is never going to be the same again. It was my first and only experience of this monumental magnitude, and it will stay with me until my dying day.

For first-time parents like Caroline and me, the next startling revelation is that you're now perfectly free to take this tiny new person home with you (no questions asked). With absolutely no knowledge whatsoever about bringing up a child, everyone was astoundingly comfortable with having us whisk this helpless being out from under their careful supervision. To Caroline and me, this seemed contrary to basic logic. Heck, they didn't even provide us with an instruction manual. Not even a diagram of the basic parts. I guess they simply trusted that we would be caring and responsible parents. At the time, I could only hope they knew what they were doing.

Although we were far from rich, some basic financial planning went a long way. Upon learning that we were expecting, we started putting as much money aside as possible. The plan was to save up about twenty-five grand or so, such that Caroline could stay home and take care of our daughter for the first year of her life. The thought of immediately putting her into daycare (as an infant) held no appeal whatsoever. My job seemed reasonably steady at the time, so why not get the kid off to the best possible start. Things were certainly tight for that first year, but it was probably one of the best decisions we ever made.

As a new parent, I found the learning curve quite steep. But like most things that require a great deal of effort and care, the rewards were great. Not only had we settled into a routine with regard to the basics of child-rearing, but the kid actually seemed to be thriving. I guess you never know what you're truly capable of until you set forth and do it. Perhaps the hospital folks did know a thing or two. Despite all my previous misgivings and doubts, I somehow turned into a dedicated and devoted parent. As someone whose sleep would not have been interrupted by a bomb going off in the bedroom, I was suddenly jolted awake by our baby's slightest stirrings. If the kid was fussing and upset, my world was also out of sorts. If she was happy and content, then all was bliss.

Our friends and family used to say that our daughter looked like Caroline but sounded like me. As she very definitely adopted my wry wit and offbeat sense of humor, I'd certainly have to agree. I can't recall how many times we'd lay in her bedroom just before bed, laughing hysterically over just about anything. Our shared humor was a true bond which survives to this day. Naturally, I quickly introduced her to my vast repertoire of old camp songs (as well as other familiar tunes that I knew she'd love). Among her favorites were *Charlie and The MTA*, *The Sloop John B*, and of course, *Sneaky Snake*. In addition to a book, our nightly bedtime ritual always included at least one of these tunes.

When it came to entertaining our child, there were of course those activities that were just more "dad-like." We had a vaulted ceiling toward the main entrance of our house. It provided ample space for a small child to be launched up into the air with no fear of obstruction. While it usually gave Caroline a coronary, this was one of my daughter's absolute favorite pastimes. With each toss (and subsequent catch), she'd cry out, "Higher!" It was a game she could play forever, though I was always careful not to overdo it. As time went by, she quickly grew to the point where I no longer had the arm strength to get the job done. One day I sadly lamented, "You're getting too big to play this game anymore." I guess that's what happens when you keep feeding them.

As any working professional will attest, family and career can be a very delicate balance. And in that regard, I realize now that I made two very bad decisions during those early childhood years. I suppose all parents have their scares when it comes to their children's health, and in this regard, we were no exception. Sometime during that first year, our daughter contracted something called a "Rotavirus." Though we had never heard of such a thing, it can be quite dangerous if not treated swiftly. It causes all form of nourishment to come right back up, thus the victim cannot even hold down liquids. If not checked, the child can become steadily dehydrated, and things can go seriously downhill from there.

Naturally, Caroline and I had been in frequent communication all throughout the day, and it was clear that things were not going well. By the time I got home from work, I was startled and horrified at the sunken look our daughter's face had adopted. I was equally as perplexed as to why Caroline hadn't already taken her to the emergency room, but there was no doubt that was where our daughter needed to be. I.V. fluids kept her from losing any further ground, but the battle with this insidious virus was no cakewalk. By the end of that evening, I was not at all convinced that we were over the hump. Though the hospital staff assured us that we'd be in for a fight with the insurance company, I insisted that they keep her overnight. Had we taken her home that evening, I was convinced that we'd only have to bring her right back the following morning. This proved an extremely wise decision.

By the next day our daughter's rosy glow had returned, and for the first time in a couple of days, she was able to keep things down. Needless to say, we were greatly relieved. Though we certainly seemed to be over the worst at this point, we were advised to keep her at the hospital for a few more hours of observation. While this seemed a worthy precaution, I now felt confident enough to return to work. When announcing to Caroline that this was my intention, she immediately became extremely irate. "Our daughter is in the hospital, and you're going back to work," she demanded. "She appears to be out of the woods," I responded. "But if things should take an unexpected turn, I will head back immediately."

As it turned out, things continued in a positive manner and our daughter was released a few hours later. Be that as it may, I never heard the end of that one. In my wife's view, the decision to return to work was nothing short of reckless abandonment. In my heart of hearts, I was fairly certain that all was well. Another day off from work, however, probably would have gone a long way toward assuaging my very anxious spouse. On the other hand, I'm not so sure how it would have been received by my boss (who was by no means a family man). Whatever decision I made that day would no doubt have angered someone. If I had it to do again, however, I surely would have stayed at the hospital.

My second extremely poor decision regarding work dedication came as the result of a rather severe snowstorm that fell on Seattle back in 1990. As the Associated Press described, "*A howling storm dumped up to 14 inches of snow in western Washington state, knocking out power to tens of thousands of homes and stranding children overnight in more than three dozen schools.*" A spokesman from the mayor's office noted, "*We are anticipating really treacherous conditions, really slick roads, and we want to do anything we can do to help keep people off the roads.*" The Seattle School Superintendent commented that "*He hadn't seen anything like this in thirty-four years.*" My history in Seattle didn't go back nearly that far, but I can certainly attest that it was one hell of a storm.

Looking back, I'm not certain as to my true motivation. Perhaps I was simply determined to be the hero of the day, or maybe it was my way of trying to climb into my boss's true inner circle. In any case, I confidently settled into my twelve-year-old Honda Accord, and set off on what was to be an extremely arduous expedition. In a word, it was "nuts". This was during the period that Tom was shuttling back and forth to Salt Lake City, and was thus enjoying yet another balmy Utah day.

Here in Seattle, there was absolutely nobody else out on the freeway that treacherous morning (why would there be?) By now, however, the road had become a ribbon of ice. Had I owned a four-wheel-drive vehicle at the time, it might have made some sort of sense. But doing it in an old beater Honda was pure madness. It was a long drive from my suburban home (some thirty-five miles south of Seattle) even under normal circumstances. On this day, however, my speed averaged somewhere between five and ten miles per hour. Any faster than that and I would have exited the freeway in a most involuntary and harrowing manner.

More than two hours later, and with my heart in my throat the entire time, I finally reached the Lake City Way exit of I-5. With my white-knuckle grip on the steering wheel finally loosening ever so slightly, I quickly noticed that the exit ramp had been barricaded. At that point, expressions all beginning with "Son Of A" started spewing from my mouth. Oh well, in for a penny, in for a pound. I'd now have to continue on to the next exit several miles down the road.

    After what seemed like an eternity, I finally reached I-5's Northgate exit. Mercifully this exit had remained open, but the ramp itself was a winding downhill affair that now resembled an Olympic ski run. Gathering too much speed or applying the break too vigorously could have sent me careening off the roadway at any given moment. By the grace of God, I somehow made it onto Lake City Way (the main thoroughfare), at a point some two miles or so north of my destination.

    This normally bustling and hectic artery was now virtually abandoned. Sometime earlier it had been plowed, the result of which was a steep wall of snow bordering both sides of the road. It now occurred to me that the mere act of making it down the street (to the company) was going to be of little consequence. Once positioned alongside the building, there would be no way to penetrate the wall of snow that now blocked my path to the company's parking lot. And even if by some miracle I could gain entrance to the parking lot, there'd be no way I'd ever get out again. I'd be stuck there for the night (possibly a couple of nights), and that level of dedication I did not possess. It was a valiant effort indeed, but the storm had simply proven too big an obstacle.

    Confident that I had given it my best shot, I noticed one establishment that had somehow remained open. The Denny's on Lake City Way was the only joint in the entire area with its lights on, and that was because it had never closed from the night before. The snow wall as well as their parking lot had been shoveled out, so I limped on in. Delirious to be off the road (and at the prospect of a hot breakfast), I made my way to the phone booth to call Tom. (Yes, this was in the days before cell phones were widespread).

    Upon hearing my harrowing story of braving the worst Seattle storm in thirty-four years, and alerting him that there was no way we were going to open for business today, Tom tersely replied as follows. "Whatever you have to do, I need you to keep it open." Perhaps my description of the current chaos had been insufficient. "You have no idea what I went through just to get here," I explained. I further emphasized that "I literally took my life in my hands by braving the trip this morning." And with that, his response was filled with irritation. "I need you to keep the place open," he callously reiterated.

    What he no doubt failed to understand was that I couldn't do that even if I tried. But somehow or other no amount of explaining was going to be sufficient. I then told him that "There was no way this was going to happen. Moreover, it would be insane to ask anyone else in the company to act as foolishly as I did. We were going to have to close today, and given the circumstances, that was the only rational decision to be made." Suffice to say that he didn't agree with me, nor did he appreciate my attitude. High atop sea level in the blue skies of Salt Lake City, however, there was little he could do about it.

When he eventually returned to Seattle, I think he finally gained an appreciation for the severity of the storm we had undergone. Despite this, the man never even thanked me for my efforts and dedication. Of the three company managers (who all lived quite a bit closer to the company than I did), I was the only one who even contemplated making the trip that morning. As the saying goes, I guess no good deed goes unpunished. After breakfast on the morning of my fateful expedition, I embarked upon the two and half-hour trip back home. The incident taught me a valuable lesson, however, about dedicating myself too fully to someone else's enterprise. A mistake I was determined never to make again.

As can easily be predicted, my time in the employ of Mr. Tom Leonard did not last much longer. Not long after Mitch's original departure, our revised managerial team hammered out a real plan for getting the staff to arrive for work on time. Unlike Mitch's general appeal to their good nature and sense of fair play, this new plan came with a real set of teeth. With Tom's total backing (or so he claimed), employees who continued to arrive late for work would be reprimanded on an escalating basis. One lateness would spark a friendly reminder, two tardy arrivals would prompt a more serious discussion, while a third incident would likely result in a dismissal. As can be imagined, this did not sit well among the staff. And while the grumbling and griping quickly commenced, the rank and file grudgingly began to realize that their world was finally going to change.

In my heart of hearts, I simply hoped that the staff would take the hint and alter their behavior accordingly. Truth be known, I had no desire to be the most hated man on campus. In the end, while some of the troops did indeed shape up, there was a goodly number that had to be shipped out. I hated doing it, but it had to be done.

It was during this "cleaning out" period that I gained a full understanding as to why Mitch couldn't take it any longer. It's one thing to be a leader when times are good and you don't have to tell people anything they don't want to hear. It's quite another when you have to make very unpopular choices and decisions. But a good leader does not shirk from these unpleasant responsibilities. I'm not necessarily crediting myself as having been a "particularly good leader" per se, but I did what the job entailed. It was indeed a very painful period that probably lasted for several months. But in the end, a new culture was born, and the lateness issue became largely a thing of the past.

To use an expression such as "A thing of the past" is rather ironic in this case, as that is what I soon became. There was a "suggestion box" located back in the warehouse, and the employees availed themselves of it at every opportunity. Every complaint in the book was registered upon me, including the fact that I made excessive use of the company restroom. It is amazing what people will come up with when they're out to get you. Personally, I think making light of a horrible stomach condition is right up there with picking on a cripple. Nonetheless, as far as they were concerned I was fair game.

In the end, I'd have to say that their suggestion-box stuffing probably paid off. It wasn't too many months later that Tom called me into his office. He made no bones about letting me know just how many complaints he'd been receiving on my behalf. Though logic might dictate that the company's hatchet man is not likely to be the most beloved person on campus, he seemed quite distraught as to my level of unpopularity. It should be noted that Tom was the kind of boss who liked to hand out hundred-dollar bills in the parking lot (to each employee) whenever profits were up. By contrast, I was the one who fired these same employees when they didn't consistently come to work on time. While feigning surprise and stark disappointment that I was not more universally beloved, I received my walking papers at the culmination of our discussion.

As I mentioned earlier, I have an uncanny ability to note what people are thinking, and how it is likely to affect their behavior. In short, I saw the handwriting on the wall. Thus my impending dismissal came as no great shock. I will now give you an excellent reason to tune into public radio on a frequent basis.

Some months prior to my fateful termination meeting with Tom, I listened to a segment on what to do when you think your employer might be planning for your departure. National Public Radio is probably one of the best investments you can possibly make. The segment to which I'm referring cost me absolutely nothing, while it enabled me to yield a tidy sum. I'm not sure how to calculate the return on investment when said investment costs you nothing. Suffice to say that it is astronomical.

Essentially the trick is to put aside the personal feelings that usually accompany getting fired, especially from an organization for which you've poured your heart and soul. Of course, this is not always the easiest thing to do, but it can prove extremely beneficial. With the personal stuff totally out of the picture, you can now direct your talking points to some final and extremely vital business aspects. Aspects that may, in fact, raise your financial standing (even considering the less than stellar circumstances).

Business aspect number one is to ask the boss what kind of severance package he or she has in mind. This is a bit like asking someone out on a date. If you don't ask, the answer is a definite no. If you do ask, the answer will be either yes or no (with yes probably weighing in at about

50/50). And in my book, 50/50 is a lot better than a definite no. Of course, the key here is preparation. A discussion of this type requires a great deal of it. The more preparation, the more successful your outcome is likely to be. Thus when Tom uttered the words that formally ended my tenure with the company, I knew exactly how to proceed. And not surprisingly, his response to my severance question was that the issue had never even entered his thinking.

Before leaving his office that afternoon, however, I had in hand a signed promissory note (on company letterhead) in the amount of fourteen thousand dollars. Not a get rich quick scheme to be sure, but certainly better than his original offer of nothing. Once we had reached our particular financial settlement, Tom then informed me that payment would take place immediately. Somehow this brought me back full circle to that first discussion when he asked me to help him run his company.

When the final figure of fourteen thousand was eventually reached, I sat back and waited for him to prepare the check. With confusion and irritation in his eyes, he asked how I could possibly expect him to prepare a check when the company accounting person had already gone home for the evening. "I really don't know," I replied. "You said payment would be immediate. And to me, immediately means immediately." Fighting the urge to audibly verify that there was probably no further need for me to "help him run his company," I asked what "immediately" meant to him. "Immediately means I'll prepare the check first thing tomorrow morning and send it to you in the mail that same day," he explained.

To my mind, however, a bird in the hand is always worth two in the bush. Thus, that is how the promissory letter came to be. In any case, I had fulfilled another tidbit of the sagely advice from the NPR story. "Always get it in writing." And with a few final meaningless platitudes from Tom, my association with his company officially came to a close. Well, almost. (And yes, the check did arrive several days later).

LXIII
An Offer They Couldn't Refuse

When I mention "meaningless platitudes," I'm referring to those things people say when they hope to cushion the blow from a traumatic event for which you are the victim. Several classics come to mind. "We can still be friends," "When one door closes...," that sort of thing. In Tom's case, it was "If there is anything I can ever do for you, please don't hesitate to ask." I would venture a guess and say that most people who make this offer are fairly confident that they will never be called upon to make good on it. And such was the case with Tom.

During my time as General Manager for his company, a wonderful product was introduced to us by a company out of Mexico. While it certainly wasn't rocket science, it was an extremely beneficial and very well-conceived item that no sign shop should be without. The rolls of vinyl used for creating signage and graphics came in a wide variety of sizes and colors. Left unchecked, they could easily clutter up the shop floor, causing all manner of disorganization (not to mention getting accidentally kicked around and damaged). What the Mexican company designed was a free-standing steel rack that easily and conveniently held up to forty-four of these cumbersome vinyl rolls. Not only did it greatly organize the shop, but it kept these pricey vinyl rolls well out of harm's way (while at the same time making them easily accessible).

Truly, it was a product whose time had come. As such, we were one of the first sign distributors to stock these units, and indeed they sold well. The only hitch was that the Mexican manufacturer couldn't possibly produce them in a timely manner. Orders took months to fill, and customers quickly grew impatient. My mission then became to find a new source for these steel wonder racks, while keeping the price point manageable.

Around that time I spotted an advertisement in one of the trade journals for some fancy hanging steel sign brackets ("scroll brackets," as they were known). There is a quality in some people that has become known as "intelligent ignorance." The concept is that these folks are just too ignorant to realize that something can't be done. So extreme is their ignorance that they disregard this fact completely. The eventual result is that they wind up creating the thing that couldn't possibly be done.

It's been said that Henry Ford had intelligent ignorance. Not being all that educated a man, Henry Ford asked his engineers to create a V8 engine. The wise and knowledgeable engineers on his staff assured him that it couldn't be done. A V8 engine was a mechanical impossibility, according to these most learned men. Taking no for an answer, not being his strong suit, Henry insisted that they need to build such an engine. Once again the wise and knowing engineers left their drawing boards and explained to Henry that it simply couldn't be done. According to the story, Henry then told them that it most certainly could be done. Not only that, but they were the ones who were going to do it. Wouldn't you know that the V8 engine came along shortly thereafter?

The purpose of this little anecdote is not to suggest that I am right up there with Mr. Ford, Mr. Edison, or any of these great visionaries. With regard to intelligent ignorance, however, my lack of steel production knowledge would have more than qualified me for "ignorant" status. Though I never imagined that someone who built sign brackets could utilize that knowledge to also crank out steel storage racks, I was fairly certain that it would cost me nothing to ask. By the same token, how could I possibly imagine that such a blind and naiive inquiry would be the start of a whole new chapter in my career.

Not only were the steel sign bracket people delighted to hear from such a prized prospective client, but they were also thoroughly intrigued with the notion of manufacturing such a potentially lucrative new product. What I didn't know then (but am quite well aware of now), is that steel is steel. That is to say that the methods of fabricating all manner of steel goods have some very basic similarities. In short, a well-equipped steel fabricator can make just about anything from ashtrays to airplanes.

After a brief round of negotiations (and a prototype or two), this new Florida-based metal fabricator was more than happy to start cranking out these vinyl racks. And wouldn't you know, they could do it for right around the same price as the Mexican folks. Not bad for a chance encounter springing from a tiny advertisement in a magazine. The Florida steel company went on to be an extremely reliable source for this product, and it became a clear winner for both of us. Score one for the savvy new General Manager (the one with intelligent ignorance).

Regrettably, the savvy new General Manager was a little too savvy in this case. Knowing that we had a clear leg up on the rest of the industry regarding this item, I requested that the Florida manufacturer grant us an exclusive on the product. While I never imagined that he'd actually say yes, it was my job at the time to ask. Not being quite as savvy, however, Precision Metal Products was more than happy to grant us this exclusive. This turned out to be a very short-sighted decision on their part, as this product had the potential to be widely accepted by sign industry distributors everywhere. From my perspective, to settle for one relatively small customer in Seattle made no sense whatsoever.

Nevertheless, a letter granting us exclusive rights arrived in the mail shortly thereafter. I must admit that I was quite torn with regard to handing over this letter to my boss at the time. Even then I had the inescapable feeling that my days with the company could be numbered. Withholding this letter could be my ticket to setting up my own enterprise down the road if need be. Handing it over to my boss, however, could serve to throw up a roadblock with regard to any such future plans. A tricky decision to be sure. Hindsight is twenty/twenty so they say, and it didn't take me long to discover that once again I made the wrong choice. Out of a sense of duty to the company, I handed the letter over to the powers that be. Oh well, live and learn.

So back to Tom's parting platitude about being more than happy to help if I ever needed anything. Given how I was now seeking out my next venture, I was most definitely at a point where I needed something. Determined that I was never going to work for someone else again, I decided to call in the favor that Tom had offered on the day of my termination. The insincere platitude that I knew had no basis in reality.

I approached the issue with him on the phone with the utmost candor and humility. In seeking my next venture, I explained that I would like to set up a manufacturer's rep firm based on the products from Precision Metal Products. In essence, I asked him plain and simply if he'd be okay with my offering the vinyl racks to the various sign distributors throughout the U.S. Bearing in mind that this was by no means the main focus of Tom's revenues, I held no reservations about posing such a question. And to his apparent credit, he immediately replied that it wouldn't be a problem at all. I thanked him profusely and wished him well with his continued endeavors. He replied in kind.

His rapid recantation didn't take long to reach me, nor did it surprise me in the least. Shades of "Help me run my company" kept coming back time after time. Rather than confronting the issue with me directly, however, he assigned Al to the task (my former colleague and very close work buddy). The same guy who I did my best to counsel and console when his wife left him to pursue a gay lifestyle, was now full-on at war with me. Al calmly and coldly explained that the company's lawyers would come after me with a vengeance if I attempted to pursue my manufacturer's rep plan. No doubt they had drummed up Precision Metal's letter granting an exclusive on the vinyl racks, and were now threatening to enforce said contract in whatever legal manner was necessary. So much for mindless and empty platitudes.

While these idle threats were not of particular concern to me, they had a definite impact on Precision Metal Products. Where they were originally thrilled that I now wanted to push their line to a nationwide audience, they now backed off for fear of getting sued. I tried my best to assure them that Tom was nothing more than a barking dog, but my new potential partner stubbornly held fast. "I gave my word," Precision Metal's president solemnly informed me.

I had to choose my next words carefully, for fear of insulting the man. In plain terms, agreeing to give my old company an exclusive was a pretty ridiculous thing to do. Without a doubt, it was not one of his wisest decisions. While not wanting to make the man seem foolish, I tried my best to convince him that Tom simply had much bigger fish to fry. To pursue such a trivial matter would be quite the waste of time and effort. "He will never come after you," I implored. "He's just posturing so that you'll back down."

Despite my best arguments, it seemed that Precision Metal Products would not be swayed. A deal was a deal. At that point, I graciously thanked him for his time and told him that I certainly respected his sense of professional ethics. Certainly, this battle had been lost. The war, however, was far from over.

It was now time to consult my favorite guidebook as to how to affect a difficult deal when people are being intractable. I should mention that my favorite guidebook is *The Godfather*, thus I needed to make Precision Metal Products an *"offer that they couldn't refuse."* I pondered, what speaks louder to a manufacturer of industrial goods than any compilation of words? The answer came to me quickly. "Orders." Orders usurp words every time. Especially if those orders are coming from a client that Precision Metal Products had been wooing ever since they first got started in the sign business.

Nisco, Inc. first started selling products to the sign and graphics industry in 1875. Out of Bolton, Missouri, they are one of the largest and most respected sign industry distributors in the country. I immediately placed a call, asking to speak with whoever was in charge of reviewing new products. To my delight, I was quickly connected to the company's vice president of marketing. Having sold a thing or two in my time, I was quick to introduce myself while coming right to the point. "I represent the manufacturer that makes the new free-standing steel vinyl racks," I explained. I then inquired as to whether Nisco would be interested in taking on this particular product line.

That was my entire sales pitch, short and sweet. The answer I received was equally as succinct, albeit extremely enthusiastic. "You're the one who sells the vinyl racks?" replied the voice from Nisco. Knowing that I was still a long way from receiving Precision Metal's blessing, I offered a most cautious and carefully worded response. "Yes I Am," I immediately replied. "That's great," Mr. V.P. chimed. We've been looking for a source for those racks. Look no further," I assured him. "My partner and I will be very pleased to ship you as many units as you need. Excellent," Mr. V.P. concluded. "Give us your information and I'll have our purchasing department fax you an order before the week is out. It's been a pleasure and thank you," were my final comments to Nisco's V.P. Can you guess the recipient of my next call?

Was it true that I was not yet Precision Metal's representative when Nisco posed the question? Sure. At that point, however, what in the world did I have to lose? Though a bit befuddled as to why I was calling again, Precision Metal's president quickly came on the line. And once again I wasted no time in getting my message across. "Would you like to do business with Nisco?" I simply offered. Suffice to say, I had his full attention. "They are getting ready to submit an order for the vinyl racks as we speak," I proudly informed him. "I'm wondering if this perhaps gives you a little different perspective on our situation," I posed? With restrained jubilation, he replied, "Nisco's on-board?" "Nisco's on-board," I confidently confirmed.

Professional ethics or not, Precision Metal Products was now also firmly on-board. I have often heard it said that selling starts when the customer says no. Thinking of Precision Metal as the customer in this case, there is certainly something to that statement. And with that, the partnership was established, and my new manufacturer's rep firm (Floyd & Associates) was born.

Nisco not only ordered a goodly amount of vinyl racks, but they took on a few of Precision Metal's other sign products as well. To have the country's flagship sign distributor now proudly featuring his products, Mr. Precision Metal Products was as happy as a pig in slop. Also with Nisco on-board, many other sign industry distributors soon followed suit. In less than a year, Precision Metal Products had morphed from a fairly small regional supplier, to a national distributor. Their products were now being shipped via truckload to all corners of the U.S. And as for Tom Leonard, he made absolutely no effort to get in our way. No surprise there.

LXIV
The Happiest Place on Earth

While my new business was indeed off to a promising start, things remained rather strained on the home front. The issues were beginning to pile up, and the wife and I were just not seeing eye to eye anymore. In addition, the things we were doing to try to recapture feelings of closeness were just not working. With an equal propensity for snoring, we also reverted to separate bedrooms by this point. In short, we were discovering that we no longer shared common interests, nor did we spend much quality time together anymore. We were rapidly moving from a marriage to a semi-polite set of roommates.

I guess some of the telltale signs of this increasing separation came on a trip back to L.A. one year. The purpose of which was several-fold. We'd hit Disneyland along the way, take a day at the beach in Santa Monica, and get in a visit with Caroline's folks at the same time. While Disneyland is often referred to as "The happiest place on earth," I've certainly witnessed a lot of unhappiness there as well. For me, it's a lot of fun for most of a day. Toward the end of that day, however, I'm totally wiped and more than happy to head home.

On this particular day, we arrived at the park right at the opening hour. Suffice to say, we crammed as much into the experience as was humanly possible. By about eight o'clock in the evening it was agreed that we'd finally head it on home. The fact that my wife and daughter were happily on-board with this plan comforted me no end. We'd had a blast, but I for one was good and Disney'd out. And then it happened. I don't even remember how it happened. Out of nowhere (but most likely emanating from my daughter) came the idea to stay for the Main Street Parade.

Even before this ill-conceived notion cropped up, Caroline was already complaining that a migraine was coming on. What better reason to call it a night and exit the park, I silently reasoned. I am very fortunate to be someone who does not struggle with migraines, but I've certainly seen their effects. Now why somebody who felt a migraine coming on would think that staying for the Main Street Disneyland Parade was a good idea, I'll never know. To my great dismay, however, Caroline was seriously considering it.

Admittedly, I am not a great fan of parades to begin with. My enthusiasm for them is right up there with watching paint dry. Worse still, the thought of another hour and a half at Disneyland that night was more than my weary soul could bear. Mind you, if we were booked into a nearby hotel that evening, I would have been more than happy to tell them to go and have fun. The plan, however, was to head back to the parent's place that night, thus I would have been trapped there with no way to retreat. This put me in the very unfortunate and unpleasant position of being the bad guy. "We are not staying for the parade," I declared. "The plan was to head back, and that's what we are now going to do." This, of course, did not put me in good stead with the wife (whose migraine was now coming into full force), or my daughter.

I could not imagine for the life of me how Caroline was going to enjoy a parade when she was already in terrible pain and thoroughly sick to her stomach. As it turned out, she wasn't actually well again for the next twenty-four hours. As I recall, however, I was to blame for her migraine (as I somehow didn't allow her time to get something to eat). My only consolation that evening was knowing full well that mine is by no means the only story of a Disneyland trip that ended with tremendous anxiety.

But if our Disney adventure wasn't enough of a challenge, the beach outing that followed a couple of days later was an even bigger disaster. Truth be known, we had a perfectly good time splashing around in the waves for a goodly part of the day. Once again the problem came when it was time to head home. Another tense situation somehow arose, and a day that was filled mostly with extreme fun and frolicking managed to end with angry and deeply hurt feelings. Perhaps it was just the culmination of two people who were no longer communicating on any level.

LXV
I'm Going to Give It to Someone Else

Despite the plethora of negative lessons, one very positive quality that my father always instilled in me was to never give up. He probably over-emphasized it a time or two, but the concept did indeed take seed. And though there are times when throwing in the towel may indeed be the best plan, I never seriously contemplated the notion of abandoning a long-term and once deeply committed marriage. I believe there is also a certain "stick-to-it-iv-ness" mentioned in the wedding vows as well (in sickness and health, for better or worse, that sort of thing). In the end, I guess it boils down to just how "worse" it has to get before the acceptable level of bad is achieved.

In any case, I awoke one Saturday morning and was greeted with an expression on my wife's face that I had never before seen. I guess you could say that I was enjoying a moment of blissful ignorance. My thoughts yielded nothing more than embarking on a pleasant weekend morning. By Caroline's expression, however, it was obvious that she was entertaining no such notion. "What's wrong," I asked in a truly curious manner. "This isn't working," came her pained reply. "What isn't working," I responded with genuine cluelessness. "Us," she concluded. Ah. A shocking thing with which to be greeted first thing on a Saturday morning, but I guess I couldn't really argue with her.

I once heard a story about a couple that was undergoing a bitter divorce back in L.A. I mention the particular location for good reason. Los Angeles is a notoriously insidious place to get divorced. Perhaps it has something to do with the spate of residents possessing large amounts of disposable income, but L.A. has a tremendously high incidence of divorce. This clogs up the family court system in and of itself, but the abundance of wealth takes a very heavy toll as well. The more assets, the more there is to fight about. The more acrid the fight, the more time it takes to reach a resolution.

To make matters worse, real estate in this region is among the most valuable and prized in the nation. Possession often being nine-tenths of the law, neither member of this unhappy couple was willing to risk leaving the family home for fear they'd lose it in the divorce. And so they both stayed all throughout the long and arduous proceedings. They no longer spoke to one another, yet they continued to cohabitate. Stranger still, they even continued to share the same bed (although I'm quite certain for no other purpose than sleeping).

As Caroline stayed on at our family home for several weeks after announcing her plans to separate, I can tell you that this is a very strange feeling indeed. I'll never forget how bizarre it felt one night (during this period) while settling down to an old favorite movie. There is an irresistible urge to pretend that everything is just fine, while knowing full well that things are in turmoil. Then there's the issue of seeing your soon-to-be ex-wife coming in or out of the shower naked (or vice versa). Suffice to say, it's a very confusing and extremely unsettling situation. Having experienced it for less than a month, I cannot even imagine dealing with it for any extended length of time. In general, I think it's a good idea to have your exit strategy well planned before announcing your decision to vacate.

And speaking of decisions, I think I probably did well to take a hotel room nearby just prior to Caroline's official moving day. Best not to witness half the home's possessions being carried off and systematically loaded into a giant moving van. Not that seeing the house half-empty upon my return was any great prize, but it was certainly the lesser of the two evils. And with that (and for the first time in a quarter of a century), I was a bachelor once again.

My theory regarding the breakup of relationships is that the party who initiates the termination usually fares much better than the one being left. Perhaps it's all just an illusion, but the process of planning and orchestrating the separation tends to make one feel more in control. By contrast, the unsuspecting remaining party is usually left to feel unwanted and abandoned. Of course, in the end, the final result is the same. But somehow or other, the concept of coming out on top at the conclusion can be crucial with regard to maintaining one's self-preservation. Planning and orchestrating also involves lots of action and activity, which also lends to the feeling of moving ahead with one's life. It's all just a theory, but in our case, Caroline certainly took the breakup much better than I did.

It was indeed a dark time and being on my own as a "fifty-something" did nothing for my mental health. Though it is often thought of as a cliché for men of this age, I was now entering into a full-on-board "mid-life/identity crisis." I truly had no idea who I was anymore, nor did I have any inkling as to my role in this world. My daughter was still in high school, and she of course went with her mom. In addition to suspending my marital status, I had also lost that which made me a family man. I hadn't anticipated that for at least several years to come. Though my daughter mostly took it in stride, it was a grievous loss for me.

With a thorough sense that nothing was working for me anymore, I began to withdraw into a place that seemed hopeless and unrelenting. In years past, I could always count on my music to get me through the difficult times. As the saying goes, however, "When it rains, it pours." Upon completion of my fourth (and final) album, I had reached a very sobering conclusion. For the life of me, I could no longer fathom why I was putting so much time and effort into something that wasn't related to my actual profession. With very few people destined to listen to these recordings (or the anticipation of any level of commercial success), I questioned why I was striving so hard to produce them. In short, I began asking myself what in the world I was doing.

I've never been a praying man per se, but I'll never forget lying in bed one night with a feeling of total despair. While staring off into the darkness, I had one of the most startling and frank conversations of my entire life with whoever was "in charge." The voice that I was hearing came with great clarity and supreme authority. Oddly enough, however, it took the tone of my old L.A. boss, Tim Jameson.

During the time I worked for Tim, I intentionally neglected one of the more distant parts of my sales territory. As a single man involved in a career that was often rather solitary, I had no desire to be on the road for three or four days every couple of months. I simply decided that the extra income wasn't worth this additional dose of solitude. Eventually, Tim issued me an ultimatum. "If you're not going to cover this part of the territory, I'll give it to someone else," he plainly stated. I respectfully replied that this would pose no problem whatsoever, thus I surrendered the unwanted territory most voluntarily.

Though the voice of authority on this sleepless and particularly solemn evening had the very familiar resonance of my old L.A. boss, the message was clearly coming from an altogether different source. The information was truly earth-shattering, while the words were absolutely unmistakable. The voice simply stated the following. "Gary—If you're not going to use this musical talent that I gave you, I'm going to give it to someone else." Though this edict was truly heartbreaking, my reply came swiftly and with equal respect. I softly whispered, "Okay, give it to someone else."

My conversation with "the voice" then concluded as follows. "Okay Lord. I don't know if this is your way of telling me that I've now reached the end. But if it is, then I'm okay with that. I found love at one time, I started a family, I made some good friends, I became a pretty decent guitar player, I accomplished some things at school, and I even went on to form my own business. But most of all, I've never done anything to intentionally hurt anyone. If this is the end, then I can be proud of the life I've lived." Not a bad resume, I thought. And with that, I fitfully drifted off to sleep.

Sleep was no easy matter during this period. Bouts of extreme insomnia were becoming more the rule, as opposed to the exception. The first round of sleeping medication that the doc prescribed wasn't getting the job done, so he then prescribed an alternative. He was emphatic, however, that the new and old medications should not be taken concurrently. If so, the results could be disastrous. And with that, I could now form my own exit strategy. Why the doc even prescribed the new stuff, after I candidly explained my feelings of overwhelming depression, leaves a question mark indeed.

With regard to means, motive, and opportunity, however, the former was now certainly in place. The only question was whether I should regard this as the answer from "whoever was in charge." A valid assumption perhaps, but with no definitive way to be certain. I guess it was a question that only I could truly answer. I must say, however, that the thought of putting the period at the end of this sentence was the only thing that gave me any comfort.

I truly don't know what kept me from opting out. Perhaps it was the fact that my mom was still alive. Maybe it was out of concern for my daughter, or perhaps my father's message of never giving up was coming back to me. To this day, I really couldn't say. All I can say is that somehow one day led to the next, and so on. I don't recall turning a particular corner per se, but the passage of time introduced a certain routine that seemed at odds with a sudden interruption. It seems a silly analogy, but there's a very funny line in the movie The Very Best Exotic Marigold Hotel. The young Indian man explains that "Everything will be alright in the end. And if it's not alright, then it's not yet the end." Perhaps in my case, it was simply not yet the end.

Immediately following the night of "the conversation," I completely dismantled my recording studio. Shortly thereafter I got rid of most of my instruments and gear. I kept only those guitars and fiddles that were most near and dear to me. Those who know me best couldn't believe I could ever turn away from music. It has now been eleven years since completing that fourth (and final) album. The fact of the matter is, however, that I barely ever pick up those guitars anymore. My old musical buddies insist that I'll get back into it someday. Every time I think back on that sleepless evening, and the life-altering conversation that took place, I rather think not.

LXVI
It's My Company and We'll Do It My Way

When it comes to launching a new business, there is a very fine line between due diligence and going off half-cocked. I've certainly observed both extremes. While there is a strong argument for getting out there quickly in many cases, throwing caution completely to the wind can surely end in disaster. On the other hand, I've seen people put in so much diligence and planning, that the enterprise never even gets off the ground. Like anything else, a philosophy involving some level of moderation is usually prudent. Once the ship finally hits the open waters, however, it then becomes a case of day-to-day navigation.

As for the good ship "Floyd & Associates," I was beginning to put together a pretty respectable client list. The orders were coming in and cash flow was generating. In short, all initial indications were promising. The sails were taking on a positive arc, and the ship was indeed heading in a northerly direction. And like a sailing expedition, you never know from which direction that next gust of wind will come. If one is properly attuned, however, there is no better feeling than being driven forward by a great force of nature.

My great force of nature came about one day with a phone call from my Florida steel partner (Precision Metal Products). Seems a fellow had drifted into his shop one afternoon pretty much from out of the blue. The gentleman was seeking out a steel company to manufacture his line of tile and flooring displays. After the obligatory questioning as to what constituted a tile display, my Florida folks were quite intrigued with the products that the man was seeking to build. Moreover, this new prospective client was talking about some pretty decent quantities, as well as some rather impressive profit margins.

Suffice to say that Precision Metal Products was most favorably impressed. So much so, that they were quite happy to begin building this lucrative new line of merchandise. Along the way, my steel guy also put in a good word for me out here on the west coast. He further took the liberty of suggesting that a telephone meeting might prove extremely beneficial to all three of us. As I was most eager to take my company to the next level, this seemed an excellent idea to me as well. From the tile fellow's perspective, it represented a promising path toward entering a brand-new marketplace. From Precision Metal's view, the more widgets they manufactured, the happier they'd be. Surely, a good chance for a win-win-win, with seemingly little to lose.

When, in fact, I did receive a call from a Mr. Ed McCoy some days later, he struck me as a plainspoken, enthusiastic, and rather personable fellow. He described his experience in the tile and flooring display business, which spanned a period of some thirty years. Clearly, he had identified a nice little niche within this industry. As such, he seemed quite determined to utilize this knowledge to put together a thriving business. In fact, the more I talked to Ed, the more convinced I was becoming that he indeed had a winner.

Ed's plan was to have me represent his tile displays on the west coast. I'd receive a nice little commission for every unit I sold. And with the vast California, Washington, and Oregon markets available to me, I was just about to tell him to sign me up. As we were going over the pricing schedule one day, however, I discovered that Ed also had a hard and intractable side. Even more troubling was that the man also had a temper.

In formulating his pricing, he had to take into consideration some costs that were passed on by Precision Metal Products (i.e. handling and storage charges). As for me, I've never been a fan of "nickeling and diming" customers. While Ed was intent upon adding these accessorial charges as a separate line item on the customer's invoice, I believed that the price we advertised should indeed be the actual price. If we put forth a price of a hundred dollars, it shouldn't be a hundred and fifteen dollars when storage and handling are mysteriously added. If I'm the customer, a surprise fifteen-dollar upcharge is most likely going to upset me. What's more, it's going to lead to mistrust.

And so, I simply suggested to Ed that we adjust the unit price to account for the fifteen-dollar handling costs. Why not just make the unit a hundred and fifteen dollars, with no unpleasant upcharges that may cause our customers any possible angst? And here was Ed's most unabated reply to my suggestion. "Gary, It's my company and we'll do it my way. Is that clear?"

Up until that point, Ed had seemed a most agreeable and entirely affable sort. Most assuredly, someone quite capable of analyzing a situation from a variety of viewpoints. I was, therefore, quite taken aback at his sudden and fierce intractability. I considered Ed's angry retort for several moments before offering a reply. After taking a deep breath, I assured him that I was indeed quite clear as to his meaning. With much regret, however, I also informed him that it would probably be best if we did not work together. And with that, our short-lived partnership was dissolved.

Unfortunately for Ed, there were three things he was probably unaware of. One was that the seed of exploring the tile and flooring display business had now been thoroughly planted within me. Secondly, in matters of business, I tend to be a fast learner. And finally, I had no aversion to exploring brand new venues in search of new opportunities. Through my previous undertakings with Precision Metal Products, I had already learned a fair bit about steel fabrication. The kicker now was to familiarize myself with the tile and flooring industry. And toward that end, I figured the best approach would be to speak directly with those who did it for a living.

It's a very interesting feeling to approach people within a specific industry who've never heard of you, and have absolutely no reason to believe that you are genuine and/or credible. But that is exactly what I did. Through a quick internet search, I gathered up a list of the most prominent tile distributors in Seattle. I then hopped in the car one morning and paid them a visit. One must bear in mind at this juncture that Precision Metal Products now shared a strong alliance with Ed McCoy, and under no circumstances would they betray him by building tile displays for me. This was an issue to be sure, but one I'd tackle somewhere down the line. For now, the most important aspect was to gauge the reaction I'd get from these Seattle based industry professionals.

Among the first of my sales calls that morning was a company called Superior Distributing. Unfortunately, these guys are not around anymore, but my meeting with their V.P. of Sales & Marketing was most illuminating. That he would even take the time to speak with me was encouraging in it of itself, but he was actually quite attentive and very much interested in what I had to say.

I told him that I planned to set up a tile display operation here in Seattle, where we'd be ideally situated to serve a west coast clientele. I did not attempt to come off as any kind of industry expert, but rather represented myself as someone who was segueing from a different area of metal production. And from that perspective, Mr. Jack Posano was more than happy to show me around. He took me back into his showroom and pointed out the various units that his company utilized. What's more, he took it upon himself to educate me as to which features he liked, as well as those he didn't. The result of this first meeting was a very good indoctrination as to the basics of tile display engineering, as well as a very positive introduction to a key player.

While all my calls that day probably weren't quite as productive as Superior Distributing, I'd have to say that several of them certainly did bear fruit. And with each conversation, I gained more knowledge of the industry and its corresponding products. And with the accumulation of this knowledge, came an increasing degree of credibility. Before long I was casually referring to such items as "wing displays," "loose tile displays," "swiveling displays," "tile display boards," and so forth. Meeting the different players during my consultations also enabled me to drop a few prominent names along the way, thus lending added cache.

I believe it was my third meeting with Superior Distributing's Jack Posano, when he instructed the company's CFO to issue me a check in the amount of fourteen thousand dollars. This amount represented fifty percent of the total for the first order that he was now placing with me. Of course, I was only too happy to accept it. I left Superior Distributing that day with the warmest and fuzziest of feelings. "I think I'm going to like this new industry," I joyfully said to myself.

Of course, by this point I had already started grappling with the issue of how I was going to get these units made. Naturally I floated the idea to Precision Metal Products, but that possibility was definitely not in the cards. Just as well, I reasoned. Precision Metal is all the way over in Florida, and the cost of shipping clear across the country would probably be prohibitive in any case. What I now needed was a steel operation on the west coast. Perhaps even a facility that could also warehouse the units (at least for a time), much like the deal Ed McCoy was now enjoying with Precision Metal Products.

After gathering up a list of about half a dozen southern California-based metal fabricators, I placed a call to an outfit called Welded Steel Solutions. When I asked if they knew anything about making tile displays, Mr. Phil Seals confidently replied, "You mean like the one we have right here in our showroom?" Voila! Indeed Mr. Seal's company had manufactured these kinds of displays for various tile companies in his area, thus he was quite familiar with the kinds of products to which I was referring.

Upon a quick visit to L.A. to meet with Phil and check out his operation, I was indeed convinced that I had found my new supplier. In addition to having a very well-equipped shop, Phil also turned out to be a brilliant designer. His brain quickly and easily formulated new and better ways of achieving the desired result. The man could look at an existing and very standard industry product, and quickly tell you how it could be greatly improved and vastly simplified. The result being a better looking and more functional unit, while also achieving an improved price point. I didn't get the idea that people skills were necessarily his strong suit, but from a technical standpoint, he most certainly knew his stuff.

I guess it would be no exaggeration to say that Phil Seals proved to be a very big factor in my future success in this business. His brilliant product engineering provided inroads and major opportunities. Not only did he manufacture the highly customized order for Superior Distributing (and several others that soon followed), but he took a very standard industry display model and revamped it brilliantly. The result was a unit that no longer looked awkward and cumbersome (as well as being hard to assemble), but one that now had a sleek and streamlined appearance. I had my doubts at first concerning the strength of this redesign, but a few quick and dirty tests proved that it was every bit as rugged as the old model.

The three or four key players that I was fortunate enough to run into at the upcoming industry trade show took to it immediately. To them, it represented something new and different, which was exactly what they were looking for. From this most fortuitous Las Vegas tradeshow came two or three additional major west coast distribution customers. And with that, things were beginning to rock and roll. It was also at this venue that I actually met Ed McCoy in person for the first (and only) time. Although we were now direct competitors, I'd have to say that he was a most gracious fellow.

Though my admiration for Phil Seals' metal talents knew no bounds, it wasn't all fun and games concerning Welded Steel Solutions. Once the design aspects had been achieved, Phil's company started to prove quite troublesome with regard to the actual production. Mistakes began to happen which led to a great deal of tension between us. Unfortunately, I had to replace Phil's outfit with a new metal supplier after the first couple of years. The new fabricator was not without its ups and downs as well, but they eventually got the hang of it, and things went relatively smoothly from then on.

It didn't take me long to realize that the tile display industry was infinitely larger and quite a bit more lucrative than that of the steel sign products business. Clearly, a fourteen-thousand-dollar check (seemingly issued upon a whim), provided pretty solid evidence of this. Though we were still selling a goodly amount of vinyl racks, I began concentrating the greater part of my efforts on this new and emerging marketplace. This, of course, led to tension with Precision Metal Products, which was now seeing a definite drop-off regarding my involvement with their products. Though it did not come as a big surprise, Precision Metal products decided to terminate our partnership. To their credit, however, they continued paying me commissions for a year following the date of our termination. Perhaps this was done strictly out of legal concern. Nevertheless, I appreciated their extreme level of professionalism.

Though it only came to me through rumor, I heard that Precision Metal Products abandoned ship a year or two following our disassociation. That they had ceased operations was a definite, but the speculation was that my old partner liquidated the company when his wife suddenly filed for divorce. I had met the woman once, and somehow this mode of thinking seemed quite plausible. I have no idea what became of Mr. Precision Metal, but if he were still around, he'd probably be in his mid-eighties by now. Hopefully enjoying a peaceful and easy-going retirement.

Over the next several years things continued to progress nicely. We were indeed building up a rather impressive client list, and sales were climbing steadily. Mistakes were down, productivity was up, and profits were coming into line. Additionally, we were now producing one of the best-made lines of steel tile displays in the country. Our products were not only aesthetically pleasing, but they were rugged and reliable as well.

I'll never forget the feeling of walking through the plant one day and seeing my products endlessly rolling off the assembly line, and awaiting final packaging. Though it wasn't technically my plant, I imagined that this is how Henry Ford might have felt while viewing his Model T automobiles coming together right before his eyes. A kind of pride that few individuals get to experience. And even if the whole thing went bust at some point, I would be forever blessed to experience such a unique feeling of satisfaction and accomplishment.

LXVII
The Chinese Connection

Nothing in this world ever remains static. Burgeoning competition soon impacted the business, which then combined with an escalation in the cost of materials and labor. With great pressure to keep prices low (despite these increasing costs), a bold new strategy needed to be explored.

In a perfect world, I'd have liked nothing more than to keep production right there in southern California. In the real world, however, there was no way I was going to remain competitive by doing so. With a heavy heart (and much trepidation), I began putting out some feelers for Chinese metal fabricators. Though this wasn't exactly a popular route in the eyes of many of my clients, it seemed the only viable choice given the circumstances. And though I had never before done business with the Pacific Rim, I must say that locating Chinese steel manufacturers wasn't all that hard to do. In fact, I was getting emails from them on a somewhat regular basis (which up to now, I had been disregarding).

Once this proved the most prudent direction, however, negotiations proceeded with great efficiency. It is amazing how quickly business operations can progress when people are deeply motivated and determined. I quickly sent sample units to those Chinese manufacturers I considered most appropriate, and they were equally as swift in their response. To make a long story short, a product for which I was paying a hundred and thirty dollars out of California, was now going to cost seventy-five dollars from Shanghai. Even adding the cost of ocean shipping, the result was still far better than sticking with U.S. production. And with that, I suddenly entered the mysterious and complicated world of overseas importing.

And like my initial entry into steel fabrication, there was indeed much to learn. And rest assured, I probably made every mistake in the book. As I mentioned previously, however, I am a quick study when it comes to this sort of thing. And as necessity is often the mother of invention, the key points can certainly be ascertained as one plods forward. Bottom line, I was back to where I needed to be in terms of cost and competitiveness. I must admit that some of my customers weren't initially thrilled with the concept of our shift to overseas production. While I couldn't entirely blame them, this sentiment completely faded from existence within the next year or two. By then, like it or not, everyone had made the same shift.

When someone asks me how to define the term "entrepreneur," I offer the following. Simply stated, an entrepreneur is someone who is capable of making something out of nothing. I started my company in 1998 with absolutely nothing. I had no buildings or equipment, nor did I have much money in the bank (nor did anyone offer to lend me a dime). I didn't even have much expertise in the industry with which I was seeking to endeavor. I did possess one very important component, however. I was absolutely determined to never work for anyone ever again. Toward that end, I was going to do whatever it took to make my new venture a success. The faculty at Seattle Pacific University taught me that this was possible, therefore I was willing to give it my best shot.

With great risk, there is the possibility of great reward. There is an equal possibility of failure, but the relationship between risk and reward is certainly a recurring concept all throughout our lives. I started in 1998 with nothing. By 2006 I had achieved revenues in excess of one million. Once things got rolling I enjoyed an annual income well in excess of a hundred thousand. And as far as my humble lifestyle was concerned, that was just fine.

My theory is that we spend far more time regretting those things in life that we didn't have the wherewithal to do, (as opposed to the things we did do that may not have panned out the way we would have liked). And as life presents an extremely finite timeline, I'd just as soon go down swinging. Perhaps that's the real reason I chose not to "opt-out" when all had seemed so bleak.

LXVIII
A Lot of Good Talks

Those of us who have been down the divorce road with children can probably attest that there is a dramatic paradigm shift with regard to parenting. While it is certainly true that being physically separated from our kids can add significant challenge, there is an equal argument to be made that it can also make things easier. As parenting is often an issue that provides great conflict within a marriage, not always having to answer to the other party can be a most freeing experience. I'm not suggesting that we should run roughshod over our ex-spouse's wishes, but there is indeed a certain freedom that comes from knowing that our own opinions and ideas will no longer be subject to such close scrutiny. And while we all certainly strive for the ultimate well-being of our child, it's a nice feeling to be able to remove the marital/relationship element from the equation.

Not that things weren't pretty good anyway, but I'd have to say that my relationship with my daughter actually improved following the divorce. Though it took a bit more planning, we got together just about every week for some kind of one-on-one activity. We took a lot of walks, we took in quite a few movies, and we enjoyed countless lunches and dinners. Above all, we had a lot of good talks. I cannot recall a single one of our weekly get-togethers when we didn't have a good time. I guess you could say that it made our time together all the more valuable.

Although we are still in the midst of a pandemic at the time of this writing (and my daughter is now an adult), we still maintain a very consistent schedule of Zoom meetings. And when things finally do get back to some level of normality, I have no doubt that our relationship will resume in much the same manner as the pre-pandemic days. While divorce is never much fun, it's nice to know that it doesn't have to impact the relationship we have with our kids.

I have often wondered how my perspective of childhood would have differed had my own parents divorced. In those days, the wisdom was that you stayed together for the sake of the kids. From my current perspective, however, I have to wonder if our kids are really better served by growing up in a family where there is much hostility and dysfunction. Are we really doing our kids a service by showing them that marriage is about anger and bitterness (or even worse elements?) As my parents chose the traditional path, I guess it will always be a matter for speculation. Despite these observations, I am now proud and blessed to enjoy such a thoroughly fulfilling father/daughter relationship.

LXIX
Final Thoughts

As we all know, there are things in this life that we can control, and many more that we can't. Likewise, there are things we can fix, as well as things that sadly cannot be repaired. I'd love to say that I've gotten a beat on my stomach issues, and it's smooth sailing from now on. No such luck, I'm afraid. The best I've been able to achieve is a fundamental shift in my basic thinking.

The simple fact is that there are many things my condition no longer enables me to do. It would be great to go camping in the wilderness with my brother. It would be wonderful to take long hikes here in the beautiful Pacific Northwest at any time I choose to do so. This wistful list of activities is probably too numerous to name, but I have learned to live within the confines of my physical constraints. More importantly, I have come to terms with my limitations. Though probably not recognized as such, it is simply a disability like any other. If it slows us down from time to time, then so be it. Like so many other things, the trick is not to let it get us down. While this is sometimes a bit easier said than done, we must all make hay while the sun shines.

I could probably write an entire book on the subject of dating in your fifties, but I'll make no such attempt in this particular narrative. Suffice to say that it's gotten way more complicated and arduous than it ever used to be. And although the internet is responsible for bringing a great many couples together, it also introduces vast amounts of suspicion and mistrust. This is coupled with the fact that no suddenly single "fifty-something" gets to this point in life completely unscathed. Becoming a whole person once again (who is truly ready to welcome someone new) is a journey whose roads are fraught with potholes.

For those about to take this hazardous trek, I can summon no greater wisdom than the following. Under no circumstances should one let the process become a new source of bitterness, frustration, or depression.

Whataya Gonna Do?

Know that there exists a great number of wandering souls out there, each with his or her own set of unique baggage.

Following the breakup of my twenty-five-year marriage, I scaled this imposing peak for five years. There were times when the summit actually seemed within reach, only to fade completely from view. While I'm well aware of the perils, I also know that there is life on the other side. I am living proof of this, for I have once again discovered great happiness with someone new and wonderful. But like any great expedition, there is the obligatory set of highs and lows. Each existing for the purpose of the other. After all, how are we going to realize when we've reached that joyful pinnacle if we've never experienced the depths of despair? This too is only a theory.

So, whataya gonna do? With risk, there is always the possibility of reward. To choose not to risk is to guarantee that we never reach that elusive summit. Do we really want to leave this earth with regrets? Have you ever seen a gravestone that reads, "Here Lies So-and-So. At Least He Never Failed."

On her deathbed, my mom told my brother and me to "Live your life fully and pursue your dreams." Since I've never known her to give me bad advice, I think that is exactly what we all should do.

About the Author

As a twenty-five-year Brooklyn native, Gary Floyd graduated first and foremost from the school of hard knocks. Upon entering college at the age of seventeen, he knew that he absolutely hated chemistry and had no propensity for the subject whatsoever. Needless to say, he chose it as his undergraduate major. Five and half grueling years later Gary was finally presented with a B.S. degree from the College of Staten Island. He'd have to admit that "B.S." was a very appropriate designation in his case. As he owed it to himself to study something for which he had an actual passion, Gary returned to academia in his mid-thirties to pursue an MBA from Seattle Pacific University.

Throughout his career, he's been a totally inept chemist, a decent salesman, an impressive semi-professional musician, an able purchasing agent, a no-nonsense operations manager, and a successful entrepreneur. Starting at age nine, Gary spent twelve summers in northeastern Pennsylvania among the youth of Philadelphia's suburban elite (from whence many of his camp stories come.) A slow westward migration included stops in Dallas and Los Angeles, before finally settling in Seattle, WA. Soaking up these distinctly unique cultures and experiences has added much perspective to his own life adventures; thus, the basis for this most colorful and revealing memoir.

www.ingramcontent.com/pod-product-compliance
Lightning Source LLC
Chambersburg PA
CBHW070044080526
44586CB00013B/906